STUDIES
MILITARY AND DIPLOMATIC
1775–1865

STUDIES
MILITARY AND DIPLOMATIC
1775-1865

BY

CHARLES FRANCIS ADAMS

BOOKS FOR LIBRARIES PRESS
FREEPORT, NEW YORK

E181
A2

First Published 1911
Reprinted 1971

INTERNATIONAL STANDARD BOOK NUMBER:
0-8369-5681-8

LIBRARY OF CONGRESS CATALOG CARD NUMBER:
73-150168

PRINTED IN THE UNITED STATES OF AMERICA

CONTENTS

MILITARY STUDIES:

THE BATTLE OF BUNKER HILL	1
BATTLE OF LONG ISLAND	22
WASHINGTON AND CAVALRY	59
THE REVOLUTIONARY CAMPAIGN OF 1777	114
THE BATTLE OF NEW ORLEANS	174
THE ETHICS OF SECESSION	203
SOME PHASES OF THE CIVIL WAR	232
LEE'S CENTENNIAL	291

DIPLOMATIC STUDIES:

AN HISTORICAL RESIDUUM	344
QUEEN VICTORIA AND THE CIVIL WAR	375
INDEX	415

STUDIES: MILITARY AND DIPLOMATIC

I

THE BATTLE OF BUNKER HILL[1]

IN Carlyle's *Life of Frederick the Great* there is an account of a curious conversation in December, 1745, between Frederick and D'Arget, the secretary of Valori, at that juncture the French ambassador at Berlin. It was at the close of the Second Silesian War, from which Frederick, then only thirty-three years of age, had emerged victorious; thenceforth to be till he died the leading figure in European political action. He was just entering on the eleven years of more or less broken peace which preceded the Seven Years' War. D'Arget, at the instance of Valori, had suggested some grand political combinations in which Frederick was to figure as the "Pacificator of Europe." The king listened to him, and then replied: "It is too dangerous a part for playing. A reverse brings me to the verge of ruin: I know too well the mood I was in last time I left Berlin ever to expose myself to it again! If luck had been against me there, I saw myself a monarch without a throne; . . . A bad game that; . . . I am not in alarm about the Austrians. . . . They dread my army; the luck that I have. . . . I would not henceforth attack a cat except to defend myself." And so, says Carlyle, Frederick "seems to have little pride in his 'Five Victories'; or hides it well . . . and at times acknowl-

[1] *The American Historical Review*, Vol. I, 401 (April, 1896).

edges, in a fine sincere way, the omnipotence of Luck in matters of War."[1]

On the 14th of October, 1895, the centenary of the death of Colonel William Prescott, who commanded in the redoubt at Bunker Hill, was commemorated at Boston, and Dr. William Everett then delivered an address marked by a high order of eloquence and much reflection. A month later, on the 13th of November, there was unveiled at Hartford, Conn., a bronze statue of Colonel Thomas Knowlton, of Ashford, the gallant officer who commanded the Connecticut troops which covered Prescott's left, and whose death a year later at Harlem Heights was not the least of the grievous losses sustained by the American army in the disastrous New York campaign of 1776. These events, and the addresses they called forth, revived the memory of two of the most interesting and important military operations in the struggle for American Independence, in both of which, also, "the omnipotence of Luck in matters of War" made itself felt in a way not to be overlooked.

And first of Bunker Hill. The affair of the 17th of June, 1775, on the peninsula of Charlestown, opposite Boston, affords, indeed, one of the most singular examples on record of what might be called the "balancing of blunders" between opposing sides, and of the accidental inuring of all those blunders to the advantage of one side. So far as the American, or what we call the patriot cause, was concerned, the operation ought to have resulted in irretrievable disaster, for on no correct military principle could it be defended; and yet, owing to the superior capacity for blundering of the British commanders, the movement was in its actual results a brilliant success; and, indeed, could hardly have

[1] Carlyle, *Frederick II*, Book XV, Chap. XV; *Works* (Sterling Ed.), Vol. IX, 17–21, 37.

THE BATTLE OF BUNKER HILL

been made more so had the Americans controlled for that occasion the movements of both sides, and so issued orders to their opponents. Looking over the accounts of that battle and examining the ground upon which it was fought, it is difficult to understand how the Americans could knowingly have put themselves in such an untenable position; much more how the British should so utterly have failed to take advantage of the mistakes of their inexperienced antagonists.

In 1775 Charlestown, including Breed's Hill, was a peninsula of limited size and hilly formation, connected with the mainland by a single narrow causeway, which was, at times of sufficiently high tide, itself overflowed. When, therefore, on the night of the 16th-17th of June, Colonel Prescott led his force across the causeway, and established it upon Breed's Hill, he put himself and those who followed him in a trap where, with an enemy having complete control of the sea, and so commanding his rear and both flanks, it was merely necessary to snap the door and hold him, utterly powerless either to escape or to resist. He had literally thrust his head into the Lion's mouth.

Consequently, when the guns of their ships woke up the British officers in Boston on the morning of the 17th of June, had there been any, even a moderate, degree of military capacity in their commander, he would have ejaculated his fervent thanks to Heaven that his enemy had thus delivered himself into his hands; and proceeded incontinently to "bag" him. To do this, it was only necessary for him to move a sufficient detachment around by water to the causeway connecting Charlestown with the mainland, seize it securely under cover of the fire of his ships and floating batteries, there establish himself, and quietly wait a few hours for the enemy to come down to surrender, or come out to be killed. To bring this result about he might not have been compelled to fire a single gun; for his enemy had not even placed himself upon the summit of Bunker Hill, which overlooked and commanded Charlestown Neck, but had absolutely moved forward to the lower summit of Breed's Hill, between Bunker Hill and Boston, from which point, with a powerful and well-equipped enemy in undisputed control of the water, he would have been unable to escape and powerless to annoy. His position would have been much that of a rat when the door of a trap is securely sprung behind it. The only alternative to an ignominious surrender would have been a general engagement on open ground; for, with his line of communication cut off, unable to advance, unable to retreat, and unable even to strike or worry his adversary, between whom and himself he had interposed Bunker Hill, the only course open to Prescott would have been the hurried abandonment of his redoubt; and a scramble to get possession of the summit of Bunker Hill. Had he succeeded in doing that, the patriot army would still have been hopelessly cut in two, and mere starvation would within twenty-four hours have compelled the Americans to choose between surrender and an almost hopeless aggressive movement. In case of a general engagement, the patriots, a mere mob, must attack a well-armed and disciplined opponent, on ground of his own selection and protected by the guns of a fleet. Such an engagement, under the circumstances then existing, could, in all human probability, have had but one result. The patriot forces must have been routed and dispersed; for, hardly more than a partially armed militia muster, they were without organization or discipline, only inadequately supplied with weapons, artillery, or munitions, and, except on Breed's Hill, unprotected even by field works.

The untenable position into which the patriots had got themselves, and the course to pursue in dealing with them, were, from a military point of view, so obvious that, in the council of war that morning held in Boston, the proper military movement was at once urged, it is said, by a majority of the British officers with Clinton at their head. Instead of following it, a sufficient force of British was sent across to Charlestown, landed directly in the face of their enemy, and proceeded to take the American intrenchments by assault; finally, after great loss, doing so, and absolutely driving the rat out of the trap, of which the British commander had left the door wide open. A more singular exhibition of apparently unconscious temerity on one side, and professional military incapacity on the other, it would be difficult to imagine.

Under these circumstances, it becomes somewhat curious to consider the actuating causes of the operations on that day. Who was responsible for what occurred?

It is sometimes asserted that, so far as the Americans were concerned, their object was to force the fight with a view to firing the colonial heart, and that the result entirely justified the calculation. This may be true. Nevertheless, on the other side, it is apparent that, unless the American commanders calculated with absolute certainty upon the utter incapacity of their opponents, by the precise move then made they placed the cause which they had at heart in most imminent jeopardy, and came dangerously near quenching the so-called fire in the colonial heart in a sickening drench of blood, spilled in defeat; for if, instead of attacking the American line in front exactly at the point where it was prepared for attack and braced to resist, the British had operated by sea and land in their rear, it is difficult to see what could have saved the patriot cause from a complete collapse. If Colonel Prescott and his detachment had been obliged to surrender, and on the evening of June 17 had been ignominiously marched prisoners into Boston, it would only have remained for Gage, by a vigorous movement next day from Charlestown in the direction of Cambridge, distant an hour's march, to have dispersed the now demoralized patriot army and made any further organized armed resistance practically impossible. Even numerically the forces were very nearly equal. Beside the ships of war, General Gage could muster 8000 effectives operating on interior lines; while, with a force nominally 16,000 strong, General Ward could probably never have put 10,000 men in action. A general engagement was the one result the British commander ought on every consideration to have sought to bring about; while the American officers knew perfectly well that for a general engagement they were prepared in no single respect. Yet the occupation of Bunker Hill by the patriot forces meant, if met by the British with any degree of military skill, an immediate general engagement. It is quite out of the question to suppose that those who assumed to guide the patriot operations could have measured this risk, and then knowingly taken it. There are limits to any amount of rashness, except that of ignorance.

While the course which should have been pursued by the British commander was apparent, the theory on which the patriots acted is, thus, more difficult to explain. The movement on the night of June 16 had been decided upon at a council of civilians and military officers held that day at Cambridge. More than a month before, a joint committee of the council of war and the committee of safety had, after careful consideration of the ground, recommended the construction of a strong redoubt on Bunker Hill. At the same time, however, provision was to be made for apparently a simultaneous occupation of Winter, Prospect and Plowed Hills on the other, or land, side of Charlestown Neck. This plan of operations is intelligible. If, at the same time that Bunker Hill was occupied, Prospect, Winter and Plowed Hills also had been occupied, the patriot army would have commanded Charlestown Neck, and, by preventing a landing there and driving away the floating batteries, could have kept communication open between their army and the advanced and isolated force in occupation of the heights on the Charlestown peninsula. To do this successfully implied, it is true, the control of a body of artillery and munitions far in excess of what the provincial force had; but still, from a military point of view, the plan was well conceived and, if successfully carried out, would have compelled an immediate evacuation of Boston by the British.

But, had this line of operation been pursued, it would have been quite needless to occupy Breed's Hill at the outset; seeing that Breed's Hill was immediately in front of Bunker Hill and thirty-five feet lower, so that artillery posted on Bunker Hill commanded it completely. It could accordingly have been occupied at any time when a force in firm possession of Bunker Hill was ready to advance and take it.

If such was the general plan of operations under which Colonel Prescott's movement of the 16th of June was ordered, the next question is, — Who was responsible for its partial execution, and consequent failure? Its success involved two things: first, the seizing of Bunker Hill; and, secondly, and at the same time, the erection of works upon Prospect, Winter, and Plowed Hills, or the high ground at the base of those hills commanding Charlestown Neck and the adjacent water. It is impossible to ascertain conclusively whether any one was then in command of the left wing of the provincial army. If any one, it was Putnam. At the council of war he had strenuously advocated the forward movement to Bunker Hill; and, it is said, the same evening discussed with Knowlton, at the quarters of the latter, the reasons and details of the step. Knowlton was a natural soldier, and he at once, the same authority asserts, pointed out to the far from clear-headed Connecticut farmer metamorphosed into a general, that, if the proposed move was made, the enemy under cover of his floating batteries could land troops at the Neck, cutting off both reinforcements and retreat; that the approaches and flanks of the position could be enfiladed from the shipping; and, finally, that Gage could, by a judicious disposal of the land and naval forces at his command, compel the American force on the peninsula to surrender from mere starvation.[1]

This excellent advice, if really given, seems to have been thrown away on Putnam, who during the following day was most active in all parts of the field, and appears to have been recognized in a way as the general officer in command of the entire field of operations, while unquestionably Colonel Prescott was in immediate charge of the detachment on Bunker Hill. He occupied the position of a brigadier-general whose command was in action; while Putnam held in vague unmilitary fashion, the position of chief of the grand division with which Prescott's command for the time being co-operated. Certainly, on the night succeeding the engagement, General Putnam was active in holding and fortifying Prospect Hill, and was then practically recognized as in a sort of irresponsible command of the left wing of Ward's army. If, therefore, any one was to blame for the failure to carry out that essential part of the original plan

[1] Historical Address of P. Henry Woodward at the Knowlton Ceremonial, p. 20.

THE BATTLE OF BUNKER HILL

of operations which included the fortification of the ground commanding Charlestown Neck from the land side, it was Putnam.

But the truth probably is that no one was responsible. The lack of organization in the patriot army was then such that no distinctive and recognized officer was in charge of the left wing. Prescott had his orders direct from the headquarters at Cambridge; and the other officers with separate New Hampshire or Connecticut commands seem throughout what occurred to have taken orders, or declined to take them, pretty much as they saw fit.

It is, however, useless to venture surmises on this head. The essential fact is that Prescott was ordered to march across Charlestown Neck and to occupy Bunker Hill; and did so, leaving his rear wholly unprotected. After that, on his own responsibility, he exposed himself to great additional risk by advancing from the summit of Bunker Hill, from which he overlooked both Breed's Hill, in his front, and his single line of retreat across Charlestown Neck in his rear, to the lower summit before him, at which point he was helplessly in the trap, unless his opponent, by coming at him in front, drove him bodily out of the hole in which he had put himself. His opponent did just that!

It was well for the patriot cause that both Gage and Howe outranked Clinton that day. When, in the morning, with the eye of a soldier, Clinton urged Gage to pay no attention to the patriot front, but to seize the causeway in its rear, Gage seems to have replied that to do so was not in accordance with correct military principles, as, by such a movement, his force engaged might be placed between two divisions of the enemy. In other words, the movement suggested might bring on the very thing he should most have sought to bring on, — a general engagement under cover of his ships. But this was not his real reason for acting as he did. Gage was, in fact, that not uncommon type of soldier familiarly known in military parlance as a "butt-head." As such, he, as a matter of course, fell into the dangerous error of underestimating his opponent; and, while he could urge an abstractly correct military principle, he had not the capacity to judge whether it had any application to the facts before him. So much for laboring with Gage in the morning.

But Clinton on that occasion seems to have had a hard time of it. Having failed to inspire Gage with a certain degree of intelligence in the early hours of the day, he, in its later hours, tried his hand on Howe. When, at last, about four o'clock of the long June afternoon, with several hours of daylight still before him, Howe stormed the redoubt and drove Prescott's little force out of it and in pell-mell flight over Bunker Hill and across the causeway to the hills beyond, Clinton, again with the eye of a soldier to the situation, urged his superior in command to follow up his advantage, cross the causeway, and, then and there, smite and spare not.

The thing was perfectly practicable. The confusion in the patriot ranks was complete. In vain had Putnam tried to hold his own men, and rally the fugitives from the redoubt, in the partially finished works on Bunker Hill. He had been simply swept away in the panic rout. On the land side of Charlestown Neck the patriots had no works thrown up behind which they might hope to rally. Cambridge and headquarters were only two miles away. They had challenged the blow; and the blow was impending. Fortunately for the patriots and the patriot cause, Howe, and not Clinton, was now in immediate command of the king's troops. Howe, though personally brave, and really capable as a tactician, was sluggish of temperament. Subsequently, and when, succeeding Gage, he was in chief command, though personally popular with his associates, the lack of aggressive energy he uniformly evinced in the hour of victory, was with the more soldierly among them ground not only of comment but of outspoken complaint. On June 17, this deficiency stood Ward and Putnam in good stead. Howe wholly failed to avail himself of the opportunity Clinton then saw and pointed out to him.

The singular thing, however, in all these operations, as already pointed out, is that, from beginning to end, if the patriot army had been commanded by a military genius of the highest order, and gifted with absolute prescience, — having, moreover, the power to issue commands to both sides, — he could not, so far as the Americans were concerned, have bettered the course of events. The whole purpose of the move was to forestall the proposed operations of the British, who planned on the 18th, only a day later, to occupy Bunker Hill and Dorchester Heights, preliminary to an advance on the patriot lines at Cambridge. It was intended to draw their fire. If, in doing this, Prescott had, in obedience to his orders, and as technically he unquestionably should have done, contented himself with seizing Bunker Hill and there intrenching, it can hardly be questioned that the British would then have landed on Charlestown Neck, immediately in his rear, and forced him to retreat precipitately as the alternative to surrender. His very reckless audacity in moving forward to Breed's Hill led to their attacking him squarely in front.

Had Prescott directed the assaulting column, he would have ordered it to do just that. But his good fortune did not stop here. Twice he repulsed the attacking force, inflicting terrible loss upon it; and this is his great claim for credit on that memorable day. Prescott was evidently a fighter. He showed this by his forward midnight move from Bunker to Breed's Hill; and he showed it still more by the way in which he kept a levy of raw ploughmen steady there during the trying hours that preceded conflict; and then, in face of the advancing line of regulars, made them hold their fire until he gave the word. This was superb, — it deserves unstinted praise. Again, the luck of the Americans soared in the ascendant. Under the exact conditions in which they then found themselves, they had chanced on the right man in the right place, — and it was one chance in a thousand.

And then followed yet more good luck, — indeed, a crowning stroke. Twice did Prescott repulse his enemy. Had he done so a third time, he would have won a victory, held his position, and, the next day, in all human probability, the force which relieved him would have been compelled to surrender, because of properly conducted operations in its rear under cover of the British fleet. For it is impossible to suppose that Clinton's advice would not then have been followed; and had it been followed, with Clinton in charge of the operations in the field, a result not unusual in warfare would no doubt have been witnessed, — the temporary and partial success of one day would have been converted into the irretrievable disaster of the succeeding day. It was so with Napoleon himself at Ligny and Waterloo.

Fortunately for Prescott and the patriot cause, the ammunition within the Bunker Hill redoubt was pretty much consumed before the third assault was made; and so his adversaries drove the patriot commander out of his trap and into the arms of his own friends. In spite of himself Prescott was saved from ultimate disaster. Yet, curiously enough, he does not even then seem to have realized his

THE BATTLE OF BUNKER HILL 13

luck; for, instead of going back to the headquarters of General Ward, as well he might have gone, in a towering rage over the incompetence which had put him and his command in such a position, without reason or support — a position from which he had escaped only by a chance in a thousand, — in place of taking this view of the matter, he actually offered, if a fresh force 1500 strong was put under his command, to recross Charlestown Neck and recapture Bunker Hill the next day, — in other words, to go back into the trap from which the stupidity of his opponents had forcibly driven him!

The original plan of operations matured by the Cambridge council, including as it did the simultaneous occupation of both Prospect and Bunker Hills, was, therefore, bold, well-conceived, calculated to produce the results desired, and entirely practicable; assuming always that the patriot army had the necessary artillery and ammunition to equip and defend the works it was proposed to construct. Such was not the case; but, doubtless, under the circumstances, something had to be risked.

This plan, thoroughly good as a mere plan, was, however, executed in part only, and in such a way as to expose the provincial army and cause to disaster of the worst kind. And yet, through the chances of war, — the pure luck of the patriots, — every oversight of which they were guilty, every blunder they committed, worked to their advantage, and contributed to the success of their operations! They completely drew the British fire and forestalled the contemplated offensive operations, throwing the enemy on the defensive; they inspired the American militia with confidence in themselves, filling them with an aggressive spirit; they fired the continental ardor; and, finally, the force engaged was extricated from a false and impossible position, after inflicting severe punishment on its opponents. For that particular occasion and under the circumstances, Cromwell or Frederick or Napoleon in command would probably have accomplished less; for, with the means at disposal, they never would have dared to take such risks, nor would they ever have thrust themselves into such an utterly untenable position.

To penetrate the mind and plan of an opponent — to pluck out the heart of his counsel and to make dispositions accordingly — has ever been dwelt upon as one of the chief attributes of the highest military genius, — Hannibal, Cæsar, Gustavus, Marlborough, Frederick, Napoleon, all possessed it in a noticeable degree. Possibly, General Ward and Colonel Prescott may instinctively have acted in obedience to this rarest military quality on the 16th and 17th of June, 1775. If so, they certainly developed a capacity for which the world has not since given them credit; and the immediate results justified to the fullest extent their apparently almost childlike reliance on the combined professional incapacity and British bull-headedness of General Thomas Gage. Fourteen months later, as will hereafter be seen, Ward's more famous successor got himself and his army into a position on Long Island scarcely less false and difficult than Prescott's at Bunker Hill.[1] He, also, was then saved from irretrievable disaster through sheer good luck, happily combined with his opponent's incompetence. In this case, however, Fortune did not, as at Bunker Hill, positively shower its favors on the patriot cause.

Yet in one respect the battle of Bunker Hill was, in reality, epochal. Prescott did not occupy Breed's Hill and begin to throw up his intrenchments until nearly midnight on the 16th–17th of June. Thus his men had but about four

[1] *Infra*, 28–35.

hours in which to work before the break of day disclosed their whereabouts. Yet when, less than twelve hours later, the British stormed the field-works, they were amazed at their extent and completeness, and could not believe that they had all been thrown up in a single summer's night. It was something new in warfare.

There can be few things more instructive and suggestive, from a military point of view, than a visit to the battle-fields of Waterloo and Sedan, passing rapidly from the former to the latter. To one whose impressions of active warfare and military field methods are drawn from campaigns in Virginia, now thirty years ago, it is not easy, while surveying the scenes of the battles of 1815 and 1870, to understand what the English in the one case and the French in the other were doing in the hours which preceded the engagements. In the Virginia campaigns nothing was of more ordinary observation than the strength and perfect character of the intrenchments which both armies habitually threw up. Such skill in the alignment and construction of these works did the common rank and file of the armies acquire, that a few hours always sufficed to transform an ordinary bivouac into a well-protected camp. In the case of Waterloo, the Duke of Wellington had days and even weeks before selected it as his battle ground; he had even caused a topographical survey to be made of it; he arrived there from Quatre Bras twenty hours before the battle of Waterloo began; he made all his dispositions at his leisure. Yet not a spadeful of dirt seems to have been thrown; and the next day, while his line was exposed to the fury of Napoleon's famous artillery, the French cavalry rode unobstructed in and out among the English squares.

It seems to have been the same, more than half a century later, at Sedan. Strategically, the French were there in almost as false a position as the Americans at Bunker Hill. They were in a hole, — rats in a trap. Tactically, their position was by no means bad. The ancient fortifications of Sedan secured and covered their centre; while their two wings were free to operate on the high grounds behind, sloping sharply to the river. They occupied the inside of a curve, with perfect facilities for the concentration of force by interior lines. A better opportunity, so far as the character of the ground and country was concerned, for the rapid throwing up of intrenchments and field-works could not have been desired. As at Waterloo, the facilities were everywhere. McMahon's army, when surprised and cornered in Sedan, was, it is true, on its march to Metz, and all was in confusion. But they had twelve hours' notice of what was impending, and they fought on the ground on which they had slept. Yet, again, not a spadeful of dirt seems to have been thrown. What were the French thinking of or doing all those hours?

Judging by the record of Bunker Hill, and recollections of what was habitually done ninety years later in Virginia, if an army of either Federals or Confederates, as developed in 1865, had held the ground of the British at Waterloo or the French at Sedan, the lines and intrenchments which on the days of battle would have confronted Napoleon and Von Moltke could hardly have failed to give them pause. Before those temporary works they would have seen their advancing columns melt away, as did Gage at Bunker Hill, Pakenham at New Orleans, and Lee at Gettysburg.

The simple fact seems to have been, that, until the modern magazine gun made it an absolute necessity, digging was never considered a part of the soldier's training. Indeed, it was looked upon as demoralizing. In the same way, the art of designing temporary field-works and camp intrenchments was not regarded as belonging to the regimental officers' functions. The famous lines of Torres Vedras showed that Wellington knew well how to avail himself of defensive works; but they were laid out on a large scale and on scientific principles. Mere temporary field-works and improvised protections seem to have been contemptuously looked down upon as a branch of irregular warfare or Indian fighting. It was something unprofessional; even savoring of cowardice. Often, during the War of Secession, old West Point graduates, high in rank but somewhat hidebound, might be heard lamenting in the same spirit over the ever-growing tendency of the armies to protect themselves by intrenchments wherever they camped. It made soldiers afraid of exposure! As the military martinets expressed it, they wanted the rank and file "to stand up, and fight man-fashion." How often, in those days, was that expression used! Yet their idea of fighting was apparently that of Wellington at Waterloo, and of McMahon at Sedan. At either of those places our veterans of 1865, Federals or Confederates, would have protected themselves with field-works, though only bayonets were to be had for picks, and tin dippers did duty for shovels.

Putnam, therefore, showed a very profound insight when, on the eve of Bunker Hill, he remarked that, as a soldier, the Yankee was peculiar. He didn't seem to care much, the Connecticut general said, about his head, but he was dreadfully afraid of his shins; cover him half-leg high, and you could depend on him to fight. The fact seems to be that, as a fighting animal, the Yankee is unquestionably observant. Breastworks are in battle handy to the assailed; and he saw at once that breastworks admit of rapid and easy construction to men accustomed to the use of shovel and pick. Prescott taught that lesson on the 17th of June, 1775.

He did not realize it, and apparently it took almost a century for the professional soldier to master the fact thoroughly; but those light, temporary earthworks, scientifically thrown up on Bunker Hill in the closing hours of a single June night, introduced a new element into the defensive tactics of the battle-field. Its final demonstration was at Plevna, a whole century later.

The facts in this paper set forth, and the inferences drawn therefrom, are so obvious that they would naturally suggest themselves to an investigator from an examination of any topographical map of the Charlestown peninsula, and more forcibly still to one familiar with the ground. From a military point of view, they were apparent at the time; and, naturally, have not wholly escaped attention since.

In the Library of the Massachusetts Historical Society there is a copy of Israel Mauduit's "Remarks upon Gen. Howe's Account of his Proceedings on Long Island" (London, 1778), on the fly leaf of which is pasted a clipping from an issue of the *London Chronicle*, of August 3, 1779, containing a communication signed with the initials "T. P." The letter was written shortly after the reports concerning the Bunker Hill affair reached England, and with some knowledge of the locality. Every position taken and criticism advanced in the text will be there found set forth as something well understood at the time, and which did not admit of dispute. In a pamphlet entitled "A View of the Evidence Relating to the Conduct of the American War under Sir William Howe," are printed certain letters and documents entitled "Fugitive Pieces," etc. First among these is a letter from Boston, dated July 5, 1775, or eighteen days after the battle. It was written apparently by a British officer then serving under General Gage; and in it the tactics employed by Howe are severely criticised. The writer says: "Had we intended to have taken the whole rebel army prisoners, we need only have landed in their rear and occupied the high ground above Bunker Hill, by this movement we shut them up in the Peninsula as in a bag, their rear exposed to the fire of our cannon, and if we pleased our musketry; in short they must have surrendered instantly, or been blown to pieces. . . . The brave men's [i.e. British] lives were wantonly thrown away. Our conductor [Howe] as much murdered them as if he had cut their throats himself on Boston Common." See *Proceedings* of Mass. Hist. Soc., 1910, Vol. XLIV, pp. 96–103. In the library of Harvard University there is a pamphlet, entitled, "The Complaint of W. Neil Maclean to the Honorable the Commons of Great Britain in Parliament Assembled" (123 pp. 8vo). A very rare tract, this was published, apparently, about 1790, and is a severe arraignment of Sir William Howe by an officer who claims to have been most unjustly treated by him. His allegations are, accordingly, to be accepted in part only, and as indicating views held in British military circles. Speaking of what occurred on June 17, Maclean says (p. 26): " He [Howe] began . . . by the fatal attack of Bunker's Hill, where he exposed, to certain and inevitable destruction, and as far as depended on him, to woeful disgrace and dishonour, such a number of the best troops in the whole world ; before the face of an open intrenchment, that might have been attacked in the rear from both sides of the neck of land on which it was drawn, and carried without risquing the life of a single soldier."

Such were contemporaneous judgments expressed by British officers either themselves at the time on the ground or informed by participants in the operations ; yet in the extensive subsequent historical literature relating to Bunker Hill only here and there are passing references to be found to the strategic situation and tactical conditions involved; or the lessons to be derived therefrom. They are mentioned, or alluded to, in an incidental sort of way, without apparent appreciation of possible consequences, or reflection upon those on both sides responsible for what occurred. As long ago as August, 1789, however, Jeremy Belknap wrote: " I have lately been on the ground and surveyed it with my own eye, and I think it was a most hazardous and imprudent affair on both sides. Our people were extremely rash in taking so advanced a post without securing a retreat; and the British were equally rash in attacking them only in front, when they could so easily have taken them in the rear."

(*Mass. Hist. Soc. Coll.* Series 5, Vol. III, p. 159). Gordon in his history (Vol. II, p. 51) dwells upon the topic, passing a correct judgment in the assertion that the British commander "might have entrapped the provincials by landing on the narrowest part of Charlestown Neck, under the fire of the floating batteries and ships of war." But, of the modern writers, Frothingham scarcely alludes to the subject; while Devens, himself a soldier of experience, only refers to it incidentally and in a passing way (*Centennial Anniversary*, p. 87). Carrington's criticism (*Battles of the American Revolution*, p. 113) is of the most meagre possible description. Bancroft devotes to it three lines. Fiske (*The American Revolution*, I, p. 138) states the case briefly, but clearly and correctly.

Perhaps, however, the best purely military criticism is that in Stedman's *History* (Vol. I, 128). Stedman was not in Boston or attached to the British army at the time; but, subsequently, he had access to the most reliable sources of information, and was in constant personal intercourse with participants in the affair. He also wrote in the light of a wide experience in later operations during the same war. Stedman describes the British troops as marching up to the assault "in the middle of a hot summer's day, incumbered with three days' provisions, their knapsacks on their backs, which, together with cartouche-box, ammunition, and firelock, may be estimated at one hundred and twenty-five pounds weight, with a steep hill to ascend, covered with grass reaching to their knees, and intersected with the walls and fences of various inclosures, and in the face of a hot and well-directed fire . . . (from) behind a breastwork, and defended by a redoubt. But, whatever credit may be due to the valour of the troops, the plan of the attack has been severely censured.

"Had the *Symmetry* transport, which drew little water, and mounted eighteen nine-pounders, been towed up Mystic channel, and been brought to, within musket shot of the left flank, which was quite naked; or one of our covered boats, musket-proof, carrying a heavy piece of cannon, been towed close in; one charge on their uncovered flank, it was said, might have dislodged them in a moment. It has been also said, that the British troops might have been landed in the rear of the provincial intrenchment, and thereby avoided those difficulties and impediments which they had to encounter in marching up in front. By such a disposition, too, the breast-work of the Americans would have been rendered useless, and their whole detachment, being inclosed in the peninsula, must have either surrendered at discretion, or attempted, in order to get back to the main land, to cut their way through the British line. Further still, it has been said, that the success of the day was the less brilliant, from no pursuit being ordered, after the provincials had begun to take to flight."

II

THE BATTLE OF LONG ISLAND[1]

"THE dilatoriness and stupidity of the enemy saved us," wrote General Charles Lee to Washington in July, 1776, immediately after the repulse of the British fleet under Sir Peter Parker by the guns of Fort Moultrie on the first attempt at the occupation of Charleston, South Carolina. The same qualities in those opposed to Washington, combined with an almost amazing run of pure luck, saved him and the cause of American independence at New York less than two months later. Not often has a military force on which great results depended found itself in a more critical position than did the patriot army then; and seldom has any commander so completely in the toils been afforded equal opportunities for extrication.

Analyzed from any thoughtful as well as military point of view, it was a strange fiasco that enacted in and about what are now the cities of Brooklyn and New York during the months of August, September and October, 1776 — a fiasco on the part of all responsible for what occurred, though very tragic for many of those involved on the American side. So far as the British were concerned, the failure of those in command then to avail themselves of oppor-

[1] The substance of this paper appeared in two articles; the first printed in the *American Historical Review*, Vol. 1, pp. 650–670, July, 1896; the second, in the *Proceedings* of the Mass. Hist. Soc. Vol. XLIV, pp. 233–253, December, 1910. These articles have been revised and largely rewritten. Where not given, citations to authorities, etc., can be found by reference to the original publications.

tunities repeatedly offered both is, and at the time was, so apparent that the modern tendency is to attribute what they did, or failed to do, to secret instructions or, perhaps, some tacit understanding; military advantages were, for some occult reasons of state, not to be pressed too far, or to any decisive result. On the other hand, upon the American side, not only was a great cause put in extreme jeopardy, but, through the unskilful pursuance of a policy altogether wrong, many and valuable lives were unnecessarily sacrificed.

Major General Howe, afterwards Sir William Howe, K. C. B., is, as an historical character, of no great moment, and investigators are free to do with him as they may see fit; but that Washington should have then been responsible for grave errors of judgment which ought under any reasonable weighing of probabilities to have ruined the American cause and deprived the world of one of its immortalities, — that he should have involved his army in disaster and disgrace through bad judgment and because of frequent and long hesitations at a time when quick decision was essential, — these are things not readily now to be admitted; nor does the record thus in any way so read in the pages of the distinctively American historian. Though manifestly not in accord with long-accepted traditions, or, perhaps, even with the everlasting fitness of things, such seem, however, to be the only inferences fairly to be drawn from the evidence in the case, when that evidence is studied in a cold and purely critical spirit, uninspired by patriotism, and devoid of sympathy for those concerned either on the one side or the other. But, so studied, the necessary conclusion would seem to be that if there was at Bunker Hill gross military blundering on both sides, before Brooklyn and on Manhattan Island that blundering was on both sides fairly outdone. The British commander there almost wantonly threw away the certainty of a decisive and, probably, a final victory; while not even the "dilatoriness and stupidity of the enemy" saved the patriots from disasters and from disgrace which in no way, moral or otherwise, could be exploited as a victory.

The course of events leading up to the operations referred to were, briefly, as follows. The British evacuated Boston on the 16th of March. By those in charge of the patriot cause the point at which the next blow would be struck could only be surmised ; but New York naturally suggested itself. Obviously it was the strategic centre of the very extensive region in which the war had to be carried on; and, as such, invited attack. From it as a base, and from it alone of American Atlantic seaports, could large and intricate combined operations, covering all the Provinces, be conducted. A movement by the British in that direction had naturally been anticipated by the American leaders early in 1776, and General Charles Lee was, accordingly, detached from the army before Boston, and by order of Washington repaired to New York, there to make suitable provision against attack. Arriving on the 4th of February, he at once took in the difficulties of the situation. "What to do with this city," he wrote to Washington, "I own, puzzles me. It is so encircled with deep navigable water, that whoever commands the sea must command the town." The command of the sea being manifestly the key of the situation, that the British held that key was no less manifest.

Lee, nevertheless, proceeded to plan such a system of defences as seemed practicable; but, being subsequently assigned by Congress to the command of the Department of the South, he left New York on the 7th of March, leaving Major General Lord Stirling, as he was called, in temporary charge. Stirling, shortly after, was in his turn superseded by General Israel Putnam, under instructions from Washington to go on with the preparations for defence in accordance with Lee's plans. On the 13th of April, Washington himself arrived, and assumed command.

Washington had taken it for granted that, after its evacuation of Boston in March, 1776, the British armament would proceed at once to New York; but, instead of so doing, it went to Halifax, there to refit. Not until June 29 did the reënforced expedition reach Sandy Hook, inside of which it came to anchor; and, landing his army on Staten Island, General Howe there awaited the arrival of additional ships and still further reënforcements, then shortly looked for, under command of his brother, Admiral Lord Howe. These appeared in July.

Washington at that time found himself in command of some 9000 so-called effectives, "2000 of whom were entirely destitute of arms." This force was very imperfectly organized. Insufficiently armed, clothed and equipped, it was largely composed of unreliable militia. Without adequate artillery, it had no cavalry at all. Of naval support there was not even a pretence. How, with such means, to defend a place at the command of whoever controlled the sea, against a thoroughly equipped and disciplined force twice the size of his, and that force supported by a powerful fleet, was the problem with which the Commander-in-Chief found himself confronted. For two whole months did he study his problem doubtless in its every aspect; and not once in all that time does it seem to have occurred to him that it was not only insoluble, but that any considerable attempt at its solution was fraught with extreme danger. During these months he wrote many letters and prepared some formal reports; but in not one of them does he even suggest that the course pursued was opposed to his military judgment or based on incorrect strategic principles. He never even hints that under the pressure of an assumed political necessity he is taking what seems to him a dangerous military risk. On the contrary, even after the inevitable disaster had befallen him, he truthfully and frankly wrote "Till of late, I had no doubt in my own mind of defending this place."

Yet in the course of this attempt at a defence Washington was compelled to violate, and did violate, almost every recognized principle of warfare. To defend New York it was absolutely necessary to hold the heights of Brooklyn, opposite the city; for those heights, as Bunker Hill in the case of Boston, commanded New York within easy artillery range. But Brooklyn, separated from New York by deep navigable water, was on an island. Above New York, on both sides east and west, were other wide, navigable waterways, which also had to be covered by defences. Again, if, under such conditions, successful resistance was possible, it was only possible through holding to a policy of intrenchments. The patriot force should have been kept within the strongest line of defence possible to be devised; and, as at Bunker Hill, prepared to resist attack in front, it had to trust to the incompetence of its opponents that the attack would indeed be in front, and not in rear: but if, perchance, the attack should be from the rear, with the enemy in absolute control of the water, and free to strike when and where he pleased, the American army manifestly stood in imminent danger of destruction. Precipitate retreat by any route left open could alone save it.

Under these circumstances and conditions, Washington not only divided his inadequate army, but when his opponent obliged him by attacking just where alone he could hope to resist an attack, that is, in full front, instead of awaiting

THE BATTLE OF LONG ISLAND 27

the assault within his lines, as did Prescott at Bunker Hill, Washington actually went out to meet it, thus challenging the fate which befell him. Finally, even his own excellent management, in the hour of disaster he had thus provoked, could not have saved the patriot cause from irretrievable ruin and himself from hopeless failure and disgrace, had it not been combined with almost miraculous good luck, to which the "dilatoriness and stupidity of the enemy" most effectively contributed. This, too, at the very juncture when those under Howe confidently wrote that the British commander would not give his opponent "time to breathe, but push his successes like a winning gamester."

Though General Howe had come to anchor inside of Sandy Hook June 29, and been joined there by Lord Howe and the fleet July 1, it was not until August 22 that active operations on Long Island began. During that long interval of over seven weeks of the best campaigning weather of the whole year, the British army rested quietly in its summer camp on Staten Island. On July 12 two English ships, respectively of forty and twenty guns, had run by the North River defences without sustaining any injury, and gone up the Hudson to the Tappan Sea; where, until August 18, they lay in apparent perfect security, with awnings stretched, sleeping in the summer sunshine. Altogether a somewhat contemptuous demonstration of how complete was the British command of the sea, and how futile were the American efforts to obstruct the navigable channels. August 7 thirty transports, under convoy of three frigates, put to sea with the design of going around Long Island, and so threatening New York from the Sound and East River side. The line of American retreat from Brooklyn to the mainland was imperilled. All this time the two Howes were in daily communication with the royalist governor,

Tryon, of New York, who was on board one of the English ships-of-war; and, through other sympathizers on the mainland and Long Island, they could get all the information they chose to ask for, not only as to localities and roads, but in regard to the movements of the patriots. Plentifully supplied with provisions, the invaders lacked neither guides on the land nor pilots by water. Under these circumstances, it was small matter of surprise that, as the weeks dragged on, many of Washington's ablest advisers looked on the situation with ever increasing uneasiness. They feared being entrapped "on this tongue of land, where," as one of them later expressed it, "we ought never to have been."

Besides the fleet, the British commander had, by the middle of August, an army 30,000 strong in a high state of efficiency, with a large park of artillery and a small, but completely equipped, body of cavalry. Washington at the same time had nominally 17,500 men, of whom about 14,000 were reported fit for duty. With a few pieces of artillery, he still had no mounted force. And with such means at his command, incredible as it seems, he actually thought he could defend a land and water front of nearly thirty miles, open to attack front, flank and rear, besides being cut in two by a navigable channel both broad and deep. His opponent, meanwhile, was obviously free to concentrate whatever of force might be necessary for a decisive blow at any selected point. Neither did Washington indulge in any false confidence in the efficacy of his water-batteries to hold in check, at least to a certain degree, the enemy's maritime supremacy; on the contrary, as he himself wrote a whole month before actual operations against him began, he "had most religiously believed that a vessel with a brisk wind and strong tide cannot, unless by a chance shot, be stopped by a battery."

The interior works at Brooklyn alone called for a force of at least 8000 men to hold them with any prospect of success; while the exterior lines before Flatbush required an equal number, if the enemy was to be retarded there even for a day. In other words, if Howe was, as at Bunker Hill, obliging enough to attack full in front, and by land alone, the position on Long Island Washington had undertaken to defend, seeking no coöperation from the British fleet and leaving his opponent's New York rear quite unmolested, — even in this case, more than the whole force of the patriot army would be needed for the defence of Brooklyn alone.

At last, everything, after weeks of apparently needless procrastination, being in readiness, the Howes determined to strike, and on the 22d of August, Sir Henry Clinton, with 15,000 men, one regiment of cavalry, and forty pieces of artillery, crossed over from Staten to Long Island and landed, unopposed, at Gravesend. It was now evident where the blow by land was to be looked for. Brooklyn was the enemy's objective; or, at least, one of his objectives.

Why the two Howes decided on this plan of campaign is not apparent. Strategically considered, Washington had put himself in a position exactly similar to that in which Prescott had tactically been placed fourteen months before at Bunker Hill. With his opponent in undisputed command of navigable surrounding and intersecting waters, he was in a trap. The true policy of his opponents would seem to have been so to lay their plans as, not to drive him out of the trap, but to spring its door, so catching him. This they could easily have done, had Howe only learned thoroughly his 17th of June lesson. He had, however, done so only in part. He had derived from it, as will presently be seen, a wholesome caution as to bull-headed, frontal assaults, but the far-reaching significance of a command of the sea under certain conditions seems quite to have escaped his intellectual grasp, at best limited. Except on this assumption, it is still a mystery, why, under cover of the overwhelming broadsides of his brother's fleet, Howe did not go up the comparatively unobstructed Hudson to Bloomingdale, landing about where Sixtieth Street now is, three miles above the outskirts of the New York of that day; and then, crossing a strong division of his army to the East side, sweep down on Washington, by the Boston road, now Third Avenue, forcing him into the East River. To counteract such a movement it would have been necessary for the Americans precipitately to withdraw their forces from the Brooklyn side of the East River, and concentrate them at the point of British attack. This movement would have consumed much important time; if, in presence of a detachment of the British fleet in the East River, practicable at all. The combined British naval and military forces could have effected the manœuvre with certainty and ease, the broadsides of the fleet then covering the Bloomingdale, or Albany road, now Broadway, and demoralizing the flank and rear of the patriots just as they demoralized and broke the patriot line of battle a fortnight later at Kips Bay. The weight of attack being down the East side, the patriots would have been between two fires. From both the strategic and the tactical points of view the movement was so obvious and its success so certain that the failure of the Howes to adopt it must forever remain unaccountable. They elected, however, to attack Washington squarely on his Brooklyn front, with his army cut in two by the East River, and his means of communication uncovered on the water side. Even that situation was bad enough for the patriots; in fact could not have been from the purely military point of view much worse or more ill-considered. The door of the Brooklyn trap behind them might any day be snapped.

The difficulties of his situation, not to say its impossibilities, must, it would seem, now have dawned on Washington's mind. As he himself mildly put it,[1] making no allusion to a hostile fleet, operating in the broad navigable waters which on three sides compassed him, the problem was "to oppose an army of 30,000 experienced veterans with about one-third (10,514) the number of raw troops, and those scattered some fifteen miles apart."

Though the British force was transferred across from Staten Island to Gravesend August 22, it was not until the evening (9 o'clock) of the 26th, or four days later, that a forward movement was made. Constant skirmishing had meanwhile been going on, and the Americans had thus been allowed ample time in which to take the situation in, and make preparations accordingly. In the enemy's advance, there was no element of surprise. During the earlier stages of preparation for defence, General Nathanael Greene had been in charge of the Brooklyn wing of the patriot army; but he, taken down by a summer fever, had some time before been rendered wholly unfit for duty. General Sullivan succeeded him in temporary charge. All along, Washington and Greene had seen, what indeed was obvious, that, with the means at their disposal, a landing of the British on Long Island could not be prevented; but, if Brooklyn was once occupied by the enemy, New York became untenable. The British in that case would hold the heights, and the Americans the town commanded by the heights. The problem immediately involved was, therefore, the defence of Brooklyn against an attack from the land side, in all probability supported by a simultaneous

[1] *Writings* (Sparks), IV, 34.

attack on its water front, and the American rear. Greene had, accordingly, sought to cover Brooklyn by constructing a line of intrenchments and redoubts back of the village from Gowanus Cove on the south to Wallabout Bay on the north, presenting to an enemy approaching from the south and west a front of a little less than a mile in extent, well protected by creeks and morasses on either flank, and, at its centre, about one mile and a quarter from the landing-place of the East River ferry across to New York. From these intrenchments to Gravesend, the natural landing-place for the British, was some eight miles, while between the two, about five miles from Gravesend and three from Brooklyn, rose a difficult, heavily wooded ridge, forming a natural longitudinal barrier practically passable at three points: one close to the bay, the shore road; the second, three miles further inland, in front of Flatbush, being the direct and ordinary road between Gravesend and Brooklyn; and the third the Jamaica road, two miles further still to the east. Under these circumstances, assuming that they were in sufficient force and resolved to hold New York, the course to be pursued by the Americans was obvious. As soon as the landing of the British at Gravesend was known, that is, on August 22, the largest force available ought to have been concentrated under cover of the Brooklyn in-trenchments, while strong infantry outposts should have been put at each of the three passes, the roads beyond being constantly watched by mounted patrols. To do this work at least 15,000 men, with adequate artillery and cavalry, would have been required, a certain mounted force being on such extended lines indispensable to safety. The force actually there was 5500 infantry, mostly militia, none of whom had ever been in battle, with six pieces of light field artillery, and no cavalry whatever.

Under these circumstances, instead of concentrating themselves within the Brooklyn intrenchments when the English, after four days of delay, began to advance, the Americans actually went out in force to meet them on two of the roads, leaving the third, that to Jamaica, not only unprotected, but not even watched. The natural result followed. Taking advantage of their great preponderance in numbers, and excellent information and guidance, the British, advancing by three columns, found, to their great surprise, the Jamaica road unobstructed, — "a route we had never dreamed of," as an American officer engaged innocently wrote, — and, by means of it, got in the rear of the detachments under Stirling and Sullivan, who had been either posted or hurried forward to defend the two western, and more direct, approaches; and the practical destruction of those detachments followed. Both commanders were captured, and more than one-third of the entire force disposable for the defence of Brooklyn was destroyed. The American loss in killed, wounded, and missing was about 1500, out of a total engaged probably not exceeding 3500. Contemporaneous comments are sometimes the best, and it would be difficult to improve on those upon this affair shortly after jotted down by Captain Stephen Olney of the Rhode Island regiment in Stirling's command. They cover the case. "At the time, I did not pretend to know or examine the generalship of posting Sullivan's and Stirling's forces as they were, leaving the forts but poorly manned with sick and invalids. It must be on the supposition that the enemy would come on the direct road, and if our troops were overpowered, they might retreat and defend the fort. But the enemy took a circuitous route, and where it was said Colonel ——— had neglected to guard, and arrived in our rear without notice. Had it been left to the British generals to make a disposition of our troops, it is a chance if they would have made it more advantageous to themselves, and but for their tardiness they might have taken our main fort. All that seemed to prevent it was a scarecrow row of palisades from the fort to low water in the cove, which Major Box had ordered set up that morning."[1]

It is not putting it too strongly to say that Washington's position, as well as that of the American cause, was then desperate. The disaster occurred under Washington's eyes early in the day; and before two o'clock the fighting had wholly ceased. With an inadequate and demoralized command, he found himself isolated from the body of his army, such as it was; and, while a largely superior force flushed with success was marshalled before him, a fairly overwhelming naval armament threatened the ferry in his rear. In other words, he had got himself and his cause into a wholly false position. Again, luck and "the dilatoriness and stupidity of the enemy" saved him.

The course for Howe to pursue was now manifest. Six good hours of daylight remained after the commands of Stirling and Sullivan had been demolished. During those hours he should have followed up his success, striking at once and with all his force at Washington himself. Such was the decided opinion at the moment of Howe's subordinates, while the body of the British army was so flushed by victory and absolutely confident of success that it could with difficulty be restrained from immediate assault; on the other hand, so thoroughly demoralized were the defeated patriots that the general in command of one of the British divisions subsequently asserted, "the very camp women who followed his regiment took them prisoners." American historians have since asserted, on what authority does not

[1] *Battle of Long Island* (Long Island Historical Society), 518.

THE BATTLE OF LONG ISLAND

appear, that the British commander was then wise in not pressing his advantage, and that Washington "courted a storm in which he was almost sure to be victorious"; but, on the other hand, a general officer, in command of a portion of the Brooklyn lines, described them at the time as "unfinished in several places" and "so low that the rising ground immediately without it would have put it in the power of a man at 40 yards Distance to fire under my Horse's belly whenever he pleased." To the same effect another officer then present afterwards wrote, describing the line in front of where he was posted as "low and unfavorable for defence," and "commanded by the ground occupied by the enemy, who entirely enclosed the whole of our position, at the distance of but a few hundred paces"; and, he added, "as to General Howe, I have scarcely a doubt that he might have carried the intrenchments at Brooklyn." And such works as these it has since been confidently asserted could have been victoriously defended by militia, to use Washington's official language, "timid and ready to fly from their own shadows."

At Bunker Hill, Howe had been overconfident; at Brooklyn he was too cautious. The inference is natural that August 27, 1776, he remembered June 17, 1775; and, a burnt child, he feared the fire. In any event, after lying for hours with his advance within gunshot of Washington's lines, which his scouts approached so closely as to report that they could be carried almost instantly by assault, and which his subordinates begged leave to be allowed to attack and fairly "stormed with rage when ordered to retire," — after lying here for hours during a summer noon, he declared that enough had been done for one day, and, drawing back, went into camp. In his official report of these operations he stated that in his judgment the works could have been stormed, and that his soldiers were so eager for the assault "that it required repeated orders to prevail on them to desist"; but as it was apparent the opposing lines could be carried with slight loss by regular approaches, he commanded a halt.

So far "the dilatoriness of the enemy" had saved Washington from total disaster. The element of luck next made itself felt in his favor. The British fleet was lying inside of Sandy Hook. It was impossible for a moment to suppose that the numerous ships of the line and frigates there idly anchored were not to coöperate with the army in the long-planned and carefully prepared operations. They might engage the batteries on the North River, and cover a landing there, taking the enemy in the rear; or, most fatal move of all, they might run the batteries on the East River, and, destroying all means of transportation from its Brooklyn rear to the New York side, cut the American army hopelessly in two. It was now the close of August, and in the region of New York the prevailing wind at that season is from the southwest. Such a wind may, indeed, almost be counted upon; and unquestionably was counted upon by the British commanders in planning their operations. A wind from the southwest and a favoring tide would have carried the British ships swiftly up the East River, under full sail. Chance ordered otherwise. While General Howe was destroying the commands of Stirling and Sullivan, and threatening Washington's entrenchments, a strong northeast wind was blowing, against which, and the tide, five ships of the line, under command of Sir Peter Parker, in vain endeavored to work into the positions assigned them in the programme. One ship of smaller size alone succeeded in working up sufficiently far to open with its guns on the wholly inadequate battery the Americans had established at Red

THE BATTLE OF LONG ISLAND 37

Hook, on the western extremity of their Brooklyn lines; and the fire of even this single ship sufficed sadly to injure the breastworks, and dismount some of the guns. If this was so, the effect of the broadsides of the fleet may be surmised. That exceptional northeast wind in August was for Washington a stroke of luck of the description sometimes classified as "providential."

The American historians next lay much stress on the sufferings of the patriot army due to the inclemency of an August storm, — the wet and cold to which the men were subjected, and the privations to which they were compelled to submit. Active campaigning is at no season a holiday business; and, to those at all familiar with its details, alternately monotonous and terrible, it cannot but be open to question whether a cold midsummer storm, accompanied with mist, or even rain, could well in the latitude of New York afford a sufficient excuse for military inactivity, much less for demoralization. But whether it could or no, that cold, August, northeasterly storm and mist, if it did wet and chill the patriot army, also shrouded it and saved it. It prevented Admiral Lord Howe from getting between Brooklyn and New York; and it seems to have kept General Howe snug in his temporary quarters.

The most reliable regiments of the patriot army had been destroyed on the 27th in the commands of Sullivan and Stirling. Thus during the afternoon of the 27th and the morning of the 28th the position of the patriots was even more dangerous than it was forlorn. Militia — wet, cold, hungry, and demoralized by a spectacle of defeat — are not to be depended on at any hour of the day; least of all in a four-o'clock-in-the-morning assault: and had Howe ordered Clinton or Cornwallis to carry the works before them by a vigorous assault at daybreak of the 28th, there is, our patriotic historians to the contrary notwithstanding, hardly room for reasonable doubt that the course of American history would have been other than it has been. It was again the "dilatoriness of the enemy," and not this time the intervention of Providence, which saved the cause of independence.

Washington realized fully the nature of the situation. With between seven and eight thousand undisciplined men, beaten and demoralized at that, he was cooped up with an uncovered rear. Immediate retreat was impossible, and a successful resistance hardly to be hoped; so, like a good and vigilant commander, he was in the saddle before break of day of the 28th, going the rounds of the works and seeking to encourage his followers. The morning broke, lowering and dreary, only to reveal to the patriots the great superiority of the force opposed to them. It was a case of four to one. Fortunately the enemy did not move. As the day advanced they did, indeed, open with their artillery, and the usual irregular fire of sharp-shooters went on between the lines; but presently a drenching rain set in, by which the historians tell us the combatants were "driven into their tents," where they kept themselves until the latter hours of the day. There is almost a touch of humor at this point in the narrative, and it is difficult to believe that it is one of actual warfare. Yet the career of Washington and the cause of American independence actually hung in the balance, with an August rain the controlling factor! But, when it came to "dilatoriness," Sir William Howe always proved himself equal to any occasion.

Presently, while it was still early in the day, the Brooklyn situation was in a way and to a certain extent improved by the arrival of reënforcements under General Mifflin. This addition to the force consisted of three regiments considered as good as any in the army, though so reduced by sickness and other causes that they numbered all together but 1300 men. One of those regiments, however, was Glover's of Marblehead, mostly sailors and fishermen. Their coming was at least opportune ; for, with a wide and swift-flowing channel between him and his only possible line of retreat, Washington, as the result showed, then stood in quite as great need of men who could trim a sail and pull an oar as of those who could handle musket or shovel. Mifflin's command was marched at once into the weakly defended intrenchments on the left of the line, opposite Clinton.

Now one of the most extraordinary incidents of this singularly conducted campaign is said to have occurred. It sounds so like a travesty of war that it has to be told in the words of the apparently unconscious historian. A dense fog was hanging over the bay and island. A group of officers, among whom were Mifflin and Reed, Washington's adjutant-general, rode out to take a look about. As they were on the high ground at the western extremity of the lines facing towards Staten Island, a light breeze lifted the fog, disclosing to them the British ships of war. The historian then goes on: "Some movement was apparently in agitation. The idea occurred to the reconnoitring party that the fleet was preparing, should the wind hold and the fog clear away, to come up the bay at the turn of the tide, silence the feeble batteries at Red Hook and the city, and anchor in the East River. In that case, the army on Long Island would be completely surrounded and entrapped. . . . Other ships had passed round Long Island, and were at Flushing Bay on the Sound. Those might land troops on the east side of Harlem River and make themselves masters of King's Bridge; that key to Manhattan Island." These facts, as military considerations, might, it would seem, for several days, if not weeks, have been obvious; but, according to the American historians, they would appear to have now for the first time dawned on the minds of the reconnoitring officers, for, "alarmed at this perilous probability, they spurred back to headquarters, to urge the immediate withdrawal of the army (and) as this might not be acceptable advice, Reed, emboldened by his intimacy with the commander-in-chief, undertook to give it." It is curious to consider what the writer meant by the words "this might not be acceptable advice."

And it is of such material that what is called history is fabricated! This story passed into all the earlier accounts of the operations on Long Island, and, though now rejected by better authorities,[1] is still the popular legend. The incident is said to have occurred on the morning of the 29th; the disaster in front of Flatbush had occurred on the 27th; and it is safe to say that not for one moment during the slow intervening hours had the direction of the wind and the movements of the British fleet been absent from the mind not only of Washington, but of every intelligent officer or man within the Brooklyn lines. Their fate hung in the balance. The reconnoitring party may have ridden down to Red Hook in the way described — probably did ride down there; but what those composing it there saw could have suggested nothing new either to themselves or to Washington. It could only have emphasized the peril of the situation, and the necessity of immediately extricating themselves from it — if they could!

Up to this point it is not easy to see how military operations could have been carried on less skilfully on the side of the Americans. Neither the plan of defence, nor the execu-

---

[1] Bancroft. Note to Chapter V of Epoch Fourth, containing account of the retreat from Long Island.

tion of that plan, presents points for commendation; and for all that had been done, the record seems to show that Washington was responsible. In scope and detail, it was his plan; and he had personally superintended the operations involved in it. The resulting situation was to the last degree perilous. But it is just situations of this sort which bring out great qualities; and those of Washington were now revealed. He showed the *mens æqua in arduis!* Calm in outward aspect and with cool prescient mind, he looked the situation in the face, recognized the mistake he had made, and prepared to extricate himself from the consequences of it, if, indeed, extrication was yet possible. The chances were immensely against him. The withdrawal of the patriot army from Brooklyn, across the East River to New York, now accomplished, has commonly been referred to, especially by the "standard" American authorities as a feat displaying remarkable military capacity on the part of Washington. Fiske, for instance, becomes enthusiastic over it as a "brilliant incident," displaying "extraordinary skill."[1] On this point something will presently be said. Meanwhile, it cannot be denied that American historical writers have availed themselves to the utmost of the opportunity thus afforded. As Trevelyan truly observes, "it may be doubted whether any great national deliverance, since the passage of the Red Sea, has ever been more loudly acclaimed, or more adequately celebrated." For instance, one, a man himself not without military experience, thus dilates upon it: "The retreat from Brooklyn was a signal achievement, characteristic of Washington's policy and of the men who withdrew under his guidance . . . their Commander-in-Chief had his own plan, as before Boston, which he did not reveal to his officers until it

[1] *American Revolution*, I, 211, 212.

was ripe for execution." Early on the morning of August 29, orders were issued to General Heath, quartermaster-general, instructing him "'to impress every craft, on either side of New York, that could be kept afloat, and had either oars, or sails, or could be furnished with them, and to have them all in the East River by dark.' The response to these orders was so promptly made that the boats reached the foot of Brooklyn Heights just at dusk that afternoon."[1]

It is almost needless to say that, from any exact military point of view, this statement is both inaccurate and misleading. Yet Trevelyan repeats it and Fiske dilates upon it. Washington was not, however, the utter military simpleton such ill-considered admiration would indicate. He had not put himself and his army into a most dangerous position depending wholly, or in chief, on some suddenly improvised means of extrication. The order to Heath was, it is true, issued, and a certain amount of transportation, undoubtedly collected in obedience to it, was concentrated at the ferry; but the bulk of the means of transfer required was already at the point where it was needed. For weeks Washington had been moving troops, munitions, and supplies across the river, — 1300 men, for instance, on the day previous to the withdrawal, that following the disastrous Flatbush affair. The transportation thus hurriedly gathered together was, therefore, merely supplementary. The mass of what was required had already long before been provided.

Our narrative then proceeds as follows: —

> From about nine o'clock until nearly midnight, through wind and rain, — company by company, — sometimes grasping hands to keep companionship in the dense gloom, — speechless and silent, so that no sound should alarm the enemy, — feeling their way down the steep steps then leading to Fulton ferry, and feeling

[1] Carrington, *Washington the Soldier*, 110.

THE BATTLE OF LONG ISLAND 43

their way as they were passed into the waiting water-craft, these drenched and weary men took passage for New York. The wind and tide were so violent that even the seamen soldiers of Massachusetts could not spread a close reefed sail upon a single vessel; and the larger vessels, upon which so much depended, would have been swept to the ocean if once intrusted to the current. For three hours all the boats that could be thus propelled had to depend upon muffled oars. The difficulties of such a trip, on such a night, can be realized better by a moment's reflection. There is no record of the size of the waves, or of narrow escapes from upset, no intimation that there was competition in entering the boats and rivalry in choice of place — that each boat-load was landed hastily and that the boats themselves were leaky and unsafe; but any person who proposes to himself an imaginary transit over the East River under their circumstances, can supply the data he may need to appreciate the process.[1]

Re-writing this account for another edition of his work, many years later, the same authority modified it in this wise: —

As early as nine o'clock, and within an hour after the "general beat to arms," the movement began, — systematically, steadily, company by company, as orderly as if marching in their own camp. A fearful storm still raged. Drenched and weary, none complained. It was Washington's orders. Often hand-in-hand, to support each other, these men descended the steep, slippery slopes to the water's edge, and seated themselves in silence; while increasing wind and rain, with incessant violence, constantly threatened to flood, or sink, the miserable flat-boats which were to convey them to the city, only a few hundred yards away. And thus until midnight. At that hour the wind and tide became so violent that no vessel could carry even a closely reefed sail. The larger vessels, in danger of being swept out to sea, had to be held fast to shore; dashing against each other, and with difficulty kept afloat. Other boats, with muffled oars, were desperately but slowly propelled against the outgoing tide. A few sickly lanterns

[1] Carrington, *Battles of the American Revolution* (3d ed.), 217.

here and there made movement possible. The invisible presence of the Commander-in-Chief seemed to resolve all dangers and apparent confusion into some pervasive harmony of purpose among officers and men alike, so that neither leaking boats nor driving storm availed to disconcert the silent progress of embarking nearly ten thousand men.

Just after midnight, both wind and tide changed. The storm from the north which had raged thus long, kept the British fleets at their anchorage in the lower bay. At last, with the clearing of the sky and change of wind, the water became smooth, and the craft of all kinds and sizes, loaded to the water's edge, made rapid progress. Meanwhile strange to relate, a heavy fog rested over the lower bay and island, while the peninsula of New York was under clear starlight.[1]

No authorities are referred to for the somewhat highly wrought statements here so precisely and positively made.

The real weather conditions prevailing on the night in question are in vain sought for. The author whose work has been quoted says that the American and British archives and biography are full of contemporaneous data which it would require volumes to quote. A fairly careful search, on the contrary, discloses no detailed and reliable meteorological statement of the conditions hour by hour prevailing during the three days of the Brooklyn operations, and, more especially, during the night referred to in the foregoing extract.

The elementary and fundamental facts in the case are simple enough. Trevelyan says that on the morning of the 27th, the day of Howe's advance and the battle before Brooklyn, "the sun rose with a red and angry glare." A summer storm was brewing; and the wind, veering to the north from the east, must have been strong, for Lord Howe reports that "the ships could not be worked up to the dis-

Washington the Soldier (ed. 1898), 111.

THE BATTLE OF LONG ISLAND 45

tance proposed." Though the historians are silent on the point, it was, as already suggested, probably a knowledge of this fact and the consequent failure of the proposed naval coöperation, which caused General Howe to desist from following up his early success. Never to follow up a success on the field energetically was characteristic with him, — he failed so to do at Bunker Hill, on Manhattan Island and in New Jersey, and again at Brandywine and during the Valley Forge winter; but on Long Island he could hardly have helped so doing had he heard his brother's guns in the East River. He must then have gone forward, and finished up the job. All that day (27th) the storm seems to have been gathering. The next day we know it blew and rained; but while the rain apparently halted the work in the trenches and kept the soldiers in their huts, the sea was not so rough as to interfere with the operations of the ferry, or prevent the transfer of one whole brigade of Washington's army from the New York side to the Brooklyn lines. The bringing it over was an inexplicable mistake; they were simply so many more to get back again, or to be made prisoners when the wind worked into the west — to-morrow, perhaps; certainly within a few days. The atmospheric conditions this day (28th) seem to have culminated; for in the afternoon "a great rain and hail storm came on, attended with thunder and lightning." By the morning of the 29th the quite abnormal conditions had worn themselves out; "a dense fog covered land and sea," consequently there could have been no heavy rain nor driving wind. This seems to have continued pretty much all that day, necessarily holding Lord Howe's ships at their anchorage. Coöperation by land and sea was not yet possible; so General Howe waited. The succeeding night Washington got away.

During that night what weather conditions prevailed?

On this interesting topic the historians are curiously at odds among themselves. On no single point do they seem to agree; not even on the one astronomically ascertainable point, — the age of the moon, and the consequent luminous character of the atmosphere. One writer, already cited, says it was so pitchy dark that the men had to feel their way down to the ferry and into the boats; another says that "during the night the moon shone brightly." But a third comes with the assertion that, though it was the night of the full moon, these moonlit hours were marked by "a heavy rain and continued adverse wind." According to a fourth authority, "there was a strong wind from the northeast," but a "dense fog prevailed"; a most improbable meteorological combination, considering that "the atmosphere was clear on the New York side of the river." We are then informed that the strong "adverse wind" most opportunely died away and a "favoring breeze," from the opposite direction "sprang up." Not without reason is it declared that these somewhat surprising and altogether conflicting conditions "seemed almost providential." If they ever actually occurred, as is altogether improbable, they were distinctly and indisputably providential. Nothing at all resembling them is to be found in the prosaic records of the modern weather bureau; the single authenticated precedent is biblical.

Putting aside this fantastic combination — Egyptian darkness in a night of the full moon, a dense fog prevailing in the face of a driving tempest, a drenching rain on one side of a narrow river with a starlit sky on the other, a favoring breeze following immediately on the dying away of an adverse wind — putting all this aside, is it possible to ascertain the real state of the weather during the night of August 29–30, 1777? One fact is scientifically demonstrable. It was the night of the full moon.¹ The two days' storm — an August northeaster — had culminated with thunder, lightning, and hail on the 28th. The conditions then apparently prevailed which ordinarily attend the dying out of a late summer storm, and which precede a change to seasonable weather. The day of the 29th was foggy and chill, with a light draft of air from the north and east. The coöperative movement on the part of Admiral Lord Howe was still delayed, inasmuch as ships leaving their anchorage drifted, not having a sufficiency of wind to enable them to stem the tide; at times the mist lifted, and at times thickened. Later the night was still, the water quiet, the atmosphere luminous; a fog settled on the bay towards morning; every atmospheric condition aided the patriots, and, at the proper stage of the tide, the boats passed to and fro, favored by a light west breeze, and loaded to the gunwale. Not a single case of swamping or collision was recorded, or is known to have occurred. Not a boat upset; not a life was lost. These facts are under the conditions given conclusive as to the absence of wind, the quietude of the water, and the luminous character of the atmosphere.

That Washington, throughout these trying days, bore himself courageously and with great outward calmness in presence of imminent danger does not admit of question. On the other hand, divested of all gush, patriotism, hero worship and rhetoric generally, the cold historical truth would seem to be that, aided by a most happy fortuitous

¹ This point was, at the request of the writer of the present paper, referred for settlement to Professor Pickering of the Harvard University Observatory. Under date of December 5, 1910, Professor Pickering replied : —

"The full moon occurred on August 28, 1776, at 19 h. 59 m. As this is Greenwich astronomical time, the corresponding civil date at Greenwich was 7 h. 59 m. of the morning of August 29. At Boston the local civil time would have been about 4 h. 44 m. earlier."

concurrence of circumstances and the extreme supineness of his opponents, he on this occasion, keeping his head under wearing conditions and taking advantage of all the resources at his command, extricated himself and his army, at a most critical juncture, from an inherently false position into which neither he nor they ever should have either put themselves, or allowed themselves to be put. As respects skill, discipline, or careful organization of movement, if they were markedly in evidence, the fact nowhere appears in the record. That the British commanders, both military and naval, made the transfer possible, and facilitated it in every conceivable way, is indisputable. They evinced neither enterprise nor alertness. No patrol boats lurked in the fog which overhung the harbor, veiling their whereabouts from the land batteries; the opposing lines were not pried into by inquisitive or adventurous pickets. Even a negro, despatched by a female Tory sympathizer, one Mrs. Rapalye, to warn the British of the withdrawal in progress, fell into the hands of a Hessian picket, who, unable to make anything out of what he said to them, retained him till morning.[1] On the other hand, that the "speechless and silent" embarkation which nothing availed to disconcert was in fact marked by much confusion is established on the best possible authority — that of Washington himself. It is even stated that the lack of discipline was such that men absolutely tried to climb over each other's shoulders, the sooner to reach the boats. In the matter of transfer the boats themselves, meanwhile, were handled by perhaps as skilful a lot of men as could anywhere have been found, — Glover's regiment of Marblehead fishermen.

This paper relates merely to the 1776 operations on Long Island, and it is not necessary to follow the American army

[1] Irving, *Washington*, II, 390.

through its subsequent unfortunate experiences on the adjacent mainland. From a purely military point of view the further occupation of New York was, after the British got possession of Brooklyn Heights, not only useless, but it involved risk of serious disaster. With an enemy in undisputed control of the surrounding waters, the situation was one from which it was impossible to escape too soon Greene saw clearly the uselessness as well as danger of the strategic situation, and volunteered his advice to Washington, pointing out that "the only eligible plan to oppose the enemy successfully, and secure ourselves from disgrace was to evacuate Manhattan Island at once"; adding that, if the Americans continued to hold it, "we must hold it at great disadvantage." This was on the 5th of September, and the views thus set forth were shared by others who also gave to them official expression.[1] Among these was John Jay, then active and influential as a member of the New York Convention, the provisional body which had locally assumed direction of affairs. Though essentially a civilian, Jay now evinced the possession of true military instinct. He took in the situation. The policy he outlined and advocated, if severe and cruel, was at least efficacious; and it was the exact policy followed by Fabius two thousand years before, as by Wellington thirty-five years later. Of the former it is unnecessary to speak, his method of warfare has passed into a proverb; but Wellington's example is very apposite. When, in October, 1810, he found himself confronted by Messena at the head of an overwhelmingly superior army, he coldly proceeded to devastate all the region the defence of which he abandoned, and withdrew within the famous lines of Torres Vedras. This very policy then ruthlessly adopted and successfully pursued in Portugal, Jay now clearly and

[1] General Scott to John Jay. Jay's *Works*, I, p. 32.

forcibly outlined for adoption in New York. Writing to Edward Rutledge, of the Board of War, and Gouverneur Morris, chairman of a special committee, he said: —

I wish our army well stationed in the Highlands, and all the lower country desolated; we might then bid defiance to all the further efforts of the enemy in that quarter. Had I been vested with absolute power in this State, I have often said, and still think, that I would last spring have desolated all Long Island, Staten Island, the city and county of New York, and all that part of the county of Westchester which lies below the mountains. I would then have stationed the main body of the army in the mountains on the east, and eight or ten thousand men in the Highlands on the west side of the river. I would have directed the river at Fort Montgomery, which is nearly at the southern extremity of the mountains, to be so shallowed as to afford only depth sufficient for an Albany sloop, and all the Southern passes and defiles in the mountains to be strongly fortified. . . . According to this plan of defence the State would be absolutely impregnable against all the world, on the seaside, and would have nothing to fear except from the way of the lake. Should the enemy gain the river, even below the mountains, I think I foresee that a retreat would become necessary, and I can't forbear wishing that a desire of saving a few acres may not lead us into difficulties.

Such a policy as that here outlined would have been truly Fabian; that actually adopted was such only in name. As Charles Lee at the time impetuously and despairingly wrote Washington: "For my part, I would have nothing to do with the islands to which you have been clinging so pertinaciously. I would give Mr. Howe a fee-simple of them."

"Mr. Howe's" successor in command, Sir Henry Clinton, subsequently held those islands in strategic "fee simple" from after Monmouth (June, 1778) until, three years later, Washington broke camp at Tarrytown (August, 1781) to march his now solidified army to Yorktown. During those three years his tactics had been exactly those outlined and

THE BATTLE OF LONG ISLAND 51

counselled by Jay in 1776, and which at that time Washington did not adopt.

Returning to September, 1776, it was on the 5th of that month that Greene from his bed of sickness wrote to Washington urging him to adopt a policy similar to that suggested to Rutledge by Jay. Three days later Washington, acting on the divided opinion of a Council of War, adopted that most dangerous thing in military operations, a middle course "between abandoning [Manhattan Island] totally and concentrating our whole strength for its defence." His letters to Congress reveal a painful state of indecision.[1] Alive to the difficulties of his situation and conscious of his want of experience in military operations on a large scale and of his limited theoretical knowledge, there was, as he subsequently admitted, at this time "warfare in my mind and hesitation." That this was apparent to those around him is shown by the impatient exclamation of Reed in his letter to Lee written two months later: "Oh! General, an indecisive mind is one of the greatest misfortunes that can befall an army; how often have I lamented it this campaign."[2] The natural result followed.

Brooklyn was abandoned on the 29th of August; but Washington lingered on Manhattan Island with his now wholly demoralized army until the 15th of September, when his dilatory opponent attacked him, again in leisurely fashion. Then followed the shocking affair of Kips Bay, at which the same militia who had manned the entrenchments at Brooklyn when Howe restrained his men from assaulting them, ran away, abandoning their lines at the first indications of an attack. As Greene, ten days before, had written

---

[1] See letters to the President of Congress of 2, 8, 11 and 16 September, 1776, in Sparks, *Writings of Washington*, Vol. IV, 72, 80, 91.
[2] *Life and Correspondence of President Reed*, I. 256.

— "it will be difficult to get such troops to behave with proper spirit in time of action, if we should be attacked." In point of fact, they scurried off like a pack of frightened sheep; but, this time, it was the lunch hour of the enemy which saved the American cause.[1] That day, under Washington's orders, Putnam abandoned New York "leaving behind him a large quantity of provisions and military stores, and most of the heavy cannon." By pure good luck, combined once more with "the dilatoriness of the enemy," he saved himself and the force under his command from capture. This disaster was the natural, and, indeed, logical outcome of the attempt to occupy a useless position for more than two weeks after it became obviously untenable. It is difficult to see why that policy did not involve a serious military blunder; and the friendly American historian has good cause to ask: "What could be the reason of this supineness on the part of Sir William Howe?" The answer to this somewhat simple query is perhaps best given in the words of a British naval commander then on the spot. His amazement and disgust at Howe's methods of warfare found expression at the time in bitter irony, and Sir George Collier, who commanded the frigate *Rainbow*, — the single British ship which on the 27th of August had worked within range of the Red Hook battery, — Sir George Collier wrote: "The having to deal with a generous, merciful, forbearing enemy, who would take no unfair advantages, must surely

[1] The sober account of these operations reads like a travesty. The English military historian of the war remarks with apparent unconscious gravity: "As soon as the English had taken possession of New York, General Howe, and some other general officers, repaired to the house of a Mrs. Murray, with whom they remained in conversation so long, that General Putnam, with 3500 men, was enabled to make good his retreat to the main body of the American army." (Stedman, I, 207.) The officers in question took lunch with Mrs. Murray, and, during the hour devoted to lunch, active military operations would seem to have been suspended.

THE BATTLE OF LONG ISLAND 53

have been highly satisfactory to General Washington, and he was certainly very deficient in not expressing his gratitude to General Howe for his kind behavior towards him. Far from taking the rash resolution of hastily passing over the East River after Gates, and crushing at once a frightened, trembling enemy, he generously gave them time to recover from their panic, — to throw up fresh works, — to make new arrangements, — and to recover from the torpid state the rebellion appeared in from its late shock."[1]

And in truth the simple fact seems to be that, time and again, between August 20 and September 20, the errors of judgment of the American commander-in-chief exposed his army and the cause he had to defend to great and unnecessary peril; and America owes its liberty and the world an immortality to the incapacity, or supineness, of Major-General William Howe.

None the less in narrating these events and describing the situation resulting therefrom, one of the most popular and widely read of the more recent narrators of the distinctively American school, finds in them frequent indications of Washington's "subtle strategy," and "evidence of military genius such as has seldom been surpassed in the history of modern warfare." The term "modern warfare" is somewhat vague, but it would currently be supposed to include

---

[1] "But delay is not the only error imputable to the commander-in-chief (Howe) in this transaction. It has been mentioned that the American army was posted at Haarlem and King's Bridge: Its position at this latter place was for the purpose of securing a retreat to the continent, should the pressure of affairs render such a step necessary. Instead, therefore, of directing his attention to New York, Sir William Howe, (supported by the fleet) ought to have thrown his army round King's Bridge, by which means he would have hemmed in the whole American army; and such a step was not at all impracticable when we consider the extent of the naval and military resources subservient to his will." — Stedman, I, 207–208.

the operations of Frederick as well as those of Napoleon, of Moltke and of Sherman, as well as of Lee.

Returning to the operations on Long Island and the errors of strategy into which both Washington and Howe there fell, it is interesting to attempt to explain the motives which actuated each. In so doing we now have all the facts before us, and see our way clearly; Washington and Howe, with only partial information, groped their way in doubt.

In the first place, what induced Washington, with the meagre resources both in men and material at his command, to endeavor to hold certain of the islands at the mouth of the Hudson against such an armament as he well knew the British could then bring to bear? He necessarily abandoned to them Staten Island; and we now see that the attempt to retain a footing on Long Island, and to hold Manhattan, was not only hopeless from the start, but in reality there was, from a military point of view, nothing to be said in its favor. As Lee, who had in March pointed out the difficulties, subsequently wrote in September in words already quoted: "I would have nothing to do with the islands to which you have been clinging so pertinaciously. I would give Mr. Howe a fee-simple of them." In this conclusion, charlatan though he was, Lee unquestionably was right.

The campaign of Long Island was in reality Washington's first experience of active field movement in which he held chief command. That he profited greatly by it was subsequently apparent. He learned through his mistakes; but, indisputably, those mistakes were both gross and his. For, in doing what he then did, it cannot fairly be claimed that the American commander was impelled to a course his judgment did not approve by popular insistence and congressional pressure. These doubtless were great, and had

THE BATTLE OF LONG ISLAND 55

their influence; but, both before and after the well-nigh inevitable catastrophe, he put himself on record as believing his plan of defence reasonably practicable, and he clung to it to the last moment. Nowhere did he point out the excessive dangers the plan involved, or enter protest against it, or even express a preference for a radically different and safer plan.

Neither can it be claimed that the disaster at Flatbush was due to the illness of Greene and the incompetence of Putnam, who succeeded Greene on the eve of the engagement. Greene relinquished the active command at Brooklyn August 16; and it was on the 22d of August that the British landed at Gravesend. Sullivan was then acting in Greene's stead. Four days later, on the evening of the 26th, Clinton began his forward march, and on the morning of the 27th he seized the unprotected Jamaica road, and so got in the rear of Sullivan and Stirling. On the 24th, Washington himself passed the day at Brooklyn, and, not until his return to New York in the afternoon of that day did he appoint Putnam to take command on the Brooklyn side, at the same time giving him, as the result of his (Washington's) personal examination of the ground, specific written instructions in which he outlined the plan of operations to be pursued, especially on the point which led to disaster, — that of going out to meet the enemy with the best troops, leaving only militia in the interior works. "The militia, or the most indifferent troops," he wrote, "will do for the interior works; whilst your best men should at all hazards prevent the enemy's passing the woods and approaching your works." This, too, though Washington had himself that day observed with alarm the confusion and lack of coöperation among commands which prevailed on Long Island, and knew perfectly that there was no mounted force there to do outpost work. His idea, as that of Greene, seems to have been to inflict severe punishment on the enemy in the wooded hills between Gravesend and Brooklyn; and then to have the forces, withdrawn from before the enemy, take refuge in the Brooklyn entrenchments. But this was a hazardous game to play. To play it successfully required a skilful commander on the spot, an efficient staff, cool, well-seasoned troops, and perfect co-operation between commands; and not one of these essentials, as no one knew better than Washington, did the Americans enjoy.

Take, for instance, the matter of artillery and cavalry. To defend with effective results such an extended advance line required good outpost work, reliable courier service, and adequate, well-handled artillery. Clinton advanced with forty field pieces: the entire American equipment consisted of six pieces, — one five-and-a-half-inch howitzer, four six-pounders and one three-pounder! As respects cavalry, the case was still worse.

But if it is curious to observe the influence of Bunker Hill and Dorchester Heights on the mind of Washington while trying to defend New York, it is at least as curious to notice the similar influence of Concord and Fort Moultrie on the minds of the two Howes when they planned to attack New York. The extreme of rashness had given place to a caution as extreme. Yet in his operations on Long Island, Sir William Howe made the same mistake which cost him so dear at Bunker Hill. Again, instead of attacking his enemy full in front and just where he wanted to be attacked, — driving him out of the trap in which he had got himself, — Howe's effort should have been to operate on Washington's rear, seize his lines of retreat, and "bag" him and his army. No better opportunity for so doing could have been

THE BATTLE OF LONG ISLAND

offered, as was obvious at the time, and has since frequently been pointed out.

So much for the land operations of the British. It was the same on the water. On the 28th of June, just two months before Flatbush, the squadron under Sir Peter Parker was severely repulsed in its attempt on Fort Moultrie. The influence of this experience was manifest in the handling of the British ships at New York in August. Parker was himself in command of the ships which attempted to cooperate with General Howe on the 27th of August, and failed to work into position. While the Americans seem to have felt an inordinate degree of confidence in the efficacy of their land batteries to resist attack on their sea side, the inertness and even timidity of the British naval commanders throughout the operations were most noticeable and almost inexplicable. In them there was no indication of the great traditions of the British navy. Instead of attempting what Blake did at Santa Cruz de Teneriffe in 1657, and Hawke at Belle Isle in 1739; or what Nelson a few years later did at Aboukir in 1798, and again at Copenhagen in 1801, — all under circumstances of far greater difficulty and danger, — instead of attempting any operation of this sort, which would then and there have gone far to finish the war, the commanders of the British fleet hardly made its presence felt.

That Washington sustained himself and retained the confidence of the army and of Congress in the face of that series of disasters for which he was so largely responsible, is extraordinary, and stands the highest tribute which could have been paid to his character and essential qualities. Yet, in spite of what historians have since asserted, his prestige at the time was greatly diminished, and his control of the situation imperilled. All eyes turned at the moment to

General Charles Lee, just back from Charleston, resplendent with the halo of the victory which those who fought the guns of Moultrie had won for him; and won in his despite. He was "hourly expectant" by Washington's demoralized army "as if from Heaven, — with a legion of flaming swordsmen"; or, as another expressed it, "The army is continually praying most ardently for the arrival of General Lee as their Guardian Angel."[1] Even John Jay wrote to Rutledge: "If General Lee should be at Philadelphia, pray hasten his departure — he is much wanted in New York." Lee arrived in the midst of disaster, and was unsparing in criticism of the defective strategy which had led to it. There was for a time no inconsiderable danger that he, the most wretched charlatan of a war not otherwise devoid of charlatans, might supplant Washington in the confidence of the army. He certainly did greatly embarrass his superior, and thwart his combinations. But in view of what then occurred and has since taken place, it is curious to reflect how different the whole course of history would have been had "the omnipotence of Luck in matters of War" entered a little differently than it did into the events of June, 1775, and August, 1776. It is not easy to imagine a state of affairs during the nineteenth century in which the United States might have continued to be what the Dominion of Canada now is, and from which the career and memory of Washington would have been obliterated.

[1] General Scott to John Jay, September 6, 1776. *Correspondence and Public Papers of John Jay*, 1,'82.

III

WASHINGTON AND CAVALRY [1]

YESTERDAY,[2] the long-delayed equestrian statue of Count Casimir Pulaski was with suitable ceremony unveiled at Washington. Mortally wounded, October 9, 1779, in an assault on the works protecting Savannah, then occupied by the British forces, Count Pulaski died two days later. Subsequently, by a vote passed by the Continental Congress November 29, 1779, the memorial only now unveiled was ordered to be erected. Over a hundred and thirty years thus elapsed between the providing for this memorial and its actual dedication at a central point on the main thoroughfare of a city now the capital of a nation, the ground covered by which was at the time of Pulaski's death quite uninhabited.

The incident referred to has a peculiar interest in connection with the present paper; for, a forgotten historic fact, it so chanced that Casimir Pulaski was the first Chief of Cavalry in the army of the United States. Commissioned by Congress a brigadier-general, September 13, 1777, he was immediately afterwards assigned by Washington to the general command of what composed the mounted force of the patriot army; at that time, though the war was then far advanced in its third year of active operations, a quite inchoate branch of the service. It thus devolved on a Pole and an exile to make the first serious attempt to give form

[1] See *infra*, p. 109.   [2] Wednesday, May 10, 1910.

to a systematic American cavalry organization for actual use in practical warfare. Of him and it more will presently be said.

Fifteen years ago I was accidentally led into a somewhat careful as well as critical examination of the actual facts of two Revolutionary battles, as contradistinguished from the accounts thereof contained in our books of history accepted as "standard," — the two battles were that at Bunker Hill, on the 17th of June, 1775, and that before Brooklyn, N.Y., known as the Battle of Long Island, fought August 27 of the following year, 1776. In connection with the second of these engagements, that on Long Island, my attention was particularly drawn to the curious fact, which I did not remember ever to have seen noticed, that Washington, in the operations he then conducted, had apparently no conception of the use to be made of cavalry, or mounted men, in warfare. His idea of an effective military organization, at least for the work then cut out for him to do, appeared to be a command consisting of infantry of the line, with a suitable artillery contingent. He did not seem at all to grasp the idea of some mounted force as an instrument essential to ascertaining the whereabouts and movements of his opponent, or concealing his own movements; or, if it occurred to him, it was in a theoretical way, and not as something to assume shape out of material at command, to meet a present exigency.

Those who have undertaken to tell the story of our War of Independence have almost without exception been civilians, men of the library; and it is accordingly in no way surprising that in reading their narratives it is constantly apparent that, even less than Michael Cassio, had they ever "set a squadron in the field"; nor, consequently, did they the "division of a battle" know in connection with the use therein to be made of the "squadron." Indeed, if questioned on the point, it would probably have become apparent that "squadron" was in the minds of not a few of them a naval term, and one in no way applicable to military organizations. This, of course, would not be true of many of the older writers; for, in the library of Revolutionary literature, besides the so-called standard narratives, we have the *Memoirs*, left by various participants, such as "Light-Horse Harry" Lee, Graydon, Tarleton, and Stedman, all of whom were in a way experts from the military point of view; though, when they wrote from memory, perhaps long after the event, their statements are, of course, open to the suspicion which proverbially attaches to evidence of that character. It would not, however, be easy at once to recall any more recent general historical narrative relating to persons or events of the Revolutionary struggle which indicates on the part of the narrator any direct personal familiarity with military operations; and, in many of them, the absence of that familiarity is almost painfully noticeable. John Fiske is a case in point. Not only is his most readable work marred and made unreliable by a spirit of adulatory and indiscriminating hero-worship wherever Washington is concerned, but, while he has composed an interesting story, the absence of anything indicative of either military experience or strategic instinct is conspicuous. He tells the tale; but he does not understand its details, nor, from the military point of view, their significance. In connection with Washington, another instance readily suggests itself. As a contribution to history, and the great literary reputation of its author, Irving's *Washington* naturally recalls Sir Walter Scott's *Life of Napoleon;* but, in referring to the latter, Napier in his *Peninsular War* does not hesitate to allude to "that intrepidity of error which characterizes the work."

Recurring, however, to the subject of this paper, there is in our distinctive and "standard" American histories a noticeable absence of all reference to the employment of cavalry in Washington's strategy and tactics, or rather to the failure to develop as a factor therein what may best be described as an adequate mounted service. Especially is this noticeable to any reader who may chance to have had some practical experience in warfare, and most of all to one who has seen actual cavalry service. The recently published narratives of Sir George Trevelyan and Sydney G. Fisher are, it is true, less open to this criticism than those of an earlier date; but, judging by our American histories taken as a whole, whether scholarly, popular, or school, it never seems to have occurred to the writers thereof that in 1776 and later the seat of warfare in America, especially between the Hudson and the Potomac, — the field in which Washington conducted his operations, — was one singularly adapted to irregular cavalry operations. As the records show, it was a region full of horses, while every Virginian and nearly every inhabitant of Pennsylvania and the Jerseys was accustomed to the saddle. Then, as later in the Confederacy during our War of Secession, people owned their mounts. Every farming lad and every son of a farmer was, in a rude way, an equestrian; the doctors made their rounds on horseback; the lawyers rode the circuits; in fact the whole social and business life of the community was in a more or less direct way connected with the saddle and the pillion. The horses, also, were of fairly good breed; and, when brought into military use, showed solid powers of endurance, especially those raised in Virginia. Under such circumstances, subsequent experience in our own civil troubles should, it would seem, lead the modern critic and student of military operations to assume that the patriot force would naturally have drifted into that irregular mounted service which was so large and picturesque a feature both in earlier and later warfare, — not less in the operations under Prince Rupert in Cromwell's day than more recently in South Africa.

The omission referred to first becomes noticeable in connection with the narrative of events in the second year of the war, — the operations in and about New York during the latter half of 1776. Prior to that time it may safely be asserted that warfare as carried on in America had, as the unfortunate Braddock found to his cost, been waged on principles and by methods neither recognized by European students nor understood by its professionals. It was in every sense of the term distinctly irregular. Carried on almost necessarily in heavily wooded regions, it was a conflict between individuals, — a struggle in which the ranger and rifleman was pitted against the savage or the Frenchman. In its operations, except as couriers, the mounted man played no part. Scouting even was impracticable in a wilderness where an opponent might be lurking behind every cover. This held good through all the earlier Revolutionary operations from Concord and Lexington to the transfer of the scene of operations from the neighborhood of Boston to that of New York. Paul Revere, for instance, was mounted; but, when arrested in his ride, he was acting as a courier. Montgomery and Arnold led detachments into Canada, seizing Montreal and threatening Quebec; but their movements, when not by canoe, were made through a wilderness, pathless, and for the mounted man impracticable. So, from the beginning of American civilization down to August, 1776, it may be said generally that, except as a pack animal or for draft and courier purposes, the horse found no place in military operations. Cavalry was not a recognized branch of the service. Such being immemorially the case, in the early months of 1776 the seat of active Revolutionary warfare was transferred from Boston and its immediate neighborhood to the mouth of the Hudson.

As already and elsewhere pointed out,[1] it is now, and to us, apparent that, to advance the patriot cause, a wholly new system of both strategy and tactics had at this juncture become advisable. The mouth of the Hudson did not, under existing conditions, admit of successful defence. The true policy to be pursued was to abandon it to the enemy; and then to draw that enemy away from his base, and into the interior, where recourse against him could be had to the tactics of Lexington and Concord. Away from New York, he would have no strategic objective, and he could be harassed day and night, and from behind every tree and stone wall. Holding only the ground on which he camped, the more country he tried to cover the more vulnerable he would have become.

Under these conditions, not yet developed fully, during the early days of July, and seven weeks before Sir William Howe showed any signs of activity, Governor Trumbull of Connecticut sent a detachment of "light-horse," as they were called, to New York. Some four or five hundred in number, they were a body of picked men, — as Washington wrote, "most of them, if not all, men of reputation and property." Yet, on the score of expense, he refused to allow them to keep their horses and, when they declined to do infantry duty, he roughly sent them home, writing to their commander, "they can no longer be of use here, where horses

[1] *Supra*, 14–16; *infra*, 122.

cannot be brought into action, and I do not care how soon they are dismissed." It is not easy to understand how a commander of even Washington's experience could under the conditions then manifestly confronting him have reached such a conclusion, much less have expressed it so bluntly and in writing. In the first place, what had he in mind when he asserted that his operations were necessarily conducted "where horses" could not "be brought into action"? It is obvious that both New York and Brooklyn then were, as they now are, on islands; but, that fact notwithstanding, the field of operations included in those islands afforded ample space as well as constant occasion for the employment of any arm of the service, — engineers, infantry, artillery or cavalry. In the second place, to hold the town of New York it was necessary to occupy Brooklyn, and the occupation of Brooklyn implied at least a dozen miles of uncovered front, or avenues of approach, to be vigilantly guarded and unceasingly patrolled. As an historical fact, it was by means of one of these avenues of approach to Brooklyn, wholly unguarded, — though some four or five miles only to the eastward of the direct road from the place where Howe landed his army, — that, a little later on, a sufficient detachment of the British force worked its way by a flanking movement to the rear of Washington's outlying right wing, and inflicted on it and him crushing disaster. Yet Long Island then was full of forage, which afterwards was either destroyed or fed the horses of the British cavalry and artillery; and so shockingly deficient was the American mounted service that on the very day when Clinton turned, in the way referred to, the American flank, Heath, the acting quartermaster-general of the patriot army, was writing from King's Bridge, a few miles away on Manhattan Island, to Mifflin, about to cross his command over the East River to Brook-

F

lyn, — "We have not a single horse here. I have written to the General [Washington] for two or three."¹ To a military critic, the attempt to hold the outer Long Island line under such circumstances seems little short of ineptitude. General Sullivan, who was in command of that line, and who, together with Stirling, his next in command, was captured when his flank was turned, afterward claimed that he had all along felt uneasy about the Bedford road — that by which Howe effected his turning movement — and "had paid horsemen fifty dollars for patrolling [it] by night, while I had command, as I had no foot for the purpose."² The plain inference would seem to be that none of the American commanders, from Washington down, had at this stage of the war any understanding of the use and absolute necessity of mounted men in field operations. A cavalry patrol fifty strong only, on the flank of the American advanced line on Brooklyn's right front, and patrolling the approaches, might, and probably would, by giving timely notice, have saved the commands of Sullivan and Stirling from the dis-

¹ "We suffer here extremely for horses; not a single one at this Post to send on Express. General Mifflin acquaints me that he cannot spare either horse or waggon from that Post. I beg that two or three may be ordered here." — Heath to Washington, August 27, 1776, *Heath Papers.* At this very time General Howe's light-horse were pillaging and intimidating the inhabitants of Long Island, offering an example of mobility and effectiveness.

² Amory, *Life of John Sullivan*, 28. Stedman says: "This pass the enemy had neglected to secure by detachments, on account of its great distance. In order to watch it, however, they sent out occasional patroles of cavalry: But one of these being intercepted by a British advanced guard, the pass was gained without any alarm being communicated to the Americans." — *History of the American War*, I, 195. The "great distance" in this case was a short two miles, and the route the British took to get into Sullivan's rear ran, according to the excellent map in Stedman's History, just about a half a mile from Sullivan's extreme left flank. That such a route should not have been constantly patrolled seems, under the circumstances, simply inexplicable.

aster of August 27; and yet, a few weeks before, the four hundred Connecticut mounted men had been sent home by Washington for the reason that cavalry could be of no service in military operations conducted "here, where horses cannot be brought into action"![1] But, American or British, it was all of a piece; and the whole story of what occurred August 27–30, 1776, on Long Island, is on both sides suggestive only of a badly played game of chess; as the result of which the losing party escaped a checkmate only through the quite unaccountable procrastination of his opponent on land, and the inactivity of that opponent on the water.

All these happenings, as well as the subsequent transfer of the patriot army from Brooklyn across the East River to New York, occurred during the closing days of August. Four months later the affairs at Trenton and Princeton closed the campaign of 1776, and Washington's army went into its winter quarters at Morristown.

For present purposes, it is not necessary even to pass in rapid review the incidents of that melancholy campaign or its redeeming, and even brilliant, close in the Christmas week of 1776. It is sufficient to say that throughout those operations, from the ignominious Kip's Bay panic on September 15 to the splendid closing rally at Princeton on New Year's day, 1777, there is nowhere any indication of the presence of mounted men connected with the patriot army, much less of any organized auxiliary cavalry service; nor is it easy to see how the necessary courier and orderly work was done. Of patrol work, picket duty, and scouting service there was no pretence on either side. Indeed, it was to this fact, and the neglect on the part of the British of the most ordinary military precautions against surprise, that Washington owed his success at both Trenton and Princeton. Yet the second

[1] See closing paragraph, Chap. XXXI, Irving, *Washington*, II, 382.

year of active operations was drawing to a close; and, certainly, operations during the last four months of that second year were not conducted "where horses" could not "be brought into action."

It is narrated of Frederick the Great that, after his first experience in active warfare in the fortunate, but for him personally inglorious and somewhat mortifying Mollwitz campaign, he subjected himself to sharp self-examination as to the errors and oversights for which he felt himself to have been personally responsible; and especially he "meditated much on the bad figure his cavalry" cut at Mollwitz. And, thereafter, he strove incessantly to improve that branch of the Prussian service, "till at length it can be said his success became world-famous, and he had such Seydlitzes and Ziethens as were not seen before or since."

If Washington, in his Morristown winter quarters, subjected himself, as he doubtless did, to a similar rigid introspection, the first and most necessary requirement of the situation which suggested itself to him, must, it would seem, have been an adequate mounted force of some kind, attached to his command, at once his army's eyes and ears, its safeguard against surprise and his most ready weapon of offence. And, as respects safeguard against surprise, Major-General Charles Lee, then second in command in the patriot army, furnished at this juncture and in his own person an illustration most opportune, though somewhat ludicrous as well as forcible. Of Lee it is unnecessary to speak; both as man and soldier he stands condemned.[1] But, in the course of

[1] Lee did appreciate the value of cavalry. "For God's sake, my dear General, urge the Congress to furnish me with a thousand cavalry. With a thousand cavalry I could insure the safety of these Southern Provinces; and without cavalry I can answer for nothing. I proposed a scheme in Virginia for raising a body almost without any expense. The scheme was relished by the gentlemen of Virginia, but I am told the project was cen-

these operations, Howe had sent out Colonel Harcourt with a detachment apparently of the Seventeenth Light Dragoons to obtain information as to Lee's movements. This detail seems to have roamed about at will; and finally Colonel Harcourt not only learned of General Lee's whereabouts, but also got full information as to how he was accompanied through an important intercepted letter of Lee's, the carriage and delivery of which, no mounted force being available for courier service even, had been entrusted to "a countryman." Stedman says that the American commander had gone out "in order to reconnoitre," and "stopped at a house to breakfast." Fiske asserts that Lee had "foolishly taken up his quarters" at the house in question, and had there slept. However this may be, on the morning of the 13th of December, a fortnight to a day before the affair at Trenton, a mere squad of British cavalry, thirty strong only, swooped down on White's Tavern, near Baskingridge, — halfway across the State of New Jersey, — and, in leisurely fashion, carried Lee off in slippers and dressing-gown, a prisoner of war. Another point of interest in connection with this somewhat *opera bouffe* performance was the presence in it, as a participant, of Banastre Tarleton, then a cornet of light-horse,— the Tarleton who subsequently gained so great notoriety as an active and enterprising cavalry officer in the Southern Department. The capture of Charles Lee does, however, reveal the fact

sured by some members of the Congress on the principle that a military servant should not take the liberty to propose anything. . . . From want of this species of troops, we had infallibly lost this Capital, but the dilatoriness and stupidity of the enemy saved us." — To Washington, July 1, 1776, *Correspondence of the Revolution* (Sparks), I, 246. He had already written to the Virginia Committee of Secrecy: "Your resolution to raise a body of light-horse is, in my opinion, most judicious. It is a species of troops without which an army is a defective and lame machine." See also *Lee Papers*, II, 15, 100; IV, 102, 119.

that Howe's army in this campaign did boast a small force of regular cavalry, designated by Stedman "light dragoons" or "light-horse," and mention is from time to time made of it; but its only noticeable, or even recorded, performance was this bagging of Charles Lee. It is none the less apparent that, with a sufficient and effective auxiliary mounted force, such as Tarleton subsequently had under him in the Carolinas, the advantages gained in the operations about New York during the autumn months of 1776 by Howe and Cornwallis could easily have been followed up later, and Washington's straggling and demoralized army might have been effectually dispersed. On the other hand, while the British, from the lack of a mounted force adapted to irregular service and American conditions, did not, and could not, follow up their successes, the Americans, for the same reason, were wholly unable to harass their enemy and retard his advance. They could not even keep informed as to that enemy's position and movements, much less cut off his supplies, or exhaust and distract him by continually beating up his cantonments, — a system of tactics subsequently most successfully employed in the Carolina campaigns under even less advantageous conditions. That during the earlier stages of that seven years' struggle, the British failed to "catch on," so to speak, to this somewhat novel feature in warfare, as then conducted, is perhaps, considering the national characteristics, no matter for surprise. At best the British soldier is not peculiarly adaptive; and, fighting in a new country under wholly unaccustomed conditions, a Prince Rupert was not at once developed. The curious and hardly explicable fact, however, is that, later, they did "catch on" more quickly than Washington, who was to the manner born, and they did develop, in advance of the Americans, a substitute for Prince Rupert, and a tolerably good one also, in the person of Tarleton. But, with material directly at hand in the way of both horses and riders, it is fairly matter of wonder that no American Mosby developed anywhere or at any time within the field of operations presided over by Washington. Further south the partisan leader and the mounted rifleman appeared, as if by spontaneous generation, almost immediately after interior operations began; for Marion, Sumter, Pickens and the two Horrys were the Forrests and Mosbys of the earlier struggle. But north of the Chesapeake, where the initiative and personal influence of Washington set the gait, so to speak, any trace of this aggressive individual enterprise is looked for in vain. Washington subsequently had recourse to what was at the time altogether inappropriately termed a system of Fabian tactics; but the Parthian system was quite as well established historically as the Fabian,[1] and all the conditions lent themselves admirably to a recourse to the first named. The men were there; the horses were there; the forage was there: all in abundance. The organization and leaders only were lacking; nor were the leaders far to seek. Daniel Morgan, of Virginia, was there, Jersey-born, but of Welsh stock, no less a born commander of irregular horse than, eighty years later in the War of Secession was Forrest, of Tennessee, a man of exactly similar type, instinctively a strategist and cavalry leader. And again another instance: from the very commencement of hostilities, Benedict Arnold gave unmistakable evidence of the possession of every quality which went to make up the dashing cavalry commander.

Contrasting him with well-known characters familiar to a later generation, Washington seems, on the contrary, to have had more traits in common with George H. Thomas than

[1] "The ne'er yet beaten horse of Parthia
We have jaded out o' the field." — *Antony and Cleopatra*, iii, 1.

with either Sherman or Sheridan. To the military critic, he is something of a puzzle; for, though ordinarily cautious and even slow, he at times was wonderfully alert, and at other times actually audacious. In the operations in and about New York during the autumn of 1776 he failed to grasp the strategic situation, and vacillated in presence of his opponent in a way which should have led to his destruction. The decision, alertness and energy displayed by him at Princeton and Trenton were, on the other hand, remindful of Wolfe at Quebec, and of Prince Henry of Prussia at Haverswerda, thirteen days only after Quebec.[1] The next year, also, at Brandywine and Germantown, the audacity, not to say rashness, with which Washington challenged battle with an opposing force which, not only in organization and equipment but numerically even, completely outclassed his own, was, and is, simply confounding.

Returning, however, to the subject under immediate consideration, — the organization of a mounted service and its effective use in the Revolutionary operations, — Washington did not evince mental alertness. On the contrary, while his correspondence and reports reveal no trace of the consciousness of an unsupplied necessity in this direction, he, in the field, showed himself distinctly lacking in what may, for present purposes, be well enough described as the cavalry *flair*, so conspicuous in Cromwell and Frederick. There is in Sheridan's *Memoirs* a passage curiously illustrative of this divergence of view, chiefly attributable to character and temperament, but in part due to training and vocation. Sheridan was essentially a cavalry officer, — a *sabreur*. General George G. Meade, the victor of Gettysburg, originally assigned to the artillery, later served in the engineer corps until

[1] *Infra*, 143. The legend of Frederick's admiration of Washington's Trenton-Princeton operation has long been disproved; see Greene, *The Revolutionary War*, 73 n.

WASHINGTON AND CAVALRY 73

August, 1861, when he was put in command of a brigade of Pennsylvania infantry then being organized. Both were in their respective ways excellent officers, but Sheridan says of Meade (*Memoirs* I. 355): "He was filled with the prejudices that, from the beginning of the war, had pervaded the army regarding the importance and usefulness of cavalry. General Scott then predicted that the contest would be settled by artillery, and thereafter refused the services of regiment after regiment of mounted troops. General Meade deemed cavalry fit for little more than guard and picket duty." Sheridan, on the contrary, regarding the problem from the cavalry point of view, grasped the possibilities, and wanted to weld that arm of the service into an effective, and even deadly, weapon of offence. Throughout the Revolutionary operations, Washington seems to have looked upon cavalry much as did Scott and Meade in the later struggle; and, in the Revolution, no Sheridan forged to the front.

The campaign of 1777 — Washington's third — was marked by Burgoyne's invasion from Canada, and the ill-considered and altogether aimless movement of Sir William Howe on Philadelphia. The northern campaign began in the middle of June, and closed with the Saratoga surrender on the 17th of October. Burgoyne was a cavalry officer, and had won such distinction as he enjoyed by organizing the so-called "light-horse" as an arm of the English military service. Now, however, he was called upon to conduct operations in a well-nigh primeval wilderness, through which he should have moved by water whenever it was possible so to do, but elected to march by land. Accordingly, men, and Germans in some cases at that, accustomed to European roads, found themselves following woodland trails through a country intersected by creeks, and consisting in great part of impassable morasses. Under such conditions, a mounted force would have been simply an additional encumbrance. Accordingly, in the Saratoga campaign, cavalry cut, and could cut, no figure; and, as will presently be seen, a mistaken inference drawn by Gates from this chapter in his earlier experience led a year later to his final undoing.

But if there was no obvious use to be made of cavalry, or rather of an improvised force of mounted rangers, in the swampy wilderness at the head of Lake George and about Saratoga, it was quite otherwise in Maryland and southern and eastern Pennsylvania, the region which Howe selected as the field for his operations; and that in which Washington next had to figure.

During the earlier months of that summer, there had been some desultory movements on the part of Howe, from New York as a base, which Washington had contented himself with observing. He was at this juncture pursuing a true Fabian policy. He was, also, wise in so doing; for, in every branch of the service, — infantry, artillery, or even cavalry, — the force opposed to him was incomparably superior to anything he could put in motion. These operations were at the time not inaptly referred to in England as Howe's "two weeks' fooling in New Jersey"; and it is surely needless to point out how valuable any mounted force, regular or irregular, would have been to the patriot commander while they were in process. Indeed, it is not easy to see how, without even the pretence of such an arm to his service, he contrived to keep in the field. His opponent must, apparently, have been singularly devoid of anything even remotely resembling aggressive alertness. Presently Howe moved his army back to Staten Island, and, loading it on transports, disappeared from view until the last days of July, when he turned up, so to speak, at the entrance of Delaware Bay. Washington at once hurried his ill-organized command to the new field of operations. On his way he passed through Philadelphia, where the Continental Congress was then holding its sittings; and, from a letter written by John Adams to his wife, we get a glimpse of a more or less nebulous cavalry contingent as a component part of the patriot army. John Adams wrote: "Four regiments of light-horse, Bland's, Baylor's, Sheldon's, and Moylan's. Four grand divisions of the army, and the artillery with the matrosses. They marched twelve deep, and yet took up above two hours in passing by. General Washington and the other general officers with their aides on horseback. The Colonels and other field-officers on horseback." No mention is in this letter made of the First Troop, Philadelphia City Cavalry, though that body acted as Washington's escort when he passed through the city.[1]

[1] The Philadelphia City Troop is probably the oldest distinctively cavalry organization in America, and its record, both independently and as a school for officers of the national mounted service, has been noticeably creditable. A detailed and elaborate history of the Troop, from its organization in November, 1774, to 1874, was prepared and published in the latter year. A record of its service also is to be found in the Annual Report of the Adjutant-general of Pennsylvania for the year ending December 31, 1907. This Troop served under Washington's immediate command as a species of headquarters escort, not only at Trenton and Princeton but subsequently at Brandywine. Repeatedly in action, it took part in such scouting and picketing as was then done. Its record was in every way creditable; but, none the less, the detailed history of the Troop confirms the statements in the text, and forcibly illustrates the quite disorganized and wholly unreliable character of the mounted force attached to Washington's army throughout the operations described. Those in command had apparently no conception of an organized cavalry force, operating as such and as an independent unit. The service rendered by the Troop was for no particular or extended term, and consisted chiefly of courier duty, attendance at headquarters, and somewhat ineffective scouting, generally, it would appear, by individuals or small details.

Not impossibly, the usefulness of a small cavalry body constituted and serving after the manner of the Troop, may have suggested the special appeal issued by Congress on March 2, 1778, in which the desire was

Presently, the British expedition made its appearance in Chesapeake Bay; and, finally, a landing was effected near Elkton. Philadelphia, it was plain, was now the British objective, and Washington proceeded to plant himself in Howe's path. With a force some eleven thousand strong, only half-disciplined and wretchedly equipped, while Howe had eighteen thousand regulars, with an artillery contingent, this was distinctly audacious. Going by sea, Howe, of course, could not have had any considerable force of mounted men, probably only a squadron or two.[1]

What now ensued illustrated most strikingly the absence of cavalry on either side. To one trained practically in the methods of modern warfare it reads like a burlesque, exciting a sense of humor as well as a feeling of amazement. While Howe's army lay at Elkton, preparing in a leisurely way to take up its line of march to Philadelphia, Washington, it is said, accompanied by Greene and Lafayette, with a few aids,

expressed that a number of like organizations might be formed in all the States. It was urged that it was "the duty of those who enjoy in a peculiar degree the gifts of fortune and of a cultivated understanding, to stand forth in a disinterested manner in defence of their country and by laudable example to rouse and animate their countrymen to deeds worthy of their brave ancestors, and of the sacred cause of freedom." To "the young men of Property and Spirit" in the several States it was earnestly recommended that within their respective States they constitute "a Troop or Troops of Light Cavalry to serve at their own expense (except in the article of provisions for themselves for forage for their horses) until the 31st of December next."

[1] Stedman says (I. 289) that Howe's army, including "a regiment of light-horse," embarked at New York on the 5th day of July, "where both foot and cavalry remained pent up, in the hottest season of the year, in the holds of the vessels, until the 23d, when they sailed from Sandy Hook." It was the 24th of August before the expedition reached its landing-place, at the Head of Elk. Not until the 8th of September was the entire force concentrated and put in motion towards Philadelphia. Such of the horses of the expedition as survived were thus, during the most trying period of the American summer, kept exactly seven weeks in the holds of the transports.

WASHINGTON AND CAVALRY

went forward to reconnoitre. In other words, the two generals, most prominent in the army and necessary to its preservation as well as effectiveness, accompanied by a distinguished foreign guest, actually went out in person on a scout. In the early days of our Civil War, a prominent politician freshly made a general distinguished himself by attempting a close reconnoissance on a railroad train; and, in South Africa, on one memorable occasion, an English commander undertook to ascertain the whereabouts of the enemy by utilizing a park of artillery as a skirmish line: but no case except this of Washington is recorded of a commanding general going on an overnight scout himself because, apparently, he could in no other way get information of a kind, to say the least, highly desirable.

Riding forward to certain elevations, from which they got a glimpse of a few tents in the distance, Washington and his companions were caught on their return in a heavy rain, and took shelter for the night in a farm-house which chanced to be owned and occupied by a loyalist. They seem to have been without escort and ran as great a risk of being gobbled up as did Lee, eight months before. Judging by Lafayette's long subsequent account of this performance, Washington's companions passed, that night, some anxious hours. Subsequently a friendly warning was received from Virginia, to the effect that greater caution on the part of the Commander-in-Chief would in future be expedient.

It next devolved upon the patriot army to cover Philadelphia. Howe was perfectly advised as to the composition of the force opposed to him, the inadequacy of its equipment, its lack of cavalry or any mounted service, and its consequent inability to secure early and correct information as to his own whereabouts and tactics. He acted accordingly, preparing a flank movement almost exactly similar to that so successfully employed on Long Island a year previous, and at both Chancellorsville and Sadowa in the following century. The lesson administered by Clinton at Flatbush, on Long Island, had, it would appear, not been sufficiently taken to heart; so Cornwallis proceeded to administer it again at Birmingham meeting-house, on the Brandywine. The complete absence of any effective mounted force was once more apparent, as well as the utter impracticability of successfully conducting military operations in a fairly open country without the assistance of such a force. Both propositions received added and unmistakable illustration in each changing phase of an anxious day, and at every stage of its not very complicated movements. It is even now instructive to follow them in detail. Cornwallis, in immediate command of one of the two divisions into which Howe had, for this occasion, divided his army, proceeded to move around Washington's unsuspecting right, just as "Stonewall" Jackson eighty-five years later, and less than one hundred and fifty miles further south, circled Hooker's right. Trevelyan says (Pt. III, 228) that the reports which now reached Washington "were in a high degree confused and contradictory. He had not the means of getting at the positive truth, because he was very weak in cavalry"; and so the morning of a momentous day wore away "amidst distracting doubts and varying counsels." Presently, as the result of a reconnoissance made by a single horseman sent out to explore by Sullivan, who commanded the American right, Washington was erroneously advised as to his opponent's probable plan of operations, and set his forces in motion for an attack on that portion of Howe's army in his own immediate front. Other and more correct information then at last reaching him, he again changed his plan; but it was now too late. Howe's flanking movement had been completely and successfully carried out; and it only remained for the historian to record that the disaster which a few hours later overwhelmed the patriot cause was due to the fact that those in charge of it could obtain "no reliable information from the inhabitants, and had so few and insufficient cavalry that they could make no extended and rapid explorations." A year almost to a day had elapsed since this same Sullivan had found himself the victim of a precisely similar movement on Long Island, his opponent getting in his rear by a perfectly obvious roundabout route, but one over which an enemy's approach was never "dreamed of." On that occasion Sullivan, having no men at his disposal to watch the road, had, it will be remembered, "paid horsemen fifty dollars for patrolling it by night"; and now, under very similar conditions, he wrote, "I have never had any lighthorse with me since I joined the army. I found four when I came to Brentford's Ford, two of whom I sent off with Captain Hazen to Jones's Ford." In such a state of affairs, with an overpowering hostile force creeping around the army's right wing, the question naturally suggests itself, where were "Bland's, Baylor's, Sheldon's, and Moylan's four regiments of light-horse"?[1] Of them and their movements no mention is made. Howe now had Washington exactly where a vigorous and energetic commander likes to get his opponent. Demoralized and exhausted, the patriot army was driven into a *cul-de-sac* formed by the junction of the Schuylkill with the Delaware. Ruthlessly pursued, there was no escape for it. As the alternative to surrender it

[1] Fisher remarks (II. 27): "This Sullivan who learned of the flanking movement too late at Brandywine, was the same Sullivan who had failed to know of the flanking movement in time at Long Island. His *forte* did not lie in protecting an army's flank." This, possibly, is true. It is, however, equally true that on a previous notable historical occasion the *forte* of the children of Israel did not lie in the making of bricks without straw.

would have been hustled into the river. But now the absence of any cavalry contingent in Howe's army became equally apparent. An effective mounted force, energetically led, if then flung on Washington's disordered and retreating masses, could hardly have failed to convert the rout into a panic; and Washington might now have undergone the same experience at the hands of Cornwallis which Gates almost exactly three years later underwent at his and Tarleton's hands at Camden. Washington owed his salvation to the absence of a British cavalry contingent, combined perhaps with the constitutional inertness of an opponent who never saw any occasion for following up an advantage. Having won what could easily have been made a decisive victory, Sir William Howe showed no disposition to assume an active aggressive, but lay for two weeks in camp in an agreeable situation in a healthy high position within a few miles of his altogether successful battle-field.

During this inexplicable interval in active operations, the absence on the patriot side of any eyes and ears of an army received further forcible illustration in the so-called Paoli "massacre" of September 20, through which "Mad Anthony" Wayne got a rough lesson in warfare. When Washington, after the disaster on the Brandywine, withdrew across the Schuylkill, he left a small force, some fifteen hundred strong, on its further side, under Wayne, to watch Howe, and, it is said to "harass his rear" if he moved forward. The reason thus given for such a risky division of a force, insufficient at best, is not over and above intelligible; and, certainly, infantry were here left to do what was plainly the work of cavalry. Wayne also was, like Sullivan on the Brandywine, without the means of effective outpost service. Apparently he had a few very inefficient mounted men posted as videttes, who failed to give timely notice of the enemy's approach.[1] The natural result, a night surprise, followed. At about one o'clock in the morning Wayne's camp was rushed, and he lost about a fifth of his command, — lives thrown away. But historically the affair has its lesson; for the different eyes with which historians regard it and state the facts connected with it are suggestive. In Trevelyan's narrative only is there any comment on the absence of organization which made such a foot-surprise practicable, — the single military lesson to be learned from it: but one historian says of the British commander, Major-General Grey, his "only distinction in the war was in prisoner-killing"; and, in this case, he "committed, it is said, most ruthless slaughter with sword and bayonet on those he first came upon. . . . Wayne was not surprised, as has been generally supposed. . . . He was accordingly well prepared, resisted gallantly, and was able to retire, saving his artillery and stores."[2] The other historian then tells us: "The best officer in Howe's army, short of Cornwallis, was Charles Grey, who died Earl Grey of Howick in Northumberland, and who was the father of the celebrated Whig prime-minister. It once was the fashion in America to write about General Grey as if he was a pair with Governor Tryon; but, in truth, he was a high-minded and honorable gentleman, and a soldier every inch of him. . . . It was as complete a surprise, and as utter a rout, as ever occurred in modern warfare."[3] On this disputed point it can only be observed that, if the American commander was at Paoli not surprised and was "well prepared" against a midnight attack, the outcome thereof called for a great deal of explanation on his part. A loss of between three and four hundred sustained by his command was counterbalanced by "precisely a dozen casualties in the English ranks." If "well prepared" for him, Wayne certainly failed, on that

[1] Stillé's *Wayne*, 86.   [2] Fisher, II, 33.   [3] Trevelyan, Pt. III, 233.

occasion, to give his opponent what is in warfare known as a warm reception. At the bar of history the burden of further proof would appear to rest on the American investigator.

During the previous winter Congress, presumably on the suggestion of Washington, had given some more or less shadowy consideration to the idea of organizing a body of what was termed "light cavalry," in apparent distinction to the severely drilled and heavily accoutred dragoon; for, stated in general terms, in Europe the dragoon constituted the more solid mounted arm of the service, equipped with carbines, while the hussar and lancer, lighter and more dashing, depended on the sabre and lance. Both were quite unfitted to the essential, but little understood, conditions of practical warfare in America; and glimpses of the grotesque propositions at this stage of the struggle gravely pressed on the attention of the Congress are here and there obtainable through the correspondence of the time. The following, for example, is from an unpublished letter of John Adams, written to James Warren of Massachusetts from Philadelphia in June, 1775, nor would it be easy to imagine a greater contrast than that between the stagey apparition here described, and the actual American irregular mounted force which, naturally evolved, rendered such effective service under Lee and Tarleton, in the later stages of the war. "A few minutes past" wrote Adams, "a curious Phenomenon appeared at the Door of our Congress, — a German Hussar, a veteran in the Wars in Germany, in his Uniform, and on Horse back, a forlorn Cap upon his Head, with a Streamer waiving from it half down to his Waistband, with a Deaths Head painted in Front, a beautiful Hussar Cloak ornamented with Lace and Fringe and Cord of Gold, a Scarlet Waist coat under it, with shining yellow metal Buttons — a Light Gun strung over his shoulder, — and a

Turkish Sabre, much Superior to an high Land broad sword, very large and excellently fortifyed by his side-Holsters and Pistols upon his Horse — in short the most warlike and formidable Figure, I ever saw. He says he has fifty such Men ready to enlist under him immediately who have been all used to the Service as Hussars-in Germany, and desirous to ride to Boston immediately in order to see Burgoignes light Horse."

During the winter of 1776–1777 Congress once more authorized the formation of a mounted force; but whether any such force ever really came into existence, even on paper, is questionable. The historians make no mention of it. Meanwhile, Count Pulaski had now been for some time in the country and attached to Washington's headquarters as a member of his military family. Bancroft, in his not very satisfactory or intelligible account of the Brandywine operations, enigmatically says, "on that day [Pulaski] showed the daring of adventure rather than the qualities of a commander"; but, apparently because of his dashing conduct, Congress, on the recommendation of Washington, commissioned him as brigadier-general.[1] This was done, the his-

[1] Pulaski held no appointment at the time of the battle of Brandywine. He had a high opinion of his own qualities, for he asked "such rank and command in the army of these united states as will leave him subordinate to the Commander in Chief alone, or to him and the Marquis de Lafayette." — *Journals*, VIII, 673.

Washington's view of the cavalry may be measured by his recommendation of Pulaski: "This department is still without a head; as I have not, in the present deficiency of Brigadiers with the army, thought it advisable to take one from the foot for that command. The nature of the horse service with us being such, that they commonly act in detachment, a general officer with them is less necessary than at the head of the Brigades of infantry. . . . But though the horse will suffer less from the want of a general officer than the foot, a man of real capacity, experience, and knowledge in that service, might be extremely useful." Franklin, in his indorsement of Pulaski, said nothing of his special fitness for the cavalry service, and Washington doubtless only repeated the Polish

torian informs us, "in order to encourage and develop that arm which heretofore had amounted to little or nothing in the patriot service." [1]

It is, of course, easy to be wise after the event, nor, in the full light of subsequent occurrences, does it imply much perspicacity to see what ought to have been done, or left undone, at any given crisis of human affairs. Premising all this, it is yet difficult to avoid the conclusion that if, in the autumn and winter of 1777, the organization and development of an effective mounted force in the American Continental army was the end in view, the

adventurer's own claims when he told Congress that "as the principal attention in Poland has been for some time past paid to the cavalry, it is to be presumed this gentleman is not unacquainted with it." — *Writings of Washington* (Ford), VI, 57n. He was appointed to command the horse, with the rank of brigadier-general, but the experiment was short and, apparently, the reverse of fortunate. He resigned his command in March, 1778, to raise an independent mixed force of horse and foot, known in Revolutionary annals as "Pulaski's Legion." — *Journals*, X, 312.

[1] Pulaski, some months after his appointment, complained of the "ineffective state" of the cavalry. "It cannot be appropriated to any other service than that of orderlies or reconnoitring the enemy's lines, which your Excellency must be persuaded is not the only service expected from a corps, which, when on a proper footing, is so very formidable. Although it is the opinion of many, that, from the construction of the country, the cavalry cannot act to advantage, your Excellency must be too well acquainted with the many instances wherein the cavalry have been decisively serviceable, to be of this opinion, and not acknowledge that this corps has more than once completed victories. . . . What has greatly contributed to the present weak state of the cavalry was the frequent detachments ordered to the suite of general and other officers, while a colonel commanded, which were appropriated to every use, and the horses drove at the discretion of the dragoons." — *Correspondence of the Revolution* (Sparks), II, 53. Again, in December, 1777, he wrote: "While we are superior in cavalry, the enemy will not dare to extend their force, and, notwithstanding we act on the defensive, we shall have many opportunities of attacking and destroying the enemy by degrees; whereas, if they have it in their power to augment their cavalry, and we suffer ours to diminish and dwindle away, it may happen that the loss of a battle will terminate in our total defeat. Our army, once dispersed and pursued by their horse, will never be able to rally." — *Ib.* 57.

selection of Pulaski as the officer to effect that result was in no way happy. A showy, dashing Polish horseman, and, as the end showed, a most generous and gallant young fellow, Pulaski, as Chief of Cavalry for the somewhat inchoate Continental army of 1778, labored under difficulties which were in fact insuperable. With a quick temper and impatient disposition, he could not make himself understood in English; and, a stranger in a strange land, his whole former military experience was, among Americans and under American conditions, a positive drawback. He submitted to Washington a sensible memorial in which he pointed out clearly the pressing necessity of an organized and improved cavalry service; and, subsequently, he forwarded several reports setting forth in most imperfect English the difficulties he encountered. These undoubtedly were both great and irritating, if, indeed, approached in the way proposed, they were not insurmountable. But, while Pulaski addressed himself with zeal to the task he sought for and which was assigned him, he plainly did not go at it in the right way, — in the way in which, for instance, Morgan would probably have gone at it. In other words, he did not understand America, and had no correct idea as to conditions. Consequently, as Sparks very well puts it, "the officers of the several regiments, who had heretofore been in a measure independent, were not easily reconciled to the orders of a superior, particularly of a foreigner who did not understand their language, and whose ideas of discipline, arrangement, and manœuvres were different from those to which they had been accustomed."[1] The result naturally to be expected in due time ensued. Thus the first attempt at a Continental cavalry organization failed; nor can the responsibility for its failure be attributed exclusively to the inju-

[1] *Life of Count Pulaski*, Sparks' American Biography, New Series, IV.

dicious interference of an intractable Congress. It failed because it was in no way American, or entered upon with a correct, because instinctive, appreciation of existing potentialities. And so the brave and unfortunate Pulaski passed on to his early death. It was merely another case of a square peg in a round hole. But the question still presents itself — Who put the peg in that particular hole? — and did the person making the assignment exactly understand either the nature of the hole or the adaptation of the peg to it?

And this query leads to the very heart of the historical topic now under consideration. Stated broadly and as an abstract military proposition, there is no branch of the service in which a familiar acquaintance with the country to be operated in, and its conditions, is so essential to a commander's success, as in the cavalry. To any one experienced in warfare, this proposition is elementary. A man not to the manner born may be a good officer of infantry or of artillery, and an excellent engineer, even though he speaks but indifferently the language of his soldiers; not so the efficient commander of horse. To be really effective, he must be of his command; his troopers must see in him one of themselves. Especially is this so in a new country, such as the United States in all respects was during the last half of the eighteenth century. In America and in Europe, engineering and artillery were in essentials the same. That European infantry at times found themselves out of place under American conditions had been demonstrated before Fort Du Quesne and again at Bunker Hill; but still the European battalion and officers could do good work when in the open and out of the reach of rangers and riflemen. With cavalry it was altogether otherwise. American conditions called for a species of mounted service peculiar to themselves; and, in organizing and commanding it, a European had first to unlearn everything he had ever been taught, and start fresh. He must understand the country, its people and their speech; he must be familiar with its breed of horses, its roads and its forage. In a word, no less in Revolutionary times than during our War of Secession, if a leader is going to prove a cavalry success, he must be a Daniel Morgan and not a Casimir Pulaski.

To the closet historian, all this may at best be news, or at worst seem quite immaterial; but any man who in America has himself ever "set a squadron in the field" in presence of an enemy will see in it not only the alphabet, but the very crux itself, of his calling. And after two whole years of campaigning in the Jerseys and Pennsylvania, Washington, it might not unreasonably be assumed, would have grasped this elementary proposition. That he did so grasp it, there is no evidence whether in his operations or his correspondence. Yet the third year of active warfare was now drawing to its end, and while poor Pulaski was struggling in vain with the English language and a "Legion" cavalry organization at once inchoate, ill-considered and insubordinate, both Morgan and Arnold were in command of men who ought to have been on horseback with rifles on their saddle-bows, but who still marched and fought on foot with musket and bayonet.

To return, however, to the Brandywine and the course of military events. The battle was fought September 11; and towards the close of that month, Howe, skilfully out-manœuvring Washington, threw his army across the Schuylkill, and occupied Philadelphia. This has been pronounced "the cleverest piece of work" ever accomplished by him, but his success in it was again entirely due to Washington's absolute lack of any approach to an effective outpost service.

The battle of Germantown followed, involving, of course, the continued occupation of Philadelphia by the British. An audacious conception, and well planned, it came near being a brilliant success. Unfortunately, there was, as the historians say, no possibility of quick communication on the field; owing to the prevalence of dense fog the position of the enemy could not be correctly ascertained; and the small mounted force available, amounting in all perhaps to some 400 men, was divided up among the several commands for headquarter and orderly service. But, considering the nature of the locality, and the atmospheric conditions which that morning prevailed, it is at least questionable whether at Germantown any opportunity presented itself for the effective use of horse. The force there present, is, however, referred to in the accounts of the affair as "Pulaski's cavalry"; and this, so far as appears, is the first recognition of the mounted man as a distinctive branch of American army organization.

Such was the close of the campaign of 1777. Valley Forge followed; for, on the 19th of December, Washington led his now wholly demoralized following, an army in name only, along the western bank of the Schuylkill to their doleful winter quarters.

Summarizing the campaign of 1777, so far as the operations conducted by Washington in person were concerned, Trevelyan says that if Washington had "begun the campaign with a respectable force of cavalry, numerous enough to cover his own front and watch the movements of the enemy, his advance guard need never have been surprised at Paoli, and even Brandywine might have told another tale." He then adds that Washington, during the Valley Forge winter, gave much of both time and thought to the creation of such a force. The organization of what was subsequently known as

"Lee's Legion" resulted.[1] Though doubtless, as Trevelyan says, Washington gave closest attention to everything which concerned the enlistment, the equipment, and above all, the mounting of the troopers composing this body, yet that very corps, famous as it subsequently became in Revolutionary annals, and brilliant and effective as the work done by it unquestionably was, emphasizes forcibly Washington's limitations as a cavalry leader, and his failure to grasp in a large way the part which a sufficient and effective mounted service, both might and should have played in the general field of the operations which it devolved on him to conduct. Trevelyan says truly enough, "The American cavalry had small beginnings and never attained very large dimensions; but it was a serviceable instrument of war from the first moment, and ultimately it played a memorable part in deciding the campaign which preserved Georgia and the Carolinas to the Union." But, while this is undeniable so far as it goes, it is suggestive of more, — a good deal more, — to be said on the same topic.

Why was all this thus? "Lee's Legion," modelled, by the way, apparently on Pulaski's ill-conceived idea of an effective American cavalry service, consisted of some three hundred men, one-half only of whom were mounted. Instead of organizing a cavalry command of such wholly inadequate proportions, why was King's Mountain not anticipated, and a call sent out for the frontiersmen and rangers of Virginia and Pennsylvania to come riding in on their own horses? Why were not Morgan's riflemen jerked into the saddle, where they would have felt far more at home than on their feet?[2]

[1] *Journals*, XI, 545.
[2] In the paper laid before the Committee of Congress, in camp, January, 1778, Washington said: —
"The benefits arising from a superiority of horse are obvious to those who have experienced them. Independent of such as you may derive

In view of what subsequently took place during the War of Secession in this country,[1] and what took place in South Africa more recently, under conditions strikingly similar to those which obtained here during our Revolution, it is useless to say that this was impracticable; and the question next naturally presents itself — Who was responsible for this strategic and military shortcoming? The unavoidable answer suggests itself. And yet Trevelyan in a footnote to the very page in his narrative from which quotation has just

from it in the field of battle, it enables you very materially to control the inferior and subordinate motions of an enemy, to impede their knowledge of what you are doing, while it gives you every advantage of superior intelligence, and consequently facilitates your enterprise against them and obstructs theirs against you. In a defensive war, as in our case, it is peculiarly desirable, because it affords great protection to the country, and is a barrier to those inroads and depredations upon the inhabitants, which are inevitable when the superiority lies on the side of the invaders. The enemy, fully sensible of the advantages, are taking all the pains in their power to acquire an ascendancy in this respect, to defeat which, I would propose an augmentation of the cavalry." It was at this very time Washington was discussing, in the way described by Trevelyan, the formation of Lee's Legion, and he would still have only four regiments of cavalry. — *Works of Alexander Hamilton* (1850), II, 144.

That the experience was not entirely wasted on Hamilton is shown by his opinion given to Pickering in 1797: "I am much attached to the idea of a large corps of *efficient* cavalry, and I can not allow this character to militia. It is all-important to an undisciplined against a disciplined army. It is a species of force not easy to be brought by an invader, by which his supplies may be cut off, and his activity extremely checked. Were I to command an undisciplined army, I should prefer half the force with a good corps of cavalry to twice the force without one." — *Ib.* VI, 249.

[1] The most recent (1910) foreign critic on the American Civil War and its results thus expresses himself on this point: —
"Perhaps the principal military lesson (to be derived from a study of that war) is in the use of Cavalry. The problem of getting Cavalry to fight well on foot, without losing its Cavalry Spirit, is often spoken of now-a-days as a sort of ideal to be approached rather than attained; but Sheridan, Stuart, and Forrest all solved it to perfection, using mounted and dismounted action indifferently, though the two latter had few real cavalry in proportion to the size of their commands." — J. Formby, *The American Civil War*, 484.

been made, says that when Stuart was taking Washington's portrait, wishing to interest his sitter, he wrote, "I began on the revolution, the battles of Monmouth and Princeton, but he was absolutely dumb. After a while I got on horses. I had touched the right chord." Washington was at that time (*circa* 1794) President, and living in Philadelphia. Trevelyan adds he then had twenty-six horses in his stable.

The explanation seems obvious. Washington began his military career as a backwoods Indian fighter; and he never forgot the lessons then learned, nor outgrew that experience. In the wooded wildernesses of the Alleghanies cavalry could not operate. All he knew of it was from hearsay, and reading the news-letter accounts of the campaigns and battles of Frederick. And so, Virginian though he was, from the beginning to the end of his military life, there is, so far as can be discovered, no indication of any adequate conception of the value and importance of the mounted man in military operations, and more especially in that particular form of military operation which it devolved upon him to conduct. Yet it is the first business of any great soldier both to appreciate and study the nature of the weapons at his command, and then to make full and effective use of them.

In the employment of the several recognized arms of the service in the Revolutionary struggle, the British enjoyed a great, and for the patriots an insuperable, advantage as respects infantry and artillery — what is known as the line-of-battle organization. On the other hand, the Americans, from the outset, found compensation in their superior markmanship, individuality and mobility. Recourse should, accordingly, have been had to the rifle and the horse. From Lexington to King's Mountain, with Bennington by the way, the opponent the British officer most dreaded the sight of was the leather-clad ranger;[1] and, of all descriptions of rangers, the organized mounted ranger was the most potentially formidable.

It is useless to object that in 1777 the use made of mounted men and irregular cavalry in modern warfare had not yet been developed. In the first place, such is not the fact. It had been developed even in Roman times; and, as already pointed out, Parthian tactics were quite as proverbially familiar as Fabian. By the same token, in Virginia the name of Rupert was always one to conjure with. In the next place, if the use that could be made of mounted men in American open country warfare had not previously been developed, it was the province of Washington then to develop it. That is what he was there for; and a little later, at King's Mountain and Cowpens, the instinct of his people developed it for him.

The obvious objection will, of course, next be advanced that the keep of horses is costly, and Washington, when not wholly destitute, was always short of funds. This hardly merits attention. The Connecticut cavalry were dismissed and sent home on the specific ground that horses were thought to be of no use in the operations then in hand.

[1] Trevelyan, Pt. III, 259, 375; Fisher, II, 92. While the rifle as an implement in warfare seems to have been wholly unknown in the British service of the Revolutionary period, marksmanship was neither taught nor practised; and, as early as during the siege of Boston, Sir William Howe wrote home telling of the "terrible guns of the rebels." Finally he succeeded in capturing a ranger, and "sent him to England, rifle and all, and the marksman was made to perform there and exhibited as a curiosity.". Some six hundred of the Germans sent to America were riflemen, known as "Jägers"; and, in the negotiations with the landgraves, it was stipulated that as many of the recruits as possible should be riflemen. — Sawyer, *Firearms in American History*, 81–83, 140. Referring to the so-called "massacre" at Paoli, Trevelyan justly observes (Pt. III, 236): "Men always attach the idea of cruelty to modes of warfare in which they themselves are not proficient; and Americans liked the bayonet as little as Englishmen approved of taking deliberate aim at individual officers."

The riders were invited to serve on foot. Yet only a month later, because of the lack of even a pretence of a mounted service, Washington's advanced line was flanked, and the very flower of his army needlessly sacrificed. A thousand men were there lost. They represented the price of the keep of a few hundred horses for one month; while, at that very time, the majority of the dwellers on Long Island were Tories, whose fields were heavy with forage. In the next place, Washington did not then, nor afterwards, cry aloud for eyes and ears for his army, and have them denied him on the score of cost. On the contrary, until Valley Forge he does not seem to have been conscious of the absence from it of eyes and ears; at least, no allusion to the want is found in his writings. Finally, later on, the item of cost did not, in 1780 to 1782, prove an insuperable obstacle in the way of the development of a most effective mounted service in the Southern Department; though, compared with Greene's, Washington's camp chest was a purse of Fortunatus.

As respects the argument from cost, however, once for all it should be premised that war, effectively conducted, is a grim reality, and in no way a dilettante, delicately handled pastime. In it men must be armed and equipped, somehow; horses must, in some way, be had and fed. The Confederates had no great supply of money between 1862 and 1865, but they had a most effective mounted service; likewise, the South African Boers in a more recent struggle. In practical warfare the formation of a cavalry force is not so much a question of money as of the existence of an adequate supply of horses, of forage and of men accustomed to the saddle. Of all these, and of the best, the America of the Revolutionary period possessed abundance. At King's Mountain, the prospective cost of horse-keep was, so far as appears, not taken into consideration.

If this limitation of Washington's military capacity was obvious in the two campaigns of 1776 and 1777, that of 1778 emphasized the deficiency. The campaign opened, inauspiciously enough, with the somewhat inexplicable Barren Hill performance, under the leadership of a boy of twenty, for Lafayette at that time still lacked six months of attaining his majority. Though May was well advanced, active operations had not yet begun. The British army, still under the command of Sir William Howe (though being superseded by Clinton, he was about to sail for England) occupied Philadelphia; while the patriots, just again gathering strength after their terrible winter experience, remained at Valley Forge. Washington determined to feel the enemy; and, with that end in view, sent out (May 18) a detachment, some fifteen hundred strong, of his best troops, with Lafayette in command. It was, in fact, a reconnoissance in force; and, as such, should have been composed in the main of cavalry, with a strong infantry support and artillery contingent. The patriot army, however, had no cavalry to speak of, so Lafayette marched off with a command composed almost exclusively of foot. Crossing the Schuylkill by a ford some two hours' march only from Valley Forge, he advanced to Barren Hill, within twelve miles of Philadelphia, and there went into camp. What ensued illustrates several things: among them, more especially, the extreme danger of attempting without cavalry a close reconnoissance of an enemy of superior force; and, next, the utter impossibility of effecting an intelligible agreement between any two accounts of an outpost affair.

Fully informed as to the movement, the British arranged to bag Lafayette and his command. By merest chance, combined with the dull incompetence of Major-General Grant, who commanded one of the British columns, the bagging plan failed by the narrowest of margins; but it is instructive to read of the affair in the accounts of Tower,[1] of Fisher [2] and of Stedman.[3] They agree in hardly any detail; and Stedman only of the three, the one participant and military writer, gives a map of the field of operations and makes mention of the "confused galloping of some of the enemy's horsemen," through whose panicky performances Lafayette probably received his first intimation of impending danger; while "a corps of [British] cavalry took possession of a hill" which was not defended, instead of being thrown forward to seize the ford by which alone could Lafayette's frightened foot effect an escape. The whole episode afforded an interesting example both of the absence and misuse of the weapons essential to success in warfare. According to Fisher, however, Washington did profit by the experience, for he "was careful to risk no more valuable detachments to watch for the evacuation of Philadelphia." In other words, having no cavalry to send, he sent out no more infantry to do cavalry work.

All this was preliminary; and it was not until a month later (June 18) that the campaign really opened. During that month Washington was observing Clinton closely, knowing well that the British army must move, but in natural doubt as to the direction of movement. It would seem that the utmost degree of mobility on his own part should then have been present to his mind as the great necessity of the hour. If such was the case, the thought took no outward form, and remained unexpressed in correspondence. June, 1778, witnessed at last the withdrawal of the British army from Philadelphia, and its somewhat inglorious,

[1] *Lafayette in the American Revolution* (1895), I, 326–338.
[2] *The Struggle for American Independence* (1908), II, 146–148.
[3] *History of the American War* (1794), I, 376–379.

but successful, transfer across New Jersey to New York. To the absence of cavalry as a factor of efficiency in the patriot army, its escape from total destruction was then largely due. Why, at this advanced stage of the war, it should have been thus lacking is not apparent. For Trevelyan also tells us that when Clinton set out on his march from Philadelphia to New York, his army had at its disposition no less than five thousand horses, "almost all of which had been collected by requisition or purchase, during Sir William Howe's occupation of Pennsylvania."

To a like effect, the same excellent authority asserts that General Greene, Washington's quartermaster, had during the same period "secured a vast quantity of horses for the artillery and transport" of the patriot army. Pennsylvania, as well as Virginia, it would seem, was well supplied with mounts; and, with Virginia only the other side of the Potomac, troopers would naturally not have been far to seek.

Sir Henry Clinton had now succeeded Sir William Howe. For good and sufficient reasons, when his position at Philadelphia had become difficult as well as objectless, he decided to transfer himself to New York. It was in fact a withdrawal from a position no longer tenable. For equally satisfying reasons, practical as well as strategic, it was determined to make the transfer by a land march. When the British army started on its return, the movement was not unanticipated on the part of Washington; and it is curious in reading the narratives to note through incidental mentionings how very gradually it was that the use of mounted men in the kind of warfare they were then engaged in dawned on the patriot leaders. While, for instance, Clinton's troops passed out of Philadelphia and crossed the river at dawn, six hours later, Trevelyan tells us, a part of Major Lee's dragoons galloped down to the quay in time to see the English rear guard off, as it ferried the Delaware. To the same effect, Fisher says that Allan McLane with his "rough riders" was the first who entered the town. Fisher further notes that during the Valley Forge winter this Allan McLane, "a rough rider and freebooter of the most gallant type, had scouted between the Delaware and the Schuylkill, making dashes up to the gates of the redoubts," which had been thrown up for the protection of Philadelphia. Finally, he says that Washington during the season had troops between the Delaware and the Schuylkill, who, being rough riders and acting in small bands, obtained information and watched the movements of the British. Presumably there were thus attached to the patriot army the initial germs of such a mounted organization as the situation called for. It is obvious, however, it had not been organized on any large scale or comprehensive plan, and was not in such force as enabled it materially to effect subsequent strategic operations.

One thing, however, stands plainly out, — undeniable. No military movement could possibly have been much more open to fatal disaster through an application of Parthian tactics than that march of the British army from Philadelphia to Sandy Hook, in June, 1778. "When the British reached their second halting-place, the rain poured down for fourteen consecutive hours, ruining the highways, soaking the baggage, spoiling the ammunition and provisions, and drenching the soldiers to the skin." Under such conditions Clinton's progress was inordinately slow, and he "consumed a full week over the first forty miles of his journey." The heat then became intense, and Trevelyan says that the British infantry, "burdened like pack horses," were preceded by a train of carts "a dozen miles in length and frequently compelled to travel on a single causeway." The whole countryside was up in arms, bent on impeding his progress; and Sir

Henry Clinton had no cavalry. All the bridges over which the column had to pass were broken down; the road, such as it was, "was execrable, and the heat like the desert of Sahara." When the retreating army got in motion, on the torrid morning of the eleventh day, Trevelyan adds, "innumerable carriages gradually wound themselves out of the meadows where they had been parked, and covered in unbroken file the whole of the eleven miles of highway which led northward from Monmouth Court House to the village of Middletown." It was here that the American infantry, under General Charles Lee, struck the retreating column. Though since Washington's unhappy experience on Long Island in August, 1776, he had struggled through nearly two entire years of campaign work, at once active and disastrous, Charles Lee now found himself as respects mounted men and field intelligence almost exactly in the position of Sullivan before Brooklyn and on the Brandywine. It seems incredible, but so wholly without cavalry was the general in charge of Washington's leading division in the advance to Monmouth, that at seven o'clock on the evening before the battle, unable to get any precise information as to his enemies' whereabouts, Lee hurriedly wrote to Washington — "The people here are inconceivably stupid. I have sent two lively young foot men, for they have no horses, to reconnoitre." Then he added in a postscript, "I wish your Excellency would order me two or three, if they can be spared, active, well-mounted, light-horsemen."

From such a revelation, it is curious to reflect on what might, under the general conditions of time, place, season, topography and movement, have been the result had the Americans at this stage of the war resorted to Parthian tactics — anticipated the methods of the Boers instead of constantly recurring to the traditions and practice of Marlborough and Frederick, — traditions and practice wholly misleading in America. The military as well as historic truth is that, on this as on other occasions, Washington measured himself and his army up against his adversary at the point where they were strongest and he was least so. He opposed infantry to infantry; oblivious of the fact that the British infantry were of the most perfectly organized kind, while his own was at best an extemporized force. The natural result followed. Whatever the mounted force under Harry Lee or Allan McLane may have been, it is apparent that it was not sufficient to cut any figure during the momentous movement culminating at Monmouth Court House. To a wagon train, eleven miles in length, the American cavalry offered no disturbing obstacle. To have stopped that train's forward movement, and, in so doing, to have thrown the whole column into confusion, would in our day have been a simple matter. But the weapon was not at command. It was by a margin of only five days that Clinton's army escaped heavy disaster, if not total destruction. Drawing inferences from this record, would it be unfair to conclude that two thousand of the King's Mountain rangers led, we will say, by Daniel Morgan, might, during those momentous ten days of transfer, have very potently contributed towards then and there ending the War of Independence? If so, there would seem to be ground for concluding that at that juncture of Revolutionary experiences also, as well as at Flatbush and on the Brandywine, economy in horse-keep may have cost somewhat dearly.

"No more pitched battles were fought in the North. Washington never met Clinton in the field. The two commanders, one impregnably intrenched in the Highlands, and the other impregnably intrenched in the town of New York, simply watched each other, from July, 1778, until September,

1781, when Washington made his sudden move to Yorktown, Virginia." [1]

The period of active operations which has now been passed in review covered almost exactly two years, from July, 1776, to July, 1778. During nearly the whole of that period the British operations were directed by Sir William Howe. With no natural aptitude for cavalry leadership, Howe had no cavalry at his command; nor does it seem ever to have occurred to him that the key of the situation, so far as active field operations were concerned, lay in the development and use of that weapon in warfare. But of Howe and his characteristics it is not necessary here to speak. They are elsewhere discussed.[2] Suffice it now to say that both as a man and a commander he was one of a class frequently met with in all military annals, but in British military annals perhaps a little more frequently than elsewhere. Lacking in initiative, he was also inert in the hour of victory, belonging to the "enough-for-one-day" order of merit. Wellington's career once supplied a dramatic illustration of what is apt to occur when a born soldier suddenly finds himself at a moment of crisis subordinated to one of this type, — the incident eliciting from Wellington at the time a highly characteristic ejaculation. It was in Portugal, at Vimeiro, August 20, 1808, where Sir Arthur Wellesley, as he then was, in temporary command of the British expeditionary force, met the French army of occupation under Junot. That day the future Duke found himself pitted for the first time against the soldiers of the Empire. He scored a decided success; and then, a born fighter with victory in his grasp, he was replaced in command by Sir Harry Burrard, his senior in commission, who had put in his appearance while

[1] Fisher, II, 207. Morgan, at this time, wrote to Washington, "You know the cavalry are the eyes of the infantry." [2] *Infra*, 168–170.

WASHINGTON AND CAVALRY 101

the battle was still on. Junot was in exactly the position of Washington after the Brandywine. By a vigorous forward movement Junot could be cut off from Lisbon, as Washington from Philadelphia. Wellesley saw his opportunity. The French were in full retreat, and the English advance along the Torres Vedras road had begun; when, suddenly, Burrard, assuming command, ordered all pursuit to stop. In vain Wellesley expostulated, saying: "Sir Harry, now is your time to advance. The enemy are completely beaten. We shall be in Lisbon in three days." Like Howe at Flatbush and again at the Brandywine, Burrard held that "enough had been done for one day"; and it only remained for the disgusted Wellesley to turn away, remarking characteristically to his aid as he did so, "Well, then, there is nothing for us soldiers to do here except to go and shoot redlegged partridges!" Judging by his own masterly disposition and energetic pursuit of a routed enemy three years later at Camden (August 16, 1780), Cornwallis, at the Brandywine (September 11, 1777), must have been in much the same mood towards his commander as was Wellington, long afterwards, at Vimeiro. The flank movement conducted by him had been wholly successful; taken unawares and beaten, the American army was in full retreat, while Philadelphia, the British objective eighteen miles only from them, was three and twenty from the main body of the Americans, driven into a *cul-de-sac*. And, under such circumstances, Cornwallis heard Howe order his army to discontinue pursuit. As on Long Island a year before, "enough had been done for that day." In narrating the course of British operations about New York under Howe, Lord Mahon exclaims (VI, 194), "Thus was some respite obtained for the harassed and dispirited remnant of the American army. — Oh! for one hour of Clive!" Lord Clive was four years only the senior of

Sir William Howe, as he was four years Gage's junior. It is well known historically that when, in November, 1774, Clive died by his own hand, the British Ministry, in view of that appeal to the sword towards which the disputes with the American colonists were then plainly tending, had planned to avail themselves of his services. In the outcome of either Flatbush or the Brandywine, Cornwallis in command would probably have sufficed wholly to change the course of events; but it confounds the imagination to try even to conceive what history might have had to record had it been fated for Washington, in place of Major-General Thomas Gage, or Lieutenant-Generals Sir William Howe and Sir Henry Clinton, to confront Robert Clive at Boston in 1775, at New York in 1776, on the Brandywine in 1777, or at Monmouth in 1778.

After Monmouth, the seat of active Revolutionary warfare was transferred from the vicinity of New York and the Jerseys to the Carolinas, and General Nathanael Greene, in place of Washington, directed operations. Before, however, Greene superseded Gates, one incident connected with the latter's southern fiasco is suggestive in the present connection. When Gates first assumed command, some of the officers with experience in his new Department, especially Colonel White and Lieutenant-Colonel Washington, both of whom had commanded mounted men, pressed on his attention the importance of that branch of the service in the country in which he now had to operate. Gates paid no attention to their suggestions. His indifference probably resulted from his experience at Saratoga where, as already pointed out, cavalry could, from the nature of the country and the conditions under which operations were conducted, perform no obviously important service. In his *Memoirs*, "Light Horse Harry" Lee attributes to his neglect of the advice now tendered the crushing disaster which at Camden soon after befell Gates. "In no country in the world," he adds, "were the services of the cavalry more to be desired than was that which was committed to Major-General Gates, and how it was possible for an officer of his experience to have been regardless of this powerful auxiliary remains inexplicable."

It is not necessary here to enter in detail into the operations conducted in the Carolinas between the occupation of Charleston by the British, in May, 1780, and their final evacuation of South Carolina in September, 1782. It is sufficient to say that, as a military study from the cavalry point of view, those operations afford a striking contrast to what had previously taken place during an almost exactly similar space of time in the Northern Department.

There was, it is true, a large royalist faction in the Carolinas; but the same element was found in almost equal proportion in New York, New Jersey and Pennsylvania. The horse was equally at hand in each region; while forage was more plentiful in the northern than in the southern States: but it seemed as though both sides, simultaneously and as if from instinct, "caught on" in the Carolinas.[1] For instance,

[1] Describing the expedition to Savannah under Clinton, Tarleton, then a lieutenant-colonel, says (*Campaigns of* 1780 *and* 1781, 4–6) it included "a powerful detachment of artillery" and "two hundred and fifty cavalry." It left New York on the 26th of December, 1779; but, encountering a succession of storms, the fleet was dispersed, and "most of the artillery and all the cavalry horses perished." On landing in Tybee harbor Tarleton "found the condition of his corps mortifying and distressing; the horses of both officers and men, which had been embarked in excellent order, were destroyed, owing to the badness of the vessels employed to transport them, and, unfortunately, there was no substitute found in Georgia to remedy such a catastrophe." Transporting his "men and furniture" by boat to Port Royal Island, Tarleton proceeded "to collect at that place, from friends and enemies, by money or by force, all the horses belonging to the islands in that neighborhood." This was towards the end of February; but "about the middle of March" Tarleton received orders to

Savannah surrendered on the 11th of May, 1780, and, on the 29th of the same month, only eighteen days later, Tarleton had behind him seven hundred mounted men when he surprised Colonel Buford at the Waxhaws, and destroyed nearly his entire command. The British officer had covered one hundred and fifty-four miles in fifty-four hours. This was great cavalry work. Nothing like it was attempted, much less accomplished, by any of Washington's command in the Monmouth campaign.

The tactics employed on both sides in the Carolina struggle were strikingly suggestive of those employed in South Africa a century and a quarter later. They were in largest part partisan. Irregular bodies, the men mounted on their own horses, called together at a moment's notice and separating at the will of those composing the band, harried the land, cut off detached parties, showed small mercy to prisoners, and, withal, did little in the way of effective work towards bringing warfare to an end. It was a process of exhaustion. Made up chiefly of eccentric partisan operations, as studied in the voluminous detail of McCrady's two bulky volumes, the narrative conveys no lesson. The one cause

join the main command, "if he had assembled a sufficient number of horses to re-mount the dragoons; the number was complete, but the quality was inferior to those embarked at New York." Less than a month later (April 12) Tarleton, with his command thus re-mounted, surprised General Huger at the Cooper River crossing; and "four hundred horses belonging to officers and dragoons, with their arms and equipments (a valuable acquisition for the British cavalry in their present state), fell into the hands of the victors. . . . This signal instance of military advantage may be partly attributed . . . to the injudicious conduct of the American commander, who besides making a false disposition of his corps, by placing his cavalry in front of the bridge during the night, and his infantry in the rear, neglected sending patrols in front of his videttes" (*Ib.* 16, 17). Exactly one month later Charleston was surrendered, and Tarleton led his command, remounted in the way described, on the raid referred to in the text. No similar showing of energy and enterprise in the cavalry arm of the service had up to this time been seen on either side.

for wonder is, how Greene, without arms, munitions, clothing, commissariat or camp-chest, contrived to keep the field at all.

As to Greene, also, it is impossible now to say whether he possessed in any marked degree the elements of an officer of cavalry. He, however, fully realized, as a result of experience, the immense importance of that arm of the service, causing him to write to Lafayette, when the latter was conducting operations in Virginia, the enemy "are increasing their cavalry by every means in their power, and have a greater number than we have, though not of equal goodness. We are trying to increase ours. Enlarge your cavalry or you are inevitably ruined."[1]

It is a curious and very noticeable fact, also, that as respects both the organization of cavalry and its effective use, the British not only seem to have taken the initiative, but they held their advantage up to the close of the struggle. In other words, while cavalry in the campaigns of Cornwallis and Lord Rawdon acted as an adjunct in military operations, and was used effectively in this way, this on the patriot side was the case to a very limited extent only. All the cavalry Greene ever could depend upon as an effective weapon in his immediate central command, were the comparatively insignificant organizations commanded by Harry Lee and Lieutenant-Colonel Washington. On the other hand, judging by McCrady's statements, Pickens, Marion, Sumter and the rest gave Greene almost as much

[1] G. W. Greene, *Life of General Greene*, III, 320. Greene's cry for cavalry seems to have been loud and incessant, for, as he wrote to Washington, November 23, 1777, during the operations about Philadelphia, before the army went into its winter-quarters at Valley Forge: "We are greatly distressed for want of a party of light-horse;" and again, the following day, "I would wish if possible some horse might be sent, as every army is an unwieldy body without them." — *Ib.* I, 517, 519.

trouble as they rendered him assistance. He was continually making futile attempts to draw them under his personal control for some concentrated movement; while they, much older men and natives of the country, plainly more or less jealous of his, the Rhode Islander's, authority, acted on their own responsibility, obeying or neglecting to obey his orders much as they saw fit.

Two conflicts, however, which occurred in the Carolinas, the one at King's Mountain on the 6th of October, 1780, the other at the Cowpens on January 17, 1781, are especially noticeable; and King's Mountain offered what has since been admiringly referred to by the latest British investigator as an exploit which affords "as fine an example as can be found of the power of wood-craft, marksmanship and sportsmanship in war."[1] The whole patriot force engaged was less than fourteen hundred strong, "over-mountain men," as they were called. Suddenly concentrated, and covering a considerable distance with great rapidity, "as soon as they arrived near the base of the spur [on which the conflict occurred] the riflemen all dismounted and, leaving their coats and blankets strapped to the saddles, tied their horses in the woods and with scarcely a moment's delay started on foot up the three easy sides of the spur." Stedman's account of this episode is curiously suggestive: "These men . . . the wild and fierce inhabitants of Kentucky, and other settlements west of the Alleganey Mountains . . . were all well mounted on horseback and armed with rifles: each carried his own provisions in a wallet, so that no incumbrance of waggons, nor delays of public departments, impeded their movements. . . . When the different divisions of mountaineers reached Gilbert-town, which was nearly about the same time, they amounted to upwards

[1] Fortescue, *History of the British Army*, III, 323.

of three thousand men. From these fifteen hundred of the best were selected, who, mounted on fleet horses, were sent in pursuit."[1]

So, three months later, at Cowpens (January 17, 1781), Daniel Morgan there gave evidence of the possession of all the attributes of a born military commander and cavalry leader. Making his dispositions without regard for accepted military rules, he availed himself in the best way possible of the weapons at his command. He had a small force of cavalry only, amounting perhaps to one hundred and fifty troopers. They were under the command of Harry Lee; and these he flung upon Tarleton's flank at the crisis of the action, in a manner so effective that defeat became at once a rout. He hurled his little band of horsemen on his opponent, when, to use Napoleon's expression, "the battle was ripe," much as a stone is flung by a slinger. One of the very few patriot victories of the entire war, Cowpens was altogether the most neatly, though unscientifically, fought battle in it. The distinctive American attributes were there manifest both in the commander and in his command.

[1] Major Patrick Ferguson of the 2d Battalion, 71st Regiment Light Infantry, Highlanders, an excellent and enterprising officer, commanded the loyalists at King's Mountain, and there lost his life. It is a curious and most interesting historical fact in connection with the subject of the present paper that Ferguson was the inventor of the first serviceable and practical breech-loading rifled weapon ever adopted into any service. Patented in England in 1776, by it "four aimed shots a minute could be fired, as against an average of one shot in fifteen minutes with a European muzzle-loading rifle after it had become foul." — Sawyer, *Firearms in American History*, 137–139.

The only difficulty with the Ferguson breech-loader seems to have been that it was, as a weapon in practical European warfare, a full half century before its time. Even as late as our own War of Secession the West Point martinets and ordnance officers were wholly opposed to the adoption of the breech-loading weapons for use by infantry. Breech-loading cavalry carbines were in use.

So far as Greene's operations were concerned, while most skilfully as well as persistently conducted, they indicated rather the possession by him of the attributes of an excellent commander of infantry than the dashing qualities of one either accustomed to the handling of cavalry or naturally inclined to it. Both Guilford Court-House and Eutaw Springs could have been turned from defeats, or at best indecisive actions, into complete victories, had he then had attached to his command an effective force of cavalry and, like Morgan, known exactly when and how to make use of it. Even as it was, his small body of mounted men, under command of Lee and Washington, rendered on more than one occasion effective service. As to Tarleton, he proved the right arm, such as it was, of Cornwallis, and the raids led by him, both in the Carolinas and in Virginia, seem extraordinary in dash and daring.

But when it is borne in mind that the active military operations of the Revolutionary period extended from the affairs at Lexington and Concord in April, 1775, to the fall of Yorktown, in October, 1781, or through more than six years of incessant field work, while, on the other hand, the war in South Africa lasted only two years, and our own War of Secession covered not more than four years, the slowness with which the patriot side realized the nature of the situation, and learned to make the most effective use of the weapons at its command, is indisputably, to say the least, suggestive. It even gives rise to a doubt whether, after all, there was not some ground for the impatience at times felt in the Congress, and whether recourse might not well earlier have been had to a different, and much more effective, system of tactics. In any event, this phase, as yet undeveloped, of an interesting historical situation merits careful study on the part of some future investigator.

This[1] and the following paper, entitled "The Campaign of 1777," were originally prepared for submission to the Massachusetts Historical Society, and are to be found in its *Proceedings*. (Vol. XLIII, 547–593; Vol. XLIV, 13–65.) Certain facts relating to the reason of their preparation, and the process through which they assumed final shape, are there given. While appropriate enough in papers submitted to an historical society at its stated meetings, such matter, largely personal and to a certain extent at times colloquial, is manifestly out of place in a more formal publication. The two papers have, therefore, now been revised in this respect, and, in a manner, recast. The general reader is, however, always more or less careless, while the judgment of the specialist and investigator is apt to be affected by preconceptions or prejudice. In the case of these papers, misapprehensions would, therefore, almost surely rise in the minds of most, unless they read with some understanding of the purpose for which the studies were prepared, and the successive steps through which they obtained whatever they may have of both form and proportion.

For a number of years an intermittent correspondence has been carried on between Sir George Otto Trevelyan and myself. More recently we had, when together, discussed certain phases of the Revolutionary struggle in connection generally with the work on which Sir George was engaged, and more especially with persons and events necessarily to be dealt with in the forthcoming portions of his unfinished history. Chancing to be in Europe during the autumn of 1909, I had proposed a visit to Wallington, Sir George's Northumberland home, for the purpose more especially of discussing with him the use of cavalry by Washington in his military operations, or rather Washington's failure to make any use of that arm of the service; and this was to be discussed in the light of what had recently occurred in South Africa. It so chanced, however, that Sir George was, at just the time suggested for the proposed visit, leaving England for the Continent. As a personal meeting could, therefore, not be arranged, it was agreed that on my return to America I should put my suggestions in the form of a memorandum for Sir George's consideration.

[1] *Supra*, 59 n.

This accordingly was presently attempted. As originally proposed, the memorandum in question it was thought might cover at most some eight or ten pages of typewritten letter-paper. When entered upon, however, the undertaking developed, and presently assumed almost the proportions of a treatise. I then concluded that the best way for it to reach its destination was through the medium of the *Proceedings* of the Massachusetts Historical Society. The preparation of the paper in this form then brought to light new material, otherwise suggestive. One step thus led to another, until the original brief memorandum of ten typewritten pages developed into five papers covering over one hundred and fifty of the somewhat solid printed pages of the Society's *Proceedings*. The papers in question were entitled (1) "Washington and Cavalry," (2) "The Campaign of 1777," (3) "Contemporary Opinion of the Howes," (4) "The Weems Dispensation," and (5) "General Craufurd's March." In their original form, and with full references to the authorities made use of, these papers can be found in Volumes XLIII and XLIV of the *Proceedings* of the Massachusetts Historical Society. Only the more essential portions are here reproduced, together with a few additions, and the citation of some authorities brought to light since the original papers were prepared.

Obviously, the themes and events discussed are lacking in novelty. The story has been many times told; and, even now, is being retold in greater or less detail by investigators whose volumes are in course of preparation, or not yet come from the press. A justification of this reproduction must, therefore, be found, if, indeed, it exists, in the fact that, as I was step by step drawn on in my investigations, I became more and more persuaded of the truth of the following observation of Sydney G. Fisher, in his recently (1908) published work, *The Real Struggle for American Independence:* —

"Although our Revolution is said to have changed the thought of the world, like the epochs of Socrates, of Christ, of the Reformation, and of the French Revolution, yet no complete history of it has ever been written upon the plan of dealing frankly with all the contemporary evidence and withholding nothing of importance that is found in the original records. Our histories are able rhetorical efforts, enlarged Fourth of July orations, or pleasing literary essays on selected phases of the contest. . . .

"Although we are a democratic country, our history of the event which largely created our democracy has been written in the most undemocratic method — a method which conceals the real condition; a method of paternalism which seeks to let the people know only such things as the writer supposes will be good for them; a method whose foundation principle appears to be that the people cannot be trusted with the original evidence." (Preface, v, vi, ix.)

In plain language the entire already much written history of what is known as the American Revolution, but which, as Hamilton observed over a century ago, was no revolution at all,[1] but should more correctly be styled the War of American Independence, — this entire much written history needs to be, not rewritten exactly, but written *de novo*. The trouble with the existing narratives is not that those who prepared them were either superficial or inaccurate, or that stores of new material have been brought to light altering the aspect of events, or the motives which actuated individuals; on both of these heads something might be said, but nothing affecting the main issue. The difficulty — and, so far as the American school of historians is concerned, it is radical — is that pointed out by Mr. Fisher; and it is pervasive as well as radical. Our American historians have approached their task in neither a judicial frame of mind nor a detached spirit. In plain vernacular, they write under an overruling patriotism or hero-worshipping preconception; and their work is accordingly of the spread eagle and Fourth of July variety — this sometimes unconsciously and from tradition, but not infrequently through an intentional suppression of facts, a perversion of evidence or a recourse to manifest special pleading.

This, undeniably, is a sweeping indictment; yet, after years passed in the reading of narratives and the study of the original material on which they are supposed to be based, to this conclusion I have, in common with Mr. Fisher, found myself compelled. And, such being the case, the fact, if stated at all, had best be

[1] *Alexander Hamilton*, by A. McLean Hamilton, 296. Massachusetts Historical Society *Proceedings*, XLIV, 233.

stated in language which does not admit of misapprehension. Take Washington, for instance; Washington was in reality an extremely human man, one of a class; a high-minded, partially educated, Virginia country gentleman and planter of the colonial period. Of eminently lofty character, fair ability, and great common-sense, he was throughout genuine — a gentleman in the highest sense of the term. As such, he impressed himself on all with whom he came in close personal contact. He stands, and deservedly stands, second to none, not even to William of Orange, in the gallery of those world-recognized as great historical figures. Yet as one conducting critical military operations, his limitations, except in the pages of the distinctive American historian, were great and apparent. The brilliant Hamilton, his favorite aide-de-camp and confidential civil adviser, even went so far as to say that he had no military aptitude whatever;[1] and in this conclusion Pickering, his quarter-master-general, and Steuben, his inspector-general, are known to have concurred. In the eyes of the American type of historian, however, the expression of such an opinion savors strongly of something which bears a close resemblance to the questioning of the Godhead in the mind of an Orthodox minister of the old school, or to lése-majesty in a present-day German correctional court.

Washington in reality conducted active operations in five campaigns, that (1) of 1775–1776 before Boston; that (2) of 1776, in New York and New Jersey; that (3) of 1777, about Philadelphia; that (4) of 1778, culminating at Monmouth Court House; and, finally, that (5) of 1781, closing at Yorktown. Of these, the first, the operations in and about Boston, were creditable, though in no wise brilliant; but they most fortunately established Washington's reputation, winning him the confidence of his countrymen. The operations of 1776, in New York, ill-conceived at the start, in their development were, in reality, little more than a succession of blunders which by rights should have irretrievably ruined the American cause: the campaign was, however, saved, if not redeemed, by a brilliant final counterstroke made possible by the gross incapacity of the adversary. The 1777 campaign in Pennsylvania was, like the 1776 campaign in New York, in judgment a

[1] Pickering, MSS. 46, 354.

WASHINGTON AND CAVALRY 113

mistake, and in execution disastrous; in military parlance, a mess was made of it. The Monmouth campaign (1778) reflected no considerable credit on any one, American or British, wholly failing of decisive results. Finally, the Yorktown campaign of 1781 was the one real success to be set down to Washington's military account. Boldly, as well as brilliantly, conceived and in detail planned, it was carried out with prescience, judgment, skill and energy, and crowned by complete success. A fine design strategically, too much praise cannot be awarded to its execution.

Yet to-day, in the accepted rendering, there is as much need of a re-writing of the military record of Washington as there was of that of Cromwell, when Carlyle took up the theme. The former has, up to this time, been as much written up as the latter had to as late a period as 1845 been written down. Yet to-day, if an effort is made to discuss Washington, the Soldier, dispassionately, intelligently and critically — applying to his operations recognized strategic rules and precedents — the answer is made that Frederick, Napoleon, Lee, all made mistakes in war, so why call attention to those of Washington; to which the proper reply is that the mistakes made are in the case of each of those named pointed out, acknowledged and criticized. In the case of Washington, they are on the contrary by the American "standard" historian, literary or school — but more especially by those writing for the young — ignored, palliated, or flatly denied, and that on principle and as a habit.

In short, when dealing with the Revolutionary period, to make out America's case on every occasion has been the manifest, almost the avowed, purpose of the American historian. As to hero-worship, Lord Rosebery has recently [1] found occasion, when referring to Thomas Carlyle, tersely to observe that it "makes bad history." Finally, while Dr. Johnson energetically defined "patriotism" as "the last refuge of a scoundrel," it might with equal point, and far more truth, be otherwise denominated the Stumbling Block of the Historian.

[1] *Lord Chatham*, 186.

IV

THE REVOLUTIONARY CAMPAIGN OF 1777 [1]

"WHEN Sylla, after all his victories, styled himself a happy, rather than a great, general, he discovered his profound knowledge of the military art. Experience taught him that the speed of one legion, the inactivity of another, the obstinacy, the ignorance, or the treachery of a subordinate officer, was sufficient to mar the best concerted plan, — that the intervention of a shower of rain, an unexpected ditch, or any apparently trivial accident, might determine the fate of a whole army. It taught him that the vicissitudes of war are so many, disappointment will attend the wisest combinations; that a ruinous defeat, the work of chance, often closes the career of the boldest and most sagacious of generals; and that to judge of a commander's conduct by the event alone is equally unjust and unphilosophical, a refuge for vanity and ignorance." [2]

In penning these reflections, while writing of the tragic outcome of Sir John Moore's Corunna campaign, Sir William Napier might well have added to his vicissitudes of warfare the good fortune of a commander who finds himself confronted with a succession of dull incompetents, or unenterprising professional strategists; and when the caliber and temperaments of those opposed in command to him, and

[1] A paper submitted to the Massachusetts Historical Society at its October meeting, 1910; and printed in its *Proceedings* (XLIV, 13-65.). See *supra*, 109-113. Citations of authorities can be found by reference to the Proceedings of the Massachusetts Historical Society.

[2] Napier, *War in the Peninsula*, Bk. IV, Chap. VI.

THE REVOLUTIONARY CAMPAIGN OF 1777   115

with whom only he was fated to measure himself, are taken into account, there may possibly be grounds for concluding that Washington, even more than Sylla, might have had cause to style "himself a happy, rather than a great, general." The names of Major-General Thomas Gage, Sir William Howe and Sir Henry Clinton do not readily associate themselves with any considerable military achievements. Indeed, those who bore them are remembered only as having been opposed to Washington; who, again, stands out in world history far more conspicuously than does Sylla. And yet an English contemporary, writing in 1778 of the operations of 1777, summed the matter up by saying "in short, I am of the opinion . . . that any other General in the world than General Howe would have beaten General Washington; and any other General in the world than General Washington would have beaten General Howe."

The purpose of this paper is to analyze the Revolutionary campaign of 1777 — the third of that conflict — from a purely critical point of view, as distinguished from the points of view — partisan, patriotic or hero-cult — from which it has been seen and described by the distinctively "standard" American historians.

In our great Civil War the thing known as "Strategy" was first and last much, and not always over-wisely, discussed; the most popular definition of the term, and the one generally accepted among the more practically experienced, being that attributed to the Confederate leader, Nathan B. Forrest. A somewhat uncouth Tennessean, taught, like Cromwell, in the school of practical warfare and actual fighting, General Forrest is reported to have remarked that, so far as his observation went, the essence of all successful strategy was simply "to get there fust, with most men." With all due respect, however, to General

Forrest, — unquestionably a born soldier of high grade, — while his may be accepted as a definition so far as it goes, it hardly covers the whole ground. The getting "there" first with most men is undeniably of the essence of all sound strategy; but the word "there" in this connection implies another word, — "Where?" Put in a different way, there is a key to about every military situation; but that key has to be both found and properly made use of. When found and properly utilized, there is apt to result what in chess is known as a check, or, possibly, a checkmate. Strategy, therefore, is nothing more nor less than the art of playing, more or less skilfully, a complicated game of chess with a considerable, not seldom with a vast, area of broken country as its board, on which geographic points, cities and armies, are the Kings, Queens and Castles, while smaller commands and individual men serve as Pawns. In the present case, therefore, — that of the Revolutionary campaign of 1777, — as in every similar case, it is essential to any correct understanding of the game and its progress to describe the board, and to arrange the pieces in antagonism.

The board of 1777 was extensive; but, for present purposes, both simple and familiar. It calls for no map to render it visually comprehensible. With the Canada boundary and Lake Champlain for a limit to the north, it extends to Chesapeake Bay on the south, — a distance of approximately four hundred and fifty miles. Bordering on the ocean, this region was almost everywhere vulnerable by water, while its interior depth at no point exceeded two hundred and fifty miles, and for all practical purposes was limited to one hundred miles; Oswego, on Lake Ontario, being the farthest point from New York (250 miles) on the northwest, and Reading the farthest point westward (100 miles) from the Jersey coast. Practically New York City

THE REVOLUTIONARY CAMPAIGN OF 1777

was at the strategic centre, — that is, where movement was concerned, it was about equidistant from Albany and Fort Edward at one extreme, and from the capes of the Delaware and the head-waters of Chesapeake Bay on the other. In either sphere and in both directions the means of communication and of subsistence were equally good, or equally inadequate or insufficient. Philadelphia, the obvious but unessential military objective at the south, was practically one hundred miles from New York; while Albany, the equally obvious but far more important military objective at the north, was one hundred and fifty miles from it. The average day's march of an army is fifteen miles; by a forced march thirty miles or more can be covered. From New York as a strategic starting-point, Albany was therefore a ten days' march distant, while Philadelphia was three less, or a march of seven days.

Such being the board on which the game of war was to be played, it remains to locate the pieces as they stood upon it. The June of 1777 was well advanced before active operations were begun. After the brilliant and redeeming Trenton-Princeton stroke with which Washington, in the Christmas week of that year, brought the 1776 campaign to a close, Sir William Howe had drawn the British invading forces together within the Manhattan lines, and there, comfortably established in winter quarters, had awaited the coming of spring, and the arrival of reënforcements and supplies from England. Washington had placed himself in a strong defensive position at Morristown, there holding together as best he could the remnants of an army. Nearly due west of the town of New York, and about twenty-five miles from the Jersey shore of the Hudson, Morristown was a good strategic point from which to operate in any direction, whether towards Peekskill, — the gateway to the Hudson

Highlands on the road to Albany, fifty miles away, — or towards Trenton, forty miles off in the direction of Philadelphia. When, therefore, Sir William Howe, moving with that inexplicable and unsoldierly deliberation always characteristic of him, began at last to bestir himself, the situation was simple. Washington's army, some seven thousand strong, but being rapidly increased by the arrival of fresh levies, was at Morristown, waiting for Howe to disclose a plan of operations; General Israel Putnam, quite incompetent and with only a nominal force under his command, made a pretence of holding the Hudson Highlands, the stronghold of the patriots, in which they had stored their supplies, "muskets, cannon, ammunition, provisions and military tools and equipments of all kinds."[1] Farther north, General St. Clair, with some thirty-five hundred men all told, occupied the defences of Ticonderoga at the foot of Lake George, a strategic outpost erroneously supposed to be well-nigh impregnable, and hence utilized as a sort of arsenal and supply-depot; in point of fact, however, it was, in face of any skilfully directed attack, wholly untenable. Here, accordingly, had been collected a great number of cannon — some one hundred and twenty pieces — and a large amount of ammunition, together with a quantity of beef and flour. Elsewhere the patriots had nothing with which the British commanders would be compelled to reckon. Opposed to this half-organized, poorly armed, unclad and scattered musterfield gathering, numbering perhaps an aggregate of fifteen thousand, insufficiently supplied with artillery and

[1] Fisher, *Struggle for American Independence*, II, 101. In the present paper this work is used as the standard and for recurring reference because of its detailed and systematic citations. In the preface to his narrative (p. x) Mr. Fisher takes occasion to lament the "great mistake" made by the historians of our Revolution "in abandoning the good, old-fashioned plan of referring to the original evidence by foot-note citations."

THE REVOLUTIONARY CAMPAIGN OF 1777   119

with no mounted auxiliary force, the British arrayed two distinct armies counting, together, thirty-three thousand effectives; eight thousand under General Burgoyne in Canada, and twenty-five thousand under Sir William Howe in and about New York. Perfectly organized and equipped, well disciplined and supplied, they had a sufficient artillery contingent, though few cavalry; and what of mounted force they mustered was ill adapted to American conditions. The British control of the sea was undisputed, but ineffective as respects blockade.

Thus, making full allowance for every conceivable drawback on the part of the British, and conceding every possible advantage to the patriots, the outlook for the latter was, in the early summer of 1777, ominous in the extreme. To leave their opponents even a chance of winning, it was plain that the British commanders would have to play their game very badly. And they did just that! Displaying, whether on land or water, an almost inconceivable incompetence, they lost the game, even though their opponents, beside failing to take advantage of their blunders, both fundamental and frequent, committed almost equal blunders of their own.

What has in recent years come to be known as the General Staff was in the eighteenth century undreamed of as part of a military organization; but, viewed from a modern General-Staff standpoint, the contrast of what actually was done on either side in that campaign with what it is obvious should have been done, affords a study of no small historical interest. Such a contrast is also one now easy to make, for not only is hind-sight, so called, proverbially wiser and more penetrating than fore-sight, but a century's perspective lends to events and situations a proper relative proportion. That becomes clear which was at the time obscure.

For instance, the merest tyro in the study of the conditions on which great military movements depend can now point out with precision and confidence the errors of policy and strategy for which Napoleon was responsible in 1812 and 1813, and which lured him to destruction. What is obvious in the case of Napoleon less than forty years later is, of course, even more obvious in the case of Sir William Howe and General Washington in 1777.

Coming then to the point now at issue, the military policy and line of strategic action Howe would have pursued had he, in May, 1777, firmly grasped the situation and risen to an equality with it, are now so manifest as to be hardly open to discussion; they need but to be set forth. Having a complete naval and a great military superiority, he would have sought to open from his base at New York, and securely hold, a connection with Montreal and Canada by way of the Hudson and Lake Champlain, thus severing his enemy's territory and, in great degree, paralyzing his military action. The means at disposal with which to accomplish this result were ample, — Howe's own army, twenty-five thousand strong at New York, moving north on the easy line of the Hudson, could, coöperating with the fleet, easily open the route, while a naval support would insure the invading column constant and ample supplies. In close contact with an open and navigable river, there need be no fear of a repetition of the tactics of Concord and Lexington. Beyond any question, Sir William, leaning on Lord Howe's arm as he advanced on this line, would be able to connect with the army of Burgoyne, eight thousand strong, moving down from Montreal. His single other military objective would then be the patriot army under Washington, in every respect inferior to the force at Howe's own disposal; and this army it would be his aim to bring to the issue of pitched battle on almost any terms, with a view to its total destruction or dispersal. If he succeeded in so doing, the struggle would be ended, he holding the dividing strategic line of the Hudson; if, however, he failed to get at and destroy Washington's army, he would still hold the line of the Hudson, and the navy under Lord Howe then seizing for permanent occupation Wilmington, at the mouth of the Delaware, and Hampton Roads on the Chesapeake, the brothers Howe could securely depend on the blockade [1] and the gradual securing of other strategic points to bring to their opponent sure death through inanition, — or, in the language of General Charles Lee in the "Plan" of operations prepared by him during his New York captivity, and then submitted to Howe, would "unhinge and dissolve the whole system of [patriot] defence." [2] Such a strategy, in pursuance of a

[1] The crushing influence of an effective blockade on the revolted Provinces was at the time forcibly set forth by the Philadelphia renegade and exiled loyalist, Joseph Galloway, in his pamphlet entitled "A Letter to the Right Honorable Lord Viscount H—e, on His Naval Conduct in the American War," London, 1779. Galloway shows that the naval force put at Lord Howe's disposal was more than ample for an effective blockade; that to establish and maintain such a blockade was wholly practicable; and, finally, that had one been thus established and maintained, "the whole commerce of the revolted Colonies must have ceased. Their army and navy must have been ruined, from the utter impracticability of procuring for them the necessary provisions, clothing and supplies. Their produce must have perished on their hands." Salt, for instance, was almost wholly imported. In Philadelphia "this commodity, which before the rebellion was commonly bought for 15 to 20 pence now (1776-77) sold from £15 to £20 in currency of the same value."

[2] N. Y. Hist. Soc., *Lee Papers*, IV, 408. The story of this traitorous "plan" of Charles Lee is told by George H. Moore, and can be found in New York Historical Society *Collections*, 1874, vol. IV, p. 406. Fisher refers to it as "a plan of no military merit" (ii, 76) ; but on what ground he thus condemned it is not apparent. There is, on the contrary, reason for concluding that it was based on a thorough and correct understanding of existing conditions, and evinced a clear strategic insight. Speaking of the course of events at that time, Hamilton, in a conversation with

policy at once aggressive and passive, was not only safe, but obvious. Secure in control of the sea, Howe had but to divide his opponent's territory, and then destroy his army or starve it out.

The policy and strategy to be adopted and pursued by the Patriots were, on the other hand, hardly less plain. With no foothold at all on the sea, except through a sort of maritime letter-of-marque militia, on land they were hopelessly outclassed, — outclassed in numbers, in organization, in weapons, in discipline, and in every form and description of equipment. They had three things only in their favor: (1) space, (2) time, and (3) interior lines of communication, implying mobility. In any pitched battle they would necessarily take the chances heavily against themselves. Their manifest policy was, therefore, to fight only in positions of their own choosing and with every advantage on their side, striking as opportunity offered with their whole concentrated strength on an enemy necessarily more or less detached, and his detachments beyond supporting distance of each other. Put in simpler form, and drawing examples from actual experience, Bunker Hill, Lexington and Concord pointed the way so far as policy and positions were concerned, and Princeton and Trenton perfectly illustrated the system of harassing and destroying segregated detachments. On the other hand, the bitter lessons received on Long Island and in and about Manhattan in 1776 should have

Pontigibaud about the year 1792, remarked — "All the English need have done was to blockade our ports with twenty-five frigates and ten ships of the line. But, thank God, they did nothing of the sort." (Allen McLane Hamilton, *Hamilton*, 295.) This, Charles Lee at the time distinctly saw, and counselled Sir William Howe accordingly. The utter failure of the two Howes to avail themselves of the sea power by instituting a rigid blockade of the Chesapeake and Delaware bays can be explained only on grounds of professional incapacity. They neither of them knew how to make effective use of the weapons at their command.

taught the patriot leaders that, face to face in ordered battle, their half-equipped, undisciplined levies, when opposed to the European mercenaries, stood just about the chance of a rustic plough-boy if pitted in a twelve-foot ring against a trained prize fighter. It was challenging defeat.

Such, as is now apparent, being the manifest and indisputable conditions under which each party moved, and must win or lose the game or in it hold its own, it possibly is not passing a too sweeping criticism to say that every one of these conditions was either ignored or disregarded equally, and on both sides, throughout that momentous campaign. In other words, British or Patriot, it was a campaign of consecutive and sustained blundering. The leisurely fashion in which it was opened has already been referred to. Washington, holding together with difficulty what was hardly more than a skeleton organization, remained prudently in his lines at Morristown. There, his army as a military objective was apparently within Howe's grasp all through the months of April and May, — practically at his mercy. It could easily have been manœuvred out of its positions, and dispersed or sent on its wanderings; it continued to hold together only so long as its antagonist failed to avail himself of his superiority and the situation. Howe, meanwhile, in his usual time-killing way, was perfecting his arrangements in New York; Burgoyne, at Montreal, was similarly engaged. Not until May was well advanced, and what is for that region some of the best campaigning weather in the whole year was over, did Washington voluntarily emerge from his winter-quarters, and, so to speak, look about to see what his opponent might be up to; for, that he must be up to something, seemed only likely. That opponent had, however, apparently not yet roused himself from his winter's lethargy, and it was not until June was half over that he at last gave signs of active life. Burgoyne at the same time (June 17) moved on his path towards Ticonderoga, the first stage in his march to Albany. Now was Howe's opportunity. It dangled before his eyes, plain and unmistakable. Washington's army should have been his objective. Only seven thousand strong, Howe could oppose twenty thousand to it either for direct attack or purposes of manœuvre. Washington's army disposed of or held off, Howe, following the dictates of simple common sense, would then have turned his face northwards, and marched, practically unopposed, to Albany, by way of Peekskill. Co-operating with the British fleet, Clinton four months later did this with four thousand men only; capturing on his way "vast supplies of muskets, cannon, ammunition, provisions and military tools and equipments of all kinds which the patriots had stored in their great stronghold," the Hudson Highlands. Howe thus wholly failed to avail himself of what was obviously the opportunity of a good soldier's lifetime. Both what he did do and what he failed to do were and remain enigmas to both friends and foes. As a strategic operation it resembled nothing so much as the traditional and familiar movement of the unspecified King of France. Howe marched his twice ten thousand men over into New Jersey; and then marched them back again. Well might Stedman afterwards plaintively ask: "Why did he not march round either on the North or South to the rear of that enemy, where he might have been assaulted without any other hazard than such as must, in the common course of war, be unavoidably incurred?"[1] The query to this day remains unanswered; but, certainly, the British commander did not then make any considerable effort to bring matters

[1] *History of the American War*, I, 288.

"to the issue of pitched battle on almost any terms." When, shortly after, severely criticised for his conduct, Howe simply said: "I did not think it advisable to lose so much time as must have been employed upon that march during the intense heat of the season." The march in question could not very well have been made to cover much more than fifty miles; though it might have implied some discomfort from heat and dust. Washington was wholly unable to account for his opponent's proceedings; those who participated in the subsequent midsummer marchings and fightings of our Civil War have been unable to account for them since. Howe's explanation was puerile.

This military "fooling" over, Howe next evacuated New Jersey altogether, leaving the astonished Washington and his army free to go where they liked and to do what they pleased, quite unmolested; but, instead of turning his face north, and marching up to meet Burgoyne, thus making secure the Hudson line of communication with Canada, the British commander next shipped his army on a mighty fleet of transports, gathered in New York Bay, and, after idly lingering there some precious weeks, sailed away with it into space. The contemporary verdict on these performances was thus expressed by a participant, in language none too strong: —

"In the spring and summer it is impossible for the mind of man to conceive the gloom and resentment of the army, on the retreat from the Jerseys, and the shipping them to the southward : nothing but being present and seeing the countenances of the soldiers, could give an impression adequate to the scene; or paint the astonishment and despair that reigned in New York, when it was found that the North River was deserted, and Burgoyne's army abandoned to its fate. All the former opportunities lost through indolence or rejected through design, appeared innocent when compared with this fatal movement. The ruinous and dreadful consequences were instantly foreseen and foretold; and despondence or execration filled every mouth.

" Had there been no Canada army to desert or to sacrifice, the voyage to the southward could only originate from the most profound ignorance or imbecility."[1]

Disappearing from sight on the 24th of July, on the 30th the British armament was reported as being off the entrance of the Delaware River; again vanishing, not until the 21st of August did it at last make its appearance in the Chesapeake. Howe's objective then was apparent. He was moving on Philadelphia, — the town in which the Congress was holding its sittings, — the seat of Government, — the Capital of the provinces in rebellion!

As a move on the strategic chess-board this further proceeding on the part of Sir William was at the time incomprehensible; nor has it since been accounted for. Had he marched to Philadelphia overland (ninety miles), he would at least have relieved Burgoyne by keeping Washington's entire available force occupied; possibly he might have brought on a pitched battle in which every chance would have been in his favor. He would also have been free at any moment to countermarch north, with or without a battle. Electing to go by sea, when he got into Delaware Bay the Admiral in command of the fleet apparently bethought himself of Sir Peter Parker's dismal experience before Charleston just a year before, and did not like to face on a river water-front the guns of the several forts below the

[1] *View of the Evidence relative to the Conduct of the American War under Sir William Howe*, etc., 152.

" Sir Henry Clinton, in his manuscript notes to Stedman's *American War*, says, ' I owe it to truth to say there was not, I believe, a man in the army, except Lord Cornwallis and General Grant, who did not reprobate the move to the Southward, and see the necessity of a co-operation with General Burgoyne.' " — Fisher, II, 71.

town covering obstructions in the channel;[1] so, instead of landing his army at Wilmington, and proceeding thence to Philadelphia, Howe had recourse to another of those flanking movements to which, after his Bunker Hill frontal experiment, he always showed himself addicted. The front door to Philadelphia being closed, he made for the back door, sailing south around Cape Charles and up Chesapeake Bay to what was known as the Head of Elk, close to Havre de Grace, some fifty miles southwest of Philadelphia; Wilmington being at that time not only wholly unprotected and perfectly accessible, but lying on the Delaware almost exactly half the distance from Philadelphia to the Head of Elk, and, as every one making a trip from New York to Washington now knows, on the direct road between the two first-mentioned points. By this move, very cunning of its kind, Sir William Howe, unquestionably, though in most unaccountable fashion, flanked the defences of his objective point, which now lay at his mercy; but the move had taken him as far away from the line of the Hudson as he could conveniently and comfortably, at that hot season of the year, arrange to get, and had consumed four weeks of precious time. But, with Sir William Howe, time was never of moment! Such a thing is not to be suggested, and, in the case of Sir William Howe, is inconceivable, but had he deliberately and in cold blood designed the ruin of Burgoyne, — as was, indeed, charged by his more hostile critics, — he would not have done other than he did. He not only took himself off and out of the way, but, by hovering in sight of the mouth of Delaware Bay and then sailing southward, he gave Washington the broadest of hints that he need apprehend no interference on Howe's part with any northward

[1] On this point see the passage and note in J. W. Fortescue's *History of the British Army*, III, 212.

movement the patriots might see fit to decide upon. Theirs was the chance! The blunder — for disloyalty and treachery, though at the time suspected, are not gravely alleged — the blunder of which the British general had now been guilty was, in short, gross and manifest; so gross and manifest, indeed, that it could only be retrieved by a blunder of equal magnitude on the part of his adversary. This followed in due time; meanwhile, Howe, wholly losing sight of his proper immediate objective, — Washington's army, — had moved away from the sphere of vital operations, — the severance of New England from New York and the Middle Provinces, — and made himself and the force under him practically negligible quantities for the time being. Off the board, he was out of the game.

Even now, any plausible explanation of Howe's course at this time must be looked for in the mental make-up and physical inclinations of the man. Of him and them, as revealed in the record, something will be said later on in this paper. It is sufficient here to observe that if, as held from the beginning of time, it is one of the distinctive traits of a great soldier to read the mind of an opponent so truly as to be able immediately to forecast his line of conduct, Washington now certainly did not evince a conspicuous possession of that particular trait.

The explanation, at once most plausible and most charitable, of Howe's performance is that, during the winter of 1776-77, he had conceived an exaggerated and wholly erroneous idea of the importance of the possession of Philadelphia as a moral as well as strategic factor in the struggle the conduct of which had been entrusted to him. There were, indeed, good grounds for believing that a large and influential element in the population of the middle provinces — New Jersey, Pennsylvania and Maryland — were distinctly of loyalist proclivity, and that they only needed countenance and protection to assert themselves. Doubtless also Howe counted largely on his own personal magnetism and kindliness of temper, as elements of political conciliation. He then, in his military operations, proceeded to discard every sound strategic rule and consideration in favor of moral effect and social influence. He also seems to have looked on Philadelphia as if it had been a Paris or a Berlin or a Vienna; and he recalled the vital importance of those capitals in the wars of Marlborough and Frederick, — the legendary past of the British army. He was accordingly under an obsession; possessed by what was from a strictly military point of view a pure delusion. Thirty-five years later one infinitely greater than Howe suffered in the same way, but with results far more serious. In his work, *How England saved Europe*, W. H. Fitchett says (IV, 81) of Napoleon's Russian campaign, "Russia, like Spain, to quote Professor Sloane, 'had the strength of low organisms.' Its vitality was not centred in a single organ. It could lose a capital and survive." If this was true of Russia, as Napoleon in 1812 to his cost found, it was yet more true of the American federated States in 1777; for, practically, in Revolutionary warfare Philadelphia in itself, in that respect wholly unlike Albany, was of no more strategic importance than any other considerable town. When, therefore, Howe carried off the bulk and flower of the army of British invasion and set it down in Philadelphia, he made as false a move as was possible in the game assigned him to play.

It then remained for his opponent to avail himself of the great and unlooked-for opportunity thus offered him, — to call a check in the game, possibly even a checkmate. This Washington wholly failed to do; on the contrary, he actually played his opponent's game for him, redeeming Howe's blunders by the commitment of blunders of his own, fortunately less fatal in their effect, though scarcely in nature less gross. When Howe, after disappearing with his armament below the sea-line on the 24th of July, reappeared off the mouth of the Delaware on the 30th of the month, and his general objective thus became obvious, the relation to each other, and to the game, of the remaining pieces on the military chess-board would seem to have been plain. No matter where Howe now went, it was settled that he was not going up the Hudson. That made clear, he might go where he pleased. Using a shallow artifice, he tried to induce Washington to think he was going to Boston, thence to make a juncture with Burgoyne. "Silly" is the only term to apply to such a weak invention of the enemy.[1] Why go to Boston to march overland to Albany, when the shorter way by the Hudson lay open before him? Had he really proposed so to do, Washington might pleasantly have bade him God-speed, and pointed out that his best route lay through Lexington and Concord, or, possibly, up Bennington way. Under conditions similar to those then confronting Washington, it is not difficult to imagine the nervous energy or "stern contentment" with which Frederick or Wellington, or still more Napoleon, with his "tiger spring," would have contemplated the arrangement of the strategic board. The game would have been thrown into their hands. His opponent had hopelessly divided his forces beyond the possibility of effective mutual support, and Washington held the interior line. On which of the three should he pounce? And this question seemed to answer itself. Howe was not only too strong for successful attack, but, for every immediate strategic purpose, he had made of himself a negligible quantity. Placed where he had put himself, or plainly proposed

[1] Irving, *Washington* (Geoffrey Crayon ed.), III, 164.

THE REVOLUTIONARY CAMPAIGN OF 1777 131

to put himself, he could not greatly affect results. Clinton, at New York, was equally negligible; for, while the force — some six thousand men — left there with him by Howe was not sufficient properly to man the defences, much less to assume a dangerous aggressive, the place was secure under the protection of the British fleet. There was no victim in that quarter ripe just yet for sacrifice. There remained Burgoyne. He could incontinently be wiped from off the face of the earth, or, to speak more correctly, removed from the chess-board. That done, and done quickly; then — the next!

Extrication by retreat was now no longer possible; Burgoyne was hopelessly entangled. His bridges were burned; he had to get through to Albany, and thence to New York, with destruction as his sole alternative. Six weeks before (June 17) he had set out on his southward movement, four days after Howe had crossed from New York into New Jersey for his "two weeks' fooling." On the 5th of July Burgoyne occupied Ticonderoga; on that day Howe, his "two weeks' fooling" over, was loading his army on the transports anchored in New York Bay, and Washington was observing him in a state of complete and altogether excusable mental bepuzzlement. What move on the board had the man in mind? Clearly, his true move would be up the Hudson; but why load an army — foot, horse and artillery — on ocean transports to sail up the Hudson? The idea was absurd. But, if Albany was not Howe's destination, what other destination had he in mind? At length, July 24, he put to sea, — disappeared in space. In the interval Burgoyne had made his irretrievable mistake. Hitherto his movement had been in every respect most successful. Winning victories, capturing strongholds and supplies, he had swept on, forcing the great northern barrier. He had now the choice of two routes to Albany. He could go by water to the head of Lake George on his way to Fort Edward, capture it and in ten days be in Albany; or he could try to get there by constructing a military road through the woods. He elected the latter, plunging into "a half-wilderness, rough country of creeks, marshes and woodland trails." Beside removing obstructions and repairing old bridges, he had to build forty new; and one of these "was a causeway two miles long across a swamp."[1] To withdraw was now impossible; the victim was nearing the sacrificial spot. He occupied the hastily evacuated Fort Edward on the 30th of July. On that same day "the people living at Cape Henlopen, at the entrance of Delaware Bay, saw the ocean covered with a vast fleet of nearly three hundred transports and men-of war." It was Howe's armament. He was not bound for Albany! From that moment, strategically and for immediate purposes, he was for Washington as if he did not exist. He might go where he willed to go; he was outside of the present field of vital operation, — clean off the chess-board.

Did Washington see his opportunity, and quickly avail himself of it, Burgoyne was now lost — hopelessly lost. He might indeed get to Albany; but Washington could get there "fust with most men." Washington had now twelve thousand men. A large portion of them were militia, and the militia were notoriously unreliable whether on the march or in battle; as Washington expressed it, under fire they were "afraid of their own shadows"; and so, teaching them how to cover the ground rapidly and well was mere waste of time. They would, of course, have had to be left behind to occupy the attention of the enemy. There would remain probably some eight thousand marching and fighting effectives.

[1] Fisher, II, 65; Trevelyan, Pt. III, 123.

THE REVOLUTIONARY CAMPAIGN OF 1777

Schuyler had forty-four hundred men with him when (July 30) he abandoned Fort Edward; and the militia were pouring in. A month later Gates, who relieved Schuyler in command, had seven thousand. Here was a force fifteen thousand strong, if once united, and Burgoyne, when he emerged from the wilderness, could muster less than five thousand. It was the opportunity of a lifetime; unfortunately, Washington did not so see it, failed to take full advantage of it. Instead, he again had recourse to those halfway measures always in warfare so dangerous.[1]

The possibility of such a move on the part of his adversary had indeed occurred to Howe, and, apparently, to him only; so, just before sailing from New York, he wrote to Burgoyne, congratulating him on his occupation of Ticonderoga (July 5), and added: "Washington is awaiting our motions here, and has detached Sullivan with about twenty-five hundred men, as I learn, to Albany. My intention is for Pennsylvania, where I expect to meet Washington; but if he goes to the northward, contrary to my expectations, and you can keep him at bay, be assured I shall soon be after him to relieve you."[2] The letter containing this extraordinary assurance of support did not reach Burgoyne until the middle of September. It lends a touch of the grotesque to the situation. Three weeks before Howe's missive reached Burgoyne, Washington might with perfect ease have effected a junction of his own army with that under Schuyler, and crushed Burgoyne.

That, as Commander-in-Chief, Washington had ample authority to undertake such a diversion without previously consulting Congress or obtaining its consent thereto, did not admit of doubt. The question had already been raised, and

---
[1] *Supra*, 51.
[2] Fiske, *The American Revolution*, I, 308.

it had once for all been settled; "all the American forces were under his command, whether regular troops or volunteers, and he was invested with full powers to act for the good of the service in every part of the country." The conditions were now exactly those prefigured by Charles Lee the year before at Boston, when he said to Washington: "Your situation is such that the salvation of the whole depends on your striking, at certain crises, vigorous strokes, without previously communicating your intention."[1]

When Howe was descried at the mouth of the Delaware (July 30), Washington was still in central New Jersey, in the neighborhood of the Raritan. Clinton, in New York, was looking for reënforcements, which did not reach him until October. Powerless for aggression, he could be safely disregarded. Albany was only one hundred and fifty miles away; if taken leisurely, a pleasant ten days' summer march. It was a mere question of shoe leather; and, in all successful warfare, shoes are indeed a prime factor. So much is this the case that when, some thirty-five years later, Wellington, attending to every detail which contributed to the effectiveness of his army, was preparing for that final campaign in the Peninsula which culminated one month later in the complete overthrow of the French under King Joseph, directed and dry-nursed by Marshal Jourdan, at Vittoria, it was prescribed that every British infantry soldier should carry in his knapsack three pairs of shoes, with an extra pair of spare soles and heels. Such an ample provision of foot-wear would in the summer of 1777 have probably been beyond the reach of Washington's Quartermaster-General; but, shortly before, shoes sufficient, it is said, for twenty-five thousand troops had arrived safely at Portsmouth, sent out with other munitions of war by French

[1] N. Y. Hist. Soc., *Lee Papers*, IV, 262.

sympathizers. New England, moreover, was then a community of cordwainers, and the coarse cowhide foot-wear of the period could, if called for, have hardly failed somehow to be forthcoming. In any event, the march of one hundred and twenty-five miles towards Chesapeake Bay actually made at that time was in degree only less destructive of sole leather than one twenty-five miles longer to Albany. As to the operation from any other point of view, it was exactly the experience and discipline the patriot army stood most in need of. As every one who has had any experience in actual warfare knows, there is nothing which so contributes to the health, morale and discipline of an army as steady and unopposed marching over long distances. In our own more recent experience Sherman's famous movements through Georgia and the Carolinas afforded convincing illustration of this military truism. Nothing, on the other hand, is so bad for the morale and physical health of a military force, especially one hastily levied, as long hot-weather tarrying in any one locality. For instance, at the very time now under consideration, while Washington was waiting near the Falls of the Schuylkill for Howe's movement to reveal itself, we are told that the sanitary arrangements of the patriots were "particularly unfortunate," and in the "hot August weather a most horrible stench rose all round their camp."

Had Washington, straining on the leash, broken camp and set his columns in motion for Peekskill on the Hudson during the first week in August, by the 20th of a month of easy marches he would have joined Schuyler, and the united armies, fifteen thousand strong, would have been on top of Burgoyne. At that time Gates had not yet assumed command of the Northern Department. Lincoln and Stark were wrangling; and Schuyler was issuing orders which both refused or neglected to obey. The battle at Bennington was fought on August 14. Out-flanked, surrounded, crushed by an overwhelming superiority of force, his enemy flushed with victory, Burgoyne's camp everywhere searched day and night by rifle-bullets, while cannon-balls hurtled through the air, a week at most would have sufficed; the British commander would have had to choose between surrender and destruction. The combination and catastrophe of Ulm thirty-eight years later, might, on a smaller scale and in a different field, have been anticipated; but with results not less decisive. Events would thus have been precipitated seven weeks, and the early days of September might have seen Washington moving south on his interior lines at the head of a united army, flushed with success and full of confidence in itself and its leader. Rich in the spoils of Burgoyne, it would also have been a force well armed and equipped, especially strong in artillery; for, indeed, even at this interval of more than a century and a quarter of time, it leads to something closely resembling a watering of the American eyes and mouth to read at once the account of the parade of Washington's so-called army through Philadelphia on its way to the Brandywine during the latter days of August, 1777, and the schedule of the impedimenta turned over by the vanquished to the victors at Saratoga fifty days later. Of the first Fisher says (II, 19): "The greatest pains were taken with this parade. Earnest appeals were made to the troops to keep in step and avoid straggling. . . . To give some uniformity to the motley hunting-shirts, bare feet, and rags, every man wore a green sprig in his hat. . . . But they all looked like fighting men as they marched by to destroy Howe's prospects of a winter in Philadelphia." This authority then unconsciously touches the heart of the strategic blunder in that march being perpetrated by adding: "With the policy Howe was persistently

THE REVOLUTIONARY CAMPAIGN OF 1777   137

pursuing, it might have been just as well to offer no obstacle to his taking Philadelphia. He merely intended to pass the winter there as he had done in Boston and New York." Mr. Fisher does not add that this half-organized, half-armed, half-clad, undisciplined body twelve thousand strong was on its way to measure itself in pitched battle against eighteen thousand veterans, British and German, perfectly organized, equipped and disciplined, in an effort doomed in advance to failure, — an effort to protect from hostile occupation a town of not the slightest strategic importance! It was in truth a very sad spectacle, that empty Philadelphia parade of victims on the way through a dark valley of death and defeat to Valley Forge as a destination. The cold, hard military truth is that the flower of that force — eight thousand of the best of the twelve thousand should then have been at Saratoga, dividing among themselves the contents of Burgoyne's army train — "a rich prize," consisting, as Trevelyan enumerates, almost exclusively of articles which the captors specially needed. "There were five thousand muskets, seventy thousand rounds of ball-cartridges, many ammunition wagons, four hundred sets of harness, and a fine train of brass artillery, — battering guns, field guns, howitzers, and mortars; — forty-two pieces of ordnance in all." This surrender actually occurred on October 18; it might equally well have been forced in early September, and the united, victorious and seasoned army which compelled it might on the 8th of that month — the day Howe landed at the Head of Elk on Chesapeake Bay — have been hurrying forward, well advanced on its way back to confront him.

That Washington had at this juncture no realizing sense, or indeed any conception of that fundamental strategic proposition of Frederick and Napoleon — the value and effectiveness in warfare of concentration and mobility through utilizing interior lines against a segregated enemy — was now made very manifest. For a time it was supposed that the far-wandering and elusive British armament might have Charleston for its destination. The Congress now (August 1) conferred on Washington plenary powers as to the Northern Department. Instead of acting on this empowerment instantly and decisively, in the way the situation called for, Washington excused himself on the singular ground that the situation in the Northern Department was "delicate" and might involve "interesting consequences." He then called a council of war to advise on the general strategic situation and the line of action best calculated to meet it. Assuming that Howe's objective was Charleston, the council decided in favor of a movement toward the Hudson. As such a "movement might involve the most important consequences," Washington, instead of acting, sent a letter to the President of Congress, requesting the "opinion of that body." Congress gave the seal of its approval to the conclusion of the council. When every one had thus been consulted and all possible advice solicited and received, the northward movement was initiated. But at just that juncture Howe appeared in the Chesapeake. That Philadelphia was his objective now became certain; and immediately the northern movement was countermanded. The grounds on which it was countermanded were thus set forth by Washington himself: "The state of affairs in this quarter will not admit of it. It would be the height of impolicy to weaken ourselves too much here, in order to increase our strength [in the Northern Department]; and it must certainly be considered more difficult, as well as of greater moment, to control the main army of the enemy, than an inferior, and, I may say, a dependent one; for it is pretty obvious that if General Howe can be kept at bay, and prevented from effecting his purpose, the successes of General Burgoyne, whatever they may be, must be partial and temporary." In other words, the advantages of concentration were to be ignored, and no use made of time and interior lines in the striking of blows, — now here, now there. It is quite safe to say that neither Frederick, twenty years before, nor Napoleon, twenty years later, would have viewed that particular situation in that way. They, with all their strength concentrated in one solid mass, would have struck Burgoyne first, and then Howe. They would hardly have weakened themselves by sending Morgan to help "hold Burgoyne at bay"; and then insured the loss of Philadelphia, a thing in itself of no consequence, by confronting Howe with half of an army, which, as a whole, was insufficient for the work.

As Irving shows with a delightful *naïveté*, the significance of which Fiske wholly failed to appreciate, "Washington was thus in a manner carrying on two games at once, with Howe on the seaboard and with Burgoyne on the upper waters of the Hudson, and endeavoring by a skilful movement to give check to both. It was an arduous and complicated task, especially with his scanty and fluctuating means, and the wide extent of country and great distances over which he had to move his men."[1] To attempt to carry on "two games at once" on the chess-board of war, especially with "scanty and fluctuating means," is a somewhat perilous experiment, and one rarely attempted by the great masters of the art. But, with Sir William Howe for an opponent, almost any degree of skill would suffice; opposite him at the board blundering did not count.

In the next place, the extreme slowness of movement which characterized all the operations of this campaign,

[1] *Washington* (Geoffrey Crayon ed.), III, 180–181, Chap. XIII.

whether British or patriot, is by no means their least noticeable feature. Neither side seems to have known how to march in the Napoleonic or Wellingtonian sense of the term, or as the grenadiers of Frederick covered space. Philadelphia, for instance, was only ninety measured miles from New York; it was Howe's objective, by way of the Head of Elk. Taking twenty-eight days (July 24–August 21) to get to the Head of Elk, Howe then spent nine more days in landing his army and setting it in motion; finally, having won a complete victory on the Brandywine on the 11th of September, it was not until September 26 that he occupied Philadelphia, only some twenty miles away from his successful battle-field. In all sixty-five days had been consumed in the process of getting into Philadelphia from New York. On the other hand, the patriot movements were no more expeditious. In sending reënforcements to Gates, Morgan, then at Trenton, received from Washington orders to move north, August 16; the distance to be covered was approximately two hundred miles, and the riflemen did it at the rate of ten miles a day. Reporting to Gates, September 7, Morgan was actively conspicuous in the subsequent operations, which dragged on through forty days. Burgoyne capitulated October 17, and Washington was then in sore straits after Germantown (October 4); but not until November 1 did Morgan even receive his orders to return, and it was eighteen days more before he at last reported back at Whitemarsh; having, quite unopposed and under pressing orders for haste, covered some two hundred and fifty miles in eighteen days — an average of fourteen miles a day. Under the circumstances, he should certainly have covered twenty. He had then been gone ninety-four days in all; under Wellington, Frederick or Napoleon, thirty at most would have been deemed quite enough in which to finish up the job, with a court-martial and dismissal from the service the penalty for dilatoriness. Not until eighteen days after the capitulation at Saratoga was official notice thereof communicated to Congress; and it was the 20th of November — five full weeks — after Burgoyne's surrender before the longed-for reënforcements from the Army of the North put in an appearance. "Had they arrived but ten days sooner," wrote Washington, "it would, I think, have put it in my power to save Fort Mifflin and consequently have rendered Philadelphia a very ineligible situation for the enemy this winter."[1] They ought to have been back in Howe's front ten weeks earlier; and, even as it was, allowing for both Gates's inexcusable procrastination and Putnam's wrong-headed incompetence,[2] they had moved to Washington's relief in a time of well-understood crisis at the snail-like pace of twelve miles a day. Marching in the Peninsula towards Talavera (July 28, 1809) to the assistance of his less hardly pressed chief, General Crauford's famous Light Brigade, moving over execrable roads under an almost intolerable midsummer sun, covered thirty-six miles in eighteen hours; only seventeen men having fallen out of the ranks.[3] Four years later (1813) Wellington, in a campaign

[1] Irving, *Washington*, III, 371.   [2] *Ib.* 363–367.

[3] Napier's statement is that on this occasion the Light Brigade covered sixty-two miles in twenty-six hours (B. VIII, Chap. II) and subsequent authorities have followed Napier. The statement is erroneous. See Mass. Hist. Soc., *Proceedings*, XLIV, 296. The correct time and distance are as stated in the text.

Incomparably the best and most dramatic infantry march I personally ever witnessed was that of the Sixth (Sedgwick's) Corps of the Army of the Potomac on the 2d of July, 1863, hurrying to the support of Meade, very hardly pressed by Lee on the second day of Gettysburg. Breaking camp at 9 P.M. of the 1st, and marching all the next day, under a Pennsylvania July sun, the corps, moving in solid column, covered some thirty-four miles. The leading brigade was then double-quicked into position to help hold the Little Round Top against Longstreet.

In each of those cases, that in Spain in 1809 and that in Pennsylvania

of six weeks conducted in a Spanish midsummer and over Spanish roads, marched his army six hundred miles, passed six great rivers, gained one decisive battle, invested two fortresses, and drove from Spain a homogeneous army of French veterans a fifth more numerous than his own conglomerate command.[1] As Napier in recording these events tersely observes, "the difference between a common general and a great captain is immense, the one is victorious when the other is defeated."

This, however, was thirty years subsequent to the Howe-Washington campaign in Pennsylvania; but, just twenty years before, Frederick had set a yet higher standard of concentration and mobility with which all military men were familiar in 1777. Berlin, the capital of Prussia, was raided and occupied by the imperialists on the 17th of October, 1757, and a contribution levied upon it. Frederick was then at Leipsic, eighty miles away. His confederated enemies were pressing in upon him from every side. Twenty days later (November 5) he routed the French at Rossbach on the western limits of his kingdom; and then, turning fiercely to the east, fighting battle on battle and announcing his determination to assault Prince Charles and his Austrians

in 1863, both officers and men knew how to march. I may claim to have participated in the march last mentioned; as the First Massachusetts Cavalry was then temporarily detached from the brigade, under orders to report to Sixth Corps headquarters. Its marching directions for July 2 were to follow immediately in rear of the corps, and permit no straggling whatever. That day the regiment had practically nothing to do; there was no straggling. My recollection is that, in the saddle at sunrise (4 o'clock), we reached the field of battle at about 4 P.M. As respects speed, solidity and spirit, the infantry march could not have been improved upon; and the deployment of the column as it reached the rear of the line of battle at the crisis of the day's fight was the most striking and impressive incident I remember to have witnessed during my period of service.

[1] Napier, *History of the Peninsular War*, B. XX, Chap. VIII.

THE REVOLUTIONARY CAMPAIGN OF 1777   143

"wheresoever and whensoever I may meet with them," on the 5th of December he won his great victory of Leuthen in Silesia two hundred miles from Rossbach, the odds in numbers engaged being some three to one against him. In that campaign (1757), concentrating his strength, throwing his whole force from side to side of his kingdom regardless equally of distance or of odds, he executed a multiplicity of complicated movements, fought seven pitched battles, and occupied one hundred and seven different positions. After Leuthen, without a moment's hesitation investing Breslau, with its garrison twenty thousand strong, he compelled its surrender December 19, and then, and not until then, was what was left of his war-worn and foot-sore battalions permitted to go into winter quarters. Two years later (September, 1759), during the darkest hours of Frederick's seemingly hopeless struggle for existence, his brother, Prince Henry, "a highly ingenious dexterous little man in affairs of War, sharp as needles,"[1] evaded Marshal Daun, who had everything fixed to destroy him on the Landskron, near Görlitz, at break of day, and marching in fifty-six hours through fifty miles of country "wholly in the Enemy's possession," fell upon the Austrian general, Wehla, and killed or captured his entire command, utterly wrecking the imperialist plan of campaign for that year. This was conducting mili-

---

[1] Carlyle, *Frederick the Great*, B. XIX, Chap. VI. From a literary point of view most remarkable, and indisputably a work of genius, Carlyle's *Frederick* as a military narrative is undeniably irritating. In almost every page of his very striking account of the Second Silesian War, it is apparent that the narrator was wholly devoid of familiarity with the details of matter-of-fact warfare. Had it been Carlyle's fortune to have himself lugged a knapsack and musket a few hundred miles, to have passed a winter or two in camp, and to have participated in half a dozen battles, his narrative would have been altogether other than it is, and vastly more instructive as well as realistic. Carlyle's *Frederick* smells of the lamp; Napier's *Peninsular War*, of the camp-fire.

tary operations on great strategic lines and in strict conformity with the fundamental rules governing the game; but it contrasts strangely with the performances in America exactly twenty years later.

Bearing in recollection such military operations and possibilities, conducted on interior lines to well-considered and attainable objectives under correct strategic rules, it is interesting to consider what Washington actually did in 1777. As will be seen, it is not unsafe to say that during the four months — August to November — every sound principle whether of policy or strategy was on the patriot side either disregarded or violated.

Recurring to the 24th of July, when Howe, putting out to sea from Sandy Hook, disappeared below the horizon, the pieces on the strategic chess-board, as already seen, stood as follows: Washington with some twelve thousand men, probably eight thousand of whom were marching effectives, was at Middlebrook on the Raritan. He held a controlling position on the interior line, practically midway between Peekskill, on the Hudson, and Philadelphia, on the Delaware, — one hundred and seventy miles from Albany to the north, and one hundred and forty from Elkton, at the head of Chesapeake Bay, to the south. From the military, operating point of view the two places were practically equidistant, Albany being two days' march further off than Elkton. Clinton, it will be remembered, had been left by Howe to hold the British base at the mouth of the Hudson, with hardly force enough (six thousand men) for the purpose. For the time he was a mere pawn in the game. Burgoyne, with some seven thousand effectives, was slowly approaching Fort Edward, which the patriots abandoned, and he occupied, July 30. In his front, forty miles only from Albany, was Schuyler with some forty-five hundred de-

THE REVOLUTIONARY CAMPAIGN OF 1777   145

moralized men. Howe, with the bulk of the British army, some eighteen thousand, had disappeared, — his whereabouts and destination were matters of pure conjecture. To the strategic eye of Washington two things only were clear; while the advance of Burgoyne must at any cost be checked, Howe must be watched, and, if possible, circumvented. As respects the first, he was right; as respects the second, he was in error: and, because of that error, Washington now made two egregious, and, as the result showed, well-nigh fatal mistakes. Instead of going himself at the head of the whole effective part of his army, he, in the face of an enemy already superior in every respect, divided that army, sending a large detachment, some three thousand strong including Morgan's riflemen, — the very kernel and pick of his command, — to reënforce Gates, now (August 16) in charge of the Northern Department; he himself, in his pest-hole of a summer camp near Philadelphia, continuing his anxious watch for Howe. It may have been generous, but it was not war; and, within less than a week (August 21), after he had thus depleted his previously insufficient strength, Howe put in his appearance at the Head of Elk. With his divided force to risk a pitched battle under such circumstances was to disregard the first strategic rule for his conduct, and, in so doing, to invite disaster and defeat; yet that was just what Washington did. When, in 1812, after Borodino, Kutuzof, the Russian Commander-in-Chief, was urged to risk another battle before abandoning "the holy Ancient Capital of Russia" to the hated invader, Tolstoi says that he put the case thus to the Council of War: "The question for which I have convened these gentlemen is a military one. That question is as follows: The salvation of Russia is her army. Would it be more to our advantage to risk the loss of the army and of Moscow too by accepting battle, or to abandon Moscow without a battle?" Tolstoi tells us that a long discussion ensued. At last, during one of the lulls which occurred, when all felt that nothing remained to be said, "Kutuzof drew a long sigh, as if he were prepared to speak. All looked at him; 'Eh bien, Messieurs, je vois que c'est moi qui payerai les pots cassés,' said he. And, slowly getting to his feet, he approached the table: 'Gentlemen, I have listened to your views. Some of you will be dissatisfied with me. But' — he hesitated — 'I, in virtue of the power confided to me by the sovereign and the country, I command that we retreat.'"[1] Half a loaf is proverbially better than no bread; and this homely domestic aphorism holds true also of military operations. The Russian General-in-Chief merely recognized the fact. Kutuzof lost Moscow, but, as the invader presently found out to his great cost, he saved the Russian army. Washington not only lost Philadelphia, but the wreck and remnant of the patriot army survived two unnecessary defeats only to face the privations and disease of Valley Forge.

That, strategically, and from the American point of view, the battle of the Brandywine ought never to have been fought is a point upon which there is no disagreement. It is, however, argued that it was a political and moral necessity, — that a meddling and impracticable Congress compelled it out of regard to an unreasoning public sentiment. As Marshall, a contemporary authority, and himself then serving in a Virginia regiment under Washington, assures us: "Their inferiority in numbers, in discipline, and in arms, was too great to leave the Americans a probable prospect of victory. A battle, however, was not to be avoided. Public opinion, and the opinion of Congress, required it. To have given up Philadelphia without an attempt to preserve it

[1] *War and Peace*, Pt. XI, Chap. IV.

THE REVOLUTIONARY CAMPAIGN OF 1777   147

would have excited discontents."[1] If such was indeed the case,[2] the decision announced by Kutuzof to his Council of War in 1812 would have been very apposite in the mouth of Washington in 1777. As the result of the battle, he should have lost his army; for, in addition to the fact that it ought never to have been fought at all, the battle of the Brandywine, while well and skilfully fought by the British, was very badly and blunderingly fought on the side of the Americans. They were out-manœuvred, surprised, out-fought and routed. That the chief patriot army — the mainstay of the cause of Independence — was not on that occasion utterly destroyed was, indeed, due wholly to the indolent forbearance of Howe. It was one of the pithy aphorisms of Napoleon that the art of war is to march twelve leagues in a single day, overthrow your enemy in a great battle, and then march twelve leagues more in pursuit. Sir William Howe met neither requirement; but it was in the last that he failed most conspicuously. As Galloway, the Philadelphia loyalist, with the best conceivable opportunities for forming an opinion, wrote of him, "Howe always succeeded in every attack he thought proper to make, as far as he chose to succeed." In this respect Brandywine was a mere repetition of Bunker Hill and Flatbush. Of two French officers who took part in the operations on the Brandywine, one (Lafayette) observes, "Had the enemy marched directly to Derby, the American army would have been cut up and destroyed; they lost a precious night"; the other (Du Portail) wrote, "If the English had followed their advantage that day, Washington's army would have been spoken of no more." But Howe would not do it. If he had pursued

[1] *Washington*, III, 144, 152, 164.
[2] To the same effect Irving, *Washington*, III, 241. This subject will again be referred to in this paper, *infra*, 163.

Washington, it was said, and inflicted a crushing defeat, he might have left part of his force to occupy Philadelphia, and marched the rest to the assistance of Burgoyne. This was what the ministry had expected. As matter of cold historic truth Washington had, in the great game of war, played into his opponent's hands, — done exactly what that opponent wanted him to do, and what he ought never to have done.[1] He had permitted Howe to draw him away from his true objective, — the army of Burgoyne, — then to divide his force, and, finally, in the sequence of so doing, to venture a pitched battle which he had not one chance in ten of winning. Great in ministerial circles were the gratulations when news arrived in London that Howe's false move had been thus retrieved by a move equally false on the patriot side. "I confess," wrote Lord George Germain, — and one can even now almost hear a deep-drawn breath of relief in the words, — "I confess I feared that Washington would have

[1] In his defence of his proceedings, after resigning his command and returning to England, Howe claimed that so far as Burgoyne was concerned, his Chesapeake Bay expedition was a well-designed and altogether successful movement, fully accomplishing its intended purpose. "Had I adopted the plan of going up Hudson's-river, it would have been alleged, that I had wasted the campaign with a considerable army under my command, merely to ensure the progress of the northern army, which could have taken care of itself, provided I had made a diversion in its favour, by drawing off to the southward the main army under General Washington." Therefore, acting upon the advice of the admiral, Lord Cornwallis and other general officers, believing that Washington would follow him, he "determined on pursuing that plan which would make the most effectual diversion in favour of the northern army, which promised in its consequences the most important success, and which the Secretary of State at home, and my own judgment upon the spot, had deliberately approved." — *Parliamentary History*, XX, 693, 694. And in his *Observations upon a Pamphlet entitled "Letters to a Nobleman,"* 61, Howe repeated the assertion. "I shall ever insist, and I am supported by evidence in insisting, that the southern expedition, by drawing off General Washington and his whole force, was the strongest diversion [in favor of the northern army] that could have been made."

THE REVOLUTIONARY CAMPAIGN OF 1777   149

marched all his force towards Albany, and attempted to demolish the army from Canada, but the last accounts say that he has taken up his quarters at Morristown after detaching three thousand men to Albany. If this is all he does, he will not distress Burgoyne."[1] Thus, while himself wandering off with an utterly false objective — Philadelphia — in view, by supreme good fortune Howe had not only induced Washington to follow him, but also in so doing to give the British leader a chance at his true objective, Washington's own army. In the final outcome, it is difficult to see how blundering could have gone further. Out-manœuvred and out-fought, twice beaten in pitched battles, neither of which under the circumstances he ought to have risked, Washington presently crawled into his winter-quarters at Valley Forge, while Howe ensconced himself comfortably in Philadelphia. Yet months before, Charles Lee, then a prisoner of war in New York, had traitorously but truly advised Howe, "In my opinion the taking possession of Philadelphia will not have any decisive consequences."

The undeniable fact is that from a cold military point of view, Howe's movement ought to have been encouraged by Washington, and the British occupation of Philadelphia rather facilitated than opposed. A mere show of obstruction to it should have sufficed; for, as Franklin, the shrewdest observer of the day, whether of nature or of events, is said to have remarked when the news reached him that Howe had captured Philadelphia: "No, Philadelphia has captured Howe!"

In a recent Congressional Report [2] on the proposal to erect a statue of General Nathanael Greene on the battleground at

---

[1] *Lord George Germain to General Irwin*, August 23, 1777. Hist. MSS. Com., *Report on MSS. of Mrs. Stopford-Sackville*, I, 138.
[2] House Report, No. 1698, 61st Congress, 2d Session.

Guilford Courthouse, North Carolina, it is stated with apparent correctness that when, in March, 1781, nearly four years after Howe's occupation of Philadelphia, Greene made his indecisive North Carolina fight, Washington had formed a plan to attack Clinton, who had 12,000 troops, in New York; and, the French fleet coöperating, to capture him and his army, thereby putting an end to the war. His preparations to that end were in full progress, when, suddenly, tidings of Greene's battle reached him, and of the subsequent falling back of Cornwallis on Wilmington. Though victorious, unable, because of his losses, longer to hold the field in the South, the British commander must obviously return northward through the lower part of Virginia. Grasping the essential fact that the capture of either Cornwallis or Clinton would bring the war to an end, Washington, this time, saw his opportunity. Cornwallis, as Burgoyne in 1777, was the surer victim, he having only 7000 men, while Clinton had 12,000. Washington changed his plans accordingly. Deceiving Clinton, he moved rapidly upon the weaker force, and by a masterly movement brought hostilities to a practical close at Yorktown. But it is difficult to see why a movement and combination of precisely similar character might not have brought the war to a close four years earlier. The march to Lake Champlain would, in 1777, have been both shorter and easier than the subsequent march of 1781 from the banks of the Hudson to the shores of the Chesapeake; and Howe at Philadelphia in 1777 would have been even more powerless to stay it than in 1781 was Clinton in New York.

The actual strategy of the campaign of 1777 has now been passed in view, and its merits or demerits on either side tested by the application to them of the acknowledged principles of a sound policy or rules of correct strategy, laid down in the full light of subsequent events and with our knowledge

THE REVOLUTIONARY CAMPAIGN OF 1777

of conditions then existing. The result has been stated. On neither side was the great game played with an intelligent regard to its rules; but, taken as a whole, the mistakes committed and the blunders perpetrated on the British side clearly and considerably more than counterbalanced those on the patriot side. On each side they were bad; but in Burgoyne's capitulation the British lost so to speak a queen, while in Howe's failure to destroy Washington's army after his victory on the Brandywine the British threw away the chance of mating their adversary's king, by no means impossibly of calling a checkmate.

Charles Lee was second to Washington in command of all the American armies. Captured, or rather ignominiously bagged, by the British at Basking Ridge, December 13, 1776, Lee passed the entire year 1777 a prisoner of war in New York, not being released in exchange until May, 1778. While in New York, Lee experienced a change of heart as respects the conflict in which he was a participant; and the plan of operations he then drew up for the consideration of Sir William Howe has already been referred to.[1] Charles Lee was not a man who inspired either confidence or respect. So lightly did his former British army associates regard him that when his capture was announced and the disposition to be made of him as a prisoner of war was mooted, it was contemptuously observed by "one of the wisest servants of the Crown" that he was so constituted that "he must puzzle everything he meddles in, and he was the worst present the Americans could receive."[2] Lee, nevertheless, did have a certain military instinct as well as training, and the scheme of operations outlined by him for Howe's consideration was in close general conformity with the principles set forth in the earlier portion

[1] *Supra*, 121. [2] N. Y. Hist. Soc. *Lee Papers*, IV, 402.

of this paper. Holding New York as a base, the British navy was also to secure the control of Chesapeake Bay; and then, cutting New England off from the Middle Provinces, was to rely on a gradual process of inanition to dissolve the patriot levies. So self-evident did this strategic proposition seem to Lee that up to the 15th of June, 1778, three days only before Howe's successor, Clinton, abandoning Philadelphia in the summer following Brandywine, began his march to New York, Lee at Valley Forge insisted, in a long letter addressed to Washington, that the plainly impending move of the British commander would be in the direction of Lancaster, Pa., with a view to manœuvring the patriot army out of its strong position at Valley Forge and forcing it to a trial of strength under conditions less advantageous to it; and then, whatever the result, Clinton purposed to take possession of some convenient tract of country effectually protected by the British command of the sea, and, by so doing, to paralyze further resistance.[1]

The French alliance, jeopardizing as it did for the time being — and until Rodney's victory (February 19, 1782) — the British control of the sea, had in June, 1778, introduced a new and controlling factor into the strategic situation, in obedience to which Clinton made his move from Philadelphia to New York. But until the news of Burgoyne's capitulation reached Europe (December, 1777), resulting in the Franco-American alliance (January, 1778), it is difficult to detect any point of weakness in "Mr. Lee's Plan." If put in operation at any time during 1777 and systematically pursued, it could hardly have failed to work. The British commander had at his disposal an ample force with which to do anything, except generally occupy the country. Had he seen fit in June, 1777, to move up the Hudson by land and

[1] *Lee Papers*, II, 401.

THE REVOLUTIONARY CAMPAIGN OF 1777   153

river to effect a junction with Burgoyne, the Americans, as their leaders perfectly well knew, could have offered to him no sort of effective opposition. "Nothing under Heaven can save us," wrote Trumbull, "but the enemy's going to the southward." [1] Chesapeake Bay, with Hampton Roads as a depot and arsenal, next lay at the mercy of the British fleet. Wilmington, carrying with it a complete control of the Delaware and the whole eastern shore of Maryland, did not admit of defence; neither, as events subsequently showed, did Charleston or the coast of the Carolinas: and the interior was subsidiary to the seaboard controlling points. The patriot army, if left to itself, behind an effectively blockaded coast, could not be held together because of a mere lack of absolute necessities in the way of food, raiment and munitions. All the British had to do was, apparently, to hold the principal points of seaboard supply and distribution, and a single line of interior communication — New York Bay to Lake Champlain — and then — wait! How utterly and completely they failed to adopt this policy, or to act on these strategic lines, is matter of record. They not only threw away their game, but they lingered out eight years in doing it.

Turning now to the other side, the conclusion to be reached is not greatly better. The sequence of events hardly needs to be recalled: at the South, Brandywine (September 11), Paoli (September 20), Germantown (October 4), Fort Mifflin (November 15), and Valley Forge (December 9) — all in 1777. An undeniably bad and ill-considered record, with a most wretched termination. At the North it was better, though somewhat checkered; Ticonderoga lost (July 5), Fort Edward abandoned (July 30), Bennington won (August 14), Fort Montgomery and the Hudson High-

[1] Fisher, II, 71.

lands lost (October 6), winding up with the Saratoga capitulation (October 17). Assuming now that the game had been played quite otherwise than it was played, and more in accord with the rules of "good generalship," it is possible, knowing as we do the characters and temperamental methods of those responsible for the movements made, approximately to predicate results. As already set forth, and for ulterior reasons once more briefly summarized, they would have been somewhat as follows: —

On July 30 Howe's armament appeared at the entrance of Delaware Bay, and again vanished. Had Washington been endowed with the keen military instinct of Frederick or of Napoleon, that one glimpse would have been enough. Holding the interior line, Washington would have realized that Howe had made himself for an indefinite but most vital period of time a purely negligible military quantity. Burgoyne, on the other hand, had compromised himself. There would have been one tiger spring; and, before the last-named British commander realized his danger, he would have been in the toils. The next move would have been a logical sequence. Working on interior lines and applying either Frederick's or Napoleon's pitiless mobility to the situation, eighteen days would have seen the patriot army either striking savagely at Clinton in the absence of a protecting fleet, or back on the Delaware.

What Frederick or Napoleon would next have done, if placed in the position of Washington, it would be foolish to undertake to say; for Frederick and Napoleon were men of genius, and, when the critic or theorist undertakes to indicate the path either of the two would have followed under any given conditions, one thing only can safely be predicated: The conclusion reached would be far from the mark! Not impossibly, however, if a guess may be ventured by a tyro,

— and in the case of Frederick such a move would have been characteristic, — the morning after Burgoyne's capitulation, the head of the patriot column would have been in motion towards Albany. Surveying the chess-board, and the character and location of the pieces upon it, Frederick might have argued somewhat as follows: Howe is in Philadelphia; if I now strike swiftly and heavily at Clinton in New York, Howe, — and I think I understand the man, — suddenly awakened to the fatal mistake he has made, and his imperilled base, will be sure to hurry by the shortest route to Clinton's rescue; and I, abandoning New York, will then meet him, with every man and gun I can muster, at a point I will myself select in New Jersey; but "I propose to fight him wheresoever and whensoever I can find him." Clinton's turn would have come next.

Wellington, on the other hand, if similarly circumstanced, would not improbably have from the outset observed Howe's performances with the same "stern contentment" with which he observed the mistaken move of Marmont at Salamanca.[1] He would have been not ill pleased to have his opponent establish himself in Philadelphia, thus dividing his command, and placing himself in an isolated spot far from his base and of no strategic importance. Looking into the necessary subsequent moves in the game, Wellington would have seen that Howe, once in Philadelphia, must as a military necessity possess himself of the forts on the Delaware; he had to communicate with the British fleet. Those forts were held by patriot garrisons, and, after the bagging of Burgoyne, their capture must be effected under the eyes of a united and well-equipped covering force awaiting its opportunity, in no degree depleted by defeat. To a hawk-eyed commander, and that Wellington unquestionably was,

[1] *Infra*, 178.

such an opportunity could hardly fail to offer itself; and the equivalent of Germantown would then have been fought under wholly different auspices. It would have been fought to cover the defences on the Delaware. It is useless to venture a surmise as to the probable outcome of such a trial of strength. One thing only can safely be predicated of it, a victory won under those conditions would have cost Howe heavily—Bunker Hill over again, in it not impossibly half his army would have melted away.

Unfortunately Washington did not, until too late, see this latter situation in any such light. On the contrary, during the aimless marching and countermarching which followed the disaster on the Brandywine, when no doubt longer existed of Howe's ultimate occupation of Philadelphia, Marshall says: "To the requisitions for completing the works on the Delaware, the general answered that the service would be essentially injured by employing upon them at this critical juncture, while another battle was contemplated, any part of the continental troops; that, if he should be enabled to oppose the enemy successfully in the field, the works would be unnecessary; if not, it would be impossible to maintain them." As the actual result showed, this conclusion was wrong at each point; the enemy was not successfully opposed in the field, and the forts should have at once been completed, to be firmly held under the watchful eyes of a covering and as yet unbeaten army.

It is related of the Duke of Wellington that, on the day following one of his Peninsular battles, he gruffly observed to an old Scotch regimental commander, "How's this, Colonel, I hear that some French cavalry got inside your square yesterday?" To which he received the no less gruff reply, "Is that so, your Grace; but ye did'na happen to hear they got out again, did ye?" It was easy enough for Howe, after

THE REVOLUTIONARY CAMPAIGN OF 1777   157

Brandywine, to get into Philadelphia; it was for Washington to see that, once in, it was not equally easy for Howe's army to open communications with the British fleet. Speaking generally, however, and making no attempt to peer too curiously into the infinite might-have-beens, the situation of the pieces on the strategic chess-board in September, 1777, and after Brandywine, was comparatively simple. Certain moves, become military necessities, may safely be predicated as having then been inevitable; for, unless they had complete control of the Delaware to the sea, "Philadelphia was nothing but a death-trap for the British."[1] Had the game therefore been played by the Americans skilfully and in accordance with the rules, Howe would have been permitted to march into the trap there, then to find the door between him and his fleet very firmly barred. In other words, avoiding a pitched battle like Germantown, but manœuvring for delay, the patriots should have perfected and provisioned the defences, throwing into them strong garrisons of the more reliable troops, under their most resolute commanders. The covering army should then menacingly have watched; for Howe would have been compelled at any cost to possess himself of the works. Nothing of the sort was done. When at last a force of some two hundred men was thrown into Fort Mifflin, it was found to be "garrisoned by thirty militia only." The whole military situation had been misconceived;[2] but Howe, after Germantown, most characteristically gave his opponent two weeks' time in which to do the long-neglected obvious, and in some slight degree save the gravely jeopardized patriot

[1] Fisher, II, 44.
[2] "It had been impracticable for the commander-in-chief to attend personally to these works, and they were entirely incomplete. The present relative position of the armies gave them a decisive importance." — Marshall, *Washington*, III, 175.

situation. With Germantown fought on October 4, not until the 19th did the British commander address himself to the imperative problem of securing the defences on the Delaware. Two weeks of time very precious to his side had been wantonly wasted. Fortunately for him, his adversary had also failed to improve them. Delays were equally divided: for, far to the north, Burgoyne, who should have been wiped off the board six weeks at least before, had capitulated on October 17; but not for over two weeks yet (November 1) did Morgan and his riflemen receive orders to rejoin Washington, and they found him at Whitemarsh, November 18. The campaign was then over. Such dilatoriness does not admit of satisfactory explanation. Warfare was not then, nor can it ever be, successfully conducted in that way.

Apparently Washington's still divided army had as a fighting unit been used up in two ill-considered and hopeless battles, that on the Brandywine (September 11) and that at Germantown (October 4), and was equal to no aggressive action during the month of Howe's operations against the forts (October 22–November 15). A golden opportunity was thus lost.

It is hardly worth while further to consider what might have been the outcome of that campaign, with Howe still in command of the British, had the patriots pursued a more active and intelligent course. But, had the fundamental rules which should have governed the game been grasped and observed, it is by no means beyond the range of reasonable possibilities that the conflict might, even as it was, have then been brought to a triumphant close. Burgoyne disposed of even by the middle of October, a united and seasoned patriot army, equipped with Burgoyne's stores and strengthened by his excellent field batteries, might have con-

THE REVOLUTIONARY CAMPAIGN OF 1777

fronted Howe in his Philadelphia death-trap; and they would then have been in position to assail him fiercely when he tried to open the securely fastened door which stood in the way of all communication with his fleet. Even as it was, those defences — neglected, half-finished only, ill-garrisoned, unsupplied and unsupported — held out six weeks, checking the more important operations against Washington's depleted and twice beaten army. During that time Howe was in great danger of being starved out of Philadelphia, as his army had to be supplied by flatboats running the gauntlet of the forts at night, and never had more than a week's rations on hand.[1] Under these circumstances it was small cause for surprise that as the days crept on the extreme gravity of the situation "was apparent in the countenance of the best officers, who began to fear that the fort would not be reduced";[2] in which case was it at all impossible that Howe might in one season have shared the fate of Burgoyne, the tactics and mobility of Princeton and Trenton having been enlarged and developed to cover the broader strategic field between Philadelphia and Saratoga? In such case Yorktown would have been anticipated by exactly four years.

Again, and finally, reviewing the campaign of 1777, it is almost undeniable as an historical and strategic proposition, that, either in its early stages or in the course of it, decisive results as respects the entire conflict were within the safe and easy reach of either party to it, who both saw and took

[1] *View of the Evidence relative to the Conduct of the American War under Sir William Howe*, etc., 114.

[2] *Letters to a Nobleman [Howe] on the Conduct of the War in the Middle Colonies*, 81. Greene, writing November 4, said: "The enemy are greatly discouraged by the forts holding out so long; and it is the general opinion of the best of citizens that the enemy will evacuate the city if the fort holds out until the middle of next week." — *Life*, I, 504.

advantage of the conditions in his favor and the opportunities offered him. Had Howe gone up the Hudson in June and effected a junction with Burgoyne on the land side, while with the navy the British seized Hampton Roads and blockaded the Delaware from Wilmington, further resistance would have been almost completely paralyzed, and the patriot army must apparently have dissolved from inanition. There would have been no visible alternative. On the other hand, when Howe, at the crisis of the campaign, disappeared in space, leaving the field free for his opponent, Saratoga, the Philadelphia death-trap and the defences of the Delaware offered almost infinite strategic and tactical possibilities.

It remains to forestall, and, if possible, in advance meet the criticisms which may not improbably be made upon the views herein taken and the conclusions reached. In the first place, it will almost inevitably be urged that due allowance has not been made for the earlier and less matured conditions existing in 1777, as compared with those of the present time or of 1861–1865. In the Revolutionary period the country was in no way self-sustaining; the present means of information did not exist; the roads and channels of communication, when as yet not still unmade, were at best crude and inadequate; and, consequently, such military mobility as that suggested, while practicable for Frederick, was impossible for Washington.

The reply to this criticism is obvious and conclusive. In answer to a call of great exigency from Albany after the evacuation of Ticonderoga (July 4) Washington, in presence of the enemy, — dividing thereby a force at best insufficient, — sent Glover's brigade and Morgan's riflemen, in all some 3000 of his most effective troops, to confront Burgoyne. They covered the ground with a fair degree of rapidity, and rendered valuable service. There is no apparent reason why what was accomplished by this large detachment with no serious difficulty should have been impracticable for the commander-in-chief with the bulk of his army. Four years later, when the operation suggested itself to him, Washington moved a larger force through a more difficult country a yet greater distance in less time; and he did it with no particular trouble. A French contingent, some fifteen hundred strong, then proceeded from Newport, R.I., through Connecticut, crossed the Hudson above New York, and marched down to the Head of Elk on Chesapeake Bay; this in midsummer and early autumn. Apparently those composing this array had a highly enjoyable outing.[1] Accompanying the movement of the allied forces from the Hudson to Yorktown, Washington, with his companions, is said to have at times got over sixty miles a day. During the intervening four years he had obviously improved both in strategy and mobility. In

[1] The entire distance, land and water, traversed by Rochambeau's command in this movement was 756 miles. Setting out from Providence June 18, Yorktown was reached October 28. The actual road-marching distance was 548 miles, which were covered in thirty-seven days, or at an average rate of fifteen miles a day. The American army set out from Dobbs Ferry August 20, and reached Williamsburg, 492 miles, September 14, having covered on an average twenty miles a day. The itinerary of the allied army in the Yorktown movement is described in graphic detail in Chapter XX of the posthumously published *France in the American Revolution* of the late James Breck Perkins. Elsewhere in his narrative (p. 319) Mr. Perkins observes, in connection with a somewht similar operation at one time considered in New York, "to attack the French [in Rhode Island] successfully and then return to meet the American army [under Washington] required decision, celerity, and boldness. Clinton possessed none of these qualities. . . . The daring that takes great risks and accomplishes great results had been common in the officers who were inspired by Chatham, but it was not found in the generals and admirals whom George III sent out to fight with his rebellious subjects." The same author speaks (p. 385) of "the dull inefficiency that seemed characteristic of the operations of the English in America," whether naval or military.

M

effecting on interior lines this really fine concentrated movement against a divided enemy, the American commander had, also, knowingly left Philadelphia quite uncovered from the direction of New York, where Sir Henry Clinton lay with 18,000 idle effectives at his disposal. It has been urged in justification of Washington's course in following Howe's movement south in 1777 and futilely striving to protect Philadelphia, that, had he done otherwise, some great disaster might have befallen the cause; his "interior lines" would have been jeopardized. He could not — it is argued — know exactly how long Howe's salt-water excursion would last, or where it might end. It is not easy to assign its proper weight to such shadowy considerations. In warfare there is always an element of doubt as to what may be occurring, as Wellington put it, "on the other side of the hill," or as to the counterstroke an opponent may meditate; but the risk in this way incurred in the Yorktown movement of 1781 was quite as great as would have been any risk incurred by a similar movement to the north in 1777. Fortunately, however, the fear lest Clinton, were he not at hand to prevent, break loose and do something terrible in the direction of Albany or Philadelphia did not hold Washington back from aggressive action in 1781. Four years before a similar fear as respects Howe had both held him back and led him astray. The real explanation of the Yorktown movement, and of Clinton's inertness while it was in process must be looked for elsewhere; nor is it far to seek. The simple fact is that both sides had at last got to a realizing sense that, strategically, Philadelphia was eccentric. A mere pawn in the game, its loss or taking, signified nothing. The sudden concentrated move on Cornwallis at Yorktown called, on the contrary, checkmate to King George.

In their deeply suggestive and intensely interesting story,

THE REVOLUTIONARY CAMPAIGN OF 1777   163

Le Conscript de 1813, which, now become a classic, excited some fifty years ago such world-wide attention, Erckmann-Chatrian describe the veteran sergeant Pinto observing through the vanishing mist the allied armies about to attack Napoleon in flank and cut his column in two, on the morning of Lützen (May 2, 1813); as he does so, "le nez en l'air et la main en visière sur les yeux," he remarks to the conscript at his side, "C'est bien vu de leur part; ils apprennent tous les jours les malices de la guerre." A similar observation might have been applied by Sir Henry Clinton to Washington and his movement in September, 1781. Meanwhile the conditions under which operations were carried on had not greatly changed since July, 1777; it was Washington who had developed.

Another objection urged will not improbably be to the effect that Washington's military action was, in July, 1777, hampered. From considerations of prestige and on political grounds he could not afford to leave Philadelphia and the Middle Provinces even temporarily uncovered, no matter what great and speedy results might by so doing be secured in the North. In the first place be it observed, Washington never suggested any such move as that against Burgoyne, leaving Philadelphia uncovered to await its outcome; nor, accordingly, did Congress in any way hamper him as respects making it. On the contrary, he seems to have acted wholly on his own volition and in accordance with his own best judgment, and is himself on record to this effect. But, even assuming the contrary, the extreme unwisdom, not to say weakness, of allowing clergymen, politicians, editors and citizens generally to influence campaign operations has been generally admitted ever since September 3, 1650, and that day's experience of Leslie's Scotch army at the hands of Cromwell, near Dunbar. Really masterful captains do not give ear, much less yield, to such influences. On the other hand, it is matter of record that Washington was noticeably given to holding councils of war, ever seeking advice and showing a somewhat excessive deference to public opinion. He did so on Long and Manhattan Islands in 1776; and again before Philadelphia, in 1777; in both cases thereby gravely jeopardizing the cause entrusted to him. He did so knowingly and avowedly; for, difficult as it is of belief, he seems actually for a time to have held himself bound to follow the opinions of the councils he had called in all cases where they diverged from his own.[1] As to Philadelphia, Washington in the summer of 1777 seems himself to have been laboring under as great a delusion as that which possessed Howe. It apparently never occurred to him that Philadelphia could most certainly be either saved or rescued by a sudden, concentrated blow struck just north of Albany. Greene, far and away the ablest of his lieutenants, also shared in the costly delusion; but with a saving hesitation due to his keener military instinct. "I think it," he wrote, on August 14, 1777, "an object of the first importance to give a check to Burgoyne, . . . [but] Philadelphia is the American Diana, she must be preserved at all events. There

[1] In March, 1777, Washington sent Greene to Philadelphia to reach a distinct understanding with the Congress on this subject, among others. The question was then formally raised, and the following recorded: "*Resolved*, that General Washington be informed that it never was the intention of Congress that he should be bound by the majority of voices in a council of war, contrary to his own judgment." — Greene, I, 348; *Journals of the Congress*, March 24, 1777. In this connection it is interesting to note the important part played by councils of war in the Parliamentary armies of the English Civil War period. Frequently held and largely attended, they seem to have been regarded almost as a matter of right, and the neglect of a commander to call them was denounced as "unconstitutional." Fairfax undertook no important operation without consulting a council. (Firth, *Cromwell's Army*, 57–59.) A study of the American Revolutionary army, similar to that made by Firth of the Parliamentary army, is much needed.

THE REVOLUTIONARY CAMPAIGN OF 1777   165

is great attention paid to this city; it is true it is one of the finest upon this continent, but in my opinion is an object of far less importance than the North River."[1] So, less wise than Kutuzof in the next generation, Washington sacrificed an army in hopeless conflict to save "the American Diana"; and, when the "Diana" in question fell a prey to the ravisher, it was in due time discovered that she was not worth saving, but, on the contrary, only a Delilah, and rather in the nature of a "death-trap" to the foreign possessor. Having, so far as the record shows, been in no respect hampered in his action, but following the dictates of his judgment, "his own valiant spirit" and "the native ardor of his character,"[2] but, unfortunately, in pursuance of a thoroughly unmilitary plan, Washington lost Philadelphia and reduced his army to impotence from repeated defeat. He then presently did what he should have done four months before, abandoned Philadelphia to the enemy and elsewhere sought salvation for the cause. Even this, however, was decided upon only after the holding of yet other useless councils of war.

These grounds of criticism anticipated, and perhaps in degree overcome, the final and fundamental objection to the views here advanced remains; and that objection, already alluded to, is in reality at the basis of all others, and consequently the one most difficult to overcome.

At the threshold of his *Life of Columbus*, Washington Irving, in a tone so earnest as to amount almost to indignation of utterance, lays down this canon for the guidance of his-

---
[1] Greene, I, 435. "Philadelphia was then the largest city in America, and even those accustomed to European capitals found in it much to admire. The population was about forty thousand, the buildings were good, the streets broad and straight, and they were even provided with sidewalks. The shops were numerous and richly supplied. Some of the brick buildings on Market St. were of such proportions that the [officers of Rochambeau's army] called them immense." Perkins, *France in the Revolution*, 370.   [2] Irving, *Washington*, III, 241–242.

torical investigation: "There is a certain meddlesome spirit, which, in the name of learned research, goes prying about the traces of history, casting down its monuments, and marring and mutilating its fairest trophies. Care should be taken to vindicate great names from such pernicious erudition. It defeats one of the most salutary purposes of history, that of furnishing examples of what human genius and laudable enterprise may accomplish."[1] This in the case of Columbus; but the same, or a very similar, canon of criticism is levelled at all those who since have ventured, or even now venture, in any way or degree to dissent from that sweeping and altogether indiscriminate estimate of Washington, whether as a man, a patriot or a captain, emanating first from Mason L. Weems, as early as 1800, and since greatly elaborated by a large and devoted school of investigators and biographers, of which Weems must ever remain the unacknowledged head. Of this school Irving is himself, perhaps, the chief and most respected exponent. Such have established a cult — almost a creed. To dissent from it in any respect may not indeed be proof of moral turpitude, but is with them suspiciously suggestive of intellectual weakness. In our historical literature this cult has been carried to such a point as to have become a proverb in Europe. Bagehot, for instance, in alluding to some exaggeration of statement, says it would be as absurd as "to describe a post-boy as a sonneteer describes his mistress, or as the Americans stick metaphors upon General Washington."[2] This almost theological desire to preserve the Washington legend in undiminished lustre, above all doubt and beyond limitation, has gone to the extent even of a systematic suppression of evidence and consequent falsification of his-

[1] *Columbus* (Geoffrey Crayon ed.), I, 71.
[2] *Literary Studies*, I, 126.

THE REVOLUTIONARY CAMPAIGN OF 1777   167

tory. In some well-established cases this has been advanced as a patriotic duty. A striking instance is afforded in the *Life of Greene* by his grandson. Among the papers consulted by G. W. Greene in the preparation of his work were the Pickering MSS., in the possession of the Massachusetts Historical Society. He there found this anecdote, recorded by Timothy Pickering,[1] Adjutant-General of Washington's army during those operations about Philadelphia in the autumn of 1777 which have just been passed in review: "On one of these dreary nights," wrote Pickering, "as the army marched upwards on the eastern side of the Schuylkill, in its rear I fell in with General Greene. We descended the bank of Perkiomen Creek together, and while our horses were drinking, I said to him: 'General Greene, before I came to the army, I entertained an exalted opinion of General Washington's military talents, but I have since seen nothing to enhance it.' I did not venture to say it was sensibly lowered, though that was the fact; and so Greene understood me, for he instantly answered in these words precisely: 'Why, the General does want decision; for my part, I decide in a moment.'"

The biographer of Greene then adds this delightful comment and *naïve* confession, breathing in its every word the whole spirit of the Weems school and Washington cult: "That Greene did decide, after a careful examination of facts, with marvellous promptitude, is asserted by all who knew him, and proved by all his independent acts. Still, I could wish that he had never permitted himself to call Washington's decision in question; for the hereditary reverence I have been trained up in for that wonderful man, and which Greene's precept and example have made traditional in his family, renders it difficult for me to enter into the feelings of those who, acting with him, and loving and revering him, and

[1] See Massachusetts Historical Society, *Proceedings*, XLIV, 233.

putting full faith in his civic talents, still permitted themselves — as Hamilton and Pickering and Steuben are known to have done — to doubt his military talents."

Then follows, in a foot-note: "I have been counselled not to repeat this anecdote; but, as I interpret the historian's duty, the suppression of a characteristic fact is a practical falsehood. Greene saw faults in Washington, but saw too that they were outbalanced by his virtues. Lafayette tells us that Washington's 'reluctance to change opinion' led him to expose himself and his suite to a serious danger. Did Lafayette look up to him with any the less reverence?"

Further comment is unnecessary. Volumes could not express more; but, followed in that spirit,

> "Science is a blind man's guess
> And History a nurse's tale."

Finally, as to the two opponents confronting each other at the chess-board of the Kriegspiel which has now been passed in review, — Howe and Washington. Of Howe it is not easy to find much that is pleasant or anything commendatory to say. Trevelyan, after his kindly fashion, tries to part from him with a few pleasantish words, but does so with at best indifferent success. He says of him that he was "an indulgent commander; who lived and let live; and who, when off duty, was as genial to his followers, high and low, as on the actual day of battle he was formidable to the enemy." But, when it came to presenting an estimate of Sir William Howe, Charles Stedman enjoyed far better opportunities for so doing than Sir George Trevelyan; and, if the cold historical truth is the thing sought, Stedman's measured but stern indictment of the British commander should be read in close conjunction with Trevelyan's words of friendly farewell. A man of unquestioned physical courage, as a soldier Howe was a

THE REVOLUTIONARY CAMPAIGN OF 1777

very passable tactician. Face to face, on the way to a field of battle or on that field itself, he never failed both to out-manœuvre and to out-fight Washington; but, on the other hand, he had no conception of a large strategy, or of the value of time and energy as factors in warfare. Most companionable, he was lax in morals, physically self-indulgent and indolent in the extreme. In no way either thoughtful or studious, he was without any proper sense of obligation, personal or professional; and, moreover, there is reason to suspect that he was somewhat disposed to jealousy of those who might be considered in the line of succession to him,[1] especially of Sir Guy Carleton and General Burgoyne, who chanced both to be his seniors, the last by no less than seven years. Receiving at Bunker Hill a severe lesson in his over-confident attempt at a frontal attack, he afterwards showed a fair degree of skill in a recourse to flanking tactics; but, judged by the higher standards of this sort of work both before and since, what he accomplished was in no degree memorable. As a man of thirty he led Wolfe's famous scaling party at Quebec on the morning of September 13, 1759; but in 1777 he was forty-eight years old, and, becoming heavy in person, had apparently lost any mental or physical alertness he might once have possessed. Certainly, it cannot be claimed that during the campaigns of either 1776 or 1777 he evinced the possession of either personal character or professional skill. In 1777 his failure to grasp the controlling factors of the situation was so gross as to excite surprise at the time, and afterwards to defy all efforts at explanation either by himself or the historian. It remains to this day a puzzle, or worse; for, in plain language, his course, as already intimated, was suggestive at least of jealousy and disloyalty, if not of actual treachery. If he did not intentionally betray him, he wan-

[1] Fisher, Chap. LIX, with authorities cited.

tonly abandoned Burgoyne to his fate. A man, in short, of the Charles II type, he set the worst possible example to his subordinates, and did much to debauch and demoralize the army entrusted to him. Altogether, it can hardly be denied that, in 1777, he was, in mess-room parlance, a rather poor shote.[1]

Washington, on the other hand, impresses one throughout as being a clear-headed, self-centred Virginia planter and gentleman of the colonial period, noble-minded, serene and courageous, upon whom, at the mature age of forty-three, had

[1] Charles Lee was two years Howe's junior, Howe in 1775 being forty-eight and Lee forty-six. They had probably known each other before our Revolutionary troubles. Both had served in America during King George's War, Lee having been with Braddock at Fort Duquesne (1755), and Howe with Wolfe at Quebec (1759). Lee was a prisoner of war in New York, where Howe was in command, from December, 1776, to April, 1778, and the two doubtless then saw more or less of each other. Subsequently Lee, writing to Benjamin Rush from the camp at Valley Forge, June 4, 1778, gave to his correspondent the following pen-and-ink sketch of Howe, who had then shortly before laid down his command and gone to England: "From my first acquaintance with Mr. Howe I liked him. I thought him friendly, candid, good natur'd, brave and rather sensible than the reverse. I believe still that he is naturally so, but a corrupt or more properly speaking no education, the fashion of the times . . . have so totally perverted his understanding and heart, that private friendship has not force sufficient to keep a door open for the admittance of mercy towards political Hereticks. . . . He is besides the most indolent of mortals. . . . I believe he scarcely ever read the letters he signed. . . . You will say that I am drawing my Friend Howe in more ridiculous colors than He has yet been represented in — but this is his real character — He is naturally good humour'd and complacent, but illiterate and ignorant to the last degree unless as executive Soldier, in which capacity He is all fire and activity, brave and cool as Julius Cæsar — his understanding is, as I observ'd before rather good than otherwise, but was totally confounded and stupify'd by the immensity of the task impos'd upon him — He shut his eyes, fought his battles, drank his bottle, had his little whore, advis'd with his Counsellors, receiv'd his orders from North and Germain, one more absurd than the other, took Galloways opinion, shut his eyes, fought again, and is now I suppose to be called to Account for acting according to instructions; but I believe his eyes are now open'd." — *Lee Papers*, II, 397–398.

THE REVOLUTIONARY CAMPAIGN OF 1777   171

been imposed the conduct of a cause through the command of the simulacrum of an army. A man of dignified presence and the purest morals, his courage, both moral and physical, was unquestioned; but, frequently puzzled and hesitating, he showed a proneness to councils of war in no way characteristic of the born commander of men. As a strategist, he was scarcely superior to Howe; while, as a tactician, Howe, mediocre as in this respect he indisputably was, distinctly and invariably outclassed him. Washington fought two pitched battles in the 1777 campaign, neither of which can be justified under the circumstances; and both of which he lost. His strategy was at the time and has since been characterized as Fabian, yet in every one of his campaigns he evinced a most un-Fabian reluctance to abandoning any position, even though of no strategic importance, or perhaps incapable of successful defence. It was so at Brooklyn and on Manhattan Island in 1776; and, again, on the Delaware in 1777. In both cases he was, in fact, altogether too ready to fight. To characterize such a strategy and tactics as Fabian is indicative of complete misconception both of terms and operations; they are the reverse of Fabian. That the tools with which he had to work were poor, unwieldy and altogether too often unreliable does not admit of question; but it is the part of great commanders to make good such deficiencies in unexpected ways. This Washington failed to do. What he lacked is obvious, though then it could not have been forthcoming, — a trained and experienced chief of staff, a man who would have been to him what Gneisenau was to Blücher in 1815, and what A. A. Humphreys was to General Meade during sixteen months of the Army of the Potomac. Among the revolutionary officers Greene unquestionably would most nearly have met the requirements of the place; but Greene, though naturally a soldier, was self-taught and lacked experience. It is doubtful if he had any correct idea of the functions of a staff, and he certainly was not familiar with the details of a complete military organization, even to the degree that organization had attained prior to the wars of Napoleon. But, probably, it is fortunate no such position then existed; for, had it existed, some foreigner would almost certainly have been selected to fill it; and it would be difficult to name any foreigner, adventurer or otherwise, who in the American service has ever yet really understood either American conditions or the American as a soldier. Almost invariably such bring to their task European notions and formulas; and such do not apply. Essentially a volunteer, a ranger and a rifleman, the American soldier has an instinctive dislike for the European martinet; and, curiously enough, Washington himself neither understood nor used the American soldier as did Greene and Morgan in the Revolution, Jackson in the War of 1812, or Grant, Sherman and Sheridan, on the one side, and Lee, Jackson and Forrest on the other in the War of Secession.

In one respect, however, and a most important respect, Washington was supremely and uniformly fortunate, — his luck as respects those opposed to him in the game of war was notable and uniform. Gage, Howe, Clinton, fairly vied with each other in their low level of the British commonplace, — what Stedman most happily terms "monotonous mediocrity." Finally, as has elsewhere been said, Washington, courageous and enduring, confident himself and inspiring confidence in others, great in saving Common Sense, was unequalled in the possession of those qualities which go to make up what men know, and bend before, as Character.

Not only in this respect but in his other limitations as well as attributes, a study of Washington is suggestive of William of Orange. Each evinced throughout life and under most trying conditions the same overruling sense of duty and obligation, — the same steadfastness and serenity in presence of adversity, an equal saneness of judgment and patient confidence in the cause to which fate had devoted him. As a soldier, William did not excel. Confronted in Alva with a really capable military opponent, he never won a battle, and his campaigns were utter failures. The Spaniard in fact did with him almost as he pleased; yet the Dutchman was indomitable. Though between the Duke of Alva and Lieutenant-General Sir William Howe no comparison can, of course, be instituted, it was much the same in this respect with Washington. Neither William nor Washington evinced in his career the possession of any highly developed military or strategic instinct. In both also there was a noticeable absence of aggressive will power; and, moreover, be it added of that dangerous and ill-boding arbitrariness of disposition almost invariably the concomitant of an excess of will power. In Washington, as in William, there was likewise noticeable a certain lack of intellectual alertness, amounting at times almost to a slowness of apprehension.

By universal admission there is no more considerable, as well as admirable, figure in all modern history than William the Silent; and, while he stands forth as the great historical prototype of Washington, it may not unfairly be asserted the latter suffers nothing in a comparison with him.

V

THE BATTLE OF NEW ORLEANS[1]

WRITING in India, in his sixty-eighth year, Sir Charles Napier, in reminiscent mood, thus referred to certain incidents in his earlier life, when, a young man of twenty-eight, he was serving under Wellington, in his famous Peninsular campaigns: —

"September 27th [1849]. — Anniversary of Busaco, where Wellington first essayed the courage of the Portuguese troops. . . . Well, Busaco was the great test, and a very beautiful fight it was. The French were in the valley, shrouded in mist when the morning broke and the running fire of the outposts began; soon an irregular but very sharp musquetry rung through the gradually dispersing mist, which, mingled with smoke, came up the mountain, and from it many wounded men broke out. The picquets then appeared, being driven back, but firing so hard that our line loudly cheered them from the crest above: following fast came the enemy's columns, and eighty pieces of cannon opened with a roar from the summit of the mountain, sending shrapnels, shells and round shot down on them. The battle was thus begun, and soon they reached us. The firing rolled loud and heavy, the shouts of our men were grand, and their charges in different parts of the line went fiercely home. I was hit, woe the while for me! Now, thirty-nine years after, the horrid suffocation of that wound

[1] From the *Proceedings* of the Massachusetts Historical Society, Second Series, Vol. XIII, 412–433. Recast, revised and enlarged.

is scarcely endurable. Oh! it shakes my very soul, the horror of this feeling does!¹ I was carried into a small chapel of the convent of Busaco. . . . [Presently] I got up from the pallet on which I had been laid, walked clean out, and got to the convent door, looking for my horse. I was however seized instantly by Edward Pakenham, and led back with this expression, 'Damn it, Napier, are you mad to think you can go back in this state to the action? Be quiet for God's sake!' I could not speak plain, as my jaw was broke, and blood flowed freely from my mouth, so my looks were worse than the reality. . . . Poor Edward Pakenham was wounded at Busaco, which was what brought him to the convent, and having been dressed he was returning to the battle when he caught me trying to do the same. Poor fellow! He was a heroic man, that Edward Pakenham, and it was a thousand pities he died in defeat: it was not his fault, that defeat."

It was at New Orleans, a little more than four years after the Busaco fight here referred to by Napier, that this Edward Pakenham thus "died in defeat." The battle in which he died, fought in the early morning hours of January 8, 1815, was the sequel of what had occurred at Bladensburg five months before. The general in command of the British force had, it is true, been changed, for Major-General Robert Ross was killed before Baltimore, and Sir Edward Pakenham, fresh from the battle fields of the Peninsula, had succeeded him. But the British regiments, which had, simply

---

¹ Sir Charles Napier, then suffering from an attack of a chronic trouble with which he was afflicted, thus wrote at Orleans, France, May 8, 1848: "Perhaps there is no better way of dying, except apoplexy: that is prince of deaths! No pain, no preparation, no trouble to friends. You go 'like shot out of a shovel.' I know it! God defend me from the suffocating feel in my nose, produced by my horrid wound at Busaco: rather would I be broke upon the wheel."

with a volley, a shout and a rush, walked over the American line at Bladensburg, all took part in the attempt to do the same at New Orleans. The tactics, if such they deserve to be called, were in each case identical, — they were those of the football field. In other words, at Bladensburg the British officers, proceeding in conformity with their simple traditional rules, endeavored to do, and succeeded in doing, exactly what they intended to do, and failed in doing, at Bunker Hill; that is, they marched up directly in face of the defending force, carried the position with little loss, routed their opponents, and then, as matter of course, captured the objective those opponents were there to defend. The proceeding was perfectly simple, — a body of superior troops carrying by frontal assault weakly defended defensive positions. Examined in this connection, however, Bunker Hill and New Orleans afford the basis of a study, not only interesting in itself, but extremely suggestive as illustrating racial characteristics as developed in actual warfare. For, in any carefully considered account of the operations of December, 1814, and January, 1815, before New Orleans the suddenly levied, and hence undisciplined force of American riflemen and rangers, under command of Andrew Jackson, must necessarily be brought in striking contrast with the highly organized battalions of British veterans directed and led by an officer trained in the school of Wellington.

And, first, something needs to be said of Sir Edward Pakenham, and his record in the Spanish peninsula. In Great Britain, even more than in America, Pakenham is an almost forgotten military character. The reason for this oblivion, so far as his own country is concerned, will presently appear; but, in America, so far as he is mentioned at all, he has been misunderstood when not misrepresented.

A brother of the wife of the Duke of Wellington, it is assumed that, because of family influence, he was entrusted with a command. Brave to rashness, it is next assumed that otherwise he was quite incompetent. A more careful examination of his record in the light of recently published memoirs of those closely associated with Sir Edward lead to the conclusion that he was in many respects a very different and much more interesting character, not undeserving even at this late day of kindly and appreciative mention.

James Parton was by birth English, and in his *Life of Jackson* — one of the most picturesque and vivid biographies, be it said, in the language — Parton speaks thus of the class to which Pakenham belonged; and his words were no less true of those prominent in the recent war in South Africa than of those who fought in the Peninsula, at Waterloo and at New Orleans nearly a century before. The characteristics are racial.

"The British service seems to develop every high and noble quality of man and soldier, except generalship. Up to the hour when the British soldier holds an independent command, he is the most assured and competent of men. Give him a plain, unconditional order — Go and do *that* — and he will go and do it with a cool, self-forgetting pertinacity of daring that can scarcely be too much admired. All of the man below the eyebrows is perfect. The stout heart, the high purpose, the dexterous hand, the enduring frame are his. But the work of a general in command demands *head* — a cool, calculating head, fertile in expedients; a head that is the controlling power of the man. And this article of head, which is the rarest production of nature everywhere, is one which the brave British soldier is apt to be signally wanting in; and never so much so as when responsibility rests upon him."

Turning back now to Sir William Napier's famous narrative of the Peninsular War, in it there is a spirited account of the battle of Salamanca, fought by Wellington on the 22d of July, 1812, a year after Busaco and about thirty months before New Orleans, a battle in which Pakenham won great distinction. Then thirty-five years of age, he commanded, temporarily, what was known as the Third, or Picton's Division of Wellington's army, familiarly spoken of as the "Fighting Third."

Napier, himself a combatant that day, says that at about three o'clock in the afternoon a report reached Wellington — "that the French left was rapidly fronting towards the Ciudad Rodrigo Road. Starting up he repaired to the high ground and observed their movements for some time with a stern contentment, for their left wing was then entirely separated from the center; the fault was flagrant, and he fixed it with the stroke of a thunderbolt. A few orders issued from his lips like the incantations of a wizard, and suddenly the dark mass of troops which covered the English Hermanito seemed agitated by some mighty spirit; rushing violently down the interior slope of the mountain they entered the great basin amidst a storm of bullets which appeared to shear away the whole surface of the earth over which they were moving. . . . The Third Division was, however, still hidden from (Marmont[1]) by the western heights, and he hoped the tempest of bullets under which the British line was moving in the basin beneath would check it until he could bring up his reserve divisions. . . . In this crisis, despatching officer after officer to hasten up his troops from the forest, others to stop the progress of his left wing, he with fierce and sanguine expectation still looked for victory, until he saw Pakenham with the Third Division

[1] Duc de Ragusa. Youngest of Napoleon's marshals, Marmont was born in 1774, made marshal in 1809, and died at Vienna in 1852. He had in 1811 succeeded Massena in command of the forces opposed to Wellington.

THE BATTLE OF NEW ORLEANS

shoot like a meteor across [his subordinate, General] Maucune's path; then pride and hope alike died with him, and desperately he was hurrying in person to that fatal point when an exploding shell stretched him on the earth."

Salamanca has been pronounced "the most soldierly and skilful" of all Wellington's battles, and he himself considered it the occasion which best proved his military genius. The use then made of the Third Division was the master stroke of the day. The details of what occurred, as given in the several narratives, are curious, and, in several ways, suggestive. They in the first place are in all the renderings individually as well as racially characteristic; in the next, they illustrate well the school of British soldiership in which Pakenham had that education which resulted in the assault on Jackson's lines below New Orleans; and, finally, not least suggestive of all, a good example is furnished of the extreme difficulty attendant on an effort at anything approaching accuracy on a point of historical detail. One account says that when Wellington saw the gap in his opponent's formation, he at once turned it to account. "'Now's your time, Ned,' he said to Pakenham, who stood near him. The hint was enough. Pakenham kissed his brother-in-law, and, giving the word to his division, moved on, and won the battle."[1] The next account, obviously taken almost verbatim from the foregoing, reads as follows: Watching the gap in his opponent's line widen, "'Now's your time, Ned,' (Wellington) said to Pakenham, who was standing near him; and the words were scarcely spoken before Pakenham gave the word to his division, and commenced the movement which won the battle."[2] The

---

[1] G. R. Gleig, in Appleton's *Cyclopedia of American Biography*, vol. IV, "Pakenham."
[2] *Dictionary of National Biography*, "Pakenham."

next rendering of this family incident is equally graphic, but quite different: "Pakenham was in command of 'the Fighting Third,' and Wellington's orders were given to him in person, and with unconventional bluntness. 'Do you see those fellows on the hill, Pakenham,' he said, pointing to where the French columns were now visible; 'throw your division into columns of battalions at them directly, and drive them to the devil!' Pakenham, an alert and fiery soldier, formed his battalions into column with a word, and took them swiftly forward in an attack described by admiring onlookers as 'the most spirited and most perfect thing of the kind ever seen.'"[1]

The last, and what must be considered the most official account of what the English commander-in-chief really did and actually said on this dramatic and memorable occasion is that in Sir Herbert Maxwell's *Life of Wellington* (I, 281). And, in the first place, it may not be improper to observe that, when Salamanca was fought, "Our Special Head-Quarters Correspondent" had not yet been evolved; and Wellington most distinctly discouraged the presence of civilians within the sphere of his operations. Looking upon them as interlopers, he was strongly inclined to treat them as spies. There is consequently no authentic contemporaneous report of his exact words and acts on the occasion in question. It is not unsafe, however, to surmise that Wellington then gave no "hints" to his brother-in-law, nor did the brother-in-law indulge in any osculation in return for the same. Wellington, a somewhat grim personality, was not given to "hints" on the field of battle, nor was kissing conspicuously in order in the English Peninsular service. It is tolerably safe, therefore, to dismiss these two details as, so to speak, unhistorical. Others will follow presently.

[1] Fitchet, *How England saved Europe*, III, 325–326.

This is the Maxwell account: Wellington had during the morning hours been observing Marmont's movements from the Oripile. Shortly after mid-day he had withdrawn and was snatching a hasty meal in the rear of a farm building exposed to the enemy's fire, when, as he was "stumping about and munching," word was brought him of the opening offered by Marmont's false move. Mounting at once, he galloped back to his former point of observation. Observing the movement for a time, with Napier's "stern contentment," he presently ordered the formation of the Fifth Division; he then dashed off to where the Third was resting. Riding up to Pakenham, he said, "Ned, d'ye see those fellows on the hill? Throw your division into column; at them! and drive them to the devil!" He then at once returned at speed to the Oripile, whence he came. This was at one o'clock. Movements on the field of battle take time; orders are not executed as soon as uttered; and it was five o'clock, or four whole hours later, before the head of Pakenham's division struck the advancing French formation.

Unlike the others, this rendering has a natural sound. There is in it no suggestion of "hints," no kissing, no instantaneous movement; but a doubt does suggest itself as to the exact words used. They are not quite Wellingtonian. The destination of the driving is not altogether in accordance with the somewhat picturesque as well as forcible Peninsular usage as it has come to us, and it is more probable that Wellington indicated "hell" as the terminal point of the "drive" than that he named "the devil."

However this may be, and it is not important, it is now in order to return to Napier's trumpet-toned narrative of what next occurred: "It was about five o'clock when Pakenham fell on Maucune's first division under Thomières, who had then just reached an isolated open hill at the extremity of the southern range of heights. . . . The counter stroke was terrible! Two batteries of artillery placed on the summit of the western heights suddenly took his troops in flank, Pakenham's mass of infantry supported by cavalry and guns was bearing full on his front, and two thirds of his own division, lengthened out and unconnected, were still behind in a wood where they could hear but could not see the storm which was bursting: from the chief to the lowest soldier, all felt they were lost, and in an instant Pakenham, the most frank and gallant of men, commenced the battle. . . . Bearing onwards with the might of a giant, Pakenham broke the half-formed lines into fragments and sent the whole in confusion upon the supporting columns. . . . Some French squadrons now fell on the flank of the third division; . . . but Pakenham, continuing his tempestuous course, found the remainder of Thomières' division very imperfectly arrayed on the wooded heights behind the first hill, offering two fronts. . . . In this oppressed state, while Pakenham was pressing their left with a conquering violence, while the fifth division was wasting their ranks with fire, the interval between those divisions was suddenly filled with a whirling cloud of dust which moved swiftly forward, carrying with it the trampling sound of a charging multitude. . . . Anson's cavalry had suffered little in the charge, and now passing quite over the ridge were joined by D'Urban's horsemen and took the place of Le Marchant's exhausted men. United with the third and fifth divisions and the guns, they formed one formidable line more than a mile in advance of where Pakenham had commenced the battle, and that impetuous officer, with unmitigable fury, was still pressing forward, spreading terror and confusion."

Such was the estimate of Edward Pakenham held by the

famous English field marshal, and by England's most distinguished military historian. To a like effect, Wellington, shortly after Salamanca, wrote to the Horse Guards in London, strongly commending the "celerity and accuracy" which marked Pakenham's conduct of the operations of that day, adding, "Pakenham may not be the brightest genius, but my partiality for him does not lead me astray when I tell you that he is one of the best we have." These three estimates, from such different quarters and so separated in time, certainly give a favorable impression of the chief victim of the 8th of January, — the defeated of New Orleans. Looking at that battle from his point of view, it now remains to explain, if possible, why and how it was that this "heroic soul" — "the most frank and gallant of men" — went, as he did, to his own death, while thrusting his storming columns against breastworks bristling with artillery and swarming with riflemen; thus seeking, in bull-headed fashion, to accomplish a result which could have been secured in another and more scientific way absolutely without loss. For, strange as it sounds to American ears, New Orleans was on the 8th of January, 1815, within the easy grasp of the British army.

After the death of Ross before Baltimore, September 12, 1814, the British War Office looked about for some one to take charge of active operations in America. The field of these it was proposed to transfer from Chesapeake Bay to the Gulf of Mexico, making New Orleans the military objective. The conflict with Napoleon had then been brought to a triumphant, and, apparently, final close; Napoleon, having abdicated six months before, was in exile at Elba. Though the campaign of Waterloo was to open less than six months later, Wellington's veteran army of the Peninsula had already been withdrawn from the south of France, and largely disbanded. Wellington himself was in London. Under these circumstances, it was proposed to send him to America, not only to take charge of operations in the field, but with full powers to negotiate, and bring hostilities to a close; for that struggle was after all but a side show to the great European conflict. That ended, why prolong the side show? For very sufficient reasons connected with the still disturbed aspect of continental affairs, it was not deemed expedient to have Wellington out of immediate reach, and the choice of a successor to Ross was left to him. He designated his brother-in-law, Pakenham. Sailing from Portsmouth in November, Sir Edward was accompanied among others by Brigade-Major Smith, afterward Lieutenant-General Sir Harry Smith, whose autobiography, published in 1909, affords some lifelike glimpses of his commander. Smith, having often come in contact with him in the Peninsula, thought highly of Pakenham. Referring to him as "dear Sir Edward," he describes him as "a most lighthearted fellow" and "one of the most amusing persons imaginable — high-minded and chivalrous in every idea, and to our astonishment very devoutly inclined"; he adds, "I never served under a man whose good opinion I was so desirous of having," and "to fall in his estimation would have been worse than death by far."

A brave officer, trained in the European school of actual warfare during a period in which the bayonet was still looked upon as the effective weapon, and rifle marksmanship was not yet highly regarded, Pakenham's bravery was "of that animated intrepid cast that he applied his mind vigorously at the moment to the position of his own troops as well as that of the enemy . . . but he never avoided a fight of any sort." In other words, an excellent subordinate in Spain, — a most effective weapon in the hands of

THE BATTLE OF NEW ORLEANS 185

Wellington, — he was, as an officer in independent command under American conditions, to him altogether strange, no match for Andrew Jackson.

Strategically speaking, the object of his campaign was obvious. It was the capture of New Orleans. The destruction of Jackson's army was desirable as an incident, but by no means necessary to the end in view. The British base of supplies was close to the objective point, and communication could easily be kept up either by the right bank of the river, or by the river itself; or, indeed, by the left bank, provided only Jackson could be forced from his lines. The essential thing was to compel him to leave his lines. If he did so, he must abandon New Orleans to the British. From a tactical point of view the situation was different. Through a reconnoissance in force, and as the result of an artillery action, it had been ascertained that Jackson's lines were strong, and would be extremely difficult to carry by assault. The assaulting party, whether it approached from the centre or on either wing, would be subjected to a converging fire of artillery and riflemen. Under these circumstances it would obviously have been the part of a skilful tactician to endeavor to turn Jackson out of his works by rendering them untenable. This the English commander could perfectly well have done. Being in close proximity to New Orleans, — only four miles from that, his objective, point, — all General Pakenham had to do was to pass a strong division of his army across the Mississippi to its western bank, and by it threaten, if he did not capture, New Orleans from the west side of the river, operating from that side on Jackson's flank and rear. The Mississippi was less than half a mile in width; its current, varying with the tide, did not at that season of the year exceed four miles an hour, and presented no obstacle to crossing by boat or barge, which could likewise be propelled upstream by hugging the convex or western bank. Pakenham had from the fleet an abundance of boats at his disposal, well manned by sailors; and, by establishing his artillery upon the western bank, he could enfilade Jackson's line, searching his works within easy range, and rendering them, in case of assault, practically untenable. Under such circumstances, Jackson would have had no choice but to vacate his position, and allow New Orleans to fall.

It has always been assumed that Pakenham, after the wont of the English officer, preferred a direct assault, — that, greatly underrating his antagonist, the recent Bladensburg experience lured him on. So far as that portion of the force composing his army which arrived with him was concerned, this is unquestionably true; and, in the literature of the campaign, it is curious to come across footprints of the fact. Pakenham joined the army before New Orleans on the morning of Christmas Day, 1814, — only two weeks before the battle. The English had then already met with much stiffer resistance than they had anticipated, and those whom Pakenham relieved of command recognized the difficulty of the confronting problem. Nevertheless, as the reënforcements the new commander-in-chief brought with him stepped on shore, not a few of them expressed their fears lest they should be too late to take part in the advance, as they thought New Orleans would be captured before they could get into line. On the 7th of January, the day before the battle, as one of the newly arrived regiments moved towards the front, passing another regiment which had been at Bladensburg, some of the officers of the former remarked to those of the latter that "it would be now our turn to get into New Orleans, as they had done at Washington."

On the other hand, Jackson at this juncture evinced one

of the highest and rarest attributes of a great general: he read correctly the mind of his opponent,—divined his course of action. And yet it was a narrow chance; for, it now appears that the British commander was not so completely impervious to reason and changed conditions as has been supposed. According to Smith, who was then serving as the senior officer of his staff, Pakenham, immediately after getting on the ground, reconnoitred Jackson's position. As the result of so doing he came to the conclusion that it could not be successfully assailed in front or on either flank. Smith asserts that being asked for his opinion, he then said in reply, "As yet the enemy has not occupied the opposite [right] bank of the river. We must possess the right bank, enfilade the enemy's position with our fire, and, so soon as we open a fire from the right bank, we should storm the work in two, three or more columns." This opinion, Smith says, commended itself to Pakenham, and he proceeded accordingly, giving orders for the erection of batteries. As the proposed movement assumed shape, it naturally caused Jackson anxiety. All depended on its magnitude. If it was the operation in chief of the British army, New Orleans could hardly be saved. Enfiladed, and threatened in his rear from the west bank, Jackson must fall back. If, however, the west bank movement was only a diversion in favor of a main assault planned on his front, the demonstration across the river might be checked, or prove immaterial. As the thing developed during the night preceding the battle, Commodore Patterson, who commanded the American naval contingent on the river, became alarmed, and hurried a despatch to Jackson, advising him of what was taking place, and begging immediate reënforcement. At once o'clock in the morning the messenger roused Jackson from sleep, stating his errand. Jackson listened to the despatch, and at once said: "Hurry back and tell Commodore Patterson that he is mistaken. The main attack will be on this side, and I have no men to spare. General Morgan must maintain his position at all hazards." To use a vernacular, but expressive, term, Jackson had "sized" Pakenham correctly, — when the moment came, he could be depended on not to do what the occasion required. He would not throw a sufficient force across the river, and move on his objective by a practically undefended road, merely holding his enemy in check on the east bank. Had he done so, he would have acted in disregard of that first principle both of tactics and strategy which forbade the division of a force in presence of an enemy in such a way that the two parts are not in position to support each other; — but he would have taken New Orleans! An attack in front was, on the contrary, in accordance with British military traditions and the recent experience of Bladensburg. Pakenham acted accordingly. In his main assault he sacrificed his army and lost his own life, sustaining an almost unexampled defeat; while his partial movement across the river was completely successful so far as it was pressed, opening a straight and practicable road to New Orleans, and gravely jeopardizing Jackson's position. A mere diversion or auxiliary operation, the principal attack having failed it was not persisted in.

Possibly it might by some now be argued that had Pakenham thus weakened his force on the east side of the river by operating on New Orleans and on Jackson's flank and rear from the west side, in the way suggested, a vigorous fighting opponent, such as Jackson unquestionably was, might have turned the tables on him, for thus violating an elementary rule of warfare. Leaving his lines, and boldly taking the aggressive, Jackson, it will then be urged, might have overwhelmed the British force in his front, thus cutting the column operating west of the river from the fleet and its base of supplies, — in fact, destroying the expedition. Not improbably Pakenham argued in this way; if he did, however, he simply demonstrated his incompetence for high command. He failed to grasp the situation, or put a correct estimate on its conditions; for it is the part of a skilful commander to know when to secure results by making exceptions to even the most general and the soundest rules. Pakenham, it is true, grossly exaggerated the number of the force confronting him. He, and those with him, put them at from 26,000 to 30,000; but all militia. In point of fact, however, his command outnumbered that of Jackson by about two to one; while, moreover, the British were veterans, those composing Jackson's levy were hardly more than raw recruits, — like the South African Boers, good material, well accustomed to handling rifles. As one of the best of his own brigadiers, General Adair, afterwards expressed it, "our men were militia without discipline, and if once beaten, they could not be relied on again." They were, in fact, men of exactly the same temper and stuff as those who were stampeded by a volley and a shout at Bladensburg; and the unpleasant principle of military morale thus stated by General Adair was only that learned by Washington at Kips Bay forty years previous. The force Pakenham had under his command before New Orleans was, on the other hand, composed of seasoned soldiers of the best class. In the open field and on anything approaching equality of position, he had absolutely nothing to fear. He might safely provoke attack; indeed, the very most he could ask was to get Jackson out from behind his breastworks on almost any terms. So fully, moreover, did he realize this, that it inspired him to his assault. It is useless, therefore, to suggest that he hesitated to separate his force, overestimating Jackson's numbers and aggressive capacity. Had he done so, he would hardly have ventured to assail Jackson in front. On the contrary, Pakenham's trouble lay, not in overestimating, but in underestimating, his adversary. He failed to divide his force and operate on correct principles, not because he was afraid to do so, but because he did not know enough to do so.

In case, then, dividing his command, Pakenham had thrown one half of it across the river to assail New Orleans in force and turn Jackson's rear, and then with the other half held his position on the east bank, thus keeping open his communications with the fleet, the only possible way in which Jackson could have taken advantage of the situation would have been by leaving his lines and attacking.

Now, it so happens that resisting attack under just such circumstances is the position in which the British soldier has always developed his best staying qualities. Quebec was a case directly in point. Again, the men under Pakenham before New Orleans were even more reliable than those who, only five months later at Waterloo, after the auxiliary troops had been swept from the field by the fury of the French attack, held their position from noon to a June sunset against an assaulting force of nearly twice their number commanded by the Emperor himself. The somewhat unreasoning bulldog tenacity of the English infantry under such circumstances is well known; nor needs to be dilated on. But concerning it, there is a statement of the French marshal, Bugeaud, curious, and bearing on its face evidence that it was written by a military man of practical experience, — one who knew from his own recollections that whereof he spoke. Marshal Bugeaud, in making this statement, referred not to Waterloo, but to the operations in the Peninsular War, — that school in which the soldiers under Pakenham had learned their business. What he says reveals, moreover, a curious insight into the characteristics of the French and English infantry: —

"The English generally occupied well chosen defensive positions, having a certain command, and they showed only a portion of their force. The usual artillery action first took place. Soon, in great haste, without studying the position, without taking time to examine if there were means to make a flank attack, we marched straight on, taking the bull by the horns. About 1000 yards from the English line the men became excited, spoke to one another, and hurried their march; the column began to be a little confused.

"The English remained quite silent, with ordered arms, and from their steadiness appeared to be a long red wall. This steadiness invariably produced an effect on the young soldiers.

"Very soon we got nearer, shouting 'Vive l'Empereur, en avant! à la bayonette!' Shakos were raised on the muzzles of the muskets; the columns began to double, the ranks got into confusion, the agitation produced a tumult; shots were fired as we advanced.

"The English line remained still, silent and immovable, with ordered arms, even when we were only 300 paces distant, and appeared to ignore the storm about to break.

"The contrast was striking; in our inmost thoughts, each felt that the enemy was a long time in firing, and that this fire, reserved for so long, would be very unpleasant when it did come. Our ardour cooled. The moral power of steadiness, which nothing shakes (even if it be only in appearance), over disorder which stupefies itself with noise, overcame our minds. At this moment of intense excitement, the English wall shouldered arms, an indescribable feeling rooted many of our men to the ground, — they began to fire. The enemy's steady concentrated volleys swept our ranks; decimated we turned round, seeking to recover our equilibrium: then three deafening cheers broke the silence of our opponents; at the third they were on us, pushing our disorganized flight. But to our great surprise, they did not push their advantage beyond a hundred yards, retiring calmly to their lines to await a second attack."

Those thus vividly described by an hereditary race opponent, who had himself confronted them, were the identical men Jackson would have had to attack, had he, as the only possible alternative to a precipitate retreat and the abandonment of New Orleans, found himself compelled on the 8th of January to leave his lines and assume the aggressive. Unfortunately for himself and for his command, Pakenham underestimated his opponent; and it is hardly necessary to say that, as an opponent, in a rough-and-tumble fight, whether street, political or military, Andrew Jackson was a factor not safe to regard lightly. Certainly on the 8th of January, 1815, Jackson was under about as great an obligation to Pakenham as one man can be to another. Pakenham offered Jackson his opportunity; and Jackson was equal to the occasion.

From neither the strategic nor the tactical point of view is there, or, at the time, was there, anything new to be learned from the New Orleans episode. It was, as already more than once pointed out, in every essential respect merely Bunker Hill over again, — forty years after, — a body of highly disciplined veterans led by experienced officers confronted from behind improvised breastworks by intensely individual but scarcely organized rangers and riflemen. The assaulting party enjoyed in both cases the advantage of flanking water surroundings, and, having a complete maritime control, by an obvious movement could have made the position they undertook to storm wholly untenable by their opponents. Underestimating those opponents, though of the same blood as themselves, the British commander in each case elected to throw away the lives of those subject to his orders. The American rifleman under cover was simply beyond their powers of comprehension.

Thus the one really interesting and suggestive feature at New Orleans was the instinctive recourse of the American general to what may not unfairly be termed the racial characteristics of those composing the force under him — their individuality, their adaptability to conditions, their natural inclination to ranger tactics. If it had come to a line of battle formation or battalion evolutions under fire, the seasoned veterans from the Peninsula would, as at Bladensburg, have made very short work of the American levies; but, apparently, it never occurred to Jackson, a born fighter, to measure himself and his command against his opponent in that way; and those composing his command instinctively recognized in Jackson one of themselves. He knew how to fight them for all they were worth; and they knew that he knew it. The one chance, therefore, Pakenham had was so to manœuvre as to compel Jackson either to withdraw from in front of the British objective, or to come out and fight on Pakenham's own terms — "man fashion," as the expression went. Throwing away his opportunity to compel this, he took the consequences.

And yet, studied in the light of Sir Harry Smith's autobiographic statements, it is marvellous to see how close, for both Jackson and Pakenham, the call was. The British assault was to be made at dawn of the 8th. The storming columns were all moved into position during the earlier hours of the night. The firing of two rockets was to be the signal for assault. A detachment was meanwhile to be thrown across the river, to move up the right bank, capture the batteries, and turn the guns on Jackson's flank, enfilading his works at the moment they were assailed in front. To get the boats from the fleet, anchored in the bayou, across the intervening plantations to the river it was necessary to widen slightly a canal which connected the two. The river stood at higher level than the bayou; consequently a certain amount of water had to be let into the canal, using it as a lock, so as to raise it to the necessary level. When it came to opening the river end, the bayou end was dammed; but when the banks of the river were cut, the pressure of the inflowing water drove the dam out, and the delay necessary to repair the damage thus done prevented the boats being worked into the river at the hour assigned. Smith at that time was with the column of General Lambert, one of the three formed for the assault planned on the left, or eastern, bank. What ensued he thus describes:—

"About half an hour before daylight, while I was with General Lambert's column, standing ready, Sir Edward Pakenham sent for me. I was soon with him. He was greatly agitated. 'Smith, most Commanders-in-Chief have many difficulties to contend with, but surely none like mine. The dam, as you heard me say it would, gave way, and Thornton's people will be of no use whatever to the general attack.' I said, 'So impressed have you ever been, so obvious is it in every military point of view, we should possess the right bank of the river, and thus enfilade and divert the attention of the enemy; there is still time before daylight to retire the columns now. We are under the enemy's fire so soon as discovered.' He says, 'This may be, but I have twice deferred the attack. We are strong in numbers now comparatively. It will cost more men, and the assault must be made.' I again urged delay. While we were talking, the streaks of daylight began to appear, although the morning was dull, close, and heavy, the clouds almost touching the ground. He said, 'Smith, order the rocket to be fired.' I again ventured to plead the cause of delay. He said, and very justly, 'It is now too late: the columns would be visible to the enemy before they could move out of fire, and would lose more men than it is to be hoped they will in the attack. Fire the rocket, I say, and go to Lambert.' This was done. . . . The rocket was hardly in the air before a rush of our troops was met by the most murderous and destructive fire of all arms ever poured upon column."

THE BATTLE OF NEW ORLEANS

In the diary entry with which this paper began, Sir Charles Napier, a man presumably well informed on the facts of the particular case and one generally well qualified to express an opinion professionally, spoke of Pakenham as having died in defeat — a defeat " not his fault." And to the same effect, Captain Edward Codrington, as he then was, writing home to his wife from the British fleet shortly after the battle, said that Pakenham "fell a sacrifice to the errors of others." Codrington, on the spot and a participant in the operations, was personally cognizant of the facts; Napier, writing long after the event, expressed a common understanding among contemporaries. To the same effect, Sir Harry Smith, with Pakenham up almost to the very moment of his death, writing long afterward, exclaimed: "Poor dear Sir Edward Pakenham, a hero, a soldier, a man of ability in every sense·of the word, had to contend with every imaginable difficulty, starting with the most unwise and difficult position in which he found the Army. By perseverance, determination, and that gallant bearing which so insures confidence, he overcame all but one, which he never anticipated, a check to the advance of British soldiers. . . . The fire, I admit, was the most murderous I ever beheld before or since." What then had all these in mind when each made the same or a similar reservation? What was the British army belief at the time, and tradition afterwards, in regard to the outcome of the New Orleans expedition and the fate of Wellington's brother-in-law?

Neither the Ross expedition, which resulted in the capture and burning of Washington, nor the Pakenham expedition, which ended as in this paper described, loom large in any except American military annals. As already said, they were at best a mere side show to the larger and more concentrated drama then drawing to its close in Europe.

America was in 1815 a remote region, very unfamiliar to Europeans; and, strange as such slowness in transmission now seems, the news of disaster to their arms at New Orleans, and Pakenham's death, did not reach England until early in March. This was fifty days subsequent to the event, and ten whole weeks after formal announcement of the treaty, signed at Ghent (December 24) which should have brought the trans-Atlantic hostilities to a close. Those tidings thus would, in the ordinary course of events, have been suggestive only of a dying echo of the remote last gun of a long war; but the course of events at that time was in no way "ordinary." Not only England and English army circles, but all Europe, were, in the early days of March, 1815, listening, not to the echoes of the last guns of a war which was ended, but for the deep reverberation of those which were to announce that a fresh life-and-death struggle had begun. And so, "amid the excitement caused by the return from Elba, the battle of Waterloo, and the subsequent exile of the emperor, little was heard, and less was thought, of the events that had transpired in the delta of the Mississippi. A vague, brief and incorrect bulletin was published in the official *Gazette*, and then the expedition against New Orleans was allowed to be forgotten."[1]

What then was the true inwardness of the fatal event of the morning of January 8? A formidable British fleet of sixty sail, carrying about a thousand guns and manned proportionately, made part of the New Orleans expeditionary force. Of this naval contingent, Vice-Admiral Sir Alexander Cochrane was flag officer, as he had also been of the similar naval contingent during the joint operations in Chesapeake Bay, four months before. His recollection of what had taken place at Bladensburg was fresh as well as

[1] Parton, *Jackson*, II, 326.

personal; and he would have been less than English had he not felt the deepest contempt for the resisting qualities of hastily organized and undisciplined American levies, and given most outspoken expression thereof. He had come in contact with them, and seen them routed from behind breastworks like a pack of sheep. Pakenham, on the other hand, found himself in command of an army amid surroundings and under conditions wholly strange to him. His previous military experience was in fact worse than useless; it was misleading. Though at his death not yet thirty-seven, he had already served over twenty years. Writing immediately after the battle in which he fell, Codrington spoke of him as "the flower of the flock," and wrote "there was something about him which made me look forward to a future intercourse with him as a source of great satisfaction." He had been placed in command with an eye to a particular service. It was proposed to capture New Orleans, and occupy Louisiana with a view to effect on the negotiations already (July 24) entered on, which resulted, five months later, in the Treaty of Ghent (December 24). The mouth of the Mississippi and the region adjacent thereto was to be seized and held with a view "to obtaining better terms in the pending negotiation or of exacting cession thereof as the price of peace."[1] Pakenham, it has been seen, did not join the New Orleans expeditionary force until late in December, and it was the 25th of that month before he assumed actual command. During the fourteen days which now intervened before the battle and his own death, the British commander was not only much occupied, but was mentally perplexed in the extreme. He found himself in independent control for the first time, and that in a most difficult position. At the

[1] Henry Adams, *United States*, vol. VIII, 313.

outset he seems to have shown a somewhat unexpected degree of caution. Though accustomed under Wellington to furious direct assaults, when, three days after assuming command, he came suddenly in his advance on Jackson's unfinished but still ugly-looking breastworks, they gave him pause. Things were not according to rule. Improvised earthworks were to him a novelty. Belonging to the class "Fortifications," they must be treated as such; and, according to all Peninsular precedents a practical breach in them must be effected, and the position then stormed. To proceed in this way required time and breaching artillery. So, instead of being told to advance at once and clear the way, as at Bladensburg, the army was, to the surprise of all, ordered to retire out of cannon range, and to go into camp. The order was, of course, obeyed; but, as one of those who obeyed it afterwards wrote, "there was not a man among us who failed to experience both shame and indignation." This was on the 28th of December.

Fresh from the Chesapeake, and with Bladensburg and Washington in memory, Vice-Admiral Cochrane, a man twenty years Pakenham's senior, seems to have viewed this proceeding with marked disfavor. Siege equipage had now to be brought up from the ships, and the work of bringing it up fell upon the sailors. The guns, loaded on boats, had first "with incredible labor" to be rowed from the fleet to the bayou, and then dragged through three miles of bog to the British lines. At last, by the evening of the 31st, they were in position. But, meanwhile, Jackson had not been idle; his breastworks had been perfected, and he also had mounted some heavy guns. At 8 o'clock on the morning of January 1 the British batteries opened fire; and those behind them, Pakenham least of all, "made not the slightest doubt of its effect." The opposing batteries replied, at first faintly and with seeming difficulty; but, by and by, as a British officer wrote, their "salutation became more spirited, till it gradually surpassed our own, both in rapidity and precision." About noon the British fire slackened; and, at one o'clock, it had been completely overpowered. "Never," wrote the British officer, "was any failure more remarkable or unlooked for than this." Its effect on Pakenham can be imagined. He was at his wit's ends; something must be done, and that quickly; but — what?

Having his personality and position in mind, the situation now becomes distinctly tragic; to a degree, pathetic. In his perplexity he next had recourse to something to which his brother-in-law and master in practical warfare never once had recourse in his whole long military life — if he did not actually hold a formal council of war, he sought advice; and, most naturally, of Sir Alexander Cochrane among others. There is no authentic report of what advice was given him, but it is said[1] that the strategic purpose of the expedition — the capture of New Orleans — was by some of his advisers kept in mind, and it was proposed to accomplish this result by throwing a heavy detachment across the river in the way already referred to, which should march by its west bank up to a point opposite the town, and commanding it. The only difficulty in the way of so doing lay in finding a practical method of crossing troops and artillery. The Americans had destroyed or removed all the boats. Admiral Cochrane, it is said, suggested that the Villeré canal from the Bayou connecting with Lake Borgue could easily be deepened and widened, and opened into the river, thus admitting of the passage of boats and barges from the fleet. This was obviously feasible, and was determined on.

---

[1] Z. F. Smith. *The Battle of New Orleans* (Filson Club Publications, No. 19), 91 ; Bourchier, *Codrington*, vol. I, 336.

So far, all was well; things were going swimmingly. But it is now further related that Pakenham wished the main movement to be made by the west side, and the capture of New Orleans so assured; while Jackson was to be held in a position now made useless as well as untenable by a demonstration in force on his front, supported by a renewed artillery fire. Thoroughly sensible in itself, this plan of operations could hardly have failed of success; indeed, as the event showed, it would have succeeded. Most fortunately for Jackson, most unhappily for Pakenham and numerous good officers and brave men under his command, Cochrane at this point again, as it is alleged, intervened, this time making some observation to the effect that a movement in force by the west side might be all very well, but, for his part, "if the army could not take those mudbanks, defended by ragged militia, he would undertake to do it with two thousand sailors armed only with cutlasses and pistols."[1] Gross injustice may have been done Vice-Admiral Sir Alexander Forester Inglis Cochrane, and possibly he never was guilty of so cruel a slur on a brother officer, one much his junior in years and in a trying position. But at that time Pakenham had within ten days of his assumption of command been twice balked in his operations; and, having in fresh recollection what Ross had so recently accomplished at Bladensburg and Washington, most naturally an unfavorable comparison between the two leaders was in the minds and mouths of all. Cochrane also had been on peculiarly friendly terms with Ross, writing that in him were "blended those qualities so essential to promote success where coöperation between the two services becomes necessary." He and Ross were also of nearly the same age, while Ross's successor was in the eyes

[1] Parton, *Jackson*, vol. II, 189.

of the rough old admiral hardly more than a boy. In any event, the story has a natural sound to lend probability to it, and it appears in all the narratives.[1] Curiously enough, also, a force of sailors, armed in the way described, did, at the exact time of Pakenham's failure and death on the east bank, accomplish on the west bank the very feat Cochrane had claimed they could accomplish. Armed only with cutlasses and pistols they, in the course of Colonel Thornton's successful flank movement, carried the American earthworks and captured their batteries. Their loss was also inconsiderable, about one in eight of those engaged.

Speaking historically, it will not do to yield a too implicit credence to those legends of the quarter-deck and the mess-room. But, conceding a basis of fact for the Cochrane cutlass-and-pistol taunt, both Napier's and Codrington's implications are accounted for. Nationality even becomes a factor: for Cochrane was a Scotchman; Pakenham an Irishman. Bladensburg was only four months gone, and Pakenham had succeeded the gallant and dashing Ross. The implication was obvious; what Ross had done, Pakenham could do — if he dared! And so, as Codrington at the time wrote, Pakenham, though acting against his better judgment, "did not like to countermand an order for attack a second time."

It is needless to follow further the chain of inference. It is, however, curious to consider what Pakenham's brother-in-law would have done if similarly circumstanced. In the first place, Wellington would have called no council of war, nor would he have invited suggestions. With his extraordinary eye for a military situation and keen tactical sense, he would unquestionably have moved on his objective by

[1] Latour, *Historical Memoir of the War in West Florida and Louisiana*, 162; Parton, *Jackson*, II, 189.

the west bank of the river, holding Jackson firmly by one arm while he seized New Orleans with the other; finally, if a commander in another branch of the service, either in his presence or to his knowledge, had criticised his conduct or impugned his courage, it is not difficult to imagine the cutting curtness of look and speech with which his impertinence would at once have been met and disregarded. Pakenham was differently constituted.

VI

THE ETHICS OF SECESSION [1]

'ΑΝΆΓΚΗ

"Laws derive their authority from possession and use: 'tis dangerous to trace them back to their beginning; they grow great and ennoble themselves, like our rivers, by running; follow them upward to their source, 'tis but a little spring, scarce discernible, that swells thus and thus fortifies itself by growing old. Do but consult the ancient considerations that gave the first motion to this famous torrent, so full of dignity, awe, and reverence; you will find them so light and weak that it is no wonder if these people, who weigh and reduce everything to reason, and who admit nothing by authority or upon trust, have their judgments very remote and differing from those of the public." — Montaigne, *Essays*, Book II, Chap. XII.

Two hundred and sixty-four years ago a schism, since become historic, occurred in the infant colony of Massachusetts Bay. It was rent in twain; and so, as the Father of Massachusetts has recorded, "finding, upon consultation, that two so opposite parties could not continue in the same body without apparent hazard of ruin to the whole, [those in the majority] agreed to send away some of the principal." [2] And again, "by the example of Lot in Abraham's family, and after Hagar and Ishmael, he [Governor John Winthrop] saw they must be sent away." [3] Those thus proscribed went ac-

---

[1] An address delivered at Charleston, S. C., December 24, 1902, at the annual celebration of the New England Society of that city. See *infra*, p. 227; also, Massachusetts Historical Society, *Proceedings*, Second Series, Vol. XVII, pp. 90-116.

[2] Winthrop *History* (Savage's ed.), Vol. 1, p. *245.

[3] *Ibid.*, Vol. I, p. *250.

cordingly into banishment; and so, the year following, Rhode Island came into existence. This was in 1638; and, in 1640, the chief of those thus thrust into exile having occasion to write to the magistrate who had enforced the order of banishment, said, with a pathos reached only by words of simplicity, "what myself and wife and family did endure in that removal, I wish neither you nor yours may ever be put unto";[1] but again, and at almost the same time, writing from his new home in Newport, Governor William Coddington expressed to Governor John Winthrop the approval he felt "of a speech of one of note amongst you, that we were in a heate and chafed, and were all of us to blame; in our strife we had forgotten that we were brethren."[2]

The expression is apt; the admission appropriate. More, much more than two years ago, — longer ago than the lifetime of a generation, — Massachusetts and South Carolina got in "a heate and chafed" one with the other, and fell into bitter strife. Forgetting that we were brethren, were we also "all of us to blame"?

Not long since, circumstances led me into a dispassionate reëxamination of the great issues over which the country divided in the mid-years of the last century. As a result thereof, I said in a certain Phi Beta Kappa Society address[3] delivered in June [1902], at Chicago, — "legally and technically, — not morally, again let me say, and wholly irrespective of humanitarian considerations, — to which side did the weight of argument incline during the great debate which culminated in our Civil War? . . . If we accept the judgment of some of the more modern students and investigators of his-

[1] *The Winthrop Papers*, 4 Mass. Hist. Coll., Vol. VI, p. 314.
[2] *Ibid.*, p. 317.
[3] "Shall Cromwell have a Statue?" See *Lee at Appomattox and Other Papers* (2d ed.), pp. 366, 367.

THE ETHICS OF SECESSION 205

tory,—either wholly unprejudiced or with a distinct Union bias, — it would seem as if the weight of argument falls into what I will term the Confederate scale." For instance, Goldwin Smith, — an Englishman, a life-long student of history, a friend and advocate of the Union during the Civil War, the author of one of the most compact and readable narratives of our national life, — Dr. Smith has recently said: "Few who have looked into the history can doubt that the Union originally was, and was generally taken by the parties to it to be, a compact, dissoluble, perhaps, most of them would have said, at pleasure, dissoluble certainly on breach of the articles of Union."[1] To a like effect, but in terms even stronger, Mr. Henry Cabot Lodge, now a senator from Massachusetts, has said, not in a political utterance, but in a work of historical character: "When the Constitution was adopted by the votes of States at Philadelphia, and accepted by the votes of States in popular conventions, it is safe to say that there was not a man in the country, from Washington and Hamilton, on the one side, to George Clinton and George Mason, on the other, who regarded the new system as anything but an experiment entered upon by the States, and from which each and every State had the right peaceably to withdraw, a right which was very likely to be exercised."[2] Incited by those utterances to yet further inquiry of my own, the result thereof was, to me at least, curious; — and moreover suggestive of moralizing.

The question is now one purely historic; but on that ques-

---

[1] "England and the War of Secession," *Atlantic Monthly Magazine*, March, 1902, p. 305.

[2] *Webster*, American Statesmen Series, p. 172. But see Mass. Hist. Soc. *Proceedings*, Second Series, XVI, 151–173, paper entitled "Historical Conception of the Constitution," in which the views expressed by Dr. Smith and Mr. Lodge are controverted by D. H. Chamberlain. Also, *Ib.* XVIII, 397–398.

tion of the weight of authority and argument as respects the right of secession, I found a divergence of opinion existing today so great as hardly to admit of reconciliation. On the one side it was — I am told still is [1] — taught as an article of political faith, that not only was the constitutional right of peaceable secession at will plain, manifest and expressly reserved, but that, until a comparatively recent period, it had never been even disputed. In the words of one writer of authority, "Through a period of many years, the right of secession was not seriously questioned in any quarter except under the exigencies of party politics." [2] On the other hand, in the section of the country where my lot has been cast, this alleged heresy is sternly denounced, and those propounding it are challenged to their proofs. With equal posi-

[1] During the summer of 1903 a significant discussion was carried on in the columns of the press, more especially in the New York *Evening Post* and the Boston *Transcript*. It originated in a communication which appeared in the New York *Nation* of August 7, 1902, from a professor of Randolph-Macon College, Virginia. The writer said: "This public opinion [now prevalent in the South] positively demands that teachers of history, both in the colleges and high schools, shall subscribe unreservedly to two trite oaths: (1) That the South was altogether right in seceding from the Union in 1861; and (2) that the war was not waged about the negro." During the early months of 1911 a somewhat similar controversy developed in Roanoke College, Virginia, the demand being that Elson's *History of the United States* should be put on the Southern Index Expurgatorius because of references considered objectionable to the "institution" and to the "slave-holders' rebellion." Referring to the communication in the *Nation* of August 7, 1902, a Southern writer commenting thereon, and, to a degree, controverting its statements, proceeds on the assumption that "Historical scholarship has settled the fact that according to the interpretation of the American Constitution up to the time of the Civil War the Southern States did have the right to secede from the Union." The whole opposite contention, from the days of Andrew Jackson and Daniel Webster to 1860 is thus summarily dismissed.

[2] J. William Jones, Chaplain-General of the United Confederate Veterans, on the Study of American History in Southern Schools and Colleges. The South in History, *Baltimore Sun*, August 10, 1902. See also oration by Hon. John W. Daniel on the Life, Services and Character of Jefferson Davis, January 25, 1890, pp. 33–35.

tiveness it is claimed that, from the time of the adoption of the Constitution down to a comparatively recent day, "there was not a man in the country who thought or claimed that the new system was anything but a perpetual Union." [1]

Which contention, I asked, is right? And separating myself from my present environment, I tried to go back to the past, and to see things, not as they now are, but as they were; as they appeared to those of three generations gone, — to the fathers, in short, of our grandfathers. It was a groping after forgotten facts and conditions in places dark and unfamiliar. The results reached also, were, I confess, very open to question. But, while more or less curious as well as unexpected, they were such as a Massachusetts man, forty years ago at this time in arms for the Union, need not hesitate to set forth in South Carolina, where the right of secession, no longer proclaimed as a theory, was first resorted to as a fact.

It was Alexander Pope, hard on two centuries ago (1733), who wrote: —

"Manners with fortunes, humors turn with climes,
Tenets with books, and principles with times."

And, again, Tennyson in our day has said: —

"The drift of the Maker is dark, an Isis hid by the veil.
Who knows the ways of the world, how God will bring them about?
Our planet is one, the suns are many, the world is wide.
. . . .
"We are puppets, Man in his pride, and Beauty fair in her flower;
Do we move ourselves, or are moved by an unseen hand at a game
That pushes us off from the board, and others ever succeed?"

As I delved into the record, I concluded that humors turned quite as much with climes in the nineteenth century as they did in the eighteenth; and that, in the later as in the

[1] D. H. Chamberlain, Mass. Hist. Soc. *Proceedings*, Second Series, XVI, 173.

earlier period, "principles," so called, bore a very close relation to "times." We, too, had been "puppets" moved by "an unseen hand at a game." As, in short, I pursued my inquiries, the individual became more and more minimized; chance and predestination cut larger figures; and, at last, it all assumed the form of a great fatalistic process, from which the unexpected alone was sure to result.

But to come to the record: For more than a century, lawyers, jurists and publicists — journalists, politicians and statesmen — have been arguing over the Federal Constitution. Sovereignty carries with it allegiance. Wherein rested sovereignty? Was it in the State or in the Nation? Was the United States a unit, — an indissoluble Union of indestructible States,[1] — or was it a mere confederacy of nations, held together solely by a compact, upon possible infringements of which each one, so far as it was concerned, was a final judge? Each postulate has been maintained from the beginning; for that matter, is maintained still. Each has been argued out with great legal acumen and much metaphysical skill to results wholly satisfactory to those that way inclined; and yet absolutely illogical and absurd to the faithful of the other side. It was the old case of the shield of the silver and golden sides. That the two sides were irreconcilable made no difference. Be it silver or gold, the thing to him who had eyes to see was in his sight silver or gold, as the case might be. And yet, as I pursued my inquiries, I gradually felt assured, not that the thing was in this case either silver or gold, but that it was both silver and gold. Everybody, in short, was right; no one, wrong. Merely conditions changed; and, with them, not only appearances

[1] "An indestructible Union composed of indestructible States," Chief Justice Chase, Texas v. White, 7 Wallace, 725. "An indissoluble Union of imperishable States," Bancroft, *History of the Formation of the Constitution*, Vol. II, p. 334.

but principles, and even facts. Simply, the inevitable, and yet the unexpected, had occurred.

This I propose for my thesis.

In dealing with these questions the lawyers, I find, start always with the assumption that, at a given time in the past, to wit, at or about 1788, there was in the thirteen States, then soon to become the present United States, a definite consensus of public opinion, which found expression in a written compact, since known as the Federal Constitution. But was this really the case? Public opinion, so called, is a very elusive and uncertain something, signifying things different at different times and in different places. Especially was this the case in the States of the old Federation. So far as I can ascertain, every State of the Federation became a member of the Union with mental reservations, often unexpressed, growing out of local traditions and interests, in the full and correct understanding of which the action of each must be studied.[1] Dissatisfied with the past and doubtful of the future, jealous of liberties, to the last degree provincial and suspicious of all external rule, intensely common-sensed but illogical and alive with local prejudice, the one thing our ancestry united in most apprehending was a centralized government. From New Hampshire to Georgia such a government was associated with the idea of a foreign régime. The people clung to the local autonomy, — the Sovereignty of the State. With this fundamental fact the framers of the Constitution had to deal. And they did so, in my opinion, with consummate skill. Accepting things as they were, they went as far as they could, leaving the outcome to time and

[1] "Every State has some objection to the present form [the Constitution of 1788, then under discussion], and these objections are directed to different points. That which is most pleasing to one is obnoxious to another, and so *vice versa*." George Washington to Bushrod Washington, November 10, 1787. *Writings*, Ford's ed., XI, 184.

P

the process of natural growth. The immediate result was a nation founded on a metaphysical abstraction, — a condition of unstable equilibrium. In the nature of things, such a condition could not be permanent. But the great mass of people composing a community — Lincoln's "plain people" — are not metaphysicians, and do not philosophize. Loving to argue, in argument they are not logical. Even in Virginia they were not then all abstractionists; and while, in a vague way, the Virginians wanted to become part of one people, they never proposed to cease to be Virginians, or to permit Virginia to become other than a Sovereign State. It was so with the others.

Confronted with this fact, what did the framers of the Constitution propose? Taking refuge in metaphysics, they proposed a contradiction in terms — a divided sovereignty! Sovereignty, it was argued, was in the People. But who are the People? The People of the United States, it was replied, are the aggregate of those inhabiting the particular States. Then they began to apportion sovereignty, oblivious of the fact that sovereignty does not admit of apportionment. A *modus vivendi* may, of course, be agreed on, and even work effectively as well as harmoniously, by any number of people and for an indefinite period of time, but the agreed *modus vivendi* is a proposed substitute for sovereignty, not the thing itself. The Constitution as framed and originally put in operation was, so far as sovereignty was concerned, an avowed *modus vivendi*. Agreeing on this abstraction, the framers, next pursuing some vague analogy of the solar system, and conceiving of States as planets in their orbits, caused the people of the particular States to assign to the Nation a modicum of sovereignty, to confer another modicum on the State governments, and reserve whatever remained to the People themselves. Now it is written, "No man can

THE ETHICS OF SECESSION

serve two masters: for either he will hate the one and love the other; or else he will hold to the one and despise the other." The everlasting truth of this precept in the fulness of time held good in our case. From the moment the fathers sought to divide the indivisible, the result was written on the wall. It was a mere question of years and of might. Sovereignty, in case of dissent insisting peremptorily on final arbitrament, had to be somewhere, and accepted as being there.

Thus, intentionally by some of the most far-seeing, unintentionally by others anxious to effect only a more perfect union, a pious fraud was in 1788 perpetrated on the average American, and his feet were directed into a path which inevitably led him to the goal he least designed for his journey's end.[1]

> "Through the Valley of Love I went,
>   In the lovingest spot to abide,
> And just on the verge where I pitched my tent,
>   I found Hate dwelling beside."[2]

The bond was deceptive; for, on this vital point of ultimate sovereignty, — To whom was allegiance due in cases of direct

---

[1] "The convention framed a constitution by the adoption of which thirteen peoples imagining themselves still independent and sovereign, really acknowledged themselves to be but parts of a single political whole. But they made this acknowledgment unconsciously. They continued to think of themselves as sovereigns, who indeed permitted an agent to exercise some of their functions for them, but who had not abdicated their thrones. If the constitution had contained a definite statement of the actual fact; if it had said that to adopt it was to acknowledge the sovereignty of the one American people, no part of which could sever its connections from the rest without the consent of the whole, it would probably have been rejected by every State in the Union." — J. P. Gordy, *Political Parties in the United States* (ed. 1900), Vol. I, p. 79. "To the familiar state governments which had so long possessed their love and allegiance, [the plan devised and recommended by the Federal Convention of 1787] was superadding a new and untried government, which it was feared would swallow up the states and everywhere extinguish local independence." — Fiske, *The Critical Period of American History*, p. 237.

[2] Browning, *Pippa Passes*, II, Noon.

issue and last resort? — on this crucial point of points the Constitution was not self-explanatory, — explicit. Nor was it meant to be. The framers — that is, the more astute, practical and farseeing — went as far as they dared. The difficulty — the contradiction involved — was explicitly, and again and again, pointed out. It is impossible to believe that a man so intellectually acute as Hamilton failed to see the inherent weakness of the plan proposed. He did see it; but, under existing conditions, the plan was, from his point of view, the best attainable. Madison, though a man of distinctly constructive mind, was also an abstractionist. He seems really to have had faith in the principle of an unstable political equilibrium. At a later day that faith was put to a rude test; and, in 1814, while the Hartford Convention was in session, the scales fell from his eyes. He had all he wanted of a divided sovereignty in practical operation! Lawyers, meanwhile, have since argued on this point; philosophers and publicists have refined over it; historians have analyzed the so-called original materials of history; and men with arms in their hands have fought the thing to a final result. Nevertheless, the real facts in the case seem quite clear; though altogether otherwise than they are usually assumed to have been.

When the Federal Constitution was framed and adopted, — an indissoluble Union of indestructible States, — what was the law of treason, — to what or to whom, in case of final issue, did the average citizen owe allegiance? Was it to the Union or to his State? As a practical question, seeing things as they then were, — sweeping aside all incontrovertible legal arguments and metaphysical disquisitions, — I do not think the answer admits of doubt. If put in 1788, or indeed at any time anterior to 1825, the immediate reply of nine men out of ten in the northern States, and of ninety-nine out of a hundred in the southern States, would have been that, as between the Union and the State, ultimate allegiance was due to the State.

A recurrence to the elementary principles of human nature tells us that this would have been so, and could have been no otherwise. We have all heard of a famous, much-quoted remark of Mr. Gladstone to the effect that the Constitution of the United States was "the most wonderful work ever struck off at a given time by the brain and purpose of man." This may or may not be so. I propose neither to affirm nor to controvert it, here and now; but, however wonderful it may actually have been, it would have been more than wonderful, it would have been distinctly miraculous, had it on the instant so wrought with men as at once to transfer the allegiance and affection of those composing thirteen distinct communities from their old traditional governments to one newly improvised. The thing hardly admits of discussion. The change was political and far-reaching; but it produced no immediate effect on the feelings of the people.[1] As well say that the union of the crowns of Scotland and England immediately broke up Scotch clanship. It did break it up; but the process was continuous through one hundred and fifty years. The British union became an organic and legalized fact in 1707; but, as the events of forty years later showed, the consequences of the union no Campbell nor Cameron foresaw. So with us in 1788, allegiance to State had only a few years before proved stronger than allegiance to the Crown or to the Confederation, and no one then was "foolish enough to suppose that" the executive of the Union "would dare enforce a law against the wishes of a sovereign and independent State"; the very idea was deemed "preposterous." "That this new government, this upstart of yesterday, had the

[1] Tocqueville, *Democracy in America*, Reeve's ed. (1889), I, 389, n., 394. *Infra*, 349.

power to impose its edicts on unwilling States was a political solecism to which they could in no wise assent." [1]

I am sure that all this was so in 1788. I am very confident it remained so until 1815. I fully believe it was so, though in less degree, until at least 1830. A generation of men born in the Union had then grown up, supplanting the generations born and brought up in the States. Steam and electricity had not yet begun to exert their cementing influence; but time, sentiment, tradition, — more, and most of all, the intense feeling excited North and South by our naval successes under the national flag in the War of 1812, — had in 1815 in large part done their work. The sense of ultimate allegiance was surely, though slowly as insensibly, shifting from the particular and gravitating to the general, — from the State to the Union. It was not a question of law, or of the intent of the fathers, or the true construction of a written instrument; for, on that vital point, the Constitution was silent, — wisely, and, as I hold it, intentionally silent. But, though through and because of that silence there may have been ground for a difference of opinion as to the right of secession, there is no possible room for doubt, whether doubt legal or doubt historical, on the question of a divided sovereignty.[2] That is part of the record. Only strictly limited and carefully enumerated powers were conceded by the States to the Nation; the rest were reserved. Even, therefore, though Mr.

[1] Gordy, *Political Parties in the United States*, I, 203, 341.

[2] "Every State in the Union, in every instance where its sovereignty has not been delegated to the United States, is considered to be as completely sovereign as the United States are in respect to the powers surrendered. The United States are sovereign as to all the powers of government actually surrendered; each State in the Union is sovereign as to all the powers reserved." — Mr. Justice Iredell of the United States Supreme Court, in 1793 (2 Dallas, 435). Judge Iredell was a member of the Convention of 1787, which framed the Constitution, and advocated its adoption in the North Carolina Convention.

Lodge and Goldwin Smith, and the other authorities I have referred to, may be totally wrong on the question of the right of withdrawal from the Union, and the views held in regard to a withdrawal at the time the Constitution was adopted,[1] — and I wish here distinctly to say that, in my opinion, they were wrong, and a somewhat careful examination of the record has disclosed to me no evidence on which to base their somewhat sweeping assertions, — though, I say, Mr. Lodge and Dr. Smith may be wrong, yet whether they were wrong or right does not affect the proposition that, from 1788 to 1861, in case of direct and insoluble issue between sovereign State and sovereign Nation, every man was not only free to decide, but had to decide the question of ultimate allegiance for himself; and, whichever way he decided, almost equally good grounds in justification thereof could be alleged. The Constitution gave him two masters. Both he could not serve; and the average man decided which to serve in the light of sentiment, tradition and environment. Of this I feel as historically confident as I can feel of any fact not matter of absolute record or susceptible of demonstration.

I have already referred to the academic address I some months ago had occasion to deliver. In response to it I re-

[1] As respects contemporaneous opinion, there can be no authority higher than that of Madison, cited by Mr. Chamberlain, Mass. Hist. Soc. *Proceedings*, Second Series, XVI, 167. On the point raised Fiske says: "The decisive struggle was over the question whether New York could ratify the Constitution conditionally, reserving to herself the right to withdraw from the Union in case the amendments upon which she had set her heart should not be adopted. Upon this point Hamilton reinforced himself with the advice of Madison, who had just returned to New York. Could a State once adopt the Constitution, and then withdraw from the Union if not satisfied? Madison's reply was prompt and decisive. No, such a thing could never be done. A State which had once ratified was in the federal bond forever. The Constitution could not provide for nor contemplate its own overthrow. There could be no such thing as a constitutional right of secession." — *The Critical Period of American History, 1783–1789*, pp. 343, 344.

ceived quite a number of letters, one of which, bearing on this point, seemed very notable. It was from the president of an historic Virginia college, who himself bears an historic Virginia name. In the address alluded to I had said that, "however it may have been in 1788, in 1860 a nation had grown into existence." This I take to be indisputable. In no way denying the fact, my correspondent, quoting the words I have given, thus wrote: "But is it not true that this nationality was after all a Northern nationality? Did the South share in it to any extent? On the contrary, the Confederate character of the Union was more strongly impressed upon the South in 1861 than in 1788. So that it may be more truly said that the Secessionists' recourse in 1861 was to peaceable separation, and not to the sword. If the North was really the only national part of the Union, and its national character reached out after the South, must not the responsibility for the use of the sword be visited upon the North, and not on the South? Both North and South started out from the same constitutional standpoint of secession; but, while the South adhered to the same idea, the North fused into a nation, which, in 1861, determined to conquer the other and conservative part. That the South had ever suffered *nationalization* in spirit or in fact, previous to 1861, I think your address clearly disproves."

In some of the conclusions assumed in this extract from the letter of my Virginia correspondent, it is needless to say I do not concur. I do not, as I have said, believe in the right of secession as an original "constitutional standpoint" from which, in 1788, North and South started out. Neither do I believe that a "peaceable separation" was ever contemplated as a possibility by any one; least of all by those who took the lead in the Confederate movement of 1861. I do, however, believe, and the record moreover shows, that the essential basic principle of the Constitution was a divided sovereignty, and, in the contingency of a direct insoluble issue, a consequently divided personal allegiance.[1]

But, this premised, on the main issue — the essential point involved in the extract from his letter — the writer was, I think, right. Previous to 1861, the South did not undergo nationalization, to the same extent, in any event, as the North. And why did it not? Again, Tennyson's "unseen hand at a game"! — a game in which we are "puppets." But, after all, what is that "unseen hand"? And how did it manifest itself in our national life during the three-fourths of a century between 1788 and 1861? That "unseen hand," theologically known as an "inscrutable providence," I take to be nothing more or less than those material, social, industrial and political conditions, domestic and public, which, making up our environment, mould our destiny with no very great regard for our plans, our hopes, our traditions or our aspirations. All of which is merely our nineteenth-century agnostical way of putting the fifteenth-century aphorism that "Man proposes, but God disposes." With a political instinct which now seems marvellous, Madison, in the course of debate in the Constitutional Convention of 1787, casting a prophetic glance into futurity, said: "The great danger to our general government is, that the Southern and Northern interests of the continent are opposed to each other, not from their difference of size, but from climate, and principally from the effects of their having or not having slaves. Defensive power ought to be given, not between the large and small States, but between the Northern and Southern." And again, "The greatest danger is disunion of the States"; and "It seems now well understood that the real difference of interests lies, not between the large and small, but between the Northern

[1] *Infra*, p. 300.

and Southern States." Based on this line of broad difference, the contest was "between the fear of the centripetal and the fear of the centrifugal force in the system." On the other side of the Atlantic, a shrewd observer and pioneer economist, profoundly opposed to the British policy during our War of Independence, had thus, shortly before, cast a horoscope of the American people: "The mutual antipathies and clashing interests of the Americans, their difference of governments, habitudes and manners indicate that they will have no centre of union and no common interest. They never can be united into one compact empire under any species of government whatever; a disunited people till the end of time, suspicious and distrustful of each other, they will be divided and subdivided into little commonwealths or principalities according to natural boundaries, by great bays of the sea and by vast rivers, lakes, and ridges of mountains."[1]

Into the details of the conflict over sovereignty which dragged along for seventy years, it is needless for me here to enter. A twice-told tale, I certainly have no new light to cast upon it; but in freshly reviewing it, that aspect of it which has most impressed me is its resemblance to the classic. Throughout Fate, the inevitable, "the unseen hand," are everywhere now apparent, — destiny had to be fulfilled. In connection with the history of those momentous years, we read much of men; and, indeed, it is a galaxy of great names, — Washington, Hamilton, Jefferson, Marshall, Madison, Webster, Calhoun; but, as I went back to the deeper underlying influences, — the profound currents of thought and action which in the end worked results, — one and all those bearing even these names became Tennyson's "puppets" moved by the "unseen hand at the game." In this respect

[1] Josiah Tucker, Dean of Gloucester, quoted by Bancroft, *History of the Formation of the Constitution*, I, 65.

our story is suggestive of some cosmic theory, — the process by which suns and planets and satellites are evolved; and gradually it seems as if the individual man were able to affect the course of events and final results as respects the outcome of the one as much as he does of the other.[1] The elaborate legal arguments, the metaphysical theories and historical disquisitions, — even the rights and wrongs of the case, —

[1] This assertion, I am aware, is very open to dispute, and impossible of proof. The theory that men, who, in history, appear to have given shape to their own times, and, by so doing, to subsequent times, did, after all, but represent, embody and bring to a head the tendencies of their age; which embodiment would have inevitably taken place through some other, if they had not been, — this theory of historic fatalism was first developed by Buckle in his *History of Civilization in England*, half a century ago. There is certainly an element of truth in it, inasmuch as no man can be really great except in so far as he reads his time aright, "translating its dumb inarticulate cry into some articulate language, divining its wants and satisfying them, seeing and laying hold of the helps which the time affords to carry out the work which the time requires." On the other hand, it is impossible to ignore the influence of exceptional individuality on the course of events, as evidenced by innumerable instances from Moses to Bismarck. In the case of the development of American nationality because of the adoption, and under the operation, of the Federal Constitution, the two possible individual exceptions to the general rule would seem to be Washington and Marshall. But for the respect in which Washington was held, and the general recognition of his great attributes of character, it is very questionable whether the Constitution of 1788 would have been adopted, or could have been set in successful operation. But for the solid judicial renderings of Marshall, stretching through a long period of years, our system of constitutional law would hardly have assumed consistency and shape. Yet, on the other hand, the American community made both Washington and Marshall possible. They were the natural outcome of their environment. The producing power and the thing produced had to be in harmony, and act and react on each other. While the United States that now is would almost certainly have been something quite other but for the presence and influence of Washington and Marshall as factors in the solution of the problem, Washington and Marshall would have failed to produce their results had they not been in complete and happy accord with the community and conditions in which they lived and worked. As to the others named, there is no sufficient reason to doubt that the work done and the influence exerted by them would have been done and exerted by others had they not come forward.

became quite immaterial, and altogether insignificant. In obedience to underlying influences, and in conformity with natural laws, a system is crystallizing. Discordant elements blend; assimilation, willing or reluctant, goes on. See how the sides change — how rapidly "humors turn with climes"; while, as to the principles involved, the mutation is only less complete than sincere. Nationality, as we see it to-day, had its birth in Virginia; and the sovereignty of the Union assumed shape through the agency of Washington and was slowly perfected by Marshall, both more or less consciously responding to a natural movement, and working in harmony with it. Next, Virginia and her offspring, Kentucky, are passing the resolves of 1798, and arraying themselves under the standard of decentralization. The government then passes into the hands of the protestants; and, almost at once, again in response to an underlying, unseen influence too strong to resist, the process of a more complete crystallization enters on a new phase; and, as it does so, catholic suddenly becomes protestant, and while Federalist New England formally pronounces the Union at an end, Jeffersonian Virginia supplies fresh aliment to nationality.

Meanwhile, the "unseen hand" is again at work, and the "puppets" duly respond. They thought, and we once thought, they were free agents. Not at all! In the light of development it is clear to us now that they merely went through their motions in obedience to influences of the very existence of which they were at most but vaguely conscious. The drama was drawing insensibly to a crisis; the forces were arraying themselves in opposing ranks on the lines forecast by Madison in 1787. With much confidence, I assert, in its fundamentals there was no right or wrong about it; it was an inevitable, irrepressible conflict, — the question of sovereignty was to be decided, and either side could offer good ground, historical and legal, for any attitude taken in regard to it. That shield did actually have a silver as well as a golden side.

Historically speaking, from the close of our second War of Independence, — commonly known as that of 1812, — the ebb and flow of the great currents of influence had set in new and definite channels. Gradually they assumed irresistible force therein. Side by side two civilizations — a Chang and Eng — were developing. North of the Potomac and the Ohio a community was taking shape, the whole tendency of which was national. Very fluid in its elements, commercial and manufacturing in its diversified industries, it was largely composed of Europeans or their descendants, who, knowing, little of States, cared nothing for State Sovereignty, which, indeed, like the Unknown God to the Greeks, was to them foolishness. This vast discordant migration the railroad, the common school and the newspaper were rapidly merging, coalescing and fusing into a harmonious whole. Naturally it found a mouthpiece; and that mouthpiece preached Union. It was not exactly a consistent utterance; for, less than a score of years before, the same voice had been loud and emphatic in behalf of State Sovereignty.[1]

[1] See speech on the Conscription Bill, made by Mr. Webster in the House of Representatives at Washington, December 9, 1814. *Infra*, p. 339.

In language slightly varied the speech referred to was a repetition of the words of Governor Jonathan Trumbull, addressed to the legislature of Connecticut, at the opening of its special session, February 23, 1809: "Whenever our national legislature is led to overleap the prescribed bounds of their constitutional powers, on the State legislatures, in great emergencies, devolves the arduous task — it is their right — it becomes their duty, to interpose their protecting shield between the right and liberty of the people and the assumed power of the General Government." Again, Mr. Webster did but voice, in the extract quoted, the full spirit of the famous Hartford Convention, which began its sessions six days after delivery of the speech. The following was among the resolutions there passed, following closely, in time of active foreign war, Madison's own language in drafting the Virginia Resolutions of 1798: "The mode and the

So much for Chang, north of the Potomac and the Ohio; but with Eng, south of those streams, it was altogether otherwise. Under the influence of climate, soil and a system of forced African labor the southern States irresistibly reverted to the patriarchal conditions, becoming more and more agricultural; and, as is always the case with agricultural races and patriarchal communities, they clung ever more closely to their traditions and local institutions. Then it was that Calhoun, the most rigid of logicians, in obedience to an irresistible influence of the presence and power of which he was unconscious, — Calhoun, the unionist of the War of 1812 and protectionist of 1816, turned to the Constitution; he began that "more diligent and careful scrutiny into its provisions, in order to ascertain fully the nature and character of our political system." Needless to say, he there found what he was in search of.[1] But a similar scrutiny was at the

energy of the opposition should always conform to the nature of the violation, the intention of its authors, the extent of the injury inflicted, the determination manifested to persist in it, and the danger of delay. But in cases of deliberate dangerous and palpable infractions of the Constitution, affecting the sovereignty of a State and liberties of the people, it is not only the right but the duty of such a State to interpose its authority for their protection in the manner best calculated to secure that end. When emergencies occur which are either beyond the reach of the judicial tribunals, or too pressing to admit of the delay incident to their forms, States which have no common umpire must be their own judges, and execute their own decisions."

Mr. Webster, in his reply to Hayne, said : "I do not hold that the Hartford Convention was pardonable, even to the extent of the gentleman's admission, if its objects were really such as have been imputed to it." It is somewhat curious to consider what would have been the attitude of the Massachusetts senator, if, after uttering these words, the senator from South Carolina had been able to confront him with his speech of fifteen years previous in the other hall of the Capitol. But

"Manners with fortunes, humors turn with climes,
Tenets with books, and principles with times."

[1] "Just at what time Calhoun changed from a protectionist to a free trader, from a liberal to a conservative, from a liberal constructionist to a

same time going on in New England. As a result of the two scrutinies, Chang and Eng both changed sides. Before, Chang's side of the shield was gold, while that of Eng was silver; now, Chang saw quite clearly that it was silver after all, while Eng recognized it as burnished gold of the purest stamp. Both were honest, and both fully convinced. Both also were right; the simple truth — the truth of Holy Writ — being that no man can serve two masters; and two masters the fundamental law prescribed. The inevitable ensued.

But what was the inevitable? That again, as I read the story of our development, was purely a matter of circumstance and time. Fate — the Greek 'Ανάγκη — intervened in those lists and decided the issue of battle. To my mind, the record is from its commencement absolutely clear on one point, — and that the vital point. After the 25th of July, 1788, when the last of the nine States necessary to the adoption of the

strict constructionist, from a progressionist to an obstructionist, has been difficult to determine. One thing is clear; his change followed that of the majority of the people of the State; and whatever pressure there was, was exerted by the State on him, and not by him on the State." — David Franklin Houston, *A Critical Study of Nullification in South Carolina*, Harvard Historical Studies, pp. 60, 82.

When time was ripe, however, and he had directed that "more diligent and careful scrutiny" into the provisions of the Constitution necessary "in order to ascertain fully the nature and character of our political system," he found himself compelled to a dispensation, — a dispensation new to him, to the country very old. He thus formulated it: "The great and leading principle is that the general government emanated from the people of the several States, forming distinct political communities, and acting in their separate and sovereign capacity, and not from all of the people forming one aggregate political community; that the Constitution of the United States is, in fact, a compact, to which each State is a party, in the character already described; and that the several States, or parties, have a right to judge of its infractions; and in case of a deliberate, palpable and dangerous exercise of power not delegated, they have the right, in the last resort (to use the language of the Virginia Resolutions) 'to interpose for arresting the progress of the evil, and for maintaining, within their respective limits, the authorities, rights, and liberties appertaining to them.'" — *Ibid.*

Federal Constitution acted favorably thereon, the withdrawal of a State, or States, from the Union, all theories to the contrary notwithstanding, became practically an issue of might. Into the abstract question of right I will not enter, — least of all, here and now. But, conceding everything that may be asked on the point of abstract right, — looking only on imperfect and illogical man as he is, and as he acts in this world's occasions and exigencies, — I on this point adhere to my own belief. In 1790 Rhode Island was spared from being "coerced" into the Union only by a voluntary, though very reluctant, acceptance of it; and from that day to 1861 any attempted withdrawal from the Union would, after long argument over the question of right, have ultimately resolved itself into an issue of might.

Here again the elements of the Greek drama once more confront us — the Fates, necessity. What at different epochs would have been the probable outcome of any attempt at withdrawal? That ever, at any period of our history since 1790, a single State — no matter how sovereign, even Virginia — could alone have made good, peaceably or otherwise, a withdrawal in face of her unitedly disapproving sister States, I do not believe. Naturally or as a result of force applied, the attempt would have resulted in ignominious failure. But how would it have been at any given time with a combination of States, acting in sympathy, — a combination proportionately as considerable when measured with the whole as was the Confederacy in 1861? I hold that, here again, it was merely a question of time, and that such a withdrawal as then took place would never have failed of success at any anterior period in our national history. Steam and electricity settled the issue of sovereignty; not argument, not military skill, not wealth, courage or endurance; not even men in arms. Before 1861 steam and electricity, neither on

THE ETHICS OF SECESSION 225

land nor water, had been rendered so subservient to man as to make him equal to the prodigious, the unprecedented, task then undertaken, and finally accomplished. In that case, might in the end made right; but the end was in no degree a foregone conclusion.

In my own family records I find a curious bit of contemporary evidence of this, and of the line of thought and reasoning then resulting therefrom. Following the foresight of Madison, J. Q. Adams, noting the set of the currents in 1820, became instinctively persuaded that the North and the South would be swept into collision by the forces of inherent development. Again and again did he put this belief of his on record.[1] Contemplating such an eventuality, he, in 1839, thus expressed himself in a public utterance, in words which I have of late more than once seen quoted in support of the abstract constitutional right of secession. Speaking in New York on what was called the Jubilee of the Constitution, or the fiftieth anniversary of its adoption, he said: "If the day should ever come (may Heaven avert it!) when the affections of the people of these States shall be alienated from each other, when the fraternal spirit shall give way to cold indifference, or collisions of interest shall fester into hatred, the bands of political association will not long hold together parties no longer attracted by the magnetism of conciliated interests and kindly sympathies; and far better will it be for the people of the disunited States to part in friendship from each other than to be held together by constraint. Then will be the time for reverting to the precedents which occurred at the formation and adoption of the Constitution, to form

[1] See the paper entitled "John Quincy Adams and Martial Law," Mass. Hist. Soc. *Proceedings*, Second Series, XV, 436–478. Separately printed as "John Quincy Adams, His Connection with the Monroe Doctrine (1823) and with Emancipation under Martial Law (1819–1842)," by Worthington Chauncey Ford and Charles Francis Adams.

again a more perfect union by dissolving that which could no longer bind, and to leave the separated parts to be reunited by the law of political gravitation to the centre."[1]

In other words, forecasting strife, and measuring the coercive force available at a time when steam on land and water was in its stages of earlier development, J. Q. Adams regarded the attempt at an assertion of national sovereignty as so futile that, though he most potently and powerfully believed in that sovereignty, he looked upon its exercise as quixotic, and, consequently, not to be justified. A dissolution of the Union, at least temporarily, he believed to be inevitable. So strongly was he convinced of the power of the disintegrating influence as contrasted with the cohesive force, that the late Robert C. Winthrop, then a young man of twenty-seven, writing in 1836, described him as saying, in the course of dinner-table talk, that "he despaired of the Union, believing we are destined soon to overrun not merely Texas, but Mexico, and that the inevitable result will be a break-up into two, three, four or more confederacies." "Inevitable!" the unexpected alone is inevitable. These two utterances were, the one in 1836, the other in 1839. In 1839 there were not five hundred miles of constructed railroad in the United States; steam had not been applied to naval construction; electricity was a toy. So far as he could look into the future, Mr. Adams was right; only — the unexpected was to occur! It did occur; and it settled the question. In 1788 the preponderance of popular feeling and affection was wholly in the scale of State Sovereignty as opposed to Nationality; in 1801 the Union was, in all probability, saved by being taken from the hands of its friends, and, so to speak, put out to nurse with its enemies, who from that time were converts to centralization; in 1815 the final war of independence gave a

[1] J. Q. Adams, *Jubilee of the Constitution* (April 30, 1839), p. 69.

THE ETHICS OF SECESSION

great impetus to Nationality, and the scales hung even; in 1831 the irrepressible conflict began to assert itself, and now they inclined slightly but distinctly to Nationality, the younger of the two sovereigns asserting a supremacy; between 1831 and 1861 science threw steam and electricity into his scale, and, in 1865, they made the opposite scale kick the beam. But, when all is said, merely a fresh illustration had been furnished of the truth of that scriptural adage in regard to a divided service.

Such are the conclusions reached from a renewed and somewhat careful review of a record frequently scanned by others. They found it in the outcome of great orations, labored arguments and the teaching of individuals. I cannot so see it. It is, as I read it, one long, majestic Greek tragedy.

> "Like to the Pontic sea,
> Whose icy current and compulsive course
> Ne'er feels retiring ebb, but keeps due on
> To the Propontic and the Hellespont," —

so that great drama swept on to its inevitable catastrophe, — Fate and Necessity ever the refrain of its chorus, — until, at the end, the resounding clash of arms.

The circumstances connected with the preparation of the foregoing paper, and its delivery as an address, were peculiar. Not of a merely personal and passing interest, they were in a way even of historic significance. A somewhat particular reference to them may, therefore, be justified, even if not actually called for.

During the earlier months of 1902 I chanced to be engaged in a somewhat careful study of the view generally taken at the time of the adoption of the Federal Constitution, of the right of secession. Led into a more elaborate examination than I anticipated when I began my inquiry, early in October of that year an invitation reached me from the New England Society of Charleston, S. C., to go there on Forefather's Day, December 22, and, as its guest, to address that society on any subject I might select. I had never been in Charleston; and yet I had passed well-nigh an entire year, — that is, the eight months from January to August inclusive, — almost in sight of the famous town. The only actual glimpse I had ever got of it was a distant one from James Island, looking across the harbor towards Charleston, with Fort Sumter looming up midway, flying the Confederate flag. This was in June, 1862, immediately after the engagement known by us as that of James Island, and by the Confederates as Secessionville. Remaining in South Carolina with my regiment, the First Massachusetts Cavalry, until August, we, together with all other available forces, were then ordered north. Charleston was for the time being relieved of our presence, and from apprehension. It was a respite for a city doomed. Since the stern solution less than three years later of the grave question which we had been sent to South Carolina, not to discuss but to dispose of, a period equal to that passed by the children of Israel in the wilderness had elapsed. Such being the case, it was in no way unnatural that I should have felt a strong desire actually to see the city, the possession of which we had in 1862 so greatly coveted. When the invitation I have referred to reached me, I accordingly felt disposed to accept it.

Moreover the suggestion that a Massachusetts man of my particular antecedents should go to Charleston, of all conceivable places, deliberately proposing there to canvass the constitutional ethics of secession, was undeniably startling. It was like penetrating the crater of a recently extinct volcano, and philosophizing over the causes, character, and, if the expression may be used in such a connection, the justification, of a furious eruption, the cinders of which were still warm. The very delicacy of treatment called for in so doing enhanced the desire to do it. To speak the truth on that subject there, treating it as an academic question, in a purely philosophic, dispassionate tone, was not easy. The temptation was great. I concluded to accept the invitation.

Since I, on that day in June, 1862, had viewed the place from an island across its bay, it seemed as if there was no sorrow, no humiliation, no loss of property, Charleston had not undergone. Conflagration, blockade, siege, bombardment, hostile occupation, confiscation, servile supremacy and finally earthquake had followed each other in irregular but ordered sequence. Under these circumstances I freely confess that not only was my sympathy now excited, but my admiration was stirred by the indications of resiliency I everywhere saw, and still more by the cheerfulness, and quiet, uncomplaining dignity with which all those I met discussed the past, and accepted the conditions of the present. If any bitterness of feeling existed towards those who had so largely contributed to their calamities, it was not to me as one of them apparent in word or sign. Everywhere I was received with the same simple courtesy, and listened to the same frank reference to historic and other events, as my attention was called to what remained of the household gods peculiar to the place, and pertaining to a civilization long since passed away, — the civilization of plantation and slave-owning days.

One thing was apparent: — the community having, when further repining was obviously in vain, adapted itself as best it could to the conditions imposed upon it by force or nature, the people composing it were facing the future with confidence as well as courage. And yet that future did not strike me as altogether encouraging. On the contrary, the one thing which most deeply impressed me throughout South Carolina, but in Charleston more especially, was the terrible handicap under which the community was laboring in the race of competition. As an average observer, and something of a sociologist, I by no means share in that optimistic confidence, so much in vogue in the present day, which sees only progress everywhere. On the contrary there is to my mind much truth in this observation of the late Sir Leslie Stephen, one of the keenest observers and most subtle thinkers of the last half of the nineteenth century:

"Progress is the rare exception: races may remain in the lowest barbarism, or their development be arrested at some more advanced stage during periods far surpassing that of recorded history; actual decay may alternate with progress, and even true progress implies some admixture of decay. The intellectual activity of the acuter intellects, however feeble may be its immediate influence, is the great force which stimulates and guarantees every advance of the race. It is of course opposed by a vast force of inertia. The ordinary mind is indifferent to the thoughts which occupy the philosopher, unless they promise an immediate material result. Mankind resent nothing so much as the intrusion upon them of a new and disturbing truth. The huge dead weight of stupidity and indolence is always ready to smother audacious inquiries."[1]

Thus the preponderance of the factors tending towards an uplifting is, even with the most progressive nations, but a slight percentage of the whole. That slight percentage, varying either way, makes the difference between up and down, — it causes the scales to tip.

Hence, to-day, of an hundred distinct nationalities, speaking different languages, — civilized, semi-civilized and barbarian, — white, yellow and black, — it is fairly questionable whether as many as ten are really, in themselves and of themselves, progressive. The United States, Great Britain, Germany and Japan are distinctly uplifting; but can the same, save exceptionally, be said of the Latin races on either continent, or of any of the peoples of Southern Asia or of Africa? The vast majority of mankind are, of themselves, at best merely stationary. What impetus they have is from without.

Now, as compared with ourselves, the Southern people have a dead-weight of Africanism tied to them, which is tending perpetually to hold back or pull down. It may seem heterodox, perhaps it will be stigmatized as pessimistic, to say so, but I have myself little doubt that, if left to themselves, apart from the example and sustaining energy of the white man, even the most advanced types of the African race on this continent, taken as a mass, would tend steadily to deteriorate, — they would sensibly gravitate towards the normal African conditions. In other words, it is not a self-sustaining, much less an inherently advancing human species. It is held up to any standard to which it is brought by the presence and influence of the white man. Meanwhile, on the other hand, it acts as a dead-weight on the uplifting race, tending steadily to diminish its forward impetus, even if it does not produce direct deterioration. Instinctively comparing what I saw in South Carolina with the more fortunate conditions prevailing in Massachusetts, the impression left was that the white race in the South, especially in South Carolina, were at a distinct disadvantage. In

[1] *English Thought in the Eighteenth Century*, Vol. I, p. 17.

Charleston, for instance, there are about three inhabitants of black blood to two of white. The problem before that community is, therefore, momentous. They are now making an effort, both honest and strenuous, to educate the African. What the result will be at some remote future period, I do not undertake to predict. But, so far as can be judged from present indications, the outlook, in spite of expensive schooling, is not propitious. The races are segregating, and becoming more and more antagonistic. The African does not originate, he is imitative. It is so in dress, in manners, and, to a certain extent, in morals. In all these respects an increasing separation of the two species, living perforce not side by side but together, is bad for both. From what I saw and heard I should apprehend that the great future handicap of the South would be the presence in its civilization of a vast, imperfectly assimilated mass of barbarism veneered.

The foregoing paper is, therefore, a thesis submitted in Charleston in 1902, by a Massachusetts man, there born and still there resident, who had stood in arms before Charleston in 1862. Presented in the full light of existing conditions, it related to the constitutional theories and social, political and economical influences of the earlier period which had been preparatory to those existing conditions. The why-and-wherefore problem was approached in a purely historic spirit; for, as I now see it, the question involved can never be disposed of if technically dealt with. Not a mere matter of the verbal construction of a written instrument, it far transcends legal argument, however close or logically convincing. It is a case of evolution, — the growth and development of a living organism. What was true of the American people in 1787 had become false in 1860; conditions and modes of thought which prevailed generally in the earlier period had passed out of existence in the latter. Not only were they defunct, they were actually and literally forgotten. The world had moved; and, with the passage of years, the Constitution had become transformed, if not transfigured. It was this process of historical evolution and development which interested, and not the proper construction of words and phrases. To that, and to that alone, attention was directed.

VII

SOME PHASES OF THE CIVIL WAR [1]

BASED on the careful study of a vast mass of material, patiently gathered and judicially considered, Mr. Rhodes's fifth volume is literary in tone and calm in spirit, — a thoroughly good piece of up-to-date historical work. The significance of the period dealt with will, moreover, only increase with the lapse of time, and to its history this volume is a contribution of lasting value. If for no other reason, it will so prove from the fact that it is not so removed from the time of which it treats as to cease to be contemporaneous. He who writes has in this case shared in the intensity of that of which he writes; with his own eyes he has seen many of the actors in the events of which he tells, and his ears have drunk in their own descriptive words. How great an advantage this may prove to one competent to avail himself of it has been shown more recently by Clarendon and Thiers, as in the classic times by Tacitus and Thucydides. What is more, the judgments both of men and of events now rendered by Mr. Rhodes, while based on an exhaustive study of material, are not only cautiously reached, but expressed in measured terms, quite devoid of either zeal or preconception. Neither a partisan nor a

[1] James Ford Rhodes, *History of the United States from the Compromise of 1850.* Vol. V (October, 1864 — August, 1866). This paper was prepared for submission to the Massachusetts Historical Society and appears in its *Proceedings.* (Second Series, XIX, 311–356). It has been revised, and to a certain extent remodelled for the present publication. *Supra,* 109.

theorist, Mr. Rhodes is nothing unless critical. It is, therefore, not unsafe even now to predict that in essentials the conclusions here reached by him will prove in harmony with the ultimate verdict. Nor is this something to be lightly said; for the events and men of the period of Gettysburg and Emancipation will be studied and weighed not less closely by the historians and historical investigators of the twenty-third century than were those of the Naseby and Commonwealth period by Masson, by Carlyle, by Macaulay and by Gardiner in the century recently closed.

But, in writing history, especially the narrative of events still to a large extent contemporaneous, much necessarily depends on the point of view. The direction of approach involves, indeed, nothing less than the question of perspective, — the relative proportion of parts. On these, in turn, depend to some extent the conclusions reached.

Mr. Rhodes approaches his subject in a general way. Neither a politician nor a soldier, he is as unskilled in practical diplomacy as he is innocent of any study of international law; nor can he be classed as a publicist. Once, indeed, a man of affairs, he is now a judicially-minded general investigator, bringing much hard common-sense to bear, always modestly, on the complex problems of a troubled and eventful period. Now it so chances that having myself been a participant in both the political movements and the military operations of the earlier time, I have more recently, through the study of historical material as yet unpublished, had occasion to look upon the problems discussed by Mr. Rhodes from points of view other than his. I therefore propose in this paper to discuss, in a spirit of criticism wholly friendly,[1]

[1] Both Mr. Rhodes and the writer were at this time members of the Massachusetts Historical Society. Mr. Rhodes was present at the meeting (October 12, 1905) at which the present paper was submitted.

what from those points of view seem deficiencies and shortcomings in Mr. Rhodes's treatment. They will prove not inconsiderable. Indeed, they in some repects go to the heart of the subject.

At the close of his summary of the war, in that chapter devoted to a consideration of the internal affairs of the Confederacy during the struggle, Mr. Rhodes suggests a query which many others have often put to themselves, and over which, first and last, they have pondered much. Tersely stated, it is this: How was it that we succeeded in overcoming the seceded States? A task truly Titanic! — and, looking back now through a vista of fifty years, one still instinctively asks, How did we ever accomplish it?

Seeking an answer to this far from self-explanatory query, Mr. Rhodes says: "A certain class of facts, if considered alone, can make us wonder how it was possible to subjugate the Confederates. It could not have been accomplished without great political capacity at the head of the Northern government, and a sturdy support of Lincoln by the Northern people."[1] This, assuredly, is an inadequate answer to a perplexing question, — a question which goes to the heart of any correct historical treatment of our Great Rebellion, to adopt Clarendon's title. It goes without saying that to overcome a combination of numbers, resources and territory such as that composing the Southern Confederacy implied great political capacity in the overcoming power, and the sturdy popular support of him upon whom the task devolved. As Shakespeare causes Horatio to observe in another connection, "There needs no ghost come from the grave to tell us this." But the question suggested by Mr. Rhodes, being one of a very perplexing character, cannot

[1] Vol. V, p. 481.

satisfactorily be disposed of by generalities. To formulate an answer at once definite and satisfactory, we must, descending to particulars, be more specific.

The usual and altogether conventional explanation given is the immense preponderance of strength and resources — men and material — enjoyed by one of the contending parties. The census and the statistics of the War Department are then appealed to, and figures are arrayed setting forth the relative population and wealth, — the resources, manufactures and fighting strength of the two sides. As the result of such a showing, a certain amount of astonishment is finally expressed that the Confederacy ever challenged a conflict; and the conclusion reached is that, under all the circumstances, the only real cause for wonder is that such an unequal contest was so long sustained.

But this answer to the question will hardly bear examination. After the event it looks well, — has a plausible aspect; but in 1861 a census had just been taken, and every fact and figure now open to study was then patent. The South knew them, Europe knew them; and yet in the spring of 1861, and from Bull Run in July of that year to Gettysburg and Vicksburg in 1863, no unprejudiced observer anywhere believed that the subjugation of the Confederacy and the restoration of the old Union were reasonably probable, or, indeed, humanly speaking, a possibility. Mr. Gladstone, a man wise in his generation, and as a contemporaneous observer not unfriendly to the Union side, only expressed the commonly received and apparently justified opinion of all unprejudiced onlookers, when at Newcastle, in October, 1862, he made his famous declaration in public speech that "Jefferson Davis and other leaders of the South . . . have made a nation. . . . We may anticipate with certainty the success of the Southern States so far as regards their separation from the North. I cannot but believe that that event is as certain as any event yet future and contingent can be." No community, it was argued, numbering eight millions, as homogeneous, organized and combative as the South, inhabiting a region of the character of the Confederacy, ever yet had been overcome in a civil war; and there was no sufficient reason for supposing that the present case would prove an exception to a hitherto universal rule. All this, moreover, was so. Wherefore, then, the exception? How was it that, in the result of our civil war, human experience went for nothing?

Was, then, the unexpected really due to preponderance in force? Confederate authorities have, of late, evinced a strong disposition to insist upon this as the correct and sufficient explanation. In order, however, to make out even a *prima facie* showing, the Confederate authorities have assumed, or endeavored to show, that the South never, from Sumter to Appomattox, had over 600,000 men in the aggregate in arms; and these, first and last, were opposed by, as they assert, some 2,800,000 on the part of the Union. Admitting these figures to be correct of both sides, — a large admission, and one which any careful analysis would clearly disprove, — it is none the less obvious that a force six hundred thousand strong, made up of fighting material of the most approved character, wholly homogeneous, mustered for the protection of the hearthstone, is something not easily overcome. It constitutes in itself a defensive army of almost unprecedented size; and one more especially formidable when the minds of those composing it are to the last degree embittered against an opponent whose courage, as well as capacity, they held in almost unmeasured contempt. Such a force would, under the conditions existing in 1861 and 1862, unquestionably have considered itself, and been pronounced by others, quite adequate for every purpose of Southern defence.

But this estimate of Confederate field force obviously invites criticism of another character. It calls for explanation. The Confederate historians and investigators responsible for it do not seem to realize that, in the very act of advancing it, they cast opprobrium on the community they belong to and profess to honor. If this estimate is sustained, the verdict of the historian of the future cannot be escaped. He will say that if 600,000 men were all the Confederacy, first and last, could get into the field, it is clear that the South went into the struggle in a half-hearted way, and, being in it, showed but a craven soul. No effort of the government, no inducement of pride or patriotism, sufficed to get even a moiety of its arms-bearing effectives into the fighting line.

Such a showing on the part of the Confederacy, if established, will certainly not compare favorably with the forty years later record of the Boers in the very similar South African struggle. Accepting the Confederate figures as correct, how do the two cases stand? Territorially the Confederacy covered some 712,000 square miles, — a region considerably (30,000 square miles) larger than the combined European areas of Austro-Hungary, Germany, France and Italy, with Belgium, Holland and Denmark thrown in. This vast space was inhabited by five million people of European descent, with three millions of Africans who could be depended upon to produce food for those of European blood in active service. In the course of the conflict, and before admitting themselves beaten, every white male in the Confederacy between the ages of seventeen and fifty capable of bearing arms was called out. Wherever necessary to preclude evasion of military duty, the writ of habeas corpus was suspended, and the labor, property and lives of all in the Confederacy were by legislation of the most drastic character put at the disposal of an energetic executive. The struggle lasted four full years; and during that period the eighth part of a generation grew up, yielding its quota of arms-bearing men. Consequently, under any recognized method of computation, the Confederacy, first and last, contained within itself some 1,350,000 men capable of doing military duty. This result, also, is in accordance with the figures of the census of 1860.[1] During the war the Confederate army was reënforced by over 125,000 sympathizers[2] from the sister slave States not included in the Confederacy. The upshot of the contention thus is, out of a population of 5,600,000 whites, only 475,000 put in an appearance in response to a many-tongued and often reiterated call to arms,

[1] The exact number, arithmetically computed on the census returns of 1860, but of course to a certain extent inaccurate and deceptive, was 1,356,500.

[2] An exact statistical statement of the number of sympathizers from Delaware, Maryland, West Virginia, Kentucky and Missouri, who, first and last, found their way into the ranks of the Confederate army, is of course impossible. It has been asserted that there were 316,424 "Southern men in the Northern army." This large contingent, so far as not imaginary, would naturally have come in greatest part from the "Border States," so called. It would be not unnatural to assume that these States furnished an equal number of recruits to the Confederacy; but such an assumption would, on the basis above given, be manifestly absurd, leaving a comparatively pitiful contingent of less than 300,000 to be accredited to the States which formed the Confederacy. The War Records contain lists of all military organizations of the Confederate army referred to in that publication. Including regiments, battalions and companies belonging to all branches of the service, regular and provisional, these numbered 279 from the four States, West Virginia, Maryland, Kentucky and Missouri. Included in these were 238 full regiments. If these averaged, from first to last, only 600 each, they represented an aggregate of 143,000 men. No less than 132 lesser organizations, battalions, and companies, and all individual enlistments, remain to be allowed for. In view of these facts, Colonel T. L. Livermore, who has made a specialty of this subject, writes under date of October 24, 1905, "I think a larger estimate than 135,000 in the Confederate army from these States might safely be made."

— a trifle in excess of one man to each twelve inhabitants. There were, moreover, more than 500,000 able-bodied negroes well adapted in every respect for all the numerous semi-military services, — such as teamsters, servants, hospital attendants and laborers on fortifications, the call for which always depletes the number present for duty of every army.[1] Yet it is now maintained by Confederate authorities that all the efforts of the Richmond government, backed by every feeling of pride, patriotism, protection of the domestic roof-tree and hate of the enemy, could only induce or compel a comparatively Spartan band to turn out and strike for independence.[2]

How was it, under very similar circumstances, with the South Africans? On Confederate showing they are a braver, a more patriotic and self-sacrificing race. Two communities, the Transvaal and the Orange Free State, were engaged in a defensive struggle against Great Britain. They included within their bounds an area of 160,000 square miles, — less than a fourth of that included in the Confederacy. Their entire white population was but about 325,000, and, when the war commenced, it was estimated they could muster a force not in excess of 48,000. Yet in their two years of resistance, the Boers, it is computed, had 90,000 men, first and last, in actual service, or more than one in four of their population, as against the one out of twelve in the case of the Con-

[1] "I propose to substitute slaves for all soldiers employed out of the ranks — on detached service, extra duty, as cooks, engineers, laborers, pioneers, or any kind of work. Such details for this little army amount to more than 10,000 men. Negroes would serve for such purposes better than soldiers. . . . The plan is simple and quick. It puts soldiers and negroes each in his appropriate place; the one to fight, the other to work. I need not go into particulars." — Gen. J. E. Johnston, to Confederate Senator L. T. Wigfall, January 4, 1864; Mrs. D. G. Wright, *A Southern Girl in '61*, pp. 168, 169.

[2] See note, *infra*, 282.

federacy.[1] The preponderance of force opposed to the Boers was as five to one; the preponderance of force in the case of the Confederates, according to this latest estimate of their historians, was at most but four and a half to one.[2]

Such an estimate is, however, as far from the mark as, were it based on actual facts, it would be discreditable to Confederate manhood. It is simply unbelievable that, measured by the proportion of fighting men to the total populations, the Boer spirit was to the spirit of the Confederacy as three is to one. The statement carries its own refutation; and the Southerners of that period were no such race of miching, mean-spirited, stay-at-home skulkers as their self-constituted and most ill-advised annalists would apparently make them out. On the contrary, as matter of historical fact, they did

[1] To be exact, one out of each eleven and eight-tenths.

[2] We have census (1860) figures of the population of the States of the Confederacy at the breaking out of the Civil War; but the Confederate muster-rolls, showing actual enlistments, are confessedly defective. It is not easy to reach any accurate figures as to either the population of the two South African republics, or the number of men actually put into the field by them during the war. The "total number of officers and men of all Regular and Auxiliary [British] Forces in the South African War from the beginning to the end" is officially stated as 448,435. At the beginning of the war the Intelligence Division of the British War Office estimated the total available forces of the Transvaal at 29,917, and those of the Orange Free State at 13,104, or an aggregate of 43,021 combatants. At the close of the war, however, the total number accounted for was 72,974 Transvaal and Free State combatants, with 16,400 "Rebels," "Renegades and Foreigners," or a grand total of 89,374. The British officials content themselves with saying, "It is difficult to explain the excess over the Boer official returns [preceding the conflict], unless, indeed, these purposely understated the actual strength of the burghers." — Report (1903) of "His Majesty's Commissioners appointed to Inquire into the Military Preparations and Other Matters Connected with the War in South Africa," pp. 35, 158, 168. Excluding in each case foreign sympathizers, the two South African republics apparently put into the field as combatants one man to each four and two-tenths (4.2) of their entire population; on the claim of the Southern historians the nine States of the Confederacy put into the field one combatant to each eleven and eight-tenths (11.8) of their total white population.

SOME PHASES OF THE CIVIL WAR 241

both turn out in force,[1] and they fought to a finish. Undoubtedly there was, towards the close of the contest, a large desertion from the Confederate ranks. The army melted imperceptibly away. The men would not stay by the colors. When, in April, 1865, Jefferson Davis, after his flight from Richmond, met at Greensboro', N. C., Joseph E. Johnston, then in command of the army confronting Sherman, a species of council was held, at which the course to be pursued, in the then obviously desperate condition of affairs, was discussed. Johnston, knowing well the condition of things, and the consequent feeling among his men, when appealed to for his opinion bluntly said that the South felt it was whipped, and was tired of the war. Davis, on the other hand, was eager to continue the struggle. He insisted that in spite of the "terrible" disasters recently sustained, he would in three or four weeks have a large army in the field; and, further, expressed his confident belief that the Confederates could still win, and achieve their independence, if, as he expressed it, "our people will turn out."[2]

That Davis even then honestly so thought is very probable; and, looking only to the number of fighting men on each side available for service under proper conditions, he was right. And yet under existing conditions he was altogether wrong. As respects mere numbers, it is capable of demonstration that, at the close of the struggle, the preponderance was on the side of the Confederacy, and distinctly so. The Union at that time had, it is said, a million men on its muster rolls. Possibly that number were consuming rations and drawing

[1] See note, *infra*, 282.
[2] Alfriend, *Life of Jefferson Davis*, pp. 622–626; B. T. Johnson, *Life of Joseph E. Johnston*, p. 219; Roman, *Military Operations of General Beauregard*, Vol. II, p. 665. Roman here prints a letter, dated March 30, 1868, from J. E. Johnston to Beauregard, giving his recollections of what was said and took place at the Greensboro' meeting of April 12–13, 1861. See *infra*, 241, 325.

R

pay. If such was the case, acting on the offensive, and deep in a vast hostile country, the Union might possibly have been able to put 500,000 men in the fighting line. On the other side, notwithstanding the heavy drain of four years of war, the fighting strength of the Confederacy at the close cannot have been less than two-thirds of its normal strength. The South should have been able to muster, on paper, 900,000 men. Such a force, or even the half of it, acting on the defensive in a region inadequately supplied with railroad facilities, — and these, such as they were, very open to attack, — should have been ample for every purpose. Texas alone had in 1860 a white population larger by nearly 100,000 than the white population of the Transvaal and Orange Free State combined in 1899.[1] Texas covered an area of 265,780 square miles, as against the 161,296 of the combined African republics; and this vast region was rendered accessible in 1861 by some 300 miles of railroad, or about one mile of railroad of most inferior construction to each 900 square miles of territory.[2] The character of the soil made heavy movement, slow and difficult always, at times impossible. In such a region and under such conditions, how could an invading force have been fed or transported, or kept open its lines of communication? Thus, on the face of the facts, Davis was right, and the South, if it chose to defend itself, was invincible.

And here we find ourselves face to face with one of the greatest of the many delusions in the popular conception of

[1] According to the best authorities, the combined white population of the two South African States at the beginning of hostilities was approximately 323,113; the white population of Texas was returned in the census of 1860 at 421,294.

[2] The census of 1860 returned 307 miles of railroad in operation in Texas; in 1903 it was stated that 11,256 miles were in operation. The proportion of railroad mileage to area was, in 1860, one mile to each 865 square miles of territory; in 1903 it was one mile to each 24 square miles.

practical warfare. In his remark at the Greensboro' conference about the South "turning out," Jefferson Davis seems to have fallen into it. The South, at that stage of the conflict, simply could not "turn out." So doing was a physical impossibility. It was Napoleon who said that an army was like a serpent, it moves on its belly. In dealing with practical conditions in warfare, it has always to be borne in mind that an army is a most complex organization; and its strength is measured and limited not by the census number of men available, but the means at hand of arming, equipping, clothing, feeding and transporting those men. This topic is elsewhere discussed in the present publication;[1] here, and in this connection, it is sufficient to say that, so far as its military organizations were concerned, for those of all grades, from the general in command to the camp-follower, after January, 1865, the possibility of organized resistance on the part of the Confederacy no longer existed. The choice lay between surrender and disbandment; or, as General Johnston subsequently wrote: "We, without the means of purchasing supplies of any kind, or procuring or repairing arms, could continue this war only as robbers or guerillas."[2]

The next question is: How had this result been brought about? How did it happen that five millions of people in a country of practically unlimited extent, and one almost invulnerable to attack, were physically incapable of further organized resistance? How did they come to be so devoid of arms, food, clothing and means of transport? In other words, what is the correct answer to the query suggested by Mr. Rhodes? He certainly does not give it; but, perplexing

[1] *Infra*, 325.
[2] Johnston to Beauregard, March 30, 1868; Roman, *Beauregard*, Vol. II, p. 665.

as the question is, a plausible answer can surely at this late day be at least approximated.

When it comes to rendering a judgment on passing events or on contemporaries, Lord Bacon long ago classed foreign nations and posterity together, to them making his individual appeal for "name and memory." To like effect another and more modern writer has pronounced "a foreign nation a kind of contemporaneous posterity." This, in both cases, obviously because in the opinion and estimate of a "foreign nation" it may be possible to find, in degree at least, that detachment and sense of proportion always incompatible with nearness and familiarity. A recourse to this tribunal, for what it is worth, is in the present case possible. Blackwood's *Edinburgh Magazine* for July, 1866, contains a somewhat elaborate contemporaneous paper entitled *The Principles and Issues of the American Struggle*.[1] Philosophizing over the outcome of the struggle rather more than a year after it had been brought to a close, the writer of the article thus answered Mr. Rhodes's query some thirty-eight years in advance of the time when Mr. Rhodes put it: —

"By dint of obstinate endurance — by dint of illimitable paper money and credit — by dint of foreign soldiers from Ireland and Germany who swarmed into the country, allured by bounties on enlistment varying from £100 to £200 sterling per head — by dint of sacrificing general after general, however brave and able, who could not gain a victory — by dint of a blockade of the sea-board, producing in due time a famine, or something very like it, through the most fertile portions of the South; and last, but by no means least, by dint of the cowardice or incapacity of the British government, that refused to unite with that of France in acknowledging the independence of the South — the Northern people conquered their Southern brethren."

[1] Blackwood's *Edinburgh Magazine*, July, 1866, C, 31.

Here, then, is a foreign contemporaneous explanation, and one, in some respects, close to the mark. Yet it is not wholly satisfactory. It again is too general; for, though the writer is specific enough, he generalizes in his specification, omitting nothing that suggests itself, and emphasizing everything about equally. Further elimination and a more severe analysis are necessary.

Six contributing causes are specified. Let us, through the perspective of forty years, see which still stand as material. The initial two, "obstinate endurance" and "illimitable paper dollars and credit," we may pass over. The first goes without saying; and the last would not in itself have sufficed to accomplish the end sought in 1865, any more than it had sufficed to accomplish the end then sought, when, in the struggle with its revolted American provinces which ended in 1783, Great Britain, in like manner, had at its command "illimitable paper" notes and "credit," as against a worthless Continental currency. The allegation was simply fatuous. The third count also cuts no considerable figure in a revised summary. The backbone of the Union army at the close of the struggle, as at its beginning, was made up of Americans. The number of foreigners, Irish or German, drawn to the country by the temptation of bounties may have been considerable; but, as a factor of active, fighting strength it has been misunderstood and vastly exaggerated. In the early stages of the war, more than half a million men, nearly all Americans and young, were suddenly withdrawn from industrial life. A paralysis of production should necessarily have followed. That, as a matter of fact, it did not follow was due to an inrush of foreigners, filling the void thus created. The immigrants replenished the depleted ranks of industry, not those of the army in the field. This most interesting sociological and economical fact has since been demonstrated through a careful analysis of records and statistics.[1] On the other hand, any advantage the nationalists did actually derive from bounty-drawn, immigrant enlistments was far more than counterbalanced by the drastic conscription enforced throughout the Confederacy. Three factors now only remain for consideration. One of these, the sacrificing of those leaders who failed to win victories, is a feature of all warfare, and in no way peculiar to our civil strife. As a factor in results it was not especially noticeable there; and, moreover, there is no sort of question that both communities and those in authority are as a rule so constituted that a preference is felt for commanders in the field whose names are associated with bulletins of victory rather than with the habitually "unlucky," even though plausible in their explanations of failure. The writer of the paper referred to obviously had McClellan in mind; but, in his case, history, and the coming to light of historical material have more than justified the course finally pursued by Lincoln and Stanton towards that excellent organizer, but exceedingly insufficient field commander. Of the two remaining factors of success, — the blockade and absence of foreign intervention, — the last may be left out of consideration. It is useless to discuss historical problems from the point of view of what would have happened if something had occurred which in point of fact never did occur. On this foreign and contemporaneous judgment of conditions we are thus through elimination brought down to one factor, the blockade, as the controlling condition of Union success. In other words, that success was made possible by the undisputed naval and maritime supremacy of the national

[1] Fite, *Social and Industrial Conditions in the North during the Civil War*, 5–14.

government. Cut off from the outer world and all exterior sources of supply, reduced to a state of inanition by the blockade, the Confederacy was pounded to death.[1]

Or, to put the proposition in yet another form, in the game of warfare, maritime supremacy on the part of the North — what Admiral Mahan has since developed historically as the Influence of the Sea Power — even more than compensated for the military advantage of the defensive, and its interior strategic lines, enjoyed by the South. Such being the case, the greater command of men, supplies, munitions and transportation by one party to the conflict worked its natural result.

Unquestionably much could be said in support of this contention. More than plausible, it fairly explains an outcome otherwise inexplicable now, as contrary to all foreign expectation then. Without, however, going into any elaborate discussion of the arguments for and against it as a satisfactory historical postulate, but for present purposes accepting it as such, a distinct grasp and full recognition of the advantage in the struggle pertaining to the mastery of the sea is one of the most noticeable deficiencies in Mr. Rhodes's treatment of the outcome of the conflict. In this respect his narrative is lacking in a proper sense of proportion. As compared with the space devoted to the movements on land, he fails to give to the sea operations the emphasis properly belonging to them. Towards the close of that portion of his fifth volume devoted to a summary of the preceding narrative, Mr. Rhodes, it is true, does incidentally say that the "work of the United States navy was an affair of long patience unrelieved by the prospect of brilliant exploits; lacking the incitement of battle, it required discipline and character only the more. But the reward was great; for the blockade was one of the effective agencies in deciding the issue of the war."[2] This

[1] *Infra*, 317, 320, 321.   [2] Vol. V, p. 399.

is a somewhat faint recognition of services really decisive; but, such as it is, it may pass. As one reads Mr. Rhodes's narrative, however, it would hardly be supposed that a blockade existed at all, much less that it entered into the struggle as the essential pivot on which turned many of the most important of those land movements so fully described. For instance, an undisputed maritime supremacy made possible both Grant's operations in Virginia and Sherman's march to the sea.

To this general criticism an exception must be made in the case of the action between the *Monitor* and the *Merrimac*. To that a sufficiency of space (five pages) is given; for, obviously, on its result depended McClellan's strategy. Besides being temptingly dramatic in itself, it had to be dealt with in connection with land operations. But the capture of Hatteras Inlet (August 26, 1861) and of Port Royal (November 7, 1861) are incidentally mentioned in part of a twenty-three line paragraph, though strategically they were, and subsequently proved, of the utmost consequence, distinctly foreshadowing that process of devitalization as a result of which the Confederacy ultimately collapsed. Again, the taking of New Orleans, from every point of view one of the most important events of the war, as well as one of its most striking episodes, — a knife-thrust in the very vitals of the Confederacy, — is disposed of in two pages. The sinking of the *Alabama* by the *Kearsarge* is truly enough referred to "as of no moment towards terminating the war"; but its moral effect in Europe at a critical period was very memorable. Finally, to assert that the achievements of Admiral Farragut contributed not less than those of General Sherman to the downfall of the Confederacy may or may not be an exaggeration; but, on the part of the navy, it may safely be claimed that the running of the forts at the mouth of the

Mississippi, and the consequent fall of New Orleans, was as brilliant an operation, and one as triumphantly conducted, as the march through Georgia. It struck equal dismay into the hearts of the Southern leaders. Yet the name of Farragut appears but once in the index of Mr. Rhodes's fifth volume, in which he summarizes the war; and that once is in connection with Andrew Johnson's famous "swinging-round-the-circle" performance. Twelve lines of text are devoted to the battle of Mobile Bay, while two lines only are made to suffice for the capture of Wilmington, which closed the last inlet of the Confederacy, hermetically sealing it. Here, then, from Hatteras Inlet to Fort Fisher, — between August, 1861, and January, 1865, — is a consecutive series of operations, prime factors in the final result, and they are disposed of in ninety lines of a narrative covering 1350 pages! About a sixth of one per cent of the entire space is given to them. With Hilton Head, Hatteras Inlet, New Orleans, Hampton Roads, Mobile Bay, Wilmington and Cherbourg blazing imperishably on the record, Mr. Rhodes incidentally remarks that the work of the navy was "unrelieved by the prospect of brilliant exploits"! Nor do the names of those identified with our naval triumphs thunder in the general index. Judged by that test, six lines suffice for the allusions to Farragut, and five for those to Porter; while four solid columns are judged scarcely adequate for Grant and two for Sherman. This is clearly disproportionate. In some future edition an entire chapter for each year would not be too much to devote to an account of the operations of that arm of the Union service which on the sea counterbalanced the advantage of interior lines on the land which the Confederates so confidently counted upon, and of which all the military strategists or critics, whether domestic or foreign, so everlastingly wrote. To be steadily and effectually throttled from behind is not usually considered a negligible disadvantage, if suffered by one party to an otherwise not wholly unequal life-and-death grapple; and when the throttling process is from time to time accentuated by a spear thrust in the ribs or active knife-work in the back the consequences are apt to be contributory to defeat. In the matter of our maritime supremacy, the Confederacy so found it. As a Southern writer has in long reminiscence recently said: "Aptly did camp slang name the blockade the 'Conda.' It was the crush of the 'Conda' that squeezed us to death."

Passing to another topic of scarcely less importance, Mr. Rhodes's sense of correct proportion is again at fault. The Confederacy did not go into the conflict unadvisedly. On the contrary, its leaders gave what at the time they considered full consideration to all the factors on either side essential to success.[1] As was apparent in the outcome, they reckoned without their host; but, none the less, they did reckon. Unfortunately for it, the Southern community in the years prior to 1861 was phenomenally provincial. Judged by its literature and the published utterances of its men and women, particularly its women, it seemed — intellectually, socially, economically and physically — to be conscious only of itself. This characteristic, among many other phases of development, was inordinately and most offensively apparent in an undervaluation of its prospective opponent, both for char-

[1] For instance, in the very matter of a blockade, as an incident to war, James H. Hammond, then in the Senate from South Carolina, in a speech delivered in 1858, and presently referred to, thus summarily dismissed the idea as an absurdity: "We have three thousand miles of continental seashore line so indented with bays and crowded with islands that when their shore lines are added, we have twelve thousand miles. . . . Can you hem in such a territory as that? You talk of putting up a wall of fire around eight hundred and fifty thousand square miles so situated! How absurd!" — Selections from *Letters and Speeches* of James H. Hammond, pp. 311, 312.

acter and courage,¹ and in an overvaluation of the importance of the South as a commercial world-power. As respects the undervaluation of the prospective opponent, the mental condition of the South in 1861 was fairly expressed by General L. P. Walker, the first Confederate Secretary of War, when, on the occasion of the running up of the Confederate flag on the capitol of Montgomery, Alabama, on a day in early April, 1861, he pledged himself to the excited crowd there gathered to raise at no remote time the flag in question over "Faneuil Hall in the City of Boston." Curiously as it now sounds, there is no exaggeration in the statement that "at first flush of war the masses of the South really believed that one Southerner 'could whip a half-dozen Yankees and not half try.'"²

The explanation of this and other utterances of a similar character has since been very tersely stated by General Bradley T. Johnson, himself a Confederate, though born in Maryland, — at once jurist and veteran: "The Southern people for several generations had trained themselves into a vainglorious mood toward the Northern men. They believed that they were inconquerable by the North and that the men of the North were not their physical nor mental equals."² And, reviewing the conflict and outcome through the vista of thirty years, this typical Southron reached a conclusion, bearing directly on the query suggested by Mr. Rhodes: "The Confederate States were not crushed by overwhelming resources nor overpowering numbers. They were *out-thought* by the Northern men."³ As respects the

[1] "Vulgar, fanatical, cheating Yankees — hypocritical, if as women they pretend to real virtue; and lying, if as men they pretend to be honest." — W. H. Russell, *My Diary North and South*, Chap. XIX.
[2] T. C. De Leon, *Belles, Beaux and Brains in the 60's*, pp. 56, 394.
[3] *Memoir of the Life and Public Service of Joseph E. Johnston* (1891), pp. 60, 61.

other great factor of self-deception, the overvaluation of itself by the South as a commercial world-power, the mere mention of that delusion recalls to memory the once familiar, now quite forgotten, postulate, — "Cotton is King!" To the South its infatuation on this point was the fruitful mother of calamity; for the commercial supremacy of cotton, accepted as a fundamental truth, was made the basis of political action. The unquestioning faith in which that patriarchal community cherished this belief has now passed out of memory, and the statement of it savors of exaggeration. As a matter of fact, it does not admit of exaggeration. For instance, what modern historical presentation could be so framed as to exceed in strength, broadness and color the following from a speech delivered in the United States Senate, March 4, 1858? James H. Hammond, representing South Carolina, then said: —

"But if there were no other reason why we should never have war, would any sane nation make war on cotton? Without firing a gun, without drawing a sword, should they make war on us we could bring the whole world to our feet. The South is perfectly competent to go on one, two, or three years without planting a seed of cotton. . . . What would happen if no cotton was furnished for three years? I will not stop to depict what every one can imagine, but this is certain: England would topple headlong and carry the whole civilized world with her, save the South. No, you dare not make war on cotton. No power on earth dares to make war upon it. Cotton *is* King. Until lately the Bank of England was king, but she tried to put her screws as usual, the fall before the last, upon the cotton crop, and was utterly vanquished. The last power has been conquered. Who can doubt, that has looked at recent events, that cotton is supreme?"[1]

It would not be difficult to multiply almost indefinitely utterances like the above; but for the purpose in hand this

[1] Selections from the *Letters and Speeches* of James H. Hammond (New York, 1866), pp. 316, 317.

one will suffice. Intensely provincial, the idea was vulgarly commercial; in the jargon of the Stock Exchange, the South was satisfied that she had in her hand a corner on Cotton, and, if she so willed it, the World must walk up to her counter, and settle on any terms she saw fit to prescribe! As Russell, of the London *Times*, observed: "These tall, thin, fine-faced Carolinians are great materialists. Slavery perhaps has aggravated the tendency to look at all the world through parapets of cotton-bales and rice-bags, and, though more stately and less vulgar, the worshippers here are not less prostrate before the 'almighty dollar' than the Northerners."[1]

Thus in complete provincialism and childlike faith a community was willing to venture, and actually did venture, life, fortune and sacred honor on its contempt for those composing the largest part of the community of which they were themselves but a minority, and on the soundness of a commercial theory. In regard to the extent and implicit character of the faith held on both these points, no better witness could testify than Dr. William H. Russell, the once famous *Times* Crimean correspondent just referred to. Russell certainly had no prejudice against the South, or Southern men. On the contrary, he liked both; while he did not take kindly to the North as a whole, or to its people. A foreign observer with a remarkable faculty for vivid description, he was here to take notes and to portray things as they appeared. In South Carolina immediately after the bombardment of Sumter, he there mixed freely with the exponents of public sentiment. In his *Diary* he thus describes what he heard on the subject of Southern superiority and cotton supremacy, — he is recording what occurred at the Charleston Club on the evening of April 16, 1861, ex-governors of the State,

[1] *My Diary North and South*, Chap. XV.

senators, congressmen, and other prominent South Carolinians being of the company: —

"We talked long, and at last angrily, as might be between friends, of political affairs.

"I own it was a little irritating to me to hear men indulge in extravagant broad menace and rodomontade, such as came from their lips. 'They would welcome the world in arms with hospitable hands to bloody graves.' 'They never could be conquered.' 'Creation could not do it,' and so on. I was obliged to handle the question quietly at first, — to ask them 'if they admitted the French were a brave and warlike people!' 'Yes, certainly.' 'Do you think you could better defend yourselves against invasion than the people of France?' 'Well, no; but we'd make it pretty hard business for the Yankees.' 'Suppose the Yankees, as you call them, come with such preponderance of men and *matériel*, that they are three to your one, will you not be forced to submit?' 'Never.' 'Then either you are braver, better disciplined, more warlike than the people and soldiers of France, or you alone, of all the nations in the world, possess the means of resisting physical laws which prevail in war, as in other affairs of life.' 'No. The Yankees are cowardly rascals. We have proved it by kicking and cuffing them till we are tired of it; besides, we know John Bull very well. He will make a great fuss about non-interference at first, but when he begins to want cotton he'll come off his perch.' I found this was the fixed idea everywhere. The doctrine of 'cotton is king' — to us who have not much considered the question a grievous delusion or an unmeaning babble — to them is a lively all-powerful faith without distracting heresies or schisms."[1]

The following day, Dr. Russell was one of a party on an excursion down Charleston harbor, visiting Forts Sumter and Moultrie. In the course of the trip he met, among others, L. T. Wigfall, the notorious Texan who had recently resigned

[1] *My Diary North and South*, Chap. XIII. Later, April 19, the *Times* correspondent called on the governor of the State, F. W. Pickens. Of him he wrote: "The Governor writes very good proclamations, nevertheless, and his confidence in South Carolina is unbounded. If we stand alone, sir, we must win. They can't whip us." — *Ibid.* Chap. XVI.

a seat in the Senate of the United States to throw in his fortunes with the Confederacy. Dr. Russell says in his Diary, April 17: —

"For me there was only one circumstance which marred the pleasure of that agreeable reunion. Colonel and Senator Wigfall, who had not sobered himself by drinking deeply, in the plenitude of his exultation alluded to the assault on Senator Sumner as a type of the manner in which the Southerners would deal with the Northerners generally, and cited it as a good exemplification of the fashion in which they would bear their 'whipping.'"[1]

A day or two later, Mr. Bunch, the British consul at Charleston, who not long afterwards achieved a most unhappy diplomatic notoriety, entertained Dr. Russell at dinner. It was a "small and very agreeable party," but of the talk at that table the guest recorded: —

"It was scarcely very agreeable to my host or myself to find that no considerations were believed to be of consequence in reference to England except her material interests, and that these worthy gentlemen regarded her as a sort of appanage of their cotton kingdom. 'Why, sir, we have only to shut off your supply of cotton for a few weeks, and we can create a revolution in Great Britain. There are four millions of your people depending on us for their

[1] A month later Mr. Wigfall received, through his wife, from a correspondent in Providence, R. I., an ardent sympathizer with the Confederacy, a warning curiously characteristic of the period, and most suggestive of the estimate in which the Northern community was then held by those impregnated with Southern ideals: —

"I think, however, that you at the South are wrong to undervalue the courage and resources of the Northern States. They were no doubt less accustomed to the use of firearms — there are very few who know how to ride, and they are less fiery in their impulses. They are less disposed to fight, but they are not cowardly where their interests are concerned and will *fight for their money*. Where their property is at stake they will not hesitate to risk their lives. . . . I would not advise you of the South to trust too much in the idea that the Northerners will not fight; for I believe they will, and their numbers are overwhelming." — Mrs. D. G. Wright, *A Southern Girl in '61*, pp. 52, 53.

bread, not to speak of the many millions of dollars. No, sir, we know that England must recognize us,' etc.

"Liverpool and Manchester have obscured all Great Britain to the Southern eye. I confess the tone of my friends irritated me."

He next visited the leading merchants, bankers and brokers: —

"In one office I saw an announcement of a company for a direct communication by steamers between a southern port and Europe. 'When do you expect that line to be opened?' I asked. 'The United States cruisers will surely interfere with it.' 'Why, I expect, sir,' replied the merchant, 'that if those miserable Yankees try to blockade us, and keep you from our cotton, you'll just send their ships to the bottom and acknowledge us. That will be before autumn, I think.' It was in vain I assured him he would be disappointed. 'Look out there,' he said, pointing to the wharf, on which were piled some cotton bales; 'there's the key will open all our ports, and put us into John Bull's strong box as well.'"

A guest shortly after on the island plantation of Mr. Trescot, he there met Edmund Rhett, a member of a family prominent in South Carolina public life. The Rhett dwelling house and plantation were on Port Royal Island, a few miles only from the smaller island on which Mr. Trescot dwelt. They thus were neighbors. The stranger and guest describes the South Carolinian as "a very intelligent and agreeable gentleman," but from his lips also came the same old story. "'Look,' he said, 'at the fellows who are sent out by Lincoln to insult foreign courts by their presence.' I said that I understood Mr. Adams and Mr. Dayton were very respectable gentlemen, but I did not receive any sympathy; in fact, a neutral who attempts to moderate the violence of either side is very like an ice between two hot plates. Mr. Rhett is also persuaded that the Lord Chancellor sits on a cotton bale. 'You must recognize us, sir, before the end of October.'"[1]

But perhaps the curious and complete state of misapprehension, material and moral, then pervading the Southern community, has best been described by a Southerner who himself at the time shared in it to the full extent. Writing nearly fifty years later, he said, speaking of the very time described by Russell in the above extracts: "Two ideas, however, seemed to pervade all classes. One was that keystone dogma of secession, 'Cotton is king,' the other that the war — did one come — could not last over three months. The man who ventured dissent from either idea, back it by what logic he might, was looked upon as an idiot, if his disloyalty was not broadly hinted at."[2]

As respects the outcome of what may well enough be called the South's cotton campaign, Mr. Rhodes's narrative is again distinctly deficient. In fact the most far-reaching, and, in world effect, the most important of all the campaigns inaugurated and carried out by the Confederacy, in its result they sustained complete and disastrous defeat, — a defeat which entailed on them in the midst of the contest and in presence of the enemy, an entire change of front, economical, financial and diplomatic. This nowhere appears in Mr. Rhodes's narrative; and yet on this phase of the struggle both Confederate finance and Confederate diplomacy hinged. And here again the blockade comes to the front.

Had the theory as respects the potency of cotton on which

[1] This meeting was on April 28. A few days only more than six months later both the Rhetts and Mr. Trescot hurriedly abandoned their homes, immediately after the bombardment and capture of the forts at Hilton Head, November 7, 1861, by the expedition under command of Captain, afterwards Admiral, Dupont. All of the South Carolina sea-islands, as they were called, were thenceforth occupied by the Union forces.

[2] T. C. De Leon, *Belles, Beaux and Brains of the 60's* (1907), p. 50.

s

the South went into the war been sound, the blockade would have proved the Confederacy's most potent ally; for the blockade shut off from Europe its supply of cotton as it could have been shut off by no other possible agency. In so far the government of the Union played the game of the Confederacy, and played it effectively. In the early days of the struggle, they talked at Richmond of an export duty on their one great staple, and of inhibiting its outgo altogether; the blockade made any action of this nature quite unnecessary. Through the blockade the cotton-screw, so to speak, was applied to the fullest possible extent. Nor was the overthrow of the potentate brought about easily. He was well entrenched, and dethroning him entailed on the commercial world one of the most severe trials it has ever been called upon to pass through.[1] In this phase of the struggle Lancashire was the field of central battle; and there, as the result of a torture extending through eighteen months, the Confederate ikon was tumbled down. The catastrophe was complete; and the whole Southern program, economical, fiscal, and, at last, strategic, where it did not utterly collapse, underwent great change. The summer of 1862 marked the crisis; before that, as Mr. Rhodes truly states,[2] the Confederate policy was to keep cotton at home, and by withholding it to compel foreign recognition; after that, the one effort was to get it to market with a view to its conversion into ships, munitions of war and necessaries of life. Mr. Rhodes disposes of this crucial Confederate defeat lightly. He says: "As we have seen, [England and France] when they could not get cotton from America, got it elsewhere." The authority on which this statement is made does not appear; but it is not in accordance with the facts. In the early months of 1861 the estimated weekly consump-

[1] *Infra*, 405. [2] Vol. V, p. 382.

tion of cotton in Great Britain was 50,000 bales; at the close of 1862 it had fallen to 20,000 bales, inferior in weight as well as quality. Indeed, so bad was the quality that its manufacture was destructive to machinery. Of this greatly reduced quantity, moreover, a considerable portion — some twenty per cent — was the American product, run through the blockade. So great was the dearth that in September, 1862, the staple, which two years before had sold in Liverpool for fourpence a pound, had gone up until it touched the unheard-of price of half a crown. Cotton simply was not forthcoming from any quarter, and the commercial world was everywhere in search of substitutes for it.

To this subject Mr. Rhodes might well have devoted a chapter. As it stands, it is a case of anti-climax; introduced with a loud blast of trumpets, the potentate simply vanishes, — like Macbeth's witches, he made himself air. How, and what became of him, nowhere appears. Judging by Mr. Rhodes's narrative, one would infer that it was a case of insensible dissolution, or, as Mr. Lincoln might have phrased it, a disappearance "unbeknowns't." As an historical fact, it was very far otherwise.[1] Not all that Mr. Hammond and others predicted, or that the Confederate leaders confidently looked to see happen, actually did happen; but, none the less, the process involved a commercial and industrial disturbance of the first magnitude. The episode, too, carried with it a most instructive historical lesson as to the danger even nations incur from indulging with undue confidence in a theory, — in other words, the old South furnished in 1860-1861 a very striking illustration of the homely truth that the risks incident to what is humanly known as a condition of mental "cocksureness" are not confined to individuals. In 1861 that whole Southern com-

[1] *Infra*, 315-318.

munity was socially and economically daft. But no people and no period are exempt from such states of delusion. Within the memory of those now living, this country has been subject to a dozen such; but, fortunately, as respects the extent and awful character of the consequences of a delusion, the experience of the South was exceptional; for by their excess of over-confidence and utter misconception of the real facts of the case as respects the world at large, as well as both themselves and their immediate opponent, the people of the South brought down on their devoted heads the contents of the vials of wrath to the very dregs thereof. The vividness of it is now forgotten; but, at the time, the world-wide supremacy of King Cotton was a Southern dream from which the awakening must have been terribly bitter.

The first recorded indication of this awakening may be found in a speech made by William L. Yancey at an impromptu reception given him in the rotunda of the St. Charles Hotel at New Orleans, on his return in March, 1862, from that wholly abortive mission to Europe on which he had been sent by Jefferson Davis a year before. He had learned something in the course of his travels, and he then significantly said: "It is an error to say that 'Cotton is King.' It is not. It is a great and influential power in commerce, but not its dictator." A little foreign travel had educated that particular Southern prophet out of some of his provincialism. Almost immediately his words found an echo in Richmond, a Louisiana senator there sadly declaring in debate, "We have tested the powers of King Cotton and have found him to be wanting."[1] While three months later, in June, 1862, Alexander H. Stephens enun-

[1] Appleton's *Annual Cyclopædia*, 1862, p. 261, quoted by Rhodes, Vol. V, p. 411.

ciated too late the correct principle. They had been possessed with the idea, he told them, that "cotton was a political power. There was the mistake, — it is only a commercial power."[1]

Passing to the other topics in the treatment of which the narrative of Mr. Rhodes, though sufficiently full, seems from another point of view open to criticism, reference may next be made to his account of Sherman's famous march to the sea in November, 1864, and Grant's advance on Richmond in May, 1864. Mr. Rhodes quotes General Sherman as saying in his *Memoirs:* "Were I to express my measure of the relative importance of the March to the Sea and of that from Savannah northward, I would place the former at one and the latter at ten, or the maximum." We are then told, in a foot-note to the same page,[2] that General Schofield was of a different opinion. "Considered," he said in his *Forty-six Years* (p. 348), "as to its military results, Sherman's march cannot be regarded as more than I have stated — a grand raid. The defeat and practical destruction of Hood's army in Tennessee was what paved the way to the speedy termination of the war, which the capture of Lee by Grant fully accomplished; and the result ought to have been essentially the same as to time if Sherman's march had never been made."

[1] What is known as the alternative Confederate fiscal policy is referred to, and discussed, by Mr. Rhodes (Vol. V, pp. 381, 382). There is in the appendix to Roman's *Life of Beauregard* (Vol. II, pp. 674–680) an elaborate letter on this subject written by Mr. Stephens to Beauregard in 1882, seventeen years after the close of the struggle. In the letter he quotes at length from a speech made by him at Crawfordville, Ga., in the fall of 1862. He then said: "The great error of those who supposed that King Cotton would compel the English ministry to recognize our government and break the blockade, and who will look for the same result from the total abandonment of its culture, consists in mistaking the nature of the kingdom of the potentate. His power is commercial and financial, not political." [2] Vol. V, p. 107.

On this point Mr. Rhodes expresses no opinion. He wisely leaves it for the military critics to fight it out among themselves. At the time, however, and in Europe, this view of the relative importance of operations did not obtain. Far from it. Schofield, of course, refers to Sherman's march north from Savannah, through the Carolinas; but it is open to grave doubt whether his estimate of the strategic importance of that march, or Sherman's estimate of its relative importance as compared with that through Georgia, are either of them correct. While, so far as the fall of the Confederacy was concerned, both exercised great influence on the outcome, there is good ground for belief that the march through Georgia was the more potent in influence of the two. It was so for an obvious reason. In war, as in most other affairs in which mankind gets itself involved, moral effects count for a good deal; and especially is this so with somewhat volatile and excitable communities, such as that inhabiting the South unquestionably was. But, so far as Europe was concerned, it is safe to assert that no other operation of the entire war was productive of a moral effect in any way comparable with that caused by the march to the sea. Indeed, coming as it did and when it did, it is not too much to say it was an epochal event in that it marked the turning of the tide of European and especially of English opinion as respects the United States and things American.

James Russell Lowell wrote in those years a well-remembered essay "Upon a Certain Condescension in Foreigners"; and, during the earlier stages of the Civil War, this "condescension" resolved itself quite naturally into a studied tone of scorn, in no way veiled. The change which has since become so marked in this respect began with Sherman's march. That march in a way smote the foreign imagination; and the whole course of subsequent events has

SOME PHASES OF THE CIVIL WAR 263

served to promote what has now developed into a revolution in tone and estimate. As every one realizes, Lowell's "foreigner" has undergone a total change; his "condescension" is of the past. The beginning of that change may best perhaps be traced through the utterances of the European press. Up to the autumn of 1864, and the reëlection of Lincoln, the general tone of the European and especially of the English periodicals and papers was one of exaggerated admiration for Confederate valor and leadership; while, on the other hand, the leadership and courage of the Union side were referred to with studied contumely. Sometimes, however, the contempt was equally distributed over both parties to the fray. The famous remark attributed at least to Von Moltke is still remembered, that he "did not have time to devote to the study of the combats of two armed mobs." But a much more curious and illustrative utterance was one of Charles Lever, the Irish military novelist, who, most unfortunately for himself, chose as the time and place in which to deliver himself the January *Blackwood's* of 1865. The paper was, of course, prepared some time before. By mere ill luck, however, it appeared in London just as Sherman put in his appearance at Savannah. In this paper Mr. Lever undertook to compare the American combatants to two inmates of a lunatic asylum playing chess. They went through moves similar to those of chess, but without the slightest comprehension of the game. He then goes on: "Now, does not this immensely resemble what we are witnessing this moment in America? There are the two madmen engaged in a struggle, not one single rule nor maxim of which they comprehend. Moving cavalry like infantry, artillery like a wagon train, violating every principle of the game, till at length one cries Checkmate, and the other, accepting the defeat that is claimed against him, deplores his mishap, and sets to work for another contest. ... Just, however, as I feel assured, nobody who ever played chess would have dignified with that name the strange performance of the madmen, so am I convinced that none would call this struggle a war. It is a fight — a very big fight, if you will, and a very hard fight too, but not war."[1] There is much more to the same effect, the intensely ludicrous side of which at just that juncture the genial Irishman himself subsequently appreciated most keenly. What I have quoted will, however, suffice for the purpose of present illustration. At the very time Mr. Lever was thus rashly committing himself in cold print, General Sherman was entering on his famous march; and, while that march was in progress, the daily tone of the London newspapers was pitched in much the same key as that of Mr. Lever's lucubration in the forthcoming number of *Blackwood's*. The outcome of the move of the "Yankee" general was looked for with a contemptuous interest: it clearly was not war; a harebrained effort, dictated probably by desperation, it could end only in disaster; most probably it was an ill-considered attempt at getting out of an impossible military situation. But one day the tidings came that the heads of Sherman's columns had emerged on the sea-coast, that they had made short work of the forces there found to oppose them, and that Savannah had fallen. The Union army and the Union navy had struck hands! The announcement seemed absolutely to take away the breath of the foreign critics, — social, military, journalistic. An undeniably original and brilliant strategic blow had been struck; an operation, the character of which could neither be ignored nor

---

[1] Cornelius O'Dowd upon *Men and Women and other Things in General*, Part XII, The Fight over the Way. *Blackwood's Edinburgh Magazine*, Vol. XCVII, pp. 57–59.

mistaken, had been triumphantly carried through to a momentous result; the thrust — and such a thrust! — had penetrated the vitals of the Confederacy; — what next? From that moment the end was plainly foreshadowed. Europe recognized that a new power of unknown strength, but undeniable military capacity, was thenceforth to be reckoned with.

To one feature, and one feature only, in Mr. Rhodes's account of this memorable war episode, is there occasion here to allude. The historian passes somewhat gently over the pronounced vandalism which characterized Sherman's operations from Atlanta to Savannah; and yet more from Savannah to Raleigh. It is referred to, indeed, both generally, and more especially in connection with what occurred in South Carolina, reaching a climax at Columbia; but the treatment is, notwithstanding, distinctly perfunctory.[1] The other and more realistic side is portrayed in sufficient detail, and with reference to chapter and verse, in General Bradley T. Johnson's *Life of Joseph E. Johnston*.[2] It there appears what Sherman meant by his famous aphorism "War is Hell." The truth is that in 1864–1865 the conflict had lasted too long for the patience of the combatants. The defence of the South had been unreasonably stubborn. The rules and limitations of civilized warfare, so far as non-combatants

[1] "It seems probable that the inhabitants of North Carolina were better treated than had been those of the sister State. Nevertheless correction of the bad habits engendered in the soldiery by the system of foraging upon the country was only gradually accomplished and the irregular work of stragglers was not circumscribed by State boundary lines. . . . The men who followed Sherman were probably more humane generally than those in almost any European army that marched and fought before our Civil War, but any invading host in the country of the enemy is a terrible scourge. On the other hand, there is considerable Southern evidence of depredations committed by Wheeler's cavalry." — Vol. V, pp. 102, 104.

[2] Chaps. XI, XII, XIII, pp. 119–225.

were concerned, were no longer observed, and Sherman's advancing army was enveloped and followed by a cloud of irresponsible stragglers, known throughout the country as "bummers," who were simply for the time being desperadoes bent on pillage and destruction, — subject to no discipline, amenable to no law. They were looked upon then by the North, weary of the war, with a half-humorous leniency; but, in reality, a band of Goths, their existence was a disgrace to the cause they professed to serve. It is not a pleasant admission, but the historic, if ungrateful, truth is that, as respects what are euphemistically termed the "severities" of warfare, the record made by our armies during the latter stages of the conflict will not bear comparison with that of the Army of Northern Virginia while in Pennsylvania during the Gettysburg campaign.[1] Lee's memorable general order (No. 73) dated at Chambersburg, June 27, 1863, is well known, and need not be quoted; but there was truth in the reference to those opposed to him when in it he said, "No greater disgrace could befall the army, and through it our whole people, than the perpetration of barbarous outrages upon the unarmed and defenceless, and the wanton destruction of private property, that have marked the course of the enemy in our own country. It will be remembered that we make war only upon armed men." Our own methods during the final stages of the conflict were sufficiently described by General Sheridan, when, during the Franco-Prussian War, as the guest of Bismarck, he declared against humanity in warfare, contending that the correct policy was to treat a hostile population with the utmost rigor, leaving them, as he expressed it, "nothing but their eyes to weep with over the war."[2]

[1] *Infra*, 308.
[2] *Infra*, 294.

In other words, a veteran of our civil strife, General Sheridan, advocated in an enemy's country the sixteenth-century practices of Tilly, described by Schiller, and the later devastation of the Palatinate policy of Louis XIV, commemorated by Goethe. In the twenty-first century, perhaps, partisan feeling as regards the Civil War performances having by that time ceased to exist, American investigators, no longer regardful of a victor's self-complacency, may treat the episodes of our struggle with the same even-handed and outspoken impartiality with which Englishmen now treat the revenges of the Restoration, or Frenchmen the dragonnades of the Grand Monarque. But when that time comes, the page relating to what occurred in 1864 in the valley of the Shenandoah, in Georgia, and in the Carolinas, — a page which Mr. Rhodes somewhat lightly passes over, — will probably be rewritten in characters of far more decided import.

One final topic; dealt with by Mr. Rhodes in his fourth volume rather than in the fifth, it still occupies a prominent place in his narrative, and its treatment necessarily involves a man who, first and last, for good or evil, will assuredly stand forth in history as one of Massachusetts' most conspicuous contributions to our Great Rebellion period. The topic is that Virginia campaign which made sadly memorable the spring and summer of 1864; the individual, General B. F. Butler. It may well be questioned whether Mr. Rhodes has either done justice, or fully meted out justice, to the episode or to the man.

And, primarily, something remains to be said of Grant's strategy in that campaign, no less memorable than bloody. Reasons might readily be adduced for deeming the plan for the operations this campaign necessarily involved much better considered, and more creditable to him, than would be inferred from Mr. Rhodes's narrative. Mr. Rhodes then, secondarily, fails to place where it belongs the grave responsibility for the failure of Grant's plan with the awful loss of life therein involved. Grant's original scheme assumed the active and harmonious coöperation of three distinct armies, —that of the Potomac, under General Meade; that of the James, operating in, or from, the military department of which General Butler was in command, but with General W. F. Smith in immediate charge of field movements; and, finally the Ninth Corps, 15,000 strong, under General Burnside. Grant himself, with independent and movable headquarters, was present in the field of operations, thereby insuring the necessary concentration and directness of movement. Meade, with the Army of the Potomac, was to advance and engage Lee, holding the Confederate army of NorthernVirginia fully occupied; Burnside, meanwhile, was to be in reserve, immediately in Meade's rear; and, while Lee was thus occupied, the Army of the James, composed of two corps, the Tenth and Eighteenth, and in all some 35,000 to 40,000 strong, was to push forward vigorously, threatening Richmond, and jeopardizing Lee's communications. Thus an important, if not vital, part in the plan of operations depended on the Army of the James. Opposed to that completely equipped and numerically formidable command, was a wholly inadequate and widely scattered force under General Beauregard, recently (April 15) assigned to duty, and not yet on the ground.[1] If by an offensive movement, intelligently conceived and skilfully as well as vigorously handled, the Confederate line could be broken and thrown back into Richmond, Lee's rear would

---

[1] Beauregard was at Weldon, N. C., from April 22 to May 10, waiting the development of the Union plan of campaign. He did not reach Petersburg until May 10.

SOME PHASES OF THE CIVIL WAR 269

be exposed, his lines of communication threatened, and he must, abandoning Richmond, have fallen back towards Lynchburg or the Carolinas. Grant then proposed to follow him up, hanging doggedly on his rear, and catch Lee between an upper and a nether millstone, — the Army of the James holding him in check until the Army of the Potomac, hurrying up, could force a decisive battle.

Grant's orders were framed accordingly. To Meade he wrote: "Lee's army will be your objective point. Wherever Lee goes, there you will go also. Gillmore will join Butler with about 10,000 men from South Carolina. Butler can reduce his [Fortress Monroe garrison] so as to take 23,000 men into the field directly to his front. The force will be commanded by Major-General W. F. Smith. With Smith and Gillmore, Butler will seize City Point, and operate against Richmond from the south side of the river. His movement will be simultaneous with yours."[1] At the same time Grant wrote to Butler as follows: Major-General Smith "is ordered to report to you to command the troops sent into the field from your own department. . . . The fact that Richmond is to be your objective point, and that there is to be coöperation between your force and the Army of the Potomac, must be your guide." Butler was at once to seize City Point, and there, Grant wrote, "concentrate all your troops for the field as rapidly as you can. From City Point directions cannot be given at this time for your further movements." Holding a firm base on the south bank of the James, the force from Butler's department, under the field command of Smith, was thus left free to move in any direction its commander saw fit; and "should the enemy be forced into his intrenchments in Richmond, the Army of the Potomac would follow, and by means of transports the

[1] Grant to Meade, April 9, 1864, *Personal Memoirs*, Vol. II, p. 135.

two armies would become a unit."[1] Such were Butler's instructions; meanwhile of Smith, who was "to command the troops sent into the field," Grant at the same time wrote to Halleck, General Smith "is possessed of one of the clearest military heads in the army; is very practical and industrious. No man in the service is better qualified than he for our largest commands."[2] General Smith "is really one of the most efficient officers in service, readiest in expedients, and most skilful in the management of troops in action."[3] Grant's orders were defective in one respect. Given necessarily to Butler as the major-general commanding the Military Department, they did not, regardless of Butler's feelings, ambitions or desires, distinctly specify that he was to confine himself strictly to departmental duties, with his headquarters at Norfolk or at Fortress Monroe, leaving Smith in full command of all operations in the field and in direct communication with Grant himself. Grant was yet to make himself acquainted with Butler's peculiarities as a man and his military limitations. Butler, in no way disposed to be ignored or relegated to purely departmental functions, availed himself of the opportunity thus afforded, and assumed full field command. Grant acquiesced, evidently hoping that Butler would in active operations allow himself to be guided by Smith.

Such, however, was in no way Butler's purpose. Eager for military distinction, inordinately self-confident until face-to-face with an opponent in actual battle, when, on the night of May 5, the Army of the James was landed from the transports at Bermuda Hundreds, Butler was there in full command. The movement was a complete surprise to

[1] Grant to Butler, April 2, 1864, *Butler's Book*, p. 630; *War Records*, Serial No. 95, p. 15.
[2] Grant to Stanton, November 12, 1863, *Chattanooga to Petersburg*, p. 15.
[3] Grant to Halleck, July 1, 1864, *ibid.* p. 29.

the Confederates. By mere chance General Hagood's South Carolina brigade was on its way to Richmond. Suddenly called into field service from garrison duty at Charleston, the men composing it were little better than militia, and, as subsequent operations showed, unreliable in presence of resolute attack.[1] A detachment of this brigade, some 600 strong, had been pushed forward by rail from Petersburg, and as the men jumped off the platform cars at Walthall Junction a little before five o'clock on the afternoon of May 6, to their complete surprise they found themselves in the presence of a brigade of the Army of the James, thrown forward by Butler to seize the railroad at that point. The Confederate detachment had no artillery and no supports. Those composing it should have been incontinently captured; but the opportunity, a great one, was lost. A weak attack was repulsed; and, according to the Confederate rendering, "Thus were Petersburg and Richmond barely saved by the opportune presence and gallant conduct of Hagood's command. It was upon that occasion that General Butler's forces were baffled and beaten off in their attempt to seize the Richmond railroad above Petersburg."[2] "The authorities at Richmond were now in a state of great excitement. The enemy had been repulsed on the Richmond railroad, and, to all appearance, had abandoned his original intention of investing Petersburg; but where he would next attempt to strike was the all-absorbing question."[3] At this juncture Beauregard had not yet arrived from Weldon; nor were there 3000 men all told south of Walthall Junction, or available for the defence of Petersburg. The key to the whole military situation was unprotected. "Meanwhile troops were hastily called for from all quarters," and on the 10th Beauregard

[1] Hagood, *Memoirs*, 221, 224.
[2] Roman, *Beauregard*, Vol. II, p. 198.   [3] *Ibid.* p. 199.

arrived, with the first body of reinforcements. The golden opportunity was rapidly passing. On the evening of the 9th Generals Gillmore and Smith, being then at Swift's Creek, about four miles north of Petersburg, united in a written communication to General Butler suggesting that the whole command should be directed on Petersburg, instead of Richmond, as previously agreed. They claimed that "all the work of cutting the [rail]road, and perhaps capturing the city, can be accomplished in one day." Refusing even to consider the suggestion, General Butler, the same evening, returned a reply beginning as follows: —

"GENERALS, — While I regret an infirmity of purpose which did not permit you to state to me, when I was personally present, the suggestion which you made in your written note, but left me to go to my headquarters under the impression that another and far different purpose was advised by you, I shall not yield to the written suggestions, which imply a change of plan made within thirty minutes after I left you. Military affairs cannot be carried on, in my judgment, with this sort of vacillation. The information I have received from the Army of the Potomac convinces me that our demonstration should be toward Richmond, and I shall in no way order a crossing of the Appomattox for the purpose suggested in your note." [1]

The date of this correspondence (May 9) is important. The battle of the Wilderness had been fought on May 5 and 6, that of Spottsylvania was to begin on May 10, and not until the 12th was the famous assault made on Lee's salient. The Confederate army was hard pressed. To what extent at just this juncture would sudden tidings of the capture of Petersburg, and the consequent severing of his line of southern sea-coast communication, have affected Lee's mind and the entire strategic situation? And it was

[1] *War Records*, Serial No. 68, p. 35.

just then that Butler, contemptuously and insolently ignoring the recommendations of his two subordinates, allowed Beauregard to establish himself at Petersburg, while the Army of the James made "a demonstration" toward Richmond! In his official report of the whole campaign Grant subsequently said of this "demonstration" that "the time thus consumed lost to us the benefit of the surprise and capture of Richmond and Petersburg, enabling, as it did, Beauregard to collect his loose forces in North and South Carolina, and bring them to the defence of those places."[1] The occasion was great, and Beauregard showed himself equal to it. Rapidly concentrating his scattered and scanty command, he, on the 15th, assumed the offensive. The next day (16th) he attacked Butler at Drewry's Bluff. "Butler's army was driven back, hemmed in, and reduced to comparative impotency, though not captured. The danger threatening Richmond was, for the time being, averted."[2]

The Army of the Potomac was at that juncture fighting at Spottsylvania fiercely and futilely, and not until June 3, a fortnight later, did the slaughter of Cold Harbor occur. The great opportunity of May 9, pointed out to Butler by his lieutenants, had been allowed wholly to escape; Lee's rear and communications were secure; Butler was safely "bottled up"; the Army of the Potomac, sorely crippled, had sustained losses as heavy as they were unnecessary; Grant's whole plan of campaign had gone to pieces. Had Butler on May 9, correctly taking in the military situation, complied with the suggestion of his two corps commanders, Petersburg must have fallen into his hands; Lee would perforce have been compelled to fall back on Richmond; the Cold Harbor

[1] *War Records*, Serial No. 95, p. 19.
[2] Roman, *Beauregard*, Vol. II, p. 209.

assaults would not have occurred; and all subsequent operations would have been other than they were.

Prior to this, May 7, General Butler had written a letter marked "Confidential" to Senator Wilson of Massachusetts, then on the Senate Military Committee, beginning thus: "My Dear Sir: — I must take the responsibility of asking you to bring before the Senate at once the name of General Gillmore, and have his name rejected by your body." Nominated for promotion to the rank of Major-General, the nomination of General Gillmore was then pending.[1] Under such circumstances the state of affairs in the Army of the James not unnaturally became in May so unsatisfactory that General Halleck at the request of General Grant sent (May 21) Generals Meigs and Barnard to investigate. On the 24th they gave it as their opinion that "an officer of military experience and knowledge [should be placed] in command. . . . General Butler . . . has not experience and training to enable him to direct and control movements in battle. . . . General Butler evidently desires to retain command in the field. If his desires must be gratified, withdraw Gillmore, place Smith in command of both corps under the supreme command of Butler. . . . You will thus have a command which will be a unit, and General Butler will probably be guided by Smith, and leave to him the suggestions and practical execution of army movements ordered. Success would be more certain were Smith in command untrammelled, and General Butler remanded to the administrative duties of the departments."[2] Difficulties naturally suggested themselves to the adoption of the course thus recommended. General Gillmore was relieved of his command early in June,[3] and

---

[1] *Butler's Book*, pp. 644, 1065.
[2] *War Records*, Serial No. 69, p. 178.
[3] *Butler's Book*, p. 679.

the ill-feeling between Butler and Smith culminated, June 21, in a characteristic and extremely sharp correspondence,[1] as a result of which General Smith requested to be relieved of the command of the Eighteenth Corps. Then followed one of the most extraordinary and inexplicable episodes of the war. Grant wrote (July 1) to Halleck, advising him of the situation. He said: "I regret the necessity of asking for a change of commanders here, but General Butler, not being a soldier by education or experience, is in the hands of his subordinates in the execution of all orders military." Grant, however, hesitated "to recommend his [Butler's] retirement."[2] This brought out a most suggestive reply (July 3) from Halleck. In it he said: "It was foreseen from the first that you would eventually find it necessary to relieve General B. on account of his total unfitness to command in the field, and his generally quarrelsome character."[3] The Chief of Staff then went on to discuss the several dispositions which might be made of Butler, significantly pointing out the danger to be apprehended from "his talent at political intrigue, and his facilities for newspaper abuse." He finally suggested, "Why not leave General Butler in the local command of his department, including North Carolina, Norfolk, Fort Monroe, Yorktown, &c., and make a new army corps of the part of the Eighteenth under Smith." The letter closed with a sentence indicative of the personal apprehension General Butler seemed to excite in the breasts of those put in any position antagonistic to him. The official Chief of Staff said: "As General Butler claims to rank me, I shall give him no orders wherever he may go, without the special direction of yourself or the Secretary of War." Three days later, July 6, Grant

[1] *War Records*, Serial No. 81, pp. 299–301; *From Chattanooga to Petersburg*, pp. 28, 155, 186–188.
[2] *War Records*, Serial No. 81, p. 559.   [3] *Ibid.* p. 598.

wrote to Halleck: "Please obtain an order assigning the troops of the Department of Virginia and North Carolina serving in the field to the command of Major-General W. F. Smith, and order Major-General Butler, commanding department, to his headquarters, Fortress Monroe." This request was simply a reversion, after the mischief had been done, to Grant's original plan of operations; and, in accordance with it General Order No. 225 was at once issued. Curiously enough, the original order, forwarded both to Butler and Smith,[1] read that "Maj. Gen. Smith is assigned by the President to the command of the corps," etc.; in the order as formally made public the words "by the President" do not appear. A presidential canvass was now in progress, and, apparently, Lincoln did not care to invite further complications by any act of direct interposition which would make him the objective of Butler's "talent at political intrigue, and his facilities for newspaper abuse." Under the circumstances, the omission of the words specified was probably judicious. The order, though in conformity with the recommendation of Generals Meigs and Barnard of six weeks before (May 24), was, of course, highly objectionable to General Butler. Immediately on receipt of it at Bermuda Hundred he rode over to the headquarters of General Grant, and asked if "this was his act and his desire." Grant replied: "But, I don't want this." Colonel Mordecai afterwards wrote, "Gen'l Butler returned to camp about dusk, as I recall it, and, as he dismounted from his horse, remarked to a number of his staff officers who were near him, 'Gentlemen, the order will be revoked to-morrow.'"[2] Not only was the order revoked, but General Butler's field command was extended so as to include the Nineteenth Corps, while General Smith was

[1] *Butler's Book*, p. 695; *From Chattanooga to Petersburg*, p. 33.
[2] *Chattanooga to Petersburg*, p. 189.

"relieved from the command of the Eighteenth Army Corps, and [directed to] proceed to New York, and await further orders."[1]

As respects the details of what transpired at the interview above referred to, General James H. Wilson, whose relations at the time and subsequently were intimate with both General Grant and Smith, wrote in 1904 as follows: —

"It must be confessed that Grant's explanations of his later attitude towards Smith, and of the reasons for relieving him and restoring Butler to command, were neither full nor always stated in the same terms. He ignores the subject entirely in his memoirs, but it so happens that Mr. Dana, then Assistant Secretary of War, was sitting with General Grant when Butler, clad in full uniform, called at headquarters, and was admitted. Dana describes Butler as entering the General's presence with a flushed face and a haughty air, holding out the order relieving him from command in the field, and asking: 'General Grant, did you issue this order?' To which Grant in a hesitating manner replied: 'No, not in that form.' Dana, perceiving at this point that the subject under discussion was an embarrassing one, and that the interview was likely to be unpleasant, if not stormy, at once took his leave, but the impression made upon his mind by what he saw while present was that Butler had in some measure 'cowed' his commanding officer. What further took place neither General Grant nor Mr. Dana has ever said. *Butler's Book*, however, contains what purports to be a full account of the interview, but it is to be observed that it signally fails to recite any circumstance of an overbearing nature."[2]

The disposition of commands made in Special Order No. 62, above referred to, continued in force until the Wilmington expedition and the famous powder-boat explosion of the following December. During the months intervening much had happened. July, 1864, came about during one of the most depressing, if not the most depressing, period of the whole

[1] Special Order No. 62, July 19, 1864; *Butler's Book*, p. 1087.
[2] *Life and Services of W. F. Smith*, pp. 112, 113.

struggle. Grant's movement against Richmond and Lee's army had failed, after excessive loss of life; Sherman's movement against Atlanta had not yet succeeded; Washington was threatened from the valley of the Shenandoah; a presidential election was immediately impending; the country at large, in deepest mourning because of losses in the field, was also in a state of extreme discouragement; the administration and the Union generals in the field stood in manifest fear of Butler. Six months later the whole aspect of affairs had undergone a complete and, indeed, almost magical change. Grant, it is true, was still held in firm check before Petersburg: but Sherman had marched through Georgia and captured Savannah; Sheridan had won his victories in the valley; Lincoln had been reëlected; the Confederacy was believed to be in extremities. Under these circumstances that might safely be done which in July had seemed to involve a political risk. Accordingly, on January 4, 1865, Grant wrote to the Secretary of War: "I am constrained to request the removal of Maj. Gen. B. F. Butler from the command of the Department of Virginia and North Carolina. I do this with reluctance, but the good of the service requires it. In my absence General Butler necessarily commands, and there is a lack of confidence felt in his military ability, making him an unsafe commander for a large army. His administration of the affairs of his department is also objectionable."[1] Three days later (January 7) the following was issued from the War Department: —

"General Order No. 1.
"I. By direction of the President of the United States, Maj. Gen. Benjamin F. Butler is relieved from the command of the Department of North Carolina and Virginia. . . .

[1] *War Records*, Serial No. 96, p. 29.

"II. Major-General Butler on being relieved will repair to Lowell, Mass., and report by letter to the Adjutant-General of the Army."

Of General Butler as a field officer in active military service General W. F. Smith wrote to General Grant, after asking to be relieved from further service in the Department of Virginia and North Carolina, — "I want simply... to ask you how you can place a man in command of two army corps, who is as helpless as a child on the field of battle and as visionary as an opium-eater in council?"[1] Of the same commander, Admiral David D. Porter wrote to the Secretary of the Navy, December 29, 1864, immediately after the withdrawal of the first expedition against Wilmington, subsequently to the powder-boat fiasco of December 24: "If this temporary failure succeeds in sending General Butler into private life, it is not to be regretted."[2]

Such is the military record. In his narrative Mr. Rhodes fails to develop it. He deals with Benjamin F. Butler judicially, but as a man and an official; he does not deal with him as a senior major-general standing in presence of a court of military inquiry. Judicially, the sentence he passes is severe; and the more severe because carefully restrained in expression. But it is confined to questions of mere lucre, — "beyond reasonable doubt," Mr. Rhodes says, "he [Butler] was making money [illicitly] out of his country's life struggle." That is bad; but, however bad it may be, it may not unfairly be held the rendering on a very minor count in the long indictment to which Massachusetts' senior major-general of the Civil War should be made to answer. His departmental dishonesty can be measured in dollars and cents; his headquarters incompetence cost blood and grief both unmeasured

[1] *Chattanooga to Petersburg*, p. 37; *War Records*, Serial No. 81, p. 595.
[2] *Butler's Book*, p. 1123.

and immeasurable. Who was responsible for the greater part of that awful loss of life and limb, which in May and June, 1864, littered the soil of eastern Virginia with dead, and caused the hospitals to be choked with those mutilated, — a loss in killed and maimed numerically nearly equal to the entire army Napoleon had on the field at Waterloo? Primarily, it was that commander of the Army of the James who so utterly failed in doing the work he had himself insisted should be assigned him to do;[1] and, secondarily, to the commander-in-chief who left a charlatan and an incompetent in the place to which he should have designated his trustiest lieutenant. It was a parallel case to that of Grouchy, — the fatal mistake of the man at the head in the choice of a tool. In the early days of July, 1894, it was my fortune to visit Waterloo in company with the late John C. Ropes. That Mr. Ropes was, both in this country and in Europe, an acknowledged authority on problems of strategy, is very generally known; he had also made a special study of the campaign of 1815. As respects it and its incidents, the information of no one was more exact. Viewing the field of battle from the position held by Wellington's army, we looked across toward Planchenoit, where the Prussians, first doubling back Napoleon's right, finally broke in, deciding the day. We then again discussed, as frequently before and afterwards, what turn other than that now recorded might have been given to the momentous 15th of June, 1815, had Davout, instead of being at the time Minister of War and in Paris, been, as he should have been, in command of Napoleon's right wing. It hardly admits of question that the victor of Auerstädt and Eckmühl, instinctively taking in the strate-

[1] Yet in his farewell order to the Army of the James of January 8, 1865, Butler boasted: "The wasted blood of my men does not stain my garments." — *War Records*, Serial No. 96, p. 71.

gic situation, would, during the critical hours immediately following Blücher's disaster at Ligny and subsequent movement to the rear, have kept in close touch with the Emperor, and that the Prussians would two days later have found the road from Wavre to Waterloo effectually blocked. Napoleon's right arm would not then have been paralyzed; he would have been free to throw his whole weight on Wellington's flank and rear. Fortunately for Wellington, Grouchy, and not Davout, was that day in command of Napoleon's detached wing. Butler's command and mission in the Virginia campaign of 1864 were almost exactly similar to the command and mission of Grouchy in the Waterloo campaign of 1815; and now to discuss the operations of the Army of the Potomac in the Wilderness and at Spottsylvania without constant reference to what the Army of the James was on those days doing east and south of Richmond is a treatment no less defective than it would be to try to explain what took place at Waterloo without giving any consideration to Grouchy's blundering march from Gembloux to Wavre. Butler, like Grouchy, was left by the commander-in-chief to act, under general instructions, as the conditions of time and place, and the movements of the enemy in his front, might make more expedient, the plan of campaign and general strategic situation being always clearly in mind. Both failed, and failed utterly. In each case incalculable disaster ensued; but in the narrative of Mr. Rhodes, Butler does not figure as the Grouchy of the Wilderness.

NOTES

Supra, 239, n.

In his contribution (Chapter II of Part V) entitled "The South in the War for Southern Independence" (Vol. IV, pp. 499–519) in the recent publication, *The South in the Building of the Nation* (12 vols., Southern Historical Publication Society, Richmond, Va., 1909), President L. G. Tyler, of William and Mary College, refers (p. 496, n.) to the statement in the text. He then says: "In round numbers the South had on her muster rolls from first to last about 600,000 men, and in this list the South had all it could muster; for at last it had enlisted in its armies all men between sixteen and sixty years."

This statement is not in accord with other statements relating to the same subject elsewhere contained in the same publication. The Border Slave States, so-called, those never members of the Confederacy, furnished according to President Tyler (Vol. IV, 504) approximately 316,424 men to the Federal army. In *The South* it is elsewhere stated that the same States contributed as follows to the army of the Confederacy: —

Kentucky, Vol. I, 295	30,000
Maryland, Vol. I, 205	20,000
Missouri, Vol. III, 236	60,000
West Virginia, Vol. I, 385 (minimum)	7,000
Total from Border States	117,000

That the States named, sympathizing, as at the time all Southern authorities claimed, most deeply with the Confederacy, should have furnished over 316,000 recruits to the Federal army, and only 117,000 to that of the Confederacy, is, to say the least, deserving of remark. It calls for explanation. The figures are, however, those given in *The South*, and, for present purposes, are to be accepted.

Deducting the 117,000 men from the Border States from the asserted total (600,000) on the Confederate muster-rolls, 483,000 would remain as the whole number of men supplied by the eleven States constituting the Confederacy.

SOME PHASES OF THE CIVIL WAR

Turning now to *The South*, the numbers enrolled from the several States named are given as follows: —

Alabama, Vol. II, 290 (minimum)	90,000
Arkansas, Vol. III, 308	50,000
Mississippi, Vol. II, 422	70,000
North Carolina, Vol. I, 485	120,000
South Carolina, Vol. II, 86 (minimum)	75,000
Tennessee, Vol. II, 517	115,000
Texas, Vol. III, 504 (minimum)	50,000
Virginia, Vol. I, 121	175,000
Total from eight States	745,000

Those enrolled from three States of the Confederacy — Georgia, Louisiana, and Florida — are not given even approximately in *The South*. They can, however, be supplied with sufficient accuracy from other Confederate sources.

Georgia, Avery, p. 221 } Jones, *Georgia in the War*, p. 71 }	120,000
Louisiana, *Confederate Military History*, ed. by Gen. C. A. Evans ; John Dimitry, *Louisiana*	55,000
Florida, *Rebellion Record*, Series IV, Vol. 2, pp. 648, 839	15,000
Total from three States	190,000

The figures thus furnished by Confederate authorities, or to *The South* would then stand as follows: —

Eight States of Confederacy, minimum as given in *The South*	745,000
Four Border States, as given in same	117,000
Three States of Confederacy, numbers given by Confederate authorities	190,000
Total enrolments	1,052,000

There is obviously a wide discrepancy between the results thus arrived at elsewhere from *The South*, and those given by President Tyler in the passage above quoted from his contribution to that publication. The aggregate reached from the separate State returns is, however, not only more creditable to Confederate manhood, but much more in consonance with the figures of the census than the summarized statement of President Tyler.

In the census of 1860 the eleven States composing the Confederacy reported an aggregate white population of 5,067,051; the same States reported in 1870 a similar population of 5,548,355;

and this notwithstanding the losses incurred during the Civil War (1861–1865) and the discouragements, industrial and political, incident to the period of reconstruction. The arms-bearing effectives in any community — males between 18 and 45 years of age — are roughly estimated at one in five of the population; or, allowing for exempts from all causes, at one in six. President Tyler asserts that "at last [the Confederacy] had enlisted in its armies all men between sixteen and sixty years." There is every reason to believe that this statement is not exaggerated; though the extreme age limits fixed by Confederate conscription acts (February 17, 1864) were 17 and 50. No man capable of doing duty was, however, refused permission to bear arms on the ground that he was not yet 17 or was over 50. Accepting for present purposes the statements of President Tyler, the census tables are not so arranged as to make possible any exact statement of the number of additional men between the ages of 16 and 18, at one end, and 45 and 60 at the other end, thus brought within the age of service; but it is well known that after the age of 45 the proportion of those capable of doing military service diminishes rapidly. Computations based on the census returns tend, however, to show that at the very lowest estimate the increase of time of military service would represent an increase of at least 30 per cent in effectives. The effectives of the Confederacy during the entire war period — May, 1861 to May, 1865 — would then, at the lowest computation, and allowing for no increase of population after 1860, have contained the original one million returned in 1860 as then between 18 and 45. To those must be added a further 30 per cent (300,000) composed of those between 16 and 18 and between 45 and 60. As the census of 1870 showed must have been the case, a further number also, equal to three per cent of the whole each year matured, and became military effectives during the continuance of the struggle (1861–1865) — a total of 12 per cent (150,000) additional. The figures would then stand as follows : 1,000,000 original (1860), effectives of 18 to 45 years of age; 300,000 of those less then 18 and over 45; 150,000 who reached the age of 16 between May, 1861 and May, 1865; or a total aggregate Confederate arms-bearing population of 1,450,000. From this aggregate 20 per cent is to be deducted as representing exempts of every description and all classes. There would then remain a minimum of 1,160,000 effectives. To these in the case of the Confederacy are to be added the contingent (117,000) from the Border States. The aggregate thus reached is a total Confederate enrolment of 1,277,000. The actual minimum total of separate State aggregates, given in *The South*, as above, is 1,052,000. The figures are those of the census ; the result reached is by computations based on the statement of President Tyler.

A not dissimilar result is reached through another and wholly different process of computation. The three States of Georgia, North Carolina and Virginia contained, in 1860, according to the census of that year, an arms-bearing population — that is, whites between the ages of 18 and 45 — aggregating 343,000 in round numbers — for exact figures are in such cases a delusion; West Virginia is excluded. Allowing, as in the previous computations, an increase of 30 per cent to cover the extension of the arms-bearing period, and a further increase of 12 per cent of the aggregate thus reached to represent the maturing of effectives, the number of possible enrolments in the States named would be increased to 500,000. The number reported as actually enrolled from these States was 415,000, or 84 per cent of the possible enrolment. Applying this standard to the entire Confederacy, a possible enrolment of 1,450,000 would result, 84 per cent of which would make an actual enrolment of 1,223,000; to which must be added the 117,000 admitted to have been enrolled from the Border States. The aggregate arrived at through this process of computation would be, in round numbers, 1,340,000.

No matter, therefore, on what basis a result is arrived at, whether from computations covering the whole Confederacy, or computations based on returns of certain States used as a basis for the whole, or from an analysis of the censuses of 1860 and 1870, the figures given in *The South*, as above, for enrolments from the several Confederate States are much more than confirmed not only as being substantially correct, but also as being, approximately, what would naturally and reasonably have been anticipated under the conditions then existing. In any event, the result so reached is not open to the charge of exaggeration.

On the other hand, the statement of President Tyler that the

Confederacy had from first to last "about 600,000 men" on its muster-rolls leads, when analyzed, to results difficult of acceptance. As already pointed out, deducting the 117,000 enrolments from the so-called Border States, there would remain 483,000 as the entire muster from the eleven States composing the Confederacy. Those States were returned in the Census of 1860 as containing, exclusive of West Virginia, almost exactly one million men of military age, — 18 to 45, — but a trifle in excess thereof. Allowing, as before, for extension of age of military service, and the maturing of effectives, and duly deducting the proportion of exempts, there would remain from this total a minimum of over 1,200,000 men available for military service. If then only 483,000 were actually enrolled, it would follow that, computed on the most favorable basis, and after every possible allowance had been made, and assuming also no double enrolments, less than one-half of the available effectives in the Confederacy ever bore arms in its defence. To be exact, those who bore arms were only forty out of each hundred capable of so doing. In view of the prolonged and desperate character of the conflict, and the acknowledged bravery and devotion of the people of the Confederacy, such a result, arithmetically arrived at from figures the essential correctness of which does not admit of question, cannot be considered otherwise than a *reductio ad absurdum*.

Thus, approached from any direction and reached under any conceivable method of computation, it is difficult to avoid the conclusion that the actual enrolments of the Confederate army during the entire four years of the conflict exceeded 1,100,000 rather than fell short of that number. The figures given by President Tyler, opposed to all reasonable assumption and unsupported by documentary evidence, are based on assertion only.

In certain discussions of this subject much emphasis is also laid by writers with Confederate sympathies on the large number of deserters, etc., from the armies in the field, owing to lack of proper clothing, sustenance, etc. It is difficult, however, to see how this affects the question of enrolment. To desert, a man must previously have been enrolled, and enumerated as such. Desertion, moreover, was by no means peculiar to the army of the Confederacy ; and the deserters from the Union army are not excepted by Confederate authorities from the total of Federal enlistments.

The genesis of the 600,000 legend of Confederacy military enrolments, and the basis of evidence on which it rests, have been discussed and set forth by Colonel T. L. Livermore, in a paper printed in Mass. Hist. Soc. *Proceedings* (Second Series, XVIII, 432–435), and also in *The South in the Building of the Nation*, IV, 503.

Supra, 266, n.

"Thursday, September 8, 1870. — The Chancellor gives a great dinner, the guests including the Hereditary Grand Duke of Mecklenburg-Schwerin, Herr Stephan, the Chief Director of the Post Office, and the three Americans. Amongst other matters mentioned at table were the various reports as to the affair at Bazeilles. The Minister said that peasants could not be permitted to take part in the defence of a position. Not being in uniform, they could not be recognized as combatants — they were able to throw away their arms unnoticed. The chances must be equal for both sides. Abeken considered that Bazeilles was hardly treated, and thought the war ought to be conducted in a more humane manner. Sheridan, to whom MacLean has translated these remarks, is of a different opinion. He considers that in war it is expedient, even from the political point of view, to treat the population with the utmost rigour also. He expressed himself roughly as follows: 'The proper strategy consists in the first place in inflicting as telling blows as possible upon the enemy's army, and then in causing the inhabitants so much suffering that they must long for peace, and force their Government to demand it. The people must be left nothing but their eyes to weep with over the war.' Somewhat heartless it seems to me, but perhaps worthy of consideration." — Busch, *Bismarck: Some Secret Pages of his History*, II, 127.

To the same effect General Sherman subsequently declared: "I resolved to stop the game of guarding their cities, and to destroy their cities. We were determined to produce results, and now what were those results? To make every man, woman and child in the South feel that if they dared to rebel against the flag of their country they must die or submit."

The subsequent influence on the American army of General Sherman's famous "War is Hell" aphorism, and its illustration in his campaigns in Georgia and the Carolinas, are deserving of notice. Lieutenant-General S. B. M. Young spoke to the same effect as General Sheridan, at Prince Bismarck's table, at a public dinner given by the New York Chamber of Commerce at the Arlington Hotel, Washington, in honor of the representatives of certain foreign commercial bodies then in America, November 13, 1902. General Young then pronounced "all the army's defamers densely ignorant of what constitutes the laws of war;" and added, "To carry on war, disguise it as we may, is to be cruel, it is to kill and burn, burn and kill, and again kill and burn." If the word "humane" could be applied to war, he would define it as one "fast and furious and bloody from the beginning." He added, "When war has been decided on by our nation I agree with the German Emperor's sentiments, and believe that the American army should leave such an impression that future generations would know we had been there." — New York *Tribune*, November 14, 1902.

The utterance of the German Emperor here referred to was his famous speech at Bremerhaven, July 27, 1900, to the first contingent of his army then embarking for China. He said: "When you meet the foe you will defeat them. No quarter will be given; no prisoners will be taken. Let all who fall into your mercy be at your mercy. Just as the Huns a thousand years ago, under the leadership of Attila, gained a reputation in virtue of which they still live in historical tradition, so may the name of Germany become known in such a manner in China that no Chinaman will ever again dare to look askance at a German."

At a court-martial convened in Manila twenty-one months after this utterance, Brigadier-General Jacob H. Smith declared that in operations conducted by him as general in command he had instructed a subordinate "not to burden himself with prisoners"; that he told him "that he wanted him to kill and burn in the interior and hostile country; and did also instruct him that 'The interior of Samar must be made a howling wilderness'; and did further instruct him that he wanted all persons killed who were capable of bearing arms and were actively engaged in hostilities against the United States; and that he did designate the age limit of ten years."

The court in this case found General Smith guilty of "conduct to the prejudice of good order and military discipline," and sentenced him to be admonished by the reviewing authority. The court declared itself thus lenient "in view of the undisputed evidence that the accused did not mean everything that his unexplained language implied; that his subordinates did not gather such a meaning; and that the orders were never executed in such sense." — 57th Congress, 2d Session, Senate Document No. 213.

Historically, however, it is noticeable that the instructions given by General Smith were in strict accordance with the "War is Hell" principles on which operations in a hostile country should be conducted as laid down on the occasion specified, by Lieutenant-General Sheridan, September 8, 1870, by the German Emperor, July 27, 1900, and by Lieutenant-General Young, November 13, 1902.

In his work entitled *Ohio in the War* (1868), Mr. Whitelaw Reid says of the burning of Columbia, "It was the most monstrous barbarity of the barbarous march. There is no reason to think that General Sherman knew anything of the purpose to burn the city, which had been freely talked about among the soldiers through the afternoon. But there is reason to think that he knew well enough who did it, that he never rebuked it, and made no effort to punish it. . . . He did not seek to ferret out and punish the offending parties. He did not make his army understand that he regarded this barbarity as a crime. He did not seek to repress their lawless course. On the contrary, they came to understand that the leader, whom they idolized, regarded their actions as a good joke, chuckled over them in secret, and winked at them in public. . . . In both campaigns [that from Atlanta to Savannah, and from Savannah to Goldsboro'] great bodies of men were moved over States and groups of States with the accuracy and precision of mechanism. In neither was any effort to preserve discipline apparent, save only so far as was needful for keeping up the march.

"Here, indeed, is the single stain on the brilliant record. Before his movement began, General Sherman begged permission to turn his army loose in South Carolina and devastate it. He used this permission to the full. He protested that he did not wage war on women and children. But, under the operation of his orders the last morsel of food was taken from hundreds of destitute families, that his soldiers might feast in needless and riotous abundance. Before his eyes rose, day after day, the mournful clouds of smoke on every side, that told of old people and their grandchildren driven, in midwinter, from the only roofs there were to shelter them, by the flames which the wantonness of his soldiers had kindled. With his full knowledge and tacit approval, too great a portion of his advance resolved itself into bands of jewelry-thieves and plate-closet burglars. Yet, if a single soldier was punished for a single outrage or theft during that entire movement, we have found no mention of it in all the voluminous records of the march. He did indeed say that he 'would not *protect*' them in stealing 'women's apparel or jewelry.' But even this, with no whisper of punishment attached, he said, not in general orders, nor in approval of the findings of some righteously severe court-martial, but incidentally — in a letter to one of his officers, which never saw the light till two years after the close of the war. He rebuked no one for such outrages; the soldiers understood that they pleased him. Was not South Carolina to be properly punished?

"This was not war. It was not even the revenge of a wrathful soldiery, for it was practised, not upon the enemy, but upon the defenceless 'feeble folk' he had left at home. There was indeed one excuse for it — an excuse which chivalric soldiers might be slow to plead. It injured the enemy — not by open fight, where a million would have been thought full match for less than a hundred thousand, but by frightening his men about the situation of their wives and children!" — *Ohio in the War*, I, 475-479.

VIII

LEE'S CENTENNIAL[1]

HAVING occasion once to refer in discussion to certain of the founders of our Massachusetts Commonwealth, I made the assertion that their force "lay in character"; and I added that in saying this I paid, and meant to pay, the highest tribute which in my judgment could be paid to a community or to its typical men. Quite a number of years have passed since I so expressed myself, and in those years I have grown older — materially older; but I now repeat, even more confidently than I then uttered them, these other words: "The older I have grown and the more I have studied and seen, the greater in my esteem, as an element of strength in a people, has Character become, and the less in the conduct of human affairs have I thought of mere capacity or even genius. With Character a race will become great, even though as stolid and unassimilating as the Romans; without Character, any race will in the long run prove a failure, though it may number in it individuals having all the brilliancy of the Jews, crowned with the genius of Napoleon."[2] We are here to-day to commemorate the birth of Robert Edward Lee, — essentially a Man of Character. That he was such all, I think,

[1] This address was delivered on the invitation of the president and faculty of Washington and Lee University at Lexington, Va., Saturday, January 19, 1907, the centennial anniversary of the birth of General Robert E. Lee. Having been subjected to no general revision, it is here reproduced in almost the exact form of its original publication.

[2] Massachusetts Historical Society *Proceedings*, Second Series, VIII, 408.

recognize; for, having so impressed himself throughout life on his contemporaries, he stands forth distinctly as a man of character on the page of the historian. Yet it is not easy to put in words exactly what is meant when we agree in attributing character to this man or to that, or withholding it from another; — conceding it, for instance, to Epaminondas, Cato and Wellington, but withholding it from Themistocles, Cæsar or Napoleon. Though we can illustrate what we mean by examples which all will accept, we cannot define. Emerson in his later years (1866) wrote a paper on "Character"; but in it he makes no effort at a definition. "Character," he said, "denotes habitual self-possession, habitual regard to interior and constitutional motives, a balance not to be overset or easily disturbed by outward events and opinion, and by implication points to the source of right motive. We sometimes employ the word to express the strong and consistent will of men of mixed motive; but, when used with emphasis, it points to what no events can change, that is, a will built of the reason of things." The more matter-of-fact lexicographer defines Character as "the sum of the inherited and acquired ethical traits which give to a person his moral individuality." To pursue further the definition of what is generally understood would be wearisome, so I will content myself with quoting this simile from a disciple of Emerson: "The virtues of a superior man are like the wind; the virtues of a common man are like the grass; the grass, when the wind passes over it, bends."[1]

That America has been rich in these men of superior virtues before whom the virtues of the common man have bent, is matter of history. It has also been our making as a community. Such in New England was John Winthrop, whose

[1] Thoreau, *Walden*, Chap. VIII; taken from the Analects of Confucius. *See* Mass. Hist. Soc. *Proceedings*, XLIII, 473–477.

lofty example still influences the community whose infancy he fathered. Such, in New York, was John Jay. Such, further south, was John Caldwell Calhoun, essentially a man of exalted character and representative of his community, quite irrespective of his teachings and their outcome. Such unquestionably, in Virginia, were George Washington and John Marshall; and, more recently, Robert Edward Lee. A stock, of which those three were the consummate flower, by its fruits is known.

Here to commemorate the centennial of the birth of Lee, I do not propose to enter into any eulogium of the man, to recount the well-known events of his career, or to estimate the final place to be assigned him among great military characters. All this has been sufficiently done by others far better qualified for the task. Eschewing superlatives also, I shall institute no comparisons. One of a community which then looked upon Lee as a renegade from the flag he had sworn to serve, and a traitor to the nation which had nurtured him, in my subordinate place I directly confronted Lee throughout the larger portion of the War of Secession. During all those years there was not a day in which my heart would not have been gladdened had I heard that his also had been the fate which at Chancellorsville befell his great lieutenant; and yet more glad had it been the fortune of the command in which I served to visit that fate upon him. Forty more years have since gone. Their close finds me here to-day — certainly a much older, and, in my own belief at least, a wiser man. Nay, more! A distinguished representative of Massachusetts, speaking in the Senate of the United States shortly after Lee's death upon the question of a return to Lee's family of the ancestral estate of Arlington, used these words: "Eloquent Senators have already characterized the proposition and the traitor it seeks to commemorate. I am not disposed to speak of General Lee. It is enough to say he stands high in the catalogue of those who have imbrued their hands in their country's blood. I hand him over to the avenging pen of History." It so chances that not only am I also from the State of Massachusetts, but, for more than a dozen years, I have been the chosen head of its typical historical society, — the society chartered under the name and seal of the Commonwealth considerably more than a century ago, — the parent of all similar societies. By no means would I on that account seem to ascribe to myself any representative character as respects the employment of History's pen, whether avenging or otherwise;[1] nor do I appear here as representative of the Massachusetts Historical Society: but, a whole generation having passed away since Charles Sumner uttered the words I have quoted, I do, on your invitation, chance to stand here to-day, as I have said, both a Massachusetts man and the head of the Massachusetts Historical Society, to pass judgment upon General Lee. The situation is thus to a degree dramatic.

Though in what I am about to say I shall confine myself to a few points only, to them I have given no little study, and on them have much reflected. Let me, however, once for all, and with emphasis, in advance say I am not here to instruct Virginians either in the history of their State or the principles of Constitutional Law; nor do I make any pretence to profundity whether of thought or insight. On the contrary, I shall attempt nothing more than the elaboration of what has already been said by others as well as by me, such value or

[1] Possibly, and more properly, this attribute might be considered as pertaining rather to James Ford Rhodes, also a member of the society referred to, and at present (1907) a vice-president of it. Mr. Rhodes's characterization of General Lee, and consequent verdict on the course pursued by him at the time under discussion, can be found on reference to his *History of the United States*, III, 413.

novelty as may belong to my share in the occasion being attributable solely to the point of view of the speaker. In that respect, I submit, the situation is not without novelty; for, so far as I am aware, never until now has one born and nurtured in Massachusetts — a typical bred-in-the-bone Yankee, if you please — addressed at its invitation a Virginian audience, on topics relating to the War of Secession and its foremost Confederate military character.

Coming directly to my subject, my own observation tells me that the charge still most commonly made against Lee in that section of the common country to which I belong and with which I sympathize is that, in plain language, he was false to his flag, — educated at the national academy, an officer of the United States Army, he abjured his allegiance and bore arms against the government he had sworn to uphold. In other words, he was a military traitor. I state the charge in the tersest language possible; and the facts are as stated. Having done so, and, for the purposes of the present occasion, admitting the facts, I add as the result of much patient study and most mature reflection, that under similar conditions I would myself have done exactly what Lee did. In fact, I do not see how I, placed as he was placed, could have done otherwise.

And now fairly entered on the first phase of my theme, I must hurry on; for I have much ground to traverse, and scant time in which to cover it. I must be concise, but must not fail to be explicit. And first as to the right or wrong of secession, this theoretically; then, practically, as to what secession in the year of grace 1861 necessarily involved.

If ever a subject had been thoroughly thrashed out, — so thrashed out, in fact, as to offer no possible gleaning of novelty, — it might be inferred that this was that subject. Yet I venture the opinion that such is not altogether the case. I do so, moreover, not without weighing words. The difficulty with the discussion has to my mind been that throughout it has in essence been too abstract, legal and technical, and not sufficiently historical, sociological and human. It has turned on the wording of instruments, in themselves not explicit, and has paid far too little regard to traditions and local ties. As matter of fact, however, actual men as they live, move and have their being in this world, caring little for parchments or theory, are the creatures of heredity and local attachments. Coming directly to the point, I maintain that every man in the eleven States seceding from the Union had in 1861, whether he would or no, to decide for himself whether to adhere to his State or to the Nation; and I finally assert that, whichever way he decided, if only he decided honestly, putting self-interest behind him, he decided right.

Paradoxical as it sounds, I contend, moreover, that this was indisputably so. It was a question of sovereignty — State or National; and from a decision of that question there was in a seceded State escape for no man. Yet when the national Constitution was framed and adopted that question was confessedly left undecided; and intentionally so left. Even more, the Federal Constitution was theoretically and avowedly based on the idea of a divided sovereignty, in utter disregard of the fact that, when a final issue is presented, sovereignty does not admit of division.[1]

Yet even this last proposition, basic as it is, I have heard denied. I have frequently had it replied that, as matter of fact, sovereignty is frequently divided, — divided in domestic life, — divided in the apportionment of the functions of government. Those thus arguing, however, do so confusedly. They confound sovereignty with an agreed, but artificial, *modus vivendi*.[2] The original constitution of the United States

[1] *Supra*, 210–221.   [2] *Ibid.* 218.

was, in fact, in this important respect just that, — a *modus vivendi:* — under the circumstances a most happy and ingenious expedient for overcoming an obstacle in the way of nationality, otherwise insurmountable. To accomplish the end they had in view, the framers had recourse to a metaphysical abstraction, under which it was left to time and the individual to decide, when the final issue should arise, if it ever did arise — and they all devoutly hoped it never would arise — where sovereignty lay. There is nothing in connection with the history of our development more interesting from the historical point of view than the growth, the gradual development of the spirit of nationality, carrying with it sovereignty. It has usually been treated as a purely legal question to be settled on the verbal construction of the instruments: "We, the People," etc. Webster so treated it. In all confidence I maintain that it is not a legal question; it is purely an historical question. As such, furthermore, it has been decided, and correctly decided, both ways at different times in different sections, and at different times in opposite ways in the same section.

And this was necessarily and naturally so; for, as development progressed along various lines and in different localities, the sense of allegiance shifted. Two whole generations passed away between the adoption of the Federal Constitution and the War of Secession. When that war broke out in 1861, the last of the framers had been a score of years in his grave; but evidence is conclusive that until the decennium between 1830 and 1840 the belief was nearly universal that in case of a final, unavoidable issue, sovereignty resided in the State, and to it allegiance was due. The law was so laid down in the Kentucky resolves of 1798; and to the law as thus laid down Webster assented. Chancellor Rawle so propounded the law; and such was the understanding of so unprejudiced and acute a foreign observer as Tocqueville.[1]

The technical argument — the logic of the proposition — seems plain, and, to my thought, unanswerable. The original sovereignty was indisputably in the State; in order to establish a nationality certain attributes of sovereignty were ceded by the States to a common central organization; all attributes not thus specifically conceded were reserved to the States, and no attributes of moment were to be construed as conceded by implication. There is no attribute of sovereignty so important as allegiance, — citizenship. So far all is elementary. Now we come to the crux of the proposition. Not only was allegiance — the right to define and establish citizenship — not among the attributes specifically conceded by the several States to the central nationality, but, on the contrary, it was explicitly reserved, the instrument declaring that "the citizens of each State" should be entitled to "all Privileges and Immunities of Citizens in the several States." Ultimate allegiance was, therefore, due to the State which defined and created citizenship, and not to the central organization which accepted as citizens whomever the States pronounced to be such.[2]

Thus far I have never been able to see where room was left for doubt. Citizenship was an attribute recognized by the Constitution as originating with, and of course belonging to, the several States. But, speaking historically and in a philosophical rather than in a legal spirit, it is little more than a commonplace to assert that one great safeguard of

[1] See note, *infra*, 339.
[2] See W. H. Fleming, *Slavery and the Race Problem at the South*, pp. 19, 20. An authoritative definition of United States citizenship, as distinct from the citizenship of a State, was first given in the Fourteenth Amendment to the Federal Constitution, ratified in 1868. See J. S. Wise, *A Treatise on American Citizenship*, pp. 6, 13, 31.

the Anglo-Saxon race — what might almost be termed its political palladium — has ever been that hard, if at times illogical, common-sense, which, recognizing established custom as a binding rule of action, found its embodiment in what we are wont with pride to term the Common Law. Now, just as there can, I think, be no question as to the source of citizenship, and, consequently, as to sovereignty, when the Constitution was originally adopted, there can be equally little question that during the lives of the two succeeding generations a custom of nationality grew up which became the accepted Common Law of the land, and practically binding as such. This was true in the South as well as the North, though the custom was more hardened into accepted law in the latter than in the former;[1] but the growth and acceptance as law of the custom of nationality even in the South were incontrovertibly shown in the very act of secession, — the seceding States at once crystallizing into a Confederacy. Nationality was assumed as a thing of course.

But the metaphysical abstraction of a divided sovereignty, none the less, bridged the chasm. As a *modus vivendi* it did its work. I have called it a metaphysical abstraction; but it was also a practical arrangement resulting in great advantages. It might be illogical, and fraught with possible disputes and consequent dangers; but it was an institution. And so it naturally came to pass that in many of the States a generation grew up, dating from the War of 1812, who, gravitating steadily and more and more strongly to nationality, took a wholly different view of allegiance. For them Story laid down the law; Webster was their mouthpiece; at one time it looked as if Jackson was to be their armed exponent. They were, moreover, wholly within their right. The sovereignty was confessedly divided; and it

[1] *Supra*, 224–225.

was for them to elect. The movements of both science and civilization were behind the nationalists. The railroad obliterated State lines, while it unified the nation. What did the foreign immigrants, now swarming across the ocean, care for States? They knew only the nation. Brought up in Europe, the talk of State sovereignty was to them foolishness. Its alphabet was incomprehensible. In a word, it too "was caviare to the general."

Then the inevitable issue arose; and it arose over African slavery; and slavery was sectional. The States south of a given line were arrayed against the States north of that line. Owing largely to slavery, and the practical exclusion of immigrants because thereof, the States of the South had never undergone nationalization at all to the extent those of the North had undergone it. The growing influence and power of the national government, the sentiment inspired by the wars in which we had been engaged, the rapidly improving means of communication and intercourse, had produced their effects in the South; but in degree far less than in the North. Thus the curious result was brought about that, when, at last, the long-deferred issue confronted the country, and the *modus vivendi* of two generations was brought to a close, those who believed in national sovereignty constituted the conservative majority, striving for the preservation of what then was, — the existing nineteenth-century nation, — while those who passionately adhered to State sovereignty, treading in the footsteps of the fathers, had become eighteenth-century reactionists. Legally, each had right on his side. The theory of a divided sovereignty had worked itself out to its logical consequence. "Under which King, Bezonian?" — and every man had to "speak or die."

In the North the situation was simple. State and Nation

stood together. The question of allegiance did not present itself, for the two sovereignties merged. It was otherwise in the South; and there the question became, not legal or constitutional, but practical. The life of the nation had endured so long, the ties and ligaments had become so numerous and interwoven, that, all theories to the contrary notwithstanding, a peaceable secession from the Union — a virtual exercise of State sovereignty — had become impossible. If those composing the several dissatisfied communities would only keep their tempers under restraint, and exercise an almost unlimited patience, a theoretical divided sovereignty, maintained through the agency and intervention of the Supreme Court, — in other words, the perpetuation of the *modus vivendi,* — was altogether practicable; and probably this was what the framers had in mind under such a contingency as had now arisen. But that, after seventy years of Union and nationalization, a peaceable and friendly taking to pieces was possible is now, as then it was, scarcely thinkable. Certainly, with a most vivid recollection of the state of sectional feeling which then existed, I do not believe there was a man in the United States — I am confident there was not a woman in the South — who fostered self-delusion to the extent of believing that the change was to come about without a recourse to force. In other words, practical Secession was revolution theoretically legal. Why waste time and breath in discussion! The situation becomes manifestly impossible of continuance where the issue between heated men, with weapons handy, is over a metaphysical distinction involving vast material and moral consequences. Lee, with intuitive commonsense, struck the nail squarely on the head when amidst the Babel of discordant tongues he wrote to his son: "It is idle to talk of secession"; the national government as it then was "can only be dissolved by revolution." That struggle of dissolution might be longer and fiercer, — as it was, — or shorter, and more wordy than blood-letting, — as the seceding States confidently believed would prove to be the case, — but a struggle there would be.

Historically, such were the conditions to which natural processes of development had brought the common country at the mid-decennium of the century. People had to elect; the *modus vivendi* was at an end. -- Was the State sovereign; or was the Nation sovereign? And, with a shock of genuine surprise that any doubt should exist on that head, eleven States arrayed themselves on the side of the sovereignty of the State and claimed the unquestioning allegiance of their citizens; and I think it not unsafe to assert that nowhere did the original spirit of State sovereignty and allegiance to the State then survive in greater intensity and more unquestioning form than in Virginia, — the "Old Dominion," — the mother of States and of Presidents. And here I approach a sociological factor in the problem more subtle and also more potent than any legal consideration. It has no standing in Court: but the historian may not ignore it; while, with the biographer of Lee, it is crucial. Upon it judgment hinges. I have not time to consider how or why such a result came about, but of the fact there can, I hold, be no question, — State pride, a sense of individuality, has immemorially entered more largely and more intensely into Virginia and Virginians than into any other section or community of the country. Only in South Carolina and among Carolinians, on this continent, was a somewhat similar pride of locality and descent to be found. There was in it a flavor of the Hidalgo, — or of the pride which the Macgregors and Campbells took in their clan and country. In other words, the Virginian and the Carolinian had in the middle of the last century not undergone nationalization to any appreciable extent.

But this, it will be replied, though true of the ordinary man and citizen, should not have been true of the graduate of the military academy, the officer of the Army of the United States. Winfield Scott and George H. Thomas did not so construe their allegiance; when the issue was presented, they remained true to their flag and to their oaths. Robert E. Lee, false to his oath and flag, was a renegade! The answer is brief and to the point: the conditions in the several cases were not the same, — neither Scott nor Thomas was Lee. It was our Boston Dr. Holmes who long ago declared that the child's education begins about two hundred and fifty years before it is born; and it is quite impossible to separate any man — least of all, perhaps, a full-blooded Virginian — from his prenatal traditions and living environment. From them he drew his being; in them he exists. Robert E. Lee was the embodiment of those conditions, the creature of that environment, — a Virginian of Virginians. His father was "Light Horse Harry" Lee, a devoted follower of Washington; but in January, 1792, "Light Horse Harry" wrote to Mr. Madison: "No consideration on earth could induce me to act a part, however gratifying to me, which could be construed into disregard of, or faithlessness to, this Commonwealth"; and later, when in 1798 the Virginia and Kentucky resolutions were under discussion, "Light Horse Harry" exclaimed in debate, "Virginia is my country; her will I obey, however lamentable the fate to which it may subject me." Born in this environment, nurtured in these traditions, to ask Lee to raise his hand against Virginia was like asking Montrose or the MacCallum More to head a force designed for the subjection of the Highlands and the destruction of the clans. Where such a stern election is forced upon a man as then confronted Lee, the single thing the fair-minded investigator has to take into account is the loyalty, the single-mindedness of the election. Was it devoid of selfishness, — was it free from any baser and more sordid worldly motive, — ambition, pride, jealousy, revenge or self-interest? To this question there can, in the case of Lee, be but one answer. When, after long and trying mental wrestling, he threw in his fate with Virginia, he knowingly sacrificed everything which man prizes most, — his dearly beloved home, his means of support, his professional standing, his associates, a brilliant future assured to him. Born a slaveholder in a race of slaveholders, he was himself no defender, much less an advocate of slavery; on the contrary, he did not hesitate to pronounce it in his place "a moral and political evil." Later, he manumitted his slaves. He did not believe in secession; as a right reserved under the Constitution he pronounced it "idle talk": but, as a Virginian, he also added, "if the Government is disrupted, I shall return to my native State and share the miseries of my people, and save in defence will draw my sword on none." Next to his high sense of allegiance to Virginia was Lee's pride in his profession. He was a soldier; as such rank, and the possibility of high command and great achievement, were very dear to him. His choice put rank and command behind him. He quietly and silently made the greatest sacrifice a soldier can be asked to make. With war plainly impending, the foremost place in the army of which he was an officer was now tendered him; his answer was to lay down the commission he already held. Virginia had been drawn into the struggle; and though he recognized no necessity for the state of affairs, "in my own person," he wrote, "I had to meet the question whether I should take part against my native State; I have not been able to make up my mind to raise my hand against my relatives, my children, my home." It may have been treason to take this position; the man who took it, uttering these words and sacrificing as he sacrificed, may have been technically a renegade to his flag, — if you please, false to his allegiance; but he stands awaiting sentence at the bar of history in very respectable company. Associated with him are, for instance, William of Orange, known as The Silent, John Hampden, the original *Pater Patriæ*, Oliver Cromwell, the Protector of the English Commonwealth, Sir Henry Vane, once a governor of Massachusetts, and George Washington, a Virginian of note. In the throng of other offenders I am also gratified to observe certain of those from whom I not unproudly claim descent. They were, one and all, in the sense referred to, false to their oaths — forsworn. As to Robert E. Lee, individually, I can only repeat what I have already said, — if in all respects similarly circumstanced, I hope I should have been filial and unselfish enough to have done as Lee did.[1] Such an utterance on my part may be "traitorous"; but I here render that homage.

In Massachusetts, however, I could not even in 1861 have been so placed; for, be it because of better or worse, Massachusetts was not Virginia; — no more Virginia than England once was Scotland, or the Lowlands the Highlands. The environment, the ideals, were in no respect the same. In Virginia, Lee was Macgregor; and, where Macgregor sat, there was the head of the table.

Into Lee's subsequent military career, there is no call here to enter; nor shall I undertake to compare him with other great military characters, whether contemporaneous or of all time. As I said when I began, the topic has been thoroughly discussed by others; and, moreover, the time limita-

[1] See *Lee at Appomattox and Other Papers* (2d ed.), pp. 414–417.

x

tion here again confronts me. I must press on. Suffice it for me, as one of those then opposed in arms to Lee, however subordinate the capacity, to admit at once that, as a leader, he conducted operations on the highest plane. Whether acting on the defensive upon the soil of his native State, or leading his army into the enemy's country, he was humane, self-restrained and strictly observant of the most advanced rules of civilized warfare. He respected the non-combatant; nor did he ever permit the wanton destruction of private property. His famous Chambersburg order was a model which any invading general would do well to make his own; and I repeat now what I have heretofore had occasion to say, "I doubt if a hostile force of an equal size ever advanced into an enemy's country, or fell back from it in retreat, leaving behind less cause of hate and bitterness than did the Army of Northern Virginia in that memorable campaign which culminated at Gettysburg."[1]

And yet that Gettysburg campaign is an episode in Lee's military career which I am loath wholly to pass over; for the views I entertain of it are not in all respects those generally held. Studied in the light of results, that campaign has been criticized; the crucial attack of Gettysburg's third day has been pronounced a murderous persistence in a misconception; and, among Confederate writers especially, the effort has been to relieve Lee of responsibility for final miscarriage, transferring it to his lieutenants. As a result reached from participation in those events and subsequent study of them, briefly let me say I concur in none of these conclusions. Taking the necessary chances incident to all warfare on a large scale into consideration, the Gettysburg campaign was in my opinion timely, admirably designed, energetically executed, and brought to a close with consummate military

[1] *War is Hell* (Houghton, Mifflin and Co., Boston, 1903), 40; *supra*, 266.

skill. A well-considered offensive thrust of the most deadly character, intelligently aimed at the opponent's heart, its failure was of the narrowest; and the disaster to the Confederate side which that failure might readily have involved was no less skilfully than successfully averted.

I cannot here and now enter into details. But I hold that credit, and the consequent measure of applause, in the outcome of that campaign belong to Lee's opponent, and not to him. All the chances were in Lee's favor, and he should have won a great victory; and Meade should have sustained a decisive defeat. As it was, Meade triumphantly held his ground; Lee suffered a terrible repulse, his deadly thrust was foiled, and his campaign was a failure.

So far as Lee's general plan of operations, and the movements which culminated in the battle of Gettysburg, were concerned, be it always and ever remembered, a leader must, in war, take some chances, and mistakes will occur; but the mistakes are rarely, if ever, all on one side. They tend to counterbalance each other; and, commanders and commanded being at all equal, not unseldom it is the balance of misconceptions, shortcomings, miscarriages, and the generally unforeseen, and indeed unforeseeable, which tips the scale to victory or defeat. I have said that I proposed to avoid comparisons; at best such are invidious, and, under present circumstances, might from me be considered as doubtful in matter of taste. I think, however, some things too obvious to admit of denial; or, consequently, to suggest comparison. About every crisp military aphorism is as matter of course attributed to Napoleon; and so Napoleon is alleged first to have remarked that "In war, men are nothing; a man is everything." [1] And, as formerly a soldier of the Army of the Potomac, I now stand appalled at the risk I uncon-

[1] "À la guerre les hommes ne sont rien, c'est un homme qui est tout."

sciously ran anterior to July, 1863, when confronting the Army of Northern Virginia, commanded as it then was and as we were. The situation was in fact as bad with us in the Army of the Potomac as it was with the Confederates in the southwest. There the unfortunate Pemberton simply was not in the same class as Grant and Sherman, to whom he found himself opposed. Results followed accordingly. So here, in Virginia, Lee and Jackson made an extraordinary, a most exceptional combination. They outclassed McClellan and Burnside, Pope and Hooker; outclassed them sometimes terribly, sometimes ludicrously, always hopelessly: and results in that case also followed accordingly. That we were not utterly destroyed constitutes a flat and final refutal of the truth of Napoleon's aphorism. If we did not realize the facts of the situation in this respect, our opponents did. Let me quote the words of one of them: "There was, however, one point of great interest in [the rapid succession of the Federal commanders], and that was our amazement that an army could maintain even so much as its organization under the depressing strain of those successive appointments and removals of its commanding generals. And to-day (1903) I, for one, regard the fact that it did preserve its cohesion and its fighting power under and in spite of such experiences, as furnishing impressive demonstration of the high character and intense loyalty of our historic foe, the Federal Army of the Potomac." [1]

Notwithstanding the fact that until the death of Jackson and the Gettysburg campaign we were thus glaringly outclassed, and at a corresponding disadvantage in every respect save mere men and equipment, the one noticeable feature of the succession of Virginia campaigns, from that of 1862 to that of 1864, was their obstinacy and indecisive

[1] Stiles, *Four Years under Marse Robert*, 21.

character. The advantage would be sometimes on one side, sometimes on the other: but neither side could secure an indisputable supremacy. This was markedly the case at Gettysburg; and yet, judging by the Confederate accounts of that campaign which have met my eye, the inference would be that the Union forces labored under no serious disadvantage, while Lee's plans and tactics were continually compromised by untoward accident, or the precipitation or remissness of his subordinates. My study of what then took place leads me to a wholly opposite conclusion. Well conceived and vigorously carried out as that campaign was on the part of the Confederate leader, the preponderance of the accidental — the blunders, the unforeseeable, the misconceptions and the miscarriages — was distinctly in Lee's favor. On any fair weighing of chances, he should have won a decisive victory; as a matter of actual outcome, he and his army ought to have been destroyed. As usual, on that theatre of war at the time, neither result came about.

First as to the chapter of accidents, — the misconceptions, miscarriages and shortcomings. If, as has been alleged, an essential portion of Lee's force was at one time out of reach and touch, and if, at the critical moment, a lieutenant was not promptly in place at a given hour, on the Union side an unforeseen change of supreme command went into effect when battle was already joined, and the newly appointed commander had no organized staff; his army was not concentrated; his strongest corps was over thirty miles from the point of conflict; and the two corps immediately engaged should have been destroyed in detail before reënforcements could have reached them. In addition to all this, — superadded thereto, — the most skilful general and perhaps the fiercest fighter on the Union side was killed at the outset, and, later, Meade's line of battle was almost fatally disordered by the misconception of a corps commander.

The chapter of accidents thus reads all in Lee's favor. But, while Lee on any fair weighing of chances stands in my judgment more than justified both in his conception of the campaign and in every material strategic move made in it, he none the less fundamentally misconceived the situation, with consequences which should have been fatal both to him and to his command. Frederick did the same at Kunersdorf; Napoleon, at Waterloo. In the first place, Lee had at that time supreme confidence in his command; and he had grounds for it. As he himself then wrote: "There never were such men in an army before. They will go anywhere and do anything, if properly led." And, for myself, I do not think the estimate thus expressed was exaggerated; speaking deliberately, having faced some portions of the Army of Northern Virginia at the time and having since reflected much on the occurrences of that momentous period, I do not believe that any more formidable or better organized and animated force was ever set in motion than that which Lee led across the Potomac in the early summer of 1863. It was essentially an army of fighters, — men who, individually or in the mass, could be depended on for any feat of arms in the power of mere mortals to accomplish. They would blanch at no danger. This, Lee from experience knew. He had tested them; they had full confidence in him. He also thought he knew his opponent; and here too his recent experience justified him.

The disasters which had befallen the Confederates in the Southwest in the spring and early summer of 1863 had to find compensation in the East. The exigencies of warfare necessitated it. Some risk must be incurred. So Lee determined to strike at his opponent's heart. He had what he believed to be the better weapon; and he had reason for considering himself incomparably the superior swordsman. He was; of that he had at Chancellorsville satisfied himself and the world. Then came the rapid, aggressive move; and the long, desperately contested struggle at Gettysburg, culminating in that historic charge of Pickett's Virginia division. Paradoxical as it may sound in view of the result, that charge — what those men did — justified Lee. True, those who made the charge did not accomplish the impossible; but towards it they did all that mortal men could do. But it is urged that Lee should have recognized the impossible when face to face confronted by it, and not have directed brave men to lay down their lives in the vain effort to do it. That is true; and, as Lee is said to have once remarked in another connection, "Even as poor a soldier as I am can generally discover mistakes after it is all over." After Gettysburg was over, like Frederick at Kunersdorf and Napoleon at Waterloo, Lee doubtless discovered his mistake. It was a very simple one: he undervalued his opponent. The temper of his own weapon he knew; he made no mistake there. His mistake lay in his estimate of his antagonist: but that estimate again was based on his own recent experience, though in other fields.

On the other hand, from the day I rode over the field of Gettysburg immediately following the fight to that which now is, I have fully and most potently believed that only some disorganized fragments of Lee's army should after that battle have found their way back to Virginia. The war should have collapsed within sixty days thereafter. For eighteen hours after the repulse of Pickett's division, I have always felt, and now feel, the fate of the Army of Virginia was as much in General Meade's hands as was the fate of the army led by Napoleon in the hands of Blücher on the night of Waterloo. As an aggressive force, the Confederate army was fought out. It might yet put forth a fierce defensive effort; it was sure to die game: but it was impotent for attack. Meade had one entire corps — perhaps his best, — the Sixth, commanded by Sedgwick — intact and in reserve. It lay there cold, idle, formidable. The true counter movement for the fourth day of continuous fighting would on Meade's part have been an exact reversal of Lee's own plan of battle for the third day. That plan, as described by Fitzhugh Lee, was simple. "His [Lee's] purpose was to turn the enemy's left flank with his First Corps, and, after the work began there, to demonstrate against his lines with the others in order to prevent the threatened flank from being reënforced, these demonstrations to be converted into a real attack as the flanking wave of battle rolled over the troops in their front." What Lee thus proposed for Meade's army on the third day, Meade should unquestionably have returned on Lee's army upon the fourth day. Sedgwick's corps should then have assailed Lee's right and rear. I once asked a leading Confederate general,[1] who had been in the very thick of it at Gettysburg, what would have been the outcome had Meade, within two hours of the repulse of Pickett, ordered Sedgwick to move off to the left, and, occupying Lee's line of retreat, proceeded to envelop the Confederate right, while, early the following morning, Meade had commanded a general advance. The answer I received was immediate: "Without question we would have been destroyed. We all that night fully expected it; and could not understand next day why we were unmolested. My ammunition" — for he was an officer of artillery — "was exhausted."

But in all this, as in every speculation of the sort, — and

[1] General E. P. Alexander, Chief of Artillery of the corps commanded by General Longstreet.

the history of warfare is replete with them, — the "if" is much in evidence; as much in evidence, indeed, as it is in a certain familiar Shakespearian disquisition. I here introduce what I have said on this topic simply to illustrate what may be described as the balance of miscarriages inseparable from warfare. On the other hand, the manner in which Lee met disaster at Gettysburg, and the combination of serene courage, and consequent skill, with which he extricated his army from a most critical situation commands admiration. I would here say nothing depreciatory of General Meade. He was an accomplished officer as well as a brave soldier. Placed suddenly in a most trying position, — assigned to chief command when battle was already joined, — untried in his new sphere of action, and caught unprepared, — he fought at Gettysburg a stubborn, gallant fight. With chances at the beginning heavily against him, he saved the day. Personally, I was later under deep obligation to General Meade. He too had character. None the less, as I have already pointed out, I fully believe that on the fourth day at Gettysburg Meade had but firmly to close his hand, and the Army of Northern Virginia was crushed. Perhaps under all the circumstances it was too much to have expected of him; certainly it was not done. Then Lee in turn did avail himself of his opportunity. Skilfully, proudly though sullenly, preserving an unbroken front, he withdrew to Virginia. That withdrawal was masterly.

Narrowly escaping destruction at Gettysburg, my next contention is that Lee and the Army of Northern Virginia never sustained defeat. Finally, it is true, succumbing to exhaustion, to the end they were not overthrown in fight. And here I approach a large topic, but one closely interwoven with Lee's military career; in fact, as I see it, the explanation of what finally occurred. What then was it that brought about the collapse of the Army of Northern Virginia, and the consequent downfall of the Confederacy? The literature of the War of Secession now constitutes a library in itself. Especially is this true of it in its military aspects. The shelves are crowded with memoirs and biographies of its generals, the stories of its campaigns, the records and achievements of its armies, its army corps and its regiments. Yet I make bold to say that no well and philosophically considered narrative of the struggle has yet appeared; nor has any satisfactory or comprehensive explanation been given of its extraordinary and unanticipated outcome. Let me briefly set it forth as I see it; only by so doing can I explain what I mean.

Tersely put, dealing only with outlines, the Southern community in 1861 precipitated a conflict on the slavery issue, in implicit reliance on its own warlike capacity and resources, the extent and very defensible character of its territory, and, above all, on its complete control of cotton as the great staple textile fabric of modern civilization. That the seceding States fully believed in the justice of their cause, and confidently appealed to it, I do not question, much less deny. For present purposes let this be conceded in full. But, historically, it is equally clear that to vindicate the right, next to their own manhood and determination, they relied in all possible confidence on their apparently absolute control of one commercial staple. When, therefore, in 1858, with the shadow of the impending conflict darkening the horizon, a thoughtful senator from South Carolina, one on whom the mantle of Calhoun had fallen, declared that "Cotton *is* King," that "no power on earth dares to make war on it," that "without firing a gun, without drawing a sword," the cotton-producing South could, if war was declared upon it, bring "the whole world" to its feet, he only gave utterance to what was in the South accepted as a fundamental article of political and economical faith.[1] Suggesting the contingency that no cotton was forthcoming from the South for a period of three years, the same senator declared, — "This is certain: England would topple headlong and carry the whole civilized world with her, save the South. Who," he then exclaimed, "that has looked on recent events, can doubt that cotton is supreme?" In case of conflict, cotton, if it went forth, was to supply the South with the sinews of warfare; if it did not go forth, the lack of it would bring about European civil commotion, and compel foreign intervention. In either case the South was secure. As to a maritime blockade of the South, shutting it up to die of inanition, the idea was chimerical. No such feat of maritime force ever had been accomplished, it was claimed; nor was it possible of accomplishment. To "talk of putting up a wall of fire around eight hundred and fifty thousand square miles" situated as the Confederacy was, with its twelve thousand miles of seacoast, was pronounced too "absurd" for serious discussion. And certainly, that no such thing had ever yet been done was undeniable. But, even supposing it were possible of accomplishment, the doing it would but the more effectively play the Confederate game. It would compel intervention. As well shut off bread from the manufacturing centres of Europe as stop their supply of cotton. In any or either event, and in any contingency which might arise, the victory of the Confederacy was assured. And this theory of the situation and its outcome was accepted by the Southern community as indisputable.

What occurred? In each case that which had been pronounced impossible of occurrence. On land the Confederacy had an ample force of men, they swarmed to the standards;

[1] *Supra*, 252.

and no better or more reliable material was ever gathered together. Well and skilfully marshalled, the Confederate soldier did on the march and in battle all that needed to be done. Nor were the two sides unequally matched, so far as the land arrays were concerned. As Lee with his instinctive military sense put it, even in the closing stages of the struggle: "The proportion of experienced troops is larger in our army than in that of the enemy, while his numbers exceed our own." And in warfare, experience, combined with an advantageous defensive, counts for a great deal. This was so throughout the conflict; and yet the Confederate cause sank in failure. It did so to the complete surprise of a bewildered world; for, in Europe, the ultimate success of the South was accepted as a foregone conclusion. To such an extent was this the case that the wisest and most far-seeing of English public men did not hesitate to stake their reputation for foresight upon it as a result. How was the wholly unexpected actual outcome brought about? The simple answer is: — The Confederacy collapsed from inanition! Suffering such occasional reverses and defeats as are incidental to all warfare, it was never crushed in battle or on the field, until its strength was sapped away by want of food. It died of exhaustion, — starved and gasping!

Take a living organism, whatever it may be, place it in a vessel hermetically sealed, and attach to that vessel an air-pump: — You know what follows! It is needless to describe it. No matter how strong or fierce or self-confident it may be, the victim dies; growing weaker by degrees, it finally collapses. That was the exact condition and fate of the Confederacy. What had been confidently pronounced impossible was done. The Confederacy was sealed up within itself by the blockade; and the complete exclusion of southern cotton from the manufacturing centres of Europe did not cause revolution there, nor compel intervention here. Man's foresight once more came to grief. As usual, the unexpected occurred.

Thus the two decisive defeats of the Confederacy, — those which really brought about its downfall and compelled Lee to lay down his arms, — were inflicted not before Vicksburg, nor yet in Virginia, — not in the field at all; they were sustained, the one, almost by default, on the ocean; the other, most fatal of all, after sharpest struggle in Lancashire. The story of that Lancashire Cotton Famine of 1861 to 1864 has never been adequately told in connection with our Civil War. Simply ignored by the standard historians, it was yet the Confederacy's fiercest fight, and its most decisive as well as most far-reaching defeat. A momentous conflict, the supremacy of the Union on the ocean hung on its issue; and upon that supremacy depended every considerable land operation: the retention by the Confederacy of New Orleans, and the consequent control of the Mississippi; Sherman's march to the sea; the movement through the Carolinas; the operations before Petersburg; generally, the maintenance of the Confederate armies in the field. It is in fact no exaggeration to assert that both the conception and the carrying out of every large Union operation of the war without a single exception hinged and depended on complete national maritime supremacy. It is equally indisputable that the struggle in Lancashire was decisive of that supremacy. As Lee himself admitted in the death agony of the Confederacy, he had never believed it could in the long run make good its independence "unless Foreign Powers should, directly or indirectly, assist" it in so doing. Thus, strange as it sounds, it follows as a logical consequence that Lee and his Army of Northern Virginia were first reduced to inanition, and finally compelled to succumb, as the result of events on the other side of the Atlantic, largely stimulated by a moral impulse over which they could exert no control. The great and loudly trumpeted cotton campaign of the Confederacy was its most signal failure; and that failure was decisive of the war.

It is very curious, at times almost comical, to trace historical parallels. Plutarch is, of course, the standard exemplar of that sort of treatment. Among other great careers, Plutarch, as every college boy knows, tells the story of King Pyrrhus, the Epirot. A great captain, Pyrrhus devised a military formation which his opponents could not successfully face, and his career was consequently one of victory. But at last he met his fate. Assaulting the town of Argos, he became entangled in its streets; and, fighting his way out, he was struck down, and killed, by a tile thrown from a house-top by an Argive woman. The Confederacy, and, through the Confederacy, Lee underwent a not dissimilar fate; for, as an historical fact, it was a missile from a woman's hand which was decisive of that Lancashire conflict, and so doomed the Confederacy. A startling proposition; but proof quite irrefutable of it exists in a publication to which as an authority no Southern writer at least will take exception, the organ established in London by the agents of the Confederacy in 1862. Sustained as long as the conflict continued from Confederate funds, with a view to influencing European public opinion, the *Index*, as it was called, collapsed with the Confederacy in July, 1865. Naturally those in charge of it watched with feverish interest the progress of the cotton famine. Not only was the British pocket nerve touched at its most sensitive point, but in Lancashire starvation emphasized financial distress. The pressure thus brought to bear on public opinion in Great

Britain, and, through that public opinion, on the policy of Europe, was confidently counted on for results decisive of the American struggle. Ten years before Harriet Beecher Stowe had launched through the press her *Uncle Tom's Cabin*. Translated into every civilized tongue, it had soon become world literature. In Great Britain, and especially in Lancashire, it "carried the new gospel to every cabin in the land." Whoever in those days read anything read *Uncle Tom's Cabin*. That it was a correct portrayal of conditions actually existing in the region wherein the incidents narrated were supposed to have occurred is not now to be considered. That Uncle Tom himself was a type of his race, or, indeed, even a possibility in it, few would now be disposed to contend.[1] Ethically, he was a Christian martyr of the most advanced description, and, on the large class who accepted the work as a correct portrayal, the pathetic story and cruel fate of the colored saint, moralist and philosopher made an indelible impression. Indeed, that female and sentimentalist portrayal lent a force which has not yet spent itself to the contention that the only difference between the Ethiopian and the Caucasian is epidermal; the negro being in fact merely a white man — a Yankee, if you please — who, having a black skin, has never been given a chance. Nay, more! if Uncle Tom and Legree were to be accepted as types, the black man was superior naturally to the white; for Uncle Tom was a fully developed moralist, while Legree was a demon incarnate. And this presentation of life and manners, and this portrayal of typical racial characters were in Lancashire implicitly

[1] J. C. Read, *The Brothers' War*, pp. 194–198. There is in Mr. Read's book, published fifty years after the appearance of Mrs. Stowe's historic tale, and forty years after the Proclamation of Emancipation, a chapter (IX) entitled, "Uncle Tom's Cabin," in which are to be found the views of an observant and reflecting Georgian on the statement in the text.

accepted as gospel truth! Such indisputably was the fact; and, when the final issue was joined, the fact told heavily against the Confederacy. In contemplation of it, — realizing the handicap thus imposed, the burden of which at the moment the historian has since ignored, and few consequently now appreciate, — the writers for the *Index* fairly cried aloud in agony. Their wail, long repeated, has in it as now read an element of the comic. The patience of the victims of the cotton famine, they declared was the extraordinary feature of the foreign situation; and the agents of the Confederacy noted with unconcealed dismay the absence of political demonstrations calculated to urge on a not unwilling Palmerston ministry "its duty to its suffering subjects." There was but one way of accounting for it. Uncle Tom and Legree were respectively doing their work. So it was that the *Index* despairingly at last declared : "The emancipation of the negro from the slavery of Mrs. Beecher Stowe's heroes is the one idea of the millions of British who know no better and do not care to know." Like the Cherubim with the flaming sword, this sentiment stood between Lancashire and cotton; and the inviolate blockade made possible the subjugation of the Confederacy. With Pyrrhus, it was the tile thrown by a woman from the house-top; with Lee, it was a book by a woman issued from the printing-press! The missiles were equally fatal. It was only a difference of time, and its changed conditions.

Foreign intervention being thus withheld, and the control of the sea by the Union made absolute, the blockade was gradually perfected. The fateful process then went steadily on. Armies might be resisted in the field; the working of the air-pump could not be stopped: and, day and night, season after season, the air-pump worked. So the atmosphere of the Confederacy became more and more attenuated, respiration sensibly harder. Air-hole on air-hole was closed. First New Orleans fell; then Vicksburg, and the Mississippi flowed free; next Sherman, securely counting on the control of the sea as a base of new operations on land, penetrated the vitals of the Confederacy; then, relying still on maritime coöperation, he pursued his almost unopposed way through the Carolinas; while Grant, with his base secure upon the James and Fortress Monroe, beleaguered Richmond. Lee with his Army of Northern Virginia calmly, but watchfully and resolutely, confronted him. The Confederate lines were long and thin, guarded by poorly clad and half-fed men. But, veterans, they held their assailants firmly at bay. As Lee, however, fully realized, it was only a question of time. The working of the air-pump was beyond his sphere either of influence or operations. Nothing could stop it.

As early as the close of 1863 Lee wrote of his men, — "Thousands are barefooted, a greater number partially shod, and nearly all without overcoats, blankets, or warm clothing"; and later, in the dead of winter, referring to the elementary necessities of any successful warfare, he said: "The supply, by running the blockade, has become so precarious that I think we should turn our attention to our own resources, . . . as a further dependence upon those from abroad can result in nothing but increase of suffering and want." The conclusion here drawn, while necessary, was extremely suggestive. "Our own resources!" — the Confederacy had always prided itself on being a purely agricultural community. With institutions patriarchal in character, it had looked upon the people of the North as its agents and factors, and those of Europe as its skilled workmen and artisans; and now that community, shut up within its own limits, under conditions of warfare active and severe, had only itself to rely upon for a supply of everything its defenders needed, from munitions to shoes, from blankets to medicines and even soap. Viewed in a half-century's perspective, the situation was simply and manifestly impossible of continuance. To it there could be but one outcome; and when at last on the 16th of January, 1865, the telegraph announced the fall of Fort Fisher, the Confederacy felt itself hermetically sealed. Wilmington, its last breathing-hole, was closed. Still, not the less for that, the air-pump kept on its deadly, silent work.

Three months later the long-delayed inevitable occurred. The collapse came. That under such conditions it should have been so long in coming is now the only legitimate cause of surprise. That adversity is the test of man is a commonplace; that Lee and his Army of Northern Virginia were during the long, dragging winter of 1864–1865 most direfully subjected to that test need not here be said; any more than it is needful to say that they bore the test manfully. But the handwriting was on the wall; the men were taxed beyond the limits of human endurance. And Lee knew it. "Yesterday, the most inclement day of the winter," he reported on February 8, 1865, the right wing of his army "had to be retained in line of battle, having been in the same condition the two previous days and nights. . . . Under these circumstances, heightened by assaults and fire of the enemy, some of the men had been without meat for three days, and all were suffering from reduced rations and scant clothing, exposed to battle, cold, hail and sleet. . . . The physical strength of the men, if their courage survives, must fail under this treatment." If it was so with the men, with the animals it was even worse. "Our cavalry," he added, "has to be dispersed for want of forage." Even thus Lee's army faced an opponent vastly superior in numbers, whose ranks were being constantly replenished; a force armed, clothed, equipped, fed and sheltered as no similar force in the world's history had ever been before. I state only indisputable facts. Lee proved equal to even this occasion. Bearing a bold, confident front, he was serene and outwardly calm; alert, resourceful, formidable to the last, individually he showed no sign of weakness, not even occasional petulance. Inspired by his example, the whole South seemed to lean up against him in implicit, loving reliance. It was a superlative tribute to Character. Finally, when in April the summons to conflict came, the Army of Northern Virginia, the single remaining considerable organized force of the Confederacy, seemed to stagger to its feet, and, gaunt and grim, shivering with cold and emaciated with hunger, worn down by hard, unceasing attrition, it faced its enemy, formidable still. As I have since studied that situation, listened to the accounts of Confederate officers active in the closing movements and read the letters written me by those of the rank and file, it has seemed as if Lee's command then cohered and moved by mere force of habit. Those composing it failed to realize the utter hopelessness of the situation — the disparity of the conflict. I am sure Jefferson Davis failed to realize it; so, I think, in less degree, did Lee. They talked, for instance, of recruits and of a levy in mass; Lee counselled the arming of the slaves; and when, after Lee had surrendered, Davis on the 10th of April, 1865, held his last war conference at Greensboro', he was still confident he would in a few weeks have another army in the field, and did not hesitate to express his faith that "we can whip the enemy yet, if our people will turn out." I have often pondered over what Davis had in mind when he ventured this opinion;[1] or what led Lee to advocate the enlistment of

[1] *Supra*, 241.

negroes. Both were soldiers; and, besides being great in his profession, Lee was more familiar than any other man alive with actual conditions then existing in the Confederate camps. Both Davis and Lee, therefore, must have known that, in those final stages of the conflict, if the stamp of a foot upon the ground would have brought a million men into the field, the cause of the Confederacy would thereby have been in no wise strengthened; on the contrary, what was already bad would have been made much worse. For, to be effective in warfare, men must be fed and clothed and armed. Organized in commands, they must have rations as well as ammunition, commissary and quartermaster trains, artillery horses and forage. In the closing months of the Civil War, both Lee and Davis knew perfectly well that they could not arm, nor feed, nor clothe, nor transport the forces already in the field; they were themselves without money, and the soldiers most inadequately supplied with arms, clothing, quartermaster or medical supplies, commissariat or ammunition. Notoriously, those then on the muster-rolls were going home, or deserting to the enemy, as the one alternative to death from privation — hunger and cold. If then, a million, or even only a poor hundred thousand fresh recruits had in answer to the summons swarmed to the lines around Richmond, how would it have bettered the situation? An organized army is a mighty consumer of food and material; and food and material have to be served out to it every day. It must be fed as regularly as the sun rises and sets. And the organized resources of the Confederacy were exhausted; its granaries — Georgia and the valley of the Shenandoah — were notoriously devastated and desolate; its lines of communication and supply were cut, or in the hands of the invader.

Realizing this Lee, when the time was ripe, rose to the

full height of the great occasion. The value of Character made itself felt. The service Lee now rendered to the common country, the obligation under which he placed us whether of the North or South, has not, I think, been always appreciated; and to overstate it would be difficult. Again to put on record my estimate of it brings me here to-day.

That the situation was to the last degree critical is matter of history. Further organized resistance on the part of the Confederacy was impossible. The means for it did not exist; could not be had. Cut off completely from the outer world, the South was consuming itself, — feeding on its own vitals. The single alternative to surrender was disbandment and irregular warfare. As General Johnston afterwards wrote, "without the means of purchasing supplies of any kind, or procuring or repairing arms, we could continue the war only as robbers or guerillas."[1] But that it should be so continued was wholly possible; nay more, it was in the line of precedent, — it had been done before; and, more than once, it has since been done, notably in South Africa. It was, moreover, the course advocated by many Southern participants in the struggle as that proper to be pursued; and that it would be pursued was accepted as of course by all foreign observers, and by the organ of the Confederacy in London. "A strenuous resistance and not surrender," it was there declared, "was the unalterable determination of the Confederate authorities." Lee's own son, then in the Army of Northern Virginia, but by chance not included in the surrender, has since described how surprised and incredulous he was when news of it first reached him; and, "not believing for an instant that our struggle was over," he made his way at once to Jefferson Davis, at Greensboro'. At the time of his capture Davis himself,

[1] *Supra*, 243.

wholly unsubdued in spirit, was moving in the direction of the Mississippi, intent on organizing resistance in Texas, — a resistance which the writers of the *Index* confidently predicted would "be fierce, ferocious and of long duration," — "a successful or at least a protracted resistance."

Indeed, had the veil over the immediate future then been lifted, and the outrages, and humiliations worse than outrage, of the period of so-called reconstruction, but actual servile domination, now to ensue revealed itself, no room for doubt exists that the dread alternative would have been adopted. Even as it was, the scales hung trembling. Anything or everything was possible; even that mad pistol shot of the theatrical fool which five days later so irretrievably complicated a delicate and dangerous situation. None the less, what Lee and Grant had done at Appomattox on April 9 could not be wholly undone even by the deed in Ford's theatre of April 14; much had been secured. Of Appomattox, and what there occurred, I do not care here to speak. I feel I could not speak adequately, or in words sufficiently simple; for, in my judgment, there is not in our whole history as a people any incident so creditable to our manhood, — so indicative of our racial possession of Character. Marked throughout by a straightforward dignity of personal bearing and propriety in action, it was marred by no touch of the theatrical, no effort at posturing. I know not to which of the two leaders, there face to face, preference should be given. They were thoroughly typical; the one of Illinois and the New West, the other of Virginia and the Old Dominion. Grant was considerate and magnanimous, — restrained in victory; Lee, dignified in defeat, carried himself with that sense of absolute fitness which compelled respect. Verily! — "he that ruleth his spirit is better than he that taketh a city!"

The lead that day given by Lee proved decisive of the course to be pursued by his fellows with arms in their hands. At first, and for a brief space, there was in the Confederate councils much diversity of opinion as to what should or could be done. Calm and dignified in presence of overwhelming disaster, the voice of Jefferson Davis was that of Milton's "scepter'd king": "My sentence is for open war!" Lee was not there; none the less, Lee, absent, prevailed over Davis. The sober second thought satisfied all but the most extreme that what he had done they best might do. Thus the die was cast. And now, forty years and more after the event, it is appalling to reflect what in all human probability would have resulted had the choice then been other than it was, — had Lee's personality and character not intervened. The struggle had lasted four full years; the assassination of Lincoln was as oil on the Union fire. With a million men, inured to war, on the national muster rolls, men impatient of further resistance, accustomed to license and now educated up to a belief that War was Hell, and that the best way to bring it to a close was to intensify Hell, — with such a force as this to reckon with, made more reckless in brutality by the assassin's senseless shot, the Confederacy need have looked for no consideration, no mercy. Visited by the besom of destruction, it would have been harried out of existence. Fire and sword sweeping over it, what the sword spared the fire would have consumed. Whether such an outcome of a prolonged conflict — what was recently witnessed in South Africa — would in its result have been more morally injurious to the North than it would have been destructive materially to the South, is not now to be considered. It would, however, assuredly have come about.

From that crown of sorrows Lee saved the common

country. He was the one man in the Confederacy who could exercise decisive influence. It was the night of the 8th of April, lacking ten days only of exactly four full years, — years very full for us who lived through them, — since that not dissimilar night when Lee had paced the floor at Arlington, communing with himself over the fateful issue, a decision on which was then forced upon him. A decision of even greater import was now to be reached, and reached by him. A commander of the usual cast would under such circumstances have sought advice — perhaps support; at least, a divided responsibility. Even though himself by nature and habit a masterful man and one accustomed to direct, he would have called a council, and harkened to those composing it. This Lee did not do. A singularly self-poised man, he sought no external aid. Sitting before his bivouac fire at Appomattox, he reviewed the situation. Doing so, as before at Arlington, he reached his own conclusion. That conclusion he himself at the time expressed in words, brief, indeed, but vibrating with moral triumph: "The question is, is it right to surrender this army? If it is right, then I will take all the responsibility." The conclusion reached at Arlington in the April night of 1861 to some seems to have been wrong — inexcusable even; all concur in that reached before the Appomattox camp-fire in the April vigils of 1865. He then a second time decided; and he decided right.

His work was done; but from failure he plucked triumph. Thenceforth Lee wore defeat as 'twere a laurel crown. A few days later a small group of horsemen appeared in the morning hours on the further side of the Richmond pontoons across the James. By some strange intuition it became known that General Lee was of the party; and, silent and uncovered, a crowd — Virginians all — gathered along the route the horsemen would take. "There was no excitement, no hurrahing; but as the great chief passed, a deep, loving murmur, greater than these, rose from the very hearts of the crowd. Taking off his hat, and simply bowing his head, the man great in adversity passed silently to his own door; it closed upon him; and his people had seen him for the last time in his battle harness."

From the day that he affixed his signature to the terms of surrender submitted to him by Grant at Appomattox to the day when he drew a dying breath at Lexington, Lee's subsequent course was consistent. In his case there was no vacillation, no regretful glances backward thrown. When, four months after the last hostile shot was fired, he was invited to assume the presidency of this college, though then under indictment in flagrant disregard of the immunity assured him when he gave his parole, he briefly set forth his views. "I think it," he wrote, "the duty of every citizen, in the present condition of the country, to do all in his power to aid in the restoration of peace and harmony, and in no way to oppose the policy of the State or General Governments directed to that object." And, four days later, writing to the Confederate governor of Virginia, he said: "The duty of [Virginian] citizens appears to me too plain to admit of doubt. All should unite in honest efforts to obliterate the effects of war, and to restore the blessings of peace. They should remain if possible in the country; promote harmony and good feeling; qualify themselves to vote, and elect to the State and general legislatures wise and patriotic men, who will devote their abilities to the healing of all dissensions. I have," he added, "invariably recommended this course since the cessation of hostilities, and have endeavored to practice it myself." Here was a complete exposition of duty, combined with abnegation of self;

the purest patriotism, it was also the concentrated essence of statesmanship. He counselled with a wisdom not less profound because unconscious; and what he said evinced that underlying common-sense which in politics avails more than genius.

Five years of life and active usefulness yet remained to General Lee — years in my judgment most creditable to himself, the most useful to his country of his whole life; for, during them, he set to Virginia and his own people a high example — an example of lofty character and simple bearing. Uttering no complaints, entering into no controversies, he was as one, in suffering all, that suffers nothing. His blood and judgment were well commingled; and so it fell out that he accepted fortune's buffets and rewards with equal thanks. His record and appearance during those final years are pleasant to dwell upon, for they reflect honor on our American manhood. Turning his face courageously to the future, he uttered no word of repining over the past. Yet, like the noble Moor, his occupation also was gone —

> "The royal banner, and all quality,
> Pride, pomp and circumstance of glorious war!"

But with Lee this did not imply: —

> "Farewell the tranquil mind! farewell content!"

Far from it; for as the gates closed on the old occupation, they opened on a new. And it was an occupation through which he gave to his country, North and South, a priceless gift.

Speaking advisedly and on full reflection, I say that of all the great characters of the Civil War — and it was productive of many whose names and deeds posterity will long bear in recollection — there was not one who passed away in the serene atmosphere and with the gracious bearing of Lee. From beginning to end those parting years of his will bear closest scrutiny. There was about them nothing venal, nothing querulous, nothing in any way sordid or disappointing. In his case there was no anti-climax; for those closing years were dignified, patient, useful; sweet in domesticity, they in all things commanded respect. It is pleasant to catch glimpses of the erstwhile commander in that quiet Virginia life. There is in the picture something altogether human — intensely sympathetic. "Traveller," he would write, "is my only companion; I may also say my pleasure. He and I, whenever practicable, wander out in the mountains and enjoy sweet confidence." Or again we see him, always with Traveller, the famous old charger this time "stepping very proudly" as his rider showed those two little sunbonneted daughters of a professor, astride of a plodding old horse, over a pleasant road quite unknown to them. Once more in imagination we may ride, his companions, through those mountain roads of his dearly loved Virginia, or seek shelter with him and his daughter from a thundershower in the log cabin, the inmates of which are stunned when too late they realize that the courtly, gracious intruder was no other than the idolized General Lee. Indifferent to wealth, he was scrupulous as respects those money dealings a carelessness in regard to which has embittered the lives of so many of our public men, as not infrequently it has tarnished their fame. Lee's career will be scrutinized in vain for a suggestion even of the sordid, or of an obligation he failed to meet. He was nothing if not self-respecting. He once wrote to a member of his family "'vile dross' has never been a drug with me," yet his generosity as a giver from his narrow means was limited only by his resources. Restricting his own wants to necessities, he contributed, to an extent which excites surprise, to both public calls and private needs. But the most priceless of those contributions were contained in the precepts he inculcated and in the unconscious example he set during those closing years.

Lee was at the head of Washington College from October, 1865, to October, 1870; a very insufficient time in which to accomplish any considerable work. A man of fast advancing years, he also then had sufficient cause to feel a sense of lassitude. He showed no signs of it. On the contrary, closely studied those years, and Lee's bearing in them, were in certain respects the most remarkable as well as the most creditable of his life; they impressed unmistakably upon it the stamp of true greatness. Unable to pass them wholly over, I shall deal very briefly with them. His own means of subsistence having been swept away by war, — the property of his wife as well as his own having been sequestered and confiscated in utter disregard not only of law, but — I add it regretfully — of decency, — a mere pittance, designated in courtesy "salary," under his prudent management was made to suffice for the needs of an establishment the quiet dignity of which even exceeded its severe simplicity. Within five months of the downfall of the Confederacy, he addressed himself to his new vocation. Coming to it from crushing defeat, about him there was nothing suggestive of disappointment; and thereafter through public trials and private misfortunes — for it pleased Heaven to try him with afflictions — he bore himself with serene patience, and a mingled firmness and sweetness of temper to which mere words fail to do justice. More than that, becoming interested in his new work he evinced, it would seem, as the head of a college, a grasp of educational problems not less clear and intelligent than he had previously shown of strategic conditions. It was indeed extraordinary that a man educated in a military school, first an engineer, then an officer of cavalry, and finally a general in charge of large field operations, should, when approaching his sixtieth year, have given proof of such mental activity and freshness. Fully realizing the needs and requirements of the present age, the former commandant of West Point was the ardent advocate of complete classical and literary culture. Utterly out of sympathy with the modern advocates of materialistic education, he yet recognized the fact that material well-being is, for a people, the condition of all high civilization; and, accordingly, sought to provide, in the institution of which he was the head, all means for the development of science and its practical application. With a large and correct conception, he planned, therefore, to connect all the departments of literary, scientific and professional education, and to consolidate them under a common organization. He thus outlined a true university. So at an early day he called into existence, as adjuncts of the college he found prostrate and well-nigh moribund, schools of applied mathematics, of engineering and of law; while later he submitted to its Board of Trustees a matured scheme for the complete development of the scientific and professional departments. His death, just before he had yet reached the grand climacteric, prevented the full development of his great conception. None the less, he had shown himself fully equal to the new demand upon him.

The most marked feature of his educational career was, however, the moral influence he exerted on the student body, — what has most fitly been described by one associated with him as "the mighty influence of his personal character." Here, as in the Army of Northern Virginia, this was all-powerful. It was sorely needed, too, for the young men of the South were self-willed, and resented efforts at restraint. Grown up in an environment of warfare and consequent violence, they were somewhat disposed to take matters into their own hands, — to be, in a word, a law unto themselves; but, under Lee's presidency, the elevation of tone in this respect, and the consequent improvement in student conduct were, we are on good evidence assured, marked and rapid. Acts of disorder became infrequent; and in the latter years of Lee's brief administration it is said that "hardly a single case of serious discipline occurred." A Boston student of Washington College in those years — sent there because of the feeling of profound respect for Lee entertained by his northern father — has since borne witness to me of the personal interest taken by Washington's president in the individual students. In close sympathy with the modern university spirit, the youth in question was, I have reason to suppose, far more addicted to athletics than to his text-books. "This lack of proficiency in my studies," he has recently written me, "was, of course, a matter for which I was frequently called into the presence of General Lee; and I fully appreciate now, though I did not then, the difficulties under which he labored; for, if he had expelled me, as under similar circumstances he undoubtedly would have expelled any southern student, it would have been considered a factional matter. He would plead most earnestly with me always that I should attend more to my studies and less to athletics, and never a harsh word during the entire period."

It remains to assign due weight and value to these precepts and this great example at just that juncture and from just that man. And here, bearing in mind the common country, — the community to which I belong as well as that I now address, — I feel I tread on dangerous ground. What I must necessarily say will be very susceptible of misconstruction. Speaking, however, in the true historical spirit, as throughout I have sought to do, I must deal with this topic also as best I can.

Because no blood flowed on the scaffold and no confiscations of houses or lands marked the close of our War of Secession, it has always been assumed by us of the victorious party that extreme, indeed unprecedented, clemency was shown to the vanquished, and that subsequently they had no good ground of complaint or sufficient cause for restiveness. That history will accord assent to this somewhat self-complacent conviction is open to question. On the contrary, it may not unfairly be doubted whether a people prostrate after civil strife has often received severer measure than was inflicted on the so-called reconstructed Confederate States during the years immediately succeeding the close of strife. Adam Smith somewhere defined Rebels and Heretics as "those unlucky persons who, when things have come to a certain degree of violence, have the misfortune to be of the weaker party." Spoliation and physical suffering have immemorially been their lot. The Confederate, it is true, when he ceased to resist, escaped this visitation in its usual and time-approved form. Nevertheless, he was by no means exempt from it. In the matter of confiscation, it has been computed that the freeing of the slaves by act of war swept out of existence property valued at some two thousand millions; while, over and above this, a system of simultaneous reconstruction subjected the disfranchised master to the rule of the enfranchised bondsman. For a community conspicuously masterful, and notoriously quick to resent affront, to be thus placed by alien force under the civil rule of those of a different and distinctly inferior race, only lately their property, is not physical torment, it is true, but that it is mild or considerate treatment can hardly be contended. Yet this — slave confiscation, and reconstruction under African rule — was the war penalty imposed on the States of the Confederacy. That the policy inspired at the time a feeling of bitter resentment in the South was no cause for wonder. Upon it time has already recorded a verdict. Following the high precedent set at Appomattox, it was distinctly unworthy. Conceived in passion, it ignored both science and the philosophy of statesmanship; worse yet, it was ungenerous. Lee, for instance, again setting the example, applied formally for amnesty and a restoration of civil rights within two months of his surrender. His application was silently ignored; while he died "a prisoner on parole," the suffrage denied him was conferred on his manumitted slaves. Verily, it was not alone "the base Judian" of the olden time who "threw a pearl away richer than all his tribe!"

But on such a rejection and choice of material as this was the so-called reconstruction edifice based; nor is it matter for wonder that it speedily crumbled away. It was under these conditions that Lee's bearing and example were of special national importance. The one political result the States of the Confederacy should ever have kept steadily in view after strife closed was the restoration of local self-government; and that, under the traditions and political instincts of the American community, was sure to come. It was only a question of time; and patience and self-restraint were the two qualities most sure to hasten the steps of time. "We shall have to be patient," Lee, in March, 1866, wrote to old companions in arms, "and suffer for a while at least; . . . I hope, in time, peace will be restored to the country, and that the South may enjoy some measure of prosperity. I fear, however, much suffering is still in store for her, and that her people must be prepared to exercise fortitude and forbearance." To those to whom it was addressed, no wiser or more tactful counsel could at that juncture (March, 1866) have been imparted; for, while Lee himself possessed those virtues to a well-nigh unexampled degree, patience and self-restraint have not been generally accepted as most conspicuous among the many manly and ennobling qualities of the race to which Lee belonged.

In the passage with which I began, it was observed by Emerson that "Character denotes habitual self-possession, habitual regard to interior and constitutional motives, a balance not to be overset or easily disturbed by outward events and opinion." To my knowledge I never saw General Lee; I certainly never stood in his presence, nor exchanged a word with him. On the few occasions when I was a guest in his house, he chanced to be absent. Even that was long ago; while he and his family still lived at Arlington. Thus I know him only by report, and through his letters. But, if the report of those who did know him well, and the evidence of what he wrote, may be relied on, "habitual self-possession, habitual regard to interior and constitutional motives, a balance not to be overset or easily disturbed by outward events and opinion," were his to an eminent degree, — a degree which his harshest and most prejudiced critic could not ignore. That, himself a devout man and by conviction sincerely religious, he was neither ashamed nor afraid so publicly to profess himself, may be read in his repeated army orders; or, to such as prefer there to look for it, in his family letters. What more expressive of a profound religious faith could be imagined than these words written in the very shadow of Gettysburg's disaster to the dying wife of his wounded and captured son? — "In his own good time He will relieve us, and make all things work together for our good, if we give Him our love and place in Him our trust." That his immediate family circle regarded him with the affectionate devotion founded on respect which is the surest indication of those sterling and fundamental qualities which alone can cause a man to seem a hero to those near to him, — the confidants of his privacy, — appears from those family letters and recollections which have been so freely published. That he impressed himself on those about him in his professional and public life to an uncommon extent, — that the soldiers of the Army of Northern Virginia as well as those of his staff and in high command felt not only implicit and unquestioning confidence in him, but to him a strong personal affection, is established by their concurrent testimony. He, too, might well have said with Brutus: —

"My heart doth joy that yet in all my life
I found no man but he was true to me.
I shall have glory by this losing day."

Finally, one who knew him well has written of him: "He had the quiet bearing of a powerful yet harmonious nature. An unruffled calm upon his countenance betokened the concentration and control of the whole being within. He was a kingly man, whom all men who came into his presence expected to obey." That he was gifted in a prominent degree with the *mens æqua in arduis* of the Roman poet, none deny.

And now, Virginians, a word with you in closing: "Show me the man you honor; I know by that symptom, better than by any other, what kind of man you yourself are. For you show me then what your ideal of manhood is; what kind of man you long possibly to be, and would thank the Gods, with your whole soul, for being if you could. Whom shall we consecrate and set apart as one of our sacred men? Sacred; that all men may see him, be reminded of him, and, by new example added to old perpetual precept, be taught what is real worth in man. Whom do you wish to resemble? Him you set on a high column, that all men, looking at it, may be continually apprised of the duty you expect from them." [1]

[1] Carlyle, *Latter-Day Pamphlets*, "Hudson's Statue."

"The virtues of a superior man are like the wind; the virtues of a common man are like the grass; the grass, when the wind passes over it, bends."

In regard to the early utterances of Mr. Webster (*supra*, 297), the following is from a speech by him in the National House of Representatives, December 9, 1814. It should be borne in mind that this speech was delivered in the midst of the gloomiest period of the War of 1812-15, four months after the battle of Bladensburg and the capture of Washington, and one month before the British were defeated below New Orleans. The speech was first published (1902) by C. H. Van Tyne, in his edition of the *Letters of Daniel Webster* (p. 67).

"In my opinion [the law under consideration for compulsory army and military service] ought not to be carried into effect. The operation of measures thus unconstitutional and illegal ought to be prevented, by a resort to other measures which are both constitutional and legal. It will be the solemn duty of the State Governments to protect their own authority over their own Militia and to interpose between their citizens and arbitrary power. These are among the objects for which the State Governments exist; and their highest obligations bind them to the preservation of their own rights and the liberties of their people. I express these sentiments here, Sir, because I shall express them to my constituents. Both they and myself live under a Constitution which teaches us, that 'the doctrine of non-resistance against arbitrary power and oppression is absurd, slavish, and destructive of the good and happiness of mankind.' With the same earnestness with which I now exhort you to forbear from these measures, I shall exhort them to exercise their unquestionable right of providing for the security of their own liberties."

William Rawle was in his day an eminent Philadelphia lawyer, and chancellor of the Law Association of Philadelphia. The principal author of the revised code of Pennsylvania, he stood in the foremost rank of American legal luminaries in the first third of the nineteenth century. His instincts, sympathies and connections were all national. His *View of the Constitution*, published in Philadelphia in 1825, was the standard text-book on the subject until the publication of Story's *Commentaries*, in 1833. It has been asserted that Rawle's *View* was used as a text-book for the instruction of the students at West Point until after the year 1840. (See prefatory matter to republication of paper entitled "Sectional Misunderstandings," by Robert Bingham, in *North American Review* of September, 1904; also the paper entitled "Was Secession Taught at West Point," read at the meeting, May 5, 1909, of the Military Order of the Loyal Legion of the United States Commandery of the State of Pennsylvania, by Lieut. Colonel James W. Latta.)

"If a faction should attempt to subvert the government of a State for the purpose of destroying its republican form, the paternal power of the Union could thus be called forth to subdue it. Yet it is not to be understood that its interposition would be justifiable if the people of a State should determine to retire from the Union, whether they adopted another or retained the same form of government." (Page 289.)

"The States, then, may wholly withdraw from the Union; but while they continue they must retain the character of representative republics." (Page 290.)

"The secession of a State from the Union depends on the will of the people of such State. The people alone, as we have already seen, hold the power to alter their constitution. The Constitution of the United States is, to a certain extent, incorporated into the constitutions of the several States by the act of the people. The State legislatures have only to perform certain organical operations in respect to it. To withdraw from the Union comes not within the general scope of their delegated authority. There must be an express provision to that effect inserted in the State constitutions. This is not at present the case with any of them, and it would perhaps be impolitic to confide it to them. A matter so momentous ought not to be entrusted to those who would have it in their power to exercise it lightly and precipitately upon sudden dissatisfaction, or causeless jealousy, perhaps against the interests and the wishes of a majority of their constituents.

"But in any manner by which a secession is to take place, nothing is more certain than that the act should be deliberate, clear, and unequivocal. The perspicuity and solemnity of the original obligation require correspondent qualities in its dissolution. The powers of the general government cannot be defeated or impaired by an ambiguous or implied secession on the part of the State, although a secession may perhaps be conditional. The people of the State may have some reasons to complain in respect to acts of the general government; they may in such cases invest some of their own officers with the power of negotiation, and may declare an absolute secession in case of their failure. Still, however, the secession must in such case be distinctly and peremptorily declared to take place on that event; and in such case, as in the case of an unconditional secession, the previous ligament with the Union would be legitimately and fairly destroyed. But in either case the people is the only moving power." (Pages 295, 296.)

Tocqueville cannot, of course, be cited as an authority on American Constitutional Law. Nevertheless, an acute observer, his evidence carries great weight on the question of the views generally current on all constitutional questions at the time he collected the materials for his great work (1831-32). The following extracts bearing upon the topic under discussion are found in the translation of *Democracy of America* by Henry Reeve (London, 1889).

"In America, each State has fewer opportunities of resistance and fewer temptations to non-compliance; nor can such a design be put in execution (if indeed it be entertained) without an open violation of the laws of the Union, a direct interruption of the ordinary course of justice, and a bold declaration of revolt; in a word, without taking a decisive step which men hesitate to adopt. . . . Here the term Federal government is clearly no longer applicable to a state of things which must be styled an incomplete national government: a form of government has been found out which is neither exactly national nor federal; but no further progress has been made, and the new word which will one day designate this novel invention does not yet exist." (Vol. I, pp. 156, 157.)

"The Union is a vast body which presents no definite object to patriotic feeling. The forms and limits of the State are distinct and circumscribed; since it represents a certain number of objects which are familiar to the citizens and beloved by all. It is identified with the very soil, with the right of property and the domestic affections, with the recollections of the past, the labours of the present, and the hopes of the future. Patriotism, then, which is frequently a mere extension of individual egotism, is still directed to the State, and is not excited by the Union." (Vol. I, p. 394.)

"The Federal Government is, therefore, notwithstanding the precautions of those who founded it, naturally so weak that it more peculiarly requires the free consent of the governed to enable it to subsist.

"If the Union were to undertake to enforce the allegiance of the Confederate States by military means, it would be in a position very analogous to that of England at the time of the War of Independence." (Vol. I, p. 395.)

"The Union was formed by the voluntary agreement of the States; and, in uniting together, they have not forfeited their nationality, nor have they been reduced to the condition of one and the same people. If one of the States chose to withdraw its name from the contract, it would be difficult to disprove its right of doing so; and the Federal Government would have no means of maintaining its claims directly, either by force or by right." (Vol. I, p. 396.)

"It appears to me unquestionable that if any portion of the Union seriously desired to separate itself from the other States, they would not be able, nor indeed would they attempt, to prevent it; and that the present Union will only last as long as the States which compose it choose to continue members of the confederation." (Vol. I, p. 397.)

"The dangers which threaten the American Union do not originate in the diversity of interests or of opinions, but in the various characters and passions of the Americans. The men who inhabit the vast territory of the United States are almost all the issue of a common stock; but the effects of the climate, and more especially of slavery, have gradually introduced very striking differences between the British settler of the Southern States and the British settler of the North." (Vol. I, p. 402.)

"I think that I have demonstrated that the existence of the

present confederation depends entirely on the continued assent of all the confederates; and, starting from this principle, I have inquired into the causes which may induce the several States to separate from the others. The Union may, however, perish in two different ways: one of the confederate States may choose to retire from the compact, and so forcibly to sever the Federal tie; and it is to this supposition that most of the remarks that I have made apply: or the authority of the Federal Government may be progressively entrenched on by the simultaneous tendency of the united republics to resume their independence." (Vol. I, p. 412.)

"The Constitution had not destroyed the distinct sovereignty of the States; and all communities, of whatever nature they may be, are impelled by a secret propensity to assert their independence." (Vol. I, p. 415.)

The most recent and elaborate discussion of this subject, from the historical point of view, is by Hannis Taylor, a Southerner by birth and residence, in the chapter (X) entitled "Sixty-one Years of Constitutional Growth" in his *Origin and Growth of the American Constitution* (Boston, 1911).

IX

AN HISTORICAL RESIDUUM [1]

SOME fifteen years ago the late Edward L. Pierce, the biographer of Charles Sumner, submitted to the Massachusetts Historical Society an amusing as well as interesting and suggestive paper, entitled *Recollections as a Source of History*. Buried in the rarely consulted volumes of the *Proceedings* of the Society, this paper, never having attracted any considerable notice, is now quite forgotten; but none the less as a study based on a personal experience, both long and varied, its perusal will well repay the general reader, while for the historical investigator it hangs out a veritable danger signal. Naturally, as the indefatigable student of the Sumner period, Mr. Pierce drew his instances mainly from the "Rebellion" literature, as he still designated it; and towards the close of his paper he observed: "Of all reminiscences those concerning public men at Washington are the most untrustworthy. . . . Stories of public characters have somewhat the interest of fiction, and the mass of readers care little whether they are true or not. Managers of magazines are keen in their search for them; and the result is a medley of tales, with little of truth in them, and that little of truth so compounded with falsehood as to be worse than falsehood entire. They obtain a credence with even intelligent people, who

[1] Originally prepared for submission to the Massachusetts Historical Society, at its October meeting, 1899, this paper is printed under the title *The Laird Rams* in the *Proceedings* of the Society (Second Series, XIII, 177–197). In its present form it has been recast, abbreviated in parts, and elsewhere developed by the use of new material since brought to light.

fancy that what is in type must be true. In ten, twenty or thirty years they are thought worthy of recognition as a source of history. Now and then a valuable contribution . . . appears, but generally reminiscences of Washington life and affairs should be dismissed without consideration by historians."[1]

One of this "medley of tales " it is proposed now to consider. A dramatic and interesting specimen, an effort, on behalf of the future historian, will be made to extract from it what "little of truth" may be therein. The story, as will be seen, was intimately connected with a very memorable episode ; and on its face it would seem to be entitled to absolute credence, coming as it did from a man of great respectability, one who occupied long and with credit to himself a highly responsible government position affording him access to the most secret springs of action and sources of information. If this does not constitute a basis for "credence," it is difficult to say what would; and yet, in fact, the story merely supplies one more striking, almost conclusive, illustration of the truth of Mr. Pierce's conclusion that "reminiscences of Washington life and affairs should be dismissed without consideration by historians."

During the administration of Abraham Lincoln, Mr. L. E. Chittenden was Register of the Treasury. Born in Vermont, in the year 1824, he was by profession a lawyer, though taking an active interest in politics. A member of the State Senate of Vermont between 1857 and 1859, in 1861 he was a delegate to the Peace Convention which met at Washington in February of that year. In April, 1861, he was appointed Register of the Treasury. Retiring from his position in 1865, he removed to New York, where he engaged in the practice of the law, giving at the same time considerable at-

[1] Mass. Hist. Soc. *Proceedings*, Second Series, X, 483.

tention to literary pursuits and historical study. In 1890 he wrote out his recollections of what occurred, more or less within his own observation, during his connection with public affairs. The papers drawn, as he stated, from memoranda made by him at the time, first appeared in *Harper's Magazine*, the series running through the year 1890; and in 1891 these articles, revised by the author, were published in a volume by the firm of Harper and Brothers, under the title of *Recollections of President Lincoln and his Administration*. The extraordinary story now about to be considered was told in much detail and with great particularity in that volume, filling an entire chapter, eighteen pages in length; and, at the time attracting much notice and comment, has since been the subject of constant inquiry and conjecture. Too long to quote in full, the narrative can for present purposes be briefly summarized. It is only necessary to premise that the events referred to occurred between the months of March and September, 1863. This period would probably by common consent be agreed upon as that of acute crisis in the War of Secession, — it was the period following Burnside's Fredericksburg fiasco, that marked by the great battles of Chancellorsville and Gettysburg, and by Grant's brilliant Vicksburg campaign. Taken altogether a gloomy stage of the struggle, its outcome was at the time indisputably doubtful. It must also be borne in mind that no Atlantic cable was then in operation, and communication by steam packet between America and Europe was slow and comparatively irregular.

Greatly condensed, Mr. Chittenden's narrative reads as follows: —

"At about eleven o'clock on a certain well-remembered Friday morning, in 1862," as he asserts, but in reality in March, 1863, Mr. Chittenden was called upon to go to the

AN HISTORICAL RESIDUUM 347

White House "without a moment's delay." Obeying the summons, he there found Secretaries Chase and Seward in anxious consultation with President Lincoln. They wished to know what was the shortest time within which ten millions in United States coupon five-twenty bonds could be prepared, signed and issued. With some circumlocution, the Register informed them. Both secretaries said that the time suggested could not be allowed. The bonds must be signed, and ready for use, before the following Monday, this, it will be remembered, being Friday. Moreover, there must be nothing on the face of the bonds thus signed to indicate that they were issued otherwise than in the regular course of business. Under the Act of Congress each bond issued had to be signed by the Register personally. He could not appoint a substitute. Only seventy hours were allowed, therefore, between the time of discussion and the time when the bonds must be on their way to New York. This extraordinary proceeding was necessitated by a special despatch received from Mr. Adams, the minister in London. Mr. Adams, it appeared, had for months been watching the work in progress in the Laird yards, at Birkenhead, where two armored vessels were then being constructed for the Confederate government. In tonnage, arms and speed these vessels were reported to be superior to any which the United States had at its disposal. The country was, therefore, face to face with a breaking of the blockade, and with that immediate recognition of the Confederacy by Great Britain which would unquestionably follow thereon. The question of arresting these vessels on the evidence submitted had, at the request of Mr. Adams, been referred by the British government to the Crown counsel; and, in accordance with their opinion, a restraining order had been issued, which, however, could not be enforced against the vessels until any possible damages incurred by the builders because of the restraint had been provided for. To indemnify against possible damages, a cash deposit of £1,000,000 sterling was required. The situation was critical ; the more so because of the not unnatural supposition that the Crown lawyers, never for a moment supposing that the United States minister would anticipate their decision and provide himself with funds accordingly, in reality planned that the ships would not be delayed. Mr. Chittenden then goes on as follows: —

"But the unexpected sometimes happens. The event which prevented these floating engines of destruction from entering upon their intended work was as unanticipated as a miracle. It constituted, possibly, the most signal service ever rendered by a citizen of one country to the government of another. It was all the more noble because it was intended to be anonymous. The eminently unselfish man who performed it made a positive condition that it should not be made public; that not so much as his name should be disclosed, except to the officers of our government, whose coöperation was required, in order to transact the business in a proper manner and upon correct principles. So earnest was his injunction of secrecy that his identity will not even now be disclosed, although he has long since gone to his reward.

"Within the hour after the Crown lawyers' decision, with its conditions, had been made known to Mr. Adams, and when he had given up all hope of arresting these vessels, a quiet gentleman called upon him and asked if he might be favored with the opportunity of making the deposit of coin required by the order? He observed 'that it had occurred to him that, if the United States had that amount to its credit in London, some question of authority might arise, or Mr. Adams might otherwise be embarrassed in complying with the condition, especially as communication with his government might involve delay; so that the shortest way to avoid all difficulty would be for him to deposit the coin, which he was quite prepared to do.'

"Had a messenger descended from the skies in a chariot of fire, with $5,000,000 in gold in his hands, and offered to leave it at the embassy without any security, Mr. Adams could not have been more profoundly surprised. He had accepted the condition as fatal to his efforts; he had concluded that nothing short of a miracle could prevent the departure of the vessels; and here, if not a miracle, was something much like one. He made no secret of the pleasure with which he accepted the munificent offer, provided some method of securing the liberal Englishman could be found. The latter seemed indisposed to make any suggestions on the subject. 'It might be proper,' he said, 'that some obligation should be entered into, showing that the American government recognized the deposit as made on its account; beyond that he should leave the matter wholly in the hands of Mr. Adams.'"

The narrative then goes on, stating that Mr. Adams thereupon proposed that $10,000,000 of the "five-twenties" should be delivered to this unnamed gentleman, to be returned when the order of arrest was discharged. The minister further volunteered the assurance that these bonds should be transmitted to London in the first steamer which left New York after his despatch concerning the transaction was received in the State Department.

"It was this assurance of Mr. Adams which the President and both of the secretaries desired should be made good. They regarded the faith of the government as pledged for its performance and that faith they proposed should not be violated.

"All the details of this transaction were not then disclosed. They reached the government in private, confidential despatches from Mr. Adams, some of them long afterwards."

Matters being thus arranged, it only remained to settle points of detail. Getting the bonds ready for immediate issue would involve the affixing of 12,500 signatures between twelve o'clock on Friday noon and four A.M. of the following Monday. Mr. Chittenden then goes on to describe the physical test to which he was subjected, in thus writing his name: —

"It is unnecessary to describe all the details of the devices and means resorted to prevent sleep and to continue the work. Changes of position, violent exercise, going out into the open air and walking rapidly for ten minutes, concentrated extracts, prepared food, stimulants more in kind and number than can now be recalled — every imaginable means was employed during the night of Saturday. . . .

"I have not had at any time since a very accurate memory of the events of that Sunday morning. That I could not remain in the same position for more than a few moments, that the bonds were carried from desk to table and from place to place to enable me to make ten signatures at a time, that my fingers and hand were twisted and drawn out of their natural shape — these and other facts are faintly remembered. The memory is more distinct that at about twelve o'clock, noon, the last bond was reached and signed, and the work was finished, the last hundred bonds requiring more time than the first thousand. One fact I have special cause to remember. This abuse of muscular energy eventually caused my resignation from the Treasury, and cost me several years of physical pain. . . ."

Finally, he says : —

"The ability of Mr. Adams to comply with the condition and furnish the security was accepted as the end of the controversy. It *is* known that a few months later $6,000,000 of the $10,000,000 of the bonds issued were returned to the Treasury in their original packages, with the seals of the Treasury unbroken. The remaining $4,000,000 were afterward sold for the benefit of the Treasury. . . .

"Since the publication of the foregoing facts in *Harper's Magazine* for May, 1890, I have been solicited by many correspondents to give the name of the gentleman who offered to perform such a signal service to our country. It must be obvious that nothing could give me greater pleasure than to publish his name, and to secure for him the enduring gratitude of the American people. I have, however, a special reason for my present determination not to disclose it, nor to permit myself to speculate upon the consequences of the disclosure. When we were informed that the emergency had passed, it became necessary to make a change in the entries of this large amount upon the books of the Register. This was found to be a difficult matter, unless a plain statement of the issue, to the gentleman in question, and its purpose, was made with its subsequent cancellation. This course I proposed to Secretary Chase. He was decided in his opinion that the value of the service would not have been enhanced if an actual deposit of the money had been required, and that, as the gentleman himself had imposed the obligation, he was the only authority who could possibly release it. While I regarded his conclusion as incontrovertible, I did suggest that our first duty was the official one, to our own obligation to conceal nothing, and to make our official records strictly conform to the fact.

"'We should have thought of that at the time,' said the secretary. 'We might have declined his offer, coupled as it was with the obligation to conceal his name. But I do not remember that we considered that question. Do you?'

"'No,' I said. 'Nothing was discussed in my presence except the possibility of compliance with his conditions, to the letter.'

"'Then, I think, we must continue to keep his secret, whatever the consequences may be, until he releases us from the obligation,' was the final conclusion of the secretary.

"I am, I believe, the only survivor of those to whom this gentleman's name was known. I have hitherto declined to discuss the question of his name or its disclosure. I depart from my practice far enough to say that I do not believe he was interested in the price of cotton, or that he was moved in the slightest degree by pecuniary motives, in making his offer. More than this, at present, I do not think I have the moral right to say. If I should at any time hereafter see my way clear to a different conclusion, I shall leave his name to be communicated to the Secretary of the Treasury, who will determine for himself the propriety of its disclosure."

As a result of these very mysterious and somewhat oracular utterances, a good deal of curiosity was not unnaturally aroused as to the identity of the "quiet gentleman" in question, and frequent inquiries reached all those in any way likely to be informed on the subject, or to have access to sources of information. Especially were these inquiries addressed to the custodians of the papers of Mr. Adams, he having died some two years before Mr. Chittenden's disclosure was made. In lack of a more definite identification, the process of guesswork through exclusion then began, and progressed until it seemed to centre on Mr. Joshua Bates as the one man who, in every sense of the expression, "filled the bill." Mr. Bates, by birth a Massachusetts man, had then (1863) long been the senior partner in the great British commercial firm of Baring Brothers & Co. No man was better known on the Royal Exchange, and no man there stood higher. Then in his seventy-fifth year, Mr. Bates could, if he saw fit, at any time put a million sterling on deposit, and his assurance would have been held sufficient for almost any additional amount within reason. Writing in 1890, Mr. Chittenden said of this unknown, "He has long since gone to his reward"; Joshua Bates died in London in September, 1864. Answering, with the less well informed, the requirements at every point, he must, it was argued, have been the individual whose identity Mr. Chittenden had not the "moral right" to disclose; nor, so far as known, did the whilom Register of the Treasury leave behind him any name, as he intimated he might, "to be communicated to a future Secretary" thereof. Indeed, as respects the solution of this mystery, it could be said of Mr. L. E. Chittenden, as of Shakespeare's Cardinal Beaufort, — "He dies, and makes no sign."

Such was the story of the stoppage of the famous Birkenhead rams of 1863, — its secret history as told by Mr. Lincoln's Register of the Treasury, personally cognizant of the facts whereof he spoke, knowing even the name of the mysterious stranger with the heavy bank account, who in this case proved indeed a *Deus ex machina*. Doubtless Mr. Chittenden when he wrote this story fully believed all he said. He, too, like the credible gentleman mentioned by Mr. Pierce, had told the tale so often that he had himself grown to a faith in every word of it. Repetition took the place of memory. On the other hand when, in consequence of Mr. Chittenden's revelations, inquiries poured in, Mr. Henry Adams, at the time in question his father's private secretary, and, as such, cognizant of everything that occurred, professed absolute ignorance of any transaction of the kind, or any even bearing a remote resemblance to it. He pronounced the whole statement a pure figment of Mr. Chittenden's imagination. In this he was confirmed by Colonel Hay, Mr. Lincoln's biographer, who in the course of his investigations nowhere could find any trace of the incidents described. None existed certainly in the records of the State Department, nor among the Seward papers. Finally, an examination of Mr. Adams's careful private diary brought no corroborative evidence to light. Not even an allusion was there found which by any possibility corroborated what could not have been other than the most startling as well as memorable event of a lifetime. Thus the enigma was dismissed as insoluble. It apparently only remained for Mr. Pierce's "ten, twenty, or thirty years" to pass away until the historian of the future should deem the story "worthy of recognition."

Eight of the first ten years actually had passed away, when the small residuum of historic fact at the basis of Mr. Chittenden's "yarn" — for it is entitled to no better name — was at last revealed. On the 12th of October, 1898, John M. Forbes, of Milton, Massachusetts, closed a long, and noticeably active life. Immediately after his death there appeared in the papers an obituary notice of him, manifestly prepared by some exceptionally well-informed writer, in the course of which reference was made to a mysterious mission of Mr. Forbes and Mr. William H. Aspinwall to Europe in 1863. It was clearly an unwritten Civil War episode. It appeared that the two gentlemen, hastily summoned to a conference in New York by Messrs. Chase and Welles, then respectively secretaries of the Treasury and the Navy, had been hurried off to England to prevent, if possible, the fitting out in British ports of Confederate cruisers, and more especially of the two iron-clads then well known to be in an advanced stage of construction at the yards of the Laird Brothers, at Birkenhead. Great Britain was in fact then being systematically utilized as a base from which Confederate naval operations could be conducted against the commerce and ports of the United States, a nation with which Great Britain was professedly at peace. More effectually to put a stop to any such illicit operations, the two gentlemen were, it was stated, further authorized to purchase, if need be, any vessels in course of preparation, and for that purpose took out with them "some millions of the new 5-20 bonds." The writer of the notice added that, though Mr. Forbes failed to accomplish what he was sent out to do, "our minister, the Hon. Charles Francis Adams, did all he could to second their efforts." Here was an historical clue; a sudden sending to Europe of a large amount of 5-20 bonds in connection with the Laird iron-clads. The following up of this clue was then made further possible through the publication of the *Letters and Recollections of John Murray Forbes*, by his daughter, Mrs. Hughes, in 1899. In the Forbes-Aspinwall mission of 1863 was to be found the residuum of truth at the bottom of the Chittenden legend.

From the letters and memoranda in Mrs. Hughes's volumes it appears that, on the 14th of March, 1863, Mr. Forbes, being then unwell at his house in Milton, received a brief telegram from Secretary Chase, requesting him to meet the sender the next morning in New York at the Fifth Avenue Hotel. Mr. Forbes complied, and there found both Mr. Chase and Mr. Welles. Mr. Aspinwall also was present. The secretaries wished Mr. Forbes to go forthwith to England; while Mr. Aspinwall was to follow immediately after, bringing with him $10,000,000 of that issue of United States bonds subsequently well known as "five-twenties," and so denominated because, maturing in twenty years from the date of issue, they could be redeemed at the option of the government at the end of five years from issue. Bearing interest payable in gold at the rate of 6 per cent, this issue had been recently authorized. Subsequently in great demand both at home and in Europe, the 5-20's were sold at par in currency, gold then being quoted at a premium of some 40 per cent. The five-twenties, therefore, a few years later called in and paid off at par, in the summer of 1863 were selling at a fluctuating price in gold, varying from 60 per cent to 75 per cent of their face value, with absolutely no market for them on any European exchange. With $10,000,000 of these securities at their disposal to enable them so to do, Messrs. Forbes and Aspinwall were, if possible, to stop the Confederate cruisers by purchase or otherwise.

The meeting in New York between the two Secretaries and the proposed, and secretly accredited, emissaries took place apparently on Sunday; and on Monday Mr. Forbes submitted a hastily drawn up letter of instructions, which Secretary Welles signed. The purchase of any vessels then being fitted out was the essential object in view. A formal open letter, in the nature of credentials, was also prepared and signed by Mr. Welles, enclosing another to Messrs. Baring Brothers, then the financial agents of the government in London, advising them that Messrs. Aspinwall and Forbes were authorized to arrange for a loan of a million sterling, on the security of $10,000,000 of 5-20 bonds in their hands. This was on Monday, the 16th, and Mr. Forbes sailed on the steamer of Wednesday; while, on the 17th, Mr. Welles noted in his diary that he "returned last evening from a strictly confidential visit to New York." Mr. Aspinwall, bringing with him the $10,000,000 of bonds, must have followed Mr. Forbes a week later, on the 25th, for he was in London and called on Mr. Adams on Tuesday, the 7th of April. As Mr. Chittenden is particular in specifying that it was on a "well remembered Friday morning" that he was summoned to the White House in the matter of these bonds, the morning in question must have been that of Friday, March 20 ; but March, 1863, and not, as he asserts in his recollections, 1862. He is a year out in his time; nor is there any possible question on this point, inasmuch as work had not been fairly begun on the Laird rams until the middle of July, 1862, and, under the contract for their construction, they were not to be ready for sea until March and May, 1863. Mr. Chittenden says that, when he received his directions in regard to signing the ten millions of bonds, a messenger from Mr. Adams had brought the startling intelligence that "within three days the vessels were to sail." That Mr. Adams never sent such a messenger is immaterial; the essential fact is that the statement fixes the year of the whole transaction as 1863, and not 1862, inasmuch as, owing to delays from various causes, the Laird iron-clads were not launched until July and August, 1863, nor were they ready for sea until early in the following October. As also only one lot of bonds of this magnitude was thus hurriedly signed and mysteriously transmitted to Europe, Mrs. Hughes's book fixes the time of their preparation as the week ending Tuesday, March 24, 1863, the Laird iron-clads being then still on the ways.

Messrs. Forbes and Aspinwall reached England during the gloomiest period of the War of Secession, — that darkest hour before the slowly breaking dawn which immediately preceded the fall of Vicksburg and the repulse of Lee at Gettysburg. In Europe, so far as the United States was concerned, the situation was at that time in the last degree critical. The *Alabama* was in the midst of her career of piratical depredation; the Confederate cotton loan had been successfully negotiated; the blockade-runner *Peterhoff* had just been captured under circumstances which deeply concerned English shipping interests; the *Alexandra*, another cruiser contracted for by the agents of the Confederacy and then being made ready for sea at Liverpool, was about to be seized by order of the government, with a view to making of its seizure a test case on which to get a judicial construction of the British Foreign Enlistment Act; the Confederate iron-clads at Birkenhead were being rapidly pushed to completion. Mr. Adams, while preserving a firm outward front, now privately recorded his fear that "the peace will scarcely last six months"; while Mr. John Bigelow, coming over from Paris, expressed to him the opinion that war was "inevitable." The mission of Messrs. Forbes and Aspinwall was important, and the resources at their disposal were considerable; any indiscretion on their part might involve serious consequences. They were there on behalf of the government to buy vessels not only to prevent their use by the rebels, but in certain cases for the use of the United States in the hostilities then going on; and this while Mr. Adams, the officially accredited representative of their country, was vehemently denying the legality of the construction or sale of such vessels for or to either belligerent. Seeking thus, under the exigencies of the situation, both to "run with the hare and hunt with the hounds," the government not unnaturally instructed its emissaries to "endeavor to avoid establishing a precedent that may embarrass our minister when urging the British government to stop the sailing of vessels belonging to the rebels."[1]

A sufficient account of this futile mission is given in Mrs. Hughes's volumes. A more judicious selection of agents could not have been made; and Messrs. Forbes and Aspinwall, while they did all that circumstances permitted, acted throughout with the utmost circumspection. This is made curiously, and sometimes amusingly, apparent through Mr. Adams's diary references to them and what they did. With Mr. Forbes he was of course well acquainted. Close neighbors at home, for they lived in adjoining towns, they had not only known each other long, but recently they had been in more or less active correspondence as representative and constituent during the troubled period which preceded the outbreak of the Civil War. Mr. Forbes says in his notes that immediately on reaching London, after seeing the Messrs. Baring, he called on Mr. Adams, who, he adds, "wanted to know only what was absolutely necessary of our mission, so that he might not be mixed up with our operations, which we knew might not be exactly what a diplomat would care to endorse." This was on the 31st of March; and that day Mr. Adams wrote "who should come in but Mr. John M. Forbes? He gave me some intimation of his errand, which is to investigate the practicability of obtaining contingents of troops from any quarter in Germany. I thought not; the only course was to engage the men. I did not doubt

[1] Forbes, *Letters and Recollections*, II, 6, 26.

they might be had in abundance." Thus the resurrected memory of the revolutionary Hessians seems to have been evoked by Mr. Forbes as a means of averting suspicion. During the next few days Mr. Forbes dined with Mr. Adams, and saw him frequently; and, on the 7th of April, Mr. Aspinwall also called. Owing to the capture of the *Peterhoff*, the seizure of the *Alexandra* and the destruction of the *Georgiana*, one of the minor rebel cruisers, "the city" was now in a condition of ferment, both active and noisy. Movements initiated by Mr. Adams to stop vessels in process of preparation at numerous points had, as he wrote, roused "the whole hive of sympathizers, as it was never stirred before."

Immediately on the arrival of Mr. Aspinwall, the $10,000,000 of bonds he brought with him in several small separate trunks were safely deposited in the vaults of Baring Brothers, and, on the security of a portion ($4,000,000) of them, £500,000 negotiated through Mr. Joshua Bates, was passed, as a loan, to the credit of Mr. Forbes. With that amount he began operations. Though he, of course, had no knowledge on that point, a million dollars out of the proceeds of the recently negotiated Cotton loan had been put at the control of the Confederate agents for the construction of the two Laird iron-clads, the contract price for which was £93,750 each, apart from all armament and munitions.[1] The purse of the United States emissaries was thus materially longer than that of the Confederate agents; but the money was not at the disposal of Mr. Adams, nor did it come from the pocket of Mr. Chittenden's "quiet gentleman," nor was it, either in whole or in any part, used for the purposes Mr. Chittenden states.

Three days after the arrival of Mr. Aspinwall, on the evening of Thursday, April 9, Mr. Forbes very sociably dropped

[1] Bulloch, *Secret Service*, I, 385, 386.

in to see Mr. Adams, with a view doubtless to an incidental talk on the business in hand, the stoppage of the various vessels in regard to which he had by this time informed himself. To those who knew Mr. Forbes, and understood his shrewd methods of working through indirections, Mr. Adams's comment on what took place is suggestive. "I explained to him," he wrote, "all that I had done; but he seemed to think private action might effect more. Here is an instance of the opposite nature of British and American training. The former always thinking of nothing but government action; the latter always underrating it." On the 17th Mr. Forbes again called, this time to report about the vessels over which he and Mr. Aspinwall were now exercising a joint private supervision, and Mr. Adams innocently wrote, "he made much of doing nothing to embarrass me." The next entry was more amusing still. The drift of the mission was beginning to show itself, and there was almost a groan of despair perceptible through what the minister now wrote. Mr. Robert J. Walker, formerly Secretary of the Treasury in the Polk administration, had now also put in an appearance in London, in the capacity of special agent of the Treasury. He was sent out by Secretary Chase to acquaint European capitalists with the actual circumstances and resources of the country; and, if possible, to negotiate the sale of some government securities. Messrs. Forbes and Aspinwall did not deem it expedient to admit Mr. Walker into their confidence; while Mr. Adams wrote: "He, as well as Messrs. Aspinwall and Forbes, are sent out from the Treasury to carry on operations of their own with which I have nothing to do. Of course, they will more or less, undertake to advise me, which I shall try to take in the best part. I feel sensibly that this mission is growing more and more difficult." Certainly a less conventionally diplomatic situation could hardly be conceived. The United States, in the midst of the most serious complications, was represented in London by at least three different agencies, drawing their instructions from separate sources, and each operating in secrecy so far as the others were concerned. That, under such an ingeniously bad system, a catastrophe did not result, speaks volumes for the discretion of those concerned.

On the 23d of April Mr. Forbes breakfasted with Mr. Adams, showing him "a general review of all the ship-yards of the island, and a description of every suspicious vessel. The activity of these rogues," Mr. Adams wrote, "is greater than ever. I do not know that any anxiety I have is heavier than this." Then, on the 28th, Messrs. Forbes and Aspinwall, feeling evidently that now they must face the real purpose of their errand, or they might compromise the minister, came to discuss the expediency of buying the ships then being built for the Confederacy. "I think," wrote Mr. Adams, "this is merely playing the game of the Englishmen. The competition for arms at the outset of the war raised their price more than double, and so it would be with steamers."

The situation had its grotesque as well as critical side, and casuistry played a conspicuous part in the statements and asseverations then made. For example, Messrs. Forbes and Aspinwall, privately accredited by Secretary Welles, were in London trying surreptitiously to buy the very vessels then being built in the Laird yards. The Assistant Secretary of the Navy, G. V. Fox, was writing to Mr. Forbes: "You must stop them at all hazards. . . . Let us have them in the United States for our own purposes, without any more nonsense, and at any price."[1] Shortly after, Secretary

[1] Hughes, *Forbes*, II, 23.

Welles himself wrote to Mr. Forbes to the same effect, "If we caught hold of any swift privateers which they are constructing or fitting out, the great purpose of your mission will have been accomplished." Yet in the very same letter, while his agent is feeling his way towards the purchase of ships at that very time in course of construction in the yards of the Laird Brothers, the Secretary indignantly denounces the former senior member of the firm, then in Parliament, for there asserting "that propositions had been made to him to build vessels for the United States." He declared the statement "destitute of truth" and thought it might be "advisable to expose Mr. Laird."[1] This he did in a letter to Mr. Sumner,[2] sent May 19, which Mr. Sumner made public on the 6th of the following August. In it he arraigned Mr. Laird as "a mercenary hypocrite without principle or honesty." It was certainly fortunate for all concerned, except Mr. Laird, that the purposes of the confidential mission of Messrs. Forbes and Aspinwall, and the methods pursued by them, were as yet undisclosed, as the distinction between building ships and buying ships half built and on the stocks, might not have carried conviction to all minds. Meanwhile, Messrs. Forbes and Aspinwall at about this time were settling down to the sensible conviction reached by Mr. Adams that "to offer to buy the iron-clads without success would only be to stimulate the builders to greater activity, and even to building new ones in the expectation of finding a market for them from one party or the other." And all this time on the other side, the agents and representatives of the Confederacy were protesting before high Heaven that they had no concern or interest in the Birkenhead iron-clads; and were executing fraudulent papers "in proper legal forms" making them "the property of Messrs.

---

[1] See also Welles, *Diary*, I, 291, 306, 394, 396.   [2] *Ibid.* 292.

Bravay and Co. of Paris, agents for the Pasha of Egypt." Altogether, it was a nicely complicated all-around case of fraud, deceit, duplicity, and double-dealing generally.

Throughout the month of May, Messrs. Forbes and Aspinwall remained in England, gradually reaching the conclusion that they could accomplish nothing. Meanwhile Mr. William M. Evarts had been added to the contingent of special government emissaries, he being sent out to supervise the legal proceedings in the case of the *Alexandra*. "It cannot be denied," wrote Mr. Adams, "that ever since I have been here the almost constant interference of government agents of all kinds has had the effect, however intended, of weakening the position of the minister. Most of all has it happened in the case of Mr. Evarts, whom the newspapers here have all insisted to have been sent here to superintend my office in all questions of international law. I doubt whether any minister has ever had so much of this kind of thing to contend with."

It is instructive to know that it was not Mr. Adams alone who was at this time thus encumbered with aid. The Confederate emissaries seem to have had similar cause of complaint; and in September, 1862, nine months before Mr. Adams made the foregoing entry in his diary, Captain Bulloch had written on this head as follows to the Confederate Secretary of the Navy: "I do not hesitate to say that embarrassment has already been occasioned by the number of persons from the South who represent themselves to be agents of the Confederate States Government. There are men so constituted as not to be able to conceal their connection with any affairs which may by chance add to their importance, and such persons are soon found out and drawn into confessions and statements by gossiping acquaintances, to the serious detriment of the service upon which they are engaged." [1]

During the early years of ¿Mr. Adams's mission, indeed until the autumn of 1863, when the government detained the Birkenhead iron-clads, Great Britain was, for reasons which at once suggest themselves, the special field of diplomatic activity, and the minister at London was at last driven to active remonstrance. The emissaries were of four distinct types: (1) the roving diplomat, irregularly accredited by the State Department; (2) the poaching diplomat, regularly accredited to one government, but seeking a wider field of activity; (3) the volunteer diplomat, not accredited at all, but in his own belief divinely commissioned at that particular juncture to enlighten foreign nations generally, and Great Britain in particular; and (4) the special agent, sent out by some department of the government to accomplish, if possible, a particular object.

As to these unassigned and peripatetic diplomats of the Civil War period, their name was legion, and they could only be dealt with in adequate fashion in a separate paper. To understand the system pursued it is necessary to begin with a reference to Secretary Seward's idiosyncrasies and political methods. When, in March, 1861, the ex-governor of New York, and the leading partner in the former firm of Seward, Weed & Greeley, then dissolved by the withdrawal of its junior member, — when Secretary Seward took charge (March, 1861) of the Department of State, he at once adopted a policy and inaugurated a system characteristic of New York politics. The country was face to face with what amounted to a revolution. The outcome was in large degree plainly dependent on the course of events in Europe,

---

[1] Bulloch, *Secret Service*, I, 390; also Bigelow, *Retrospections*, I, 481; II, 137.

and especially in Great Britain and France. That course of events was again necessarily much influenced by the public opinion in those countries prevailing; so, with a view to the situation, President Lincoln's foreign secretary arranged the machinery of his office on a plan peculiarly his own. He did not propose to depend altogether on the traditional accredited representatives of the country. He planned, on the contrary, to have his own private bureau of intelligence, and system of manikin wires. Accordingly, with a view to influencing, as he so considered, the European mind, while at the same time informing himself, he, first and last, precipitated on Europe a flight of generally accredited representatives and special agents, — men of eminence, dignitaries of the established churches, eminent evangelistic divines, journalists, lawyers and financiers, — whose province it was, besides educating and influencing benighted Europe, to keep him personally advised, much in the fashion of a newspaper press agency. Of those thus specially commissioned, Mr. John Bigelow was one of the more judiciously selected; and, probably, distinctly the most efficient. Without any special qualification for the post, he was appointed consul-general at Paris; with the clear further understanding that he was to use his journalistic experience acquired in the editorial rooms of the New York *Evening Post* to influence the press of continental Europe. The manipulation of the English press was at the same time entrusted to Mr. Thurlow Weed, the secretary's journalistic and political *fidus Achates*. While the private and confidential communications with the Secretary of State of those gentlemen, as of others similarly commissioned, have never as yet to any large extent seen the light, they probably contained a varied assortment of information and gossip, the nature and value of which can only be surmised.

The presence of this corps of international supernumeraries was well known abroad, and, naturally, not understood. By the foreign chancelleries, it was taken to indicate a lack of confidence in the regularly accredited representatives; and was not unskilfully manipulated to that end by the agents of the Confederacy.

Of those of the class first specified, the generally accredited or roving diplomats, lay and church, it is unnecessary here to speak. The more discreet and better informed of those invited to go declined so to do; of those who did go, Mr. Adams subsequently said they "failed entirely," while in so doing they "worried" him more than they enlightened the English.[1] Among the poaching brethren of the second class he especially mentioned Henry S. Sanford, and Cassius M. Clay, accredited respectively to Belgium and Russia. Of Mr. Sanford's private correspondence with the Secretary, nothing is known. It was probably largely made up of gossip and secret service information. Otherwise, Mr. Sanford's most active negotiation was conducted neither in Belgium nor in Great Britain, but in Italy; and was in connection with a most ill-considered move to induce Garibaldi to go to America and there accept high military command. A commission as major-general was actually offered him; but the Italian insisted on a dictatorship, civil as well as military.[2] So, most fortunately, Mr. Sanford's diplomatic activities proved altogether abortive.

In view of the subsequent career of Mr. Cassius M. Clay, and his widely published domestic episodes, it is charitable to say as little as may be of his diplomatic experiences. They were, to say the least, the reverse of either conventional or happy. Meanwhile, the late John Hay, then Lincoln's

---

[1] Mass. Hist. Soc. *Proceedings*, Second Series, XVI, 465.
[2] *Ibid.* Third Series, I, 319–325.

private secretary though himself Secretary of State thirty years afterwards, used to tell a story of Mr. Clay not only characteristic, but too entertaining to be lost. While Mr. Clay was representing the country at St. Petersburg, Charles Sumner, then chairman of the Senate Committee of Foreign Affairs, greatly offended him by some utterance, whether on the floor of the Senate or elsewhere. Mr. Clay thereupon sat down and indited an official despatch to the Secretary of State, in which he dealt with the Massachusetts Senator quite, as the expression goes, without gloves, and certainly without mercy. There were, indeed, according to Mr. Hay, few possible animadversions of an offensive nature left unexpressed. Having thus relieved himself, Mr. Clay at the close of his fulmination dropped suddenly into the diplomatic style, ending, *mutatis mutandis*, with the regulation formula, "You may read this despatch to Mr. Sumner, and should he request it you can give him a copy."

But, if Mr. Adams was "worried" by intrusions on his peculiar domain from without, if Secretary Welles can be depended on as an authority, the London situation was not wholly free from its domestic annoyances. When Mr. Adams assumed the duties of his mission, the Secretary appointed Mr. Charles L. Wilson, of Chicago, as First Secretary Legation. Wholly without diplomatic experience or familiarity with foreign or official life, Mr. Wilson was chief owner and editor of a Chicago daily newspaper of the western type of that period, which had been ardent in support of Mr. Seward in his presidential aspirations. He may have been in private communication with Mr. Seward, but Mr. Wilson certainly did not feel either at home or at ease amid his new surroundings. Accordingly, at the very time that Messrs. Forbes and Aspinwall were bestirring themselves in British shipping circles, Secretary Welles was making the following diary entry: [1] —

"Sumner tells me of a queer interview he had with Seward. The first part of the conversation was harmonious and related chiefly to the shrewd and cautious policy and management of the British ministry, who carefully referred all complex questions to the law officers of Her Majesty's government. It might have been a hint to Seward to be more prudent and considerate, and to take legal advice instead of pushing on, wordy and slovenly, as is sometimes done. . . . Our Minister, Mr. Adams, was spoken of as too reserved and retiring for his own and the general good. Sumner said, in justification and by way of excuse for him, that it would be pleasanter and happier for him if he had a Secretary of Legation whose deportment, manner, and social position were different, — if he were more affable and courteous, in short more of a gentleman, — for he could in that case make up for some of Mr. A.'s deficiencies. At this point Seward flew into a passion, and, in a high key, told Sumner he knew nothing of political (meaning party) claims and services, and accused him of a design to cut the throat of Charley Wilson, the Secretary of Legation at London. Sumner wholly disclaimed any such design or any personal knowledge of the man, but said he had been informed, and had no doubt of the fact, that it was the daily practice of Wilson to go to Morley's, seat himself in a conspicuous place, throw his legs upon the table, and, in coarse language, abuse England and the English. Whatever might be our grievances and wrong, this, Sumner thought, was not a happy method of correcting them, nor would such conduct on the part of the second officer of the legation bring about kinder feelings, or a better state of things, whereas a true gentleman could by suavity and dignity in such a position win respect, strengthen his principal, and benefit the country. These remarks only made Seward more violent, and louder in his declarations that Charley Wilson was a clever fellow and should be sustained."

Perhaps the most unfortunate of the volunteer, as distinguished from the roving, poaching, and special diplomats

[1] Welles, *Diary*, I, 300, 301.

of that period, was Mr. Moncure D. Conway. In 1863 Mr. Conway made his appearance in England, whither he had gone "to enlighten the British public in regard to the causes of the war." He almost at once invited a correspondence with Mr. Mason, the Confederate envoy, the outcome of which was bewildering rather than either happy or significant. It is now an altogether forgotten incident, and at the moment was not material. It had, however, a certain interest as illustrating the dangers inseparable from volunteer diplomacy in troublous times; and it led to some highly suggestive comments on the part of Mr. Adams, to be found in a despatch (No. 437) from that gentleman to Secretary Seward, under date of June 25, 1863.[1] Any one curious to read the Conway-Mason correspondence in connection with the history of that period, can find it in full in the columns of the London *Times* of June 18, 1863 ; while Mr. Conway subsequently (1904) gave in detail his own account of it and its consequences to himself personally, entitling it, "The Mason Incident."[2]

This divergence, though long perhaps, is still not without its interest and even value in connection with the diplomatic history of the Civil War period. It at least has the merit of novelty. But, returning now to the mission of Messrs. Forbes and Aspinwall, they, as also Mr. Evarts, were of the last description of the "accredited," — special agents sent out by some department for a particular purpose. They were men of energy, tact and discretion. Accordingly they had the good sense to confine themselves to the work they were there to do, and did not indulge in a pernicious, general activity. With his rare tact, shrewd judgment and quick insight into men, Thurlow Weed, a roving diplomat,

---

[1] *Diplomatic Correspondence*, 1863, Part I, 318; also Seward to Adams, No. 654, *ibid.* 358.   [2] *Autobiography*, I, 412–428.

made himself of use both in Great Britain and on the Continent, and relations of a friendly character grew up between him and Mr. Adams. Of others, roving, poaching or volunteer, Mr. Adams had grave and just cause of complaint; they were officious, they meddled, and they were to the last degree indiscreet. They were peculiarly addicted to the columns of the *Times*, in which their effusions appeared periodically: but not always did they confine themselves to ill-considered letter-writing or mere idle talk.

Meanwhile during the early months of 1863 the scrutiny exercised both at home and in Great Britain, be it through government officials, Union detectives or Confederate sympathizers, was altogether too close to enable men as active and prominent as Messrs. Forbes and Aspinwall to escape suspicion. The Confederate newspaper correspondents in New York almost at once got scent of their mission, and set to work to make trouble. One of them, signing himself "Manchester," spoke of the two as "delegates" about "to be followed by eight other men of note," one being Mr. W. M. Evarts, all of whom would "regulate our affairs abroad, and Mr. Adams is ordered to be their mouthpiece." This correspondent then proceeds as follows: "[Mr. Evarts] is a particular friend of W. H. Seward. The latter, it is well known, has lost all confidence in Mr. Adams, who, but for his name, would have been recalled long ago. Mr. Seward expresses himself on all occasions, early and late, that the real source of bad feeling in England towards the North has been caused by the extraordinary stupidity of Mr. Adams, our minister, and the really clever ability of all the rebel agents." This utterance seems to have caused Secretary Seward some annoyance, as the Treasury was in its turn now poaching on the domain of the State Department. Moreover, it did not require much time to satisfy

Messrs. Forbes and Aspinwall that the Confederate agents were sufficiently in funds to "render it impossible to approach the Messrs. Laird with an offer for the rams"; and, accordingly, they were forced to limit themselves to watching the effects of the legal proceedings initiated by Mr. Adams, in the hope that an opportunity would offer for "some negotiator to step in." In the interim, obviously to avert suspicion, it was thought expedient for Mr. Forbes to visit Germany, the land of Hessian mercenaries, while Mr. Aspinwall betook himself to France. They remained away until well into June; and, on their return to London, satisfied of their inability to do anything towards stopping work on the Birkenhead iron-clads, the first of which was then nearly ready to be launched, they decided to return to America. This action on their part was accelerated by the news from home ; for the crisis of the struggle was plainly at hand. It came, indeed, while they were on the ocean. For a man of Mr. Forbes's intense activity a longer absence at such a time was well-nigh impossible. Indeed, when, five weeks before, the details of the disaster at Chancellorsville reached London, he had been so much depressed by the news that, as he at the time told Mr. Adams, he had been strongly inclined to abandon his mission and start back to America that very day.

To return to the $10,000,000 of 5-20 bonds brought out by Mr. Aspinwall, and placed in the keeping of Baring Brothers. As already stated, $4,000,000 had been pledged to that firm as security for the loan of £500,000. The remaining $6,000,-000 were now withdrawn, and taken back to America. The two commissioners landed in New York on the 12th of July, just before the breaking out of the draft riots of 1863. Mr. Forbes, though not until twenty-one years later, wrote down his own recollections of how he handled on the wharf his "pile of trunks, which included three containing six millions of 5-20 bonds"; and these, doubtless, were the bonds which Mr. Chittenden refers to as being a few days later "returned to the Treasury in the original packages, with the seals of the Treasury unbroken."

Such is the residuum of authentic history at the bottom of this portion of Mr. Chittenden's recollections. Where his story was not a pure figment of the imagination, his memory deceived him at almost every point. The amount involved, and the number of bonds returned to the Treasury, together, probably, with the physical exertion he underwent in signing them, were alone accurately stated. It only remains to suggest some plausible theory through which to explain a deception so singular; for, undoubtedly, Mr. Chittenden believed what he wrote. That explanation probably is not far to seek. The heads of department undeniably concerned in the mission were Secretaries Welles and Chase. Mr. Chittenden also asserts that the President and Secretary Seward were "in anxious consultation " over it. This may or may not be so; but, undoubtedly, they were cognizant of it. In any event, the utmost secrecy was necessary to the success of the scheme, and it was highly desirable that as few persons as possible should be in any way informed as to it. The whole proceeding was to the last degree irregular, and most suggestive as to the way in which government operations were then conducted. The Navy Department was that more immediately concerned. In it the scheme originated, and by it the agents were accredited. Yet not an allusion to it of any sort is to be found in the diary of Mr. Welles, beyond the brief mention of a "strictly confidential visit to New York" on March 17, 1863. As to the Treasury, a query at once suggested itself as to how far those methods of procedure were carried in other and not dissimilar cases. Ten millions of dollars is no inconsiderable sum. Five or six trunks full of government bonds are worth looking after. In this case ten millions of bonds were withdrawn from the vaults and their official custodians, and put in the hands of two private gentlemen to take out of the country, and dispose of pretty much as they saw fit; and, so far as appears, not a receipt even was filed to indicate what had become of them. The proceeding was wrapped in impenetrable mystery. Messrs. Forbes and Aspinwall were not officers of the government, or responsible to any one. Ten million dollars were simply put at their service, and the two secretaries alone had cognizance of the transaction, knew where the securities were, what it was proposed to do with their proceeds, or who could account for them. To the heads of department during the Rebellion period, "millions of money were as star distances to ordinary men, whether two or three hundred billions of miles, what difference?"

Meanwhile, large and irregular as the Treasury operations then unquestionably were, the taking of ten millions of bonds from the Treasury and sending them in one body to Europe, where it was notorious no market or demand then existed, could not but excite comment among the officials necessarily concerned. The Register of the Treasury, suddenly called upon to authenticate this large issue by his own signature to each particular bond, might naturally be prompted to ask some explanation of a proceeding at once so large, so hasty, and so shrouded in mystery. The inference would be reasonable that the explanation given by Mr. Chittenden was in a general way concocted and agreed upon between the two secretaries, Chase and Welles, to be ready for use in case of emergency; and they tried it on the Register. He accepted it in perfect good faith, and religiously preserved it for years as a state secret. Then, at last, through a magazine of large circulation, he took the public into his confidence, verifying none of his facts or dates. Meanwhile he intimates that, at the time when he reduced his "Recollections" to paper, he was actually in possession of the name of that mysterious and altogether mythical "quiet gentleman" who "offered to perform such a signal service to our country." This is not impossible. He may have got it from Secretary Chase; and not impossibly a gleam of suppressed humor lurked in the Secretary's eye, as, with a face otherwise wholly imperturbable, he invented a name very proper to complete the grave mystification of the Register. The mystification is, however, now cleared up, one more cock-and-bull historical fiction is disposed of, and a small residuum of truth has been precipitated.

X

QUEEN VICTORIA AND THE CIVIL WAR [1]

ON the 7th of February, 1901, the New York Chamber of Commerce took occasion at its monthly meeting to observe the recent death of Queen Victoria. Speeches were made and resolutions offered and passed. Among the speeches was one by Abram S. Hewitt, then in his seventy-ninth year, and perhaps fairly entitled to the designation of New York's first citizen. A man of large experience, who had held high public office, Mr. Hewitt's word, whether on matter of opinion or of fact, carried weight; for through a long life he had shown himself conscientious and truthful. Himself conversant with the inside of affairs of state, he presumably knew that whereof he spoke. As his eulogist not untruly said of him immediately after his death, " What he wrote or said in public addresses was weighty in the best sense. . . . He was absolutely free from the slovenly profuseness in public speech with which many worthy men in American public life afflict their country." [2]

On the occasion referred to, Mr. Hewitt, though, as he said, "grown very reluctant to [speak] upon any public

---

[1] The substance of this study appeared originally in three separate papers submitted to the Massachusetts Historical Society at its meetings, respectively, of October, 1903, January, 1904, and November, 1906. (*Proceedings*, Second Series, XVII, 440-448; XVIII, 123-154; XX, 454-474.) These papers have for the present publication been revised, largely recast and materially added to, as well as compressed. For citations of authorities, etc., when not given, recourse can be had to the Mass. Hist. Soc. *Proceedings*.

[2] E. M. Shepard in *The American Monthly Review of Reviews* for February, 1903, p. 164.

occasion," accepted the invitation so to do, and by request seconded the resolutions prepared and moved by Seth Low, then President of Columbia College, later Mayor of the city of New York. Not only did he speak, but he incorporated in what he said the following noteworthy personal reminiscence and startling historical revelation: —

"President Low has referred to the *Trent* affair. It is known to all of you. I shall take no time in elaborating the incident, but it was the first occasion when the Queen had to remember the reception which had been given [here in America the year before] to the Prince of Wales and the future King of England. We are told that with her own hand she modified the harsh and unfriendly language which would undoubtedly have made it impossible, if it had been published, for Mr. Seward to extricate himself from the unfortunate dilemma in which we were placed by the arrest of the Confederate envoys by Commodore Wilkes. But other occasions arose for the Queen to show her kindly feeling, and as to one of these, I am, I suppose, the only living witness, and this explains why I accepted the invitation of your President to appear here and do what I have grown very reluctant to do, — make an address upon any public occasion. It happened that in 1862 I was sent by the Government on a confidential mission to England and France. In the course of my work I had the most intimate relations with Minister Charles Francis Adams and with Judge Dayton, who was the Minister to France. One afternoon I received a message from Judge Dayton asking me to come to the Embassy, where he asked me if I could leave for London that night. I told him I could if the matter were important. He said a piece of information had just come to his notice which he could not trust to the telegraph or even to the post. That he wished a special messenger to go to Mr. Adams and report to him what had happened. I told him I would go, and he then said, 'I have just received information from a confidential source that the Emperor Napoleon III has proposed to the British Government to recognize the Confederacy at once. I am sure that Mr. Adams has no knowledge of the fact. I want you to proceed to London to-night, see him as early as possible in the morning, and communicate the information to him.' I went to London. I saw Mr. Adams very early the next morning, as soon as he was visible, and I told him what Judge Dayton had said. I found that Mr. Adams had already an intimation from some source that the recognition was impending. However, he said he would call upon Lord John Russell, the Minister for Foreign Affairs, and ascertain what was proposed to be done. He made the call and I waited for his return. He told me that he had seen Lord John Russell and had asked him distinctly whether any proposition had been received for the recognition of the Confederacy. He received an evasive reply. It was evident to him that something of a very serious nature was on foot. But Lord John Russell declined to communicate any definite information on the subject. He told me that he then said to Lord John Russell, 'I desire an audience with the Queen.' Lord John Russell replied that it was not usual for Ministers to have an audience with the Queen; that all communications must pass through the Foreign Office. I believe — perhaps General Wilson will correct me if I am wrong — that there is a usage by which only Ambassadors can demand an interview with the Sovereign, and that Ministers — at that time we had no Ambassadors — that Ministers had no such right, but that it might be accorded as a matter of courtesy. Mr. Adams said he told Lord John Russell that he hoped he would arrange it; but at any rate he was going to Windsor that day in person, and would send a request, asking the Queen to hear him personally. He went to Windsor. Whether Lord John Russell made any communication or not, I do not know. Mr. Adams saw the Queen in the presence of Prince Albert; told her why he had come, and he said to her: 'If there is any foundation for this information which I have received, I appeal to your Majesty to prevent so great a wrong, which will result in universal war, for I can assure your Majesty that the American people are prepared to fight the whole world rather than give up the Union.' [Applause.] He said that the Queen, in the most gracious manner, replied, 'Mr. Adams, give yourself no concern. My Government will not recognize the Confederacy.' [Applause.]

"Now, this may be a very inappropriate course of remark for this occasion, but I am anxious to have these facts preserved in the records of the Chamber of Commerce. I think it very likely that the despatch of Mr. Adams to Secretary Seward contains the information which I have given you here, but I have never seen it, and I do not know that it has ever been published."

The extreme vagueness of this reminiscence cannot fail at once to attract notice. No details as respects either time or place are given, while the statements have no recognizable relation with established historical facts. Correspondence with Mr. Hewitt failed to elicit anything more specific, except that "it must have been as early as the month of July," presumably of the year 1862.[1] Indicating, as the proceedings did, an almost equal disregard of English constitutional methods and of Court etiquette, the story could have been accepted by no writer of even average care. Nevertheless, coming directly from Mr. Hewitt in so public a way and in such a specific shape, it excited curiosity. Where, in this case, was the residuum of historic fact? Presumably there must be such a residuum, could it but be precipitated.

In his paper, elsewhere referred to,[2] on *Recollections as a Source of History*, Mr. Edward L. Pierce mentions one credible gentleman who had told a tale so often that he had himself grown to a faith in every word of it; and another who had in early life heard the story of an event, and, frequently telling it, had at last come to believe that he had himself been a witness of what he described. It was probably so with Mr. Hewitt, and his Chamber of Commerce Victorian reminiscence; but while in the previous case of Mr. Chittenden's "Recollections," thanks to the publication of Mrs. Hughes's *Letters and Recollections of John M. Forbes*, a residuum of historical fact was reached,[3] in the case of Mr. Hewitt the most careful search among

---

[1] See Mass. Hist. Soc. *Proceedings*, Second Series, XVII, 444.
[2] *Supra*, 344.
[3] *Supra*, 374.

papers and records brought nothing to light. It accordingly at last became apparent that in every part — scope as well as detail — the incident was imaginary — an octogenarian's hallucination![1]

So far as internal evidence and established facts afford basis for a conclusion, the incidents described by Mr. Hewitt must have occurred during the first four months of 1862. But it so chances Mr. Adams kept a detailed diary throughout his life, and especially during his mission to Great Britain. In that diary a record of no single day of the period in question is lacking; yet in it there is no mention of any diplomatic visit to Windsor, such as that described. And here the investigation narrows. In his reminiscence Mr. Hewitt says that "Mr. Adams saw the Queen in presence of Prince Albert." But it so chances that Prince Albert had died on the 14th of December of the previous year, 1861. Subsequently, as is perfectly well known, the Queen, prostrated by the death of the Prince Consort, became practically unsettled in mind. Completely secluding herself, she thereafter, for months and even years, saw no one but members of her household, her closest personal friends and her ministers. So far as Mr. Adams was concerned, as matter of fact he never during his long mission — May, 1861, to May, 1868 — was officially at Windsor, except as a member of the diplomatic corps on the occasion of the marriage of the Prince of Wales. The Queen was not then visible from the place assigned to the American minister; and after the death of Prince Albert he did not again lay eyes on her Majesty until her reappearance on occasions of state at a "Court" held at Buckingham Palace on the 9th of April, 1864, — the time of Grant's advance upon Richmond.

This, the first function at which the Queen presided subse-

[1] Mass. Hist. Soc. *Proceedings*, Second Series, XVIII, 124.

quent to the death of the Prince Consort, took place nearly twenty-eight months later. All thought of a European intervention in the American war had then been dismissed. In the interim, Mr. Adams had been under the same roof with the Queen once only, the occasion already mentioned, the marriage of the Prince of Wales. Mr. Hewitt's alleged Windsor interview, if it took place at all, must therefore have taken place, not in 1862, but in 1861. Moreover, if it took place in 1861, it must have been prior to November 25 of that year, as on that day Mr. Adams left London to pay a visit to Lord Houghton at Frystone; nor did he return to London until after the arrival of the news of the *Trent* affair, and the first development (December 1) of the fatal illness of the Prince. But, unfortunately, Mr. Hewitt says he himself was not sent to Europe until 1862. Even supposing he was mistaken in this, and was in London in the summer of 1861, the royal family were at Balmoral from August 31 to October 22 of that year, at which date they started to come up to Windsor. The interview could, therefore, by any possibility have occurred only between October 24, 1861, when they reached Windsor, and December 1, when the Prince sickened; but during that brief space of time every day is fully accounted for in Mr. Adams's diary, and no such incident is mentioned.

It is always difficult to prove a negative to demonstration. Especially is this so when the facts alleged, or something resembling them, may have taken place anywhere during a period of years. In the present instance, however, a complete negative is proved not only as above set forth, but by the additional and decisive fact that no mention whatever of, nor even an allusion to, any such extraordinary performance as that described by Mr. Hewitt, is anywhere to be found in Mr. Adams's diary, correspondence or papers, much less in any public or private despatch of his to the Secretary of State. No accredited minister to any foreign country could, of course, have ventured on such an unprecedented and wholly irregular step without reporting it at once to his government. Mr. Adams, moreover, was of all men that one least likely to have had recourse to such a supreme effort at what could, perhaps, best be denominated shirt-waist diplomacy.

How, then, account for Mr. Hewitt's extraordinary statement? On what basis of fact was it built up? That Mr. Hewitt was in Europe during the Civil War is unquestionable. He was also in England, and saw more or less of Mr. Adams. That he interested himself greatly, and after his own energetic fashion, in the efforts to detain the Confederate cruisers and to circumvent the plans of the agents of the Confederacy goes almost without saying. That he was also at one time sent over by Mr. Dayton to advise Mr. Adams of diplomatic moves then on foot, but which subsequently failed to materialize, is altogether probable; though curiously enough a fairly careful examination fails to reveal any allusion to him in such a capacity in Mr. Adams's papers. All this, though not important, is highly probable. But, admitting all this, and, if need be, much more, it does not seem possible to avoid the conclusion that the whole account of that extremely unconventional Windsor morning call, with its royal though somewhat autocratic if informal, assurance of peace and good-will, was a pure figment of the imagination, — "such stuff as dreams are made on." In this case the most careful analysis yields positively no residuum whatever of historical fact.

But the Hewitt reminiscence naturally leads up to another Civil War legend, — the accepted tradition, now become almost an article of American faith, that somehow and in some way the cause of the Union was in its hour of trial dear to Queen Victoria, and that we of the North were then under deep and peculiar obligation to her.

It was on the 7th of February, 1901, that Mr. Hewitt put on formal record his recollection, based wholly on hearsay, of that apocryphal interview had between the American minister and Queen Victoria in the royal domesticity of Windsor, in which the latter took occasion to commit herself so unreservedly against any action of her constitutional advisers which might lead to hostilities between Great Britain and the United States. Almost exactly a year after the ex-Mayor of New York made this contribution to the diplomatic history of our Civil War, her grandson, Prince Henry of Prussia, came to Boston in the course of a tour through the United States, and, on the 6th of March, 1902, an honorary degree was conferred upon him by Harvard University. In a carefully prepared address delivered in Saunders Theatre by President Eliot, when conferring the degree, was the following: —

"Universities have long memories. Forty years ago the American Union was in deadly peril, and thousands of its young men were bleeding and dying for it. It is credibly reported that at a very critical moment the Queen of England said to her prime minister, 'My Lord, you must understand that I shall sign no paper which means war with the United States.' The grandson of that illustrious woman is sitting with us here."

To much the same effect, though nearly thirty years earlier, Mr. Joseph H. Choate thus expressed himself at a reception tendered that very true friend of ours, the Right Hon. William E. Forster, at the Union League Club of New York City, December 14, 1874: " We shall probably find out that we had [in Great Britain, during the War of Secession] more friends than we knew, both in Parliament and in the Government; and there is the best of reasons for believing that that gracious lady, the Queen herself, was from the first to the last an obstinately faithful ally of America, and was utterly averse to anything that might tend to a breach of the peace with her dearest ally."

Here in two instances, far removed from each other both in place and time, was Mr. Hewitt's story, appearing and reappearing in a slightly different form. Mr. Choate adduced in support of his statement a letter from Thurlow Weed, telling the familiar and to us pathetic story of Prince Albert's suggested modifications of Earl Russell's first draught of a despatch to Lord Lyons, in November, 1861, when news of the Mason-Slidell seizure on the *Trent* reached England. The somewhat carefully guarded statement of President Eliot was both more recent and more specific. The language quoted by him as that made use of by the Queen was substantially the same as that contained in the Hewitt reminiscence; but it was, in this version, uttered to her minister and not to the representative of a foreign country, and that country the one directly involved. In so far the Eliot version bore an aspect of much greater probability than the Hewitt version. The Eliot version was, humanly speaking, at least possible; this can scarcely be said of the Hewitt version. In reply to a letter asking his authority for the statement thus made, if indeed he had any authority except Mr. Hewitt's then comparatively recent utterance, President Eliot wrote as follows: —

"In 1874 I was at Oxford for a week. Dr. Acland, to whom I had a letter, procured for me an invitation to lunch with Prince Leopold, who was then living with a tutor in a small house at Oxford and going to some lectures. Dr. Acland went with me, and we were four at the table. In the course of luncheon the Prince told the story of the Queen's interview with Lord Russell, Dr. Acland prompting him to do so. He gave no authorities, and said nothing about the source of his information. He must have been a small boy at the time of this interview with the Queen. Dr. Acland spoke of the story as if he believed it. Naturally I remembered the Prince's statement, but I do not know that I ever talked about it. Quite lately — that is, since last March — I heard somebody else attribute this statement to Prince Leopold, but I have now forgotten who that somebody else was.[1] I have never seen any real authority for it, and that is the reason I used the expression 'credibly stated.'"

It thus appears that President Eliot spoke from his own recollection of what he had twenty-seven years previously been told by a youth of twenty-one of an occurrence and conversation which must have taken place at least twelve years before that, and when the youth in question was still a boy; for Prince Leopold, born in April, 1853, was, in 1862, as yet a child of nine. Nevertheless, here is authority, such as it is. Sir Henry Acland was in 1874 a man of fifty-nine. He had been in America, a member of the suite of the Prince of Wales during his memorable tour of 1860. In 1874 he was Regius Professor of Medicine at Oxford, and honorary physician to Prince Leopold, then an undergraduate. Thus a man very competent to form an opinion on such a point, and so situated as to have special sources of information thereon, intimated a belief in the story. This is corroborative evidence too strong to be lightly brushed aside. It indicates clearly and indisputably that an accepted tradition prevailed in the royal family and about Windsor Castle, that, at some period of crisis in the course of our Civil War, Queen Victoria did take a decided stand with the ministry in opposition to anything calculated to provoke hostil-

---

[1] The person referred to was the late Prof. N. S. Shaler. See his *Autobiography*, 264.

ities with the United States. Accepted traditions are rarely without some foundation of fact.

For this particular tradition, now welded into our American popular belief, can any clearly established foundation in fact be found? — and was the policy of the Palmerston-Russell ministry, in power throughout our War of Secession, at any juncture of that war gravely influenced by the Queen? To get at the probabilities in the case it is necessary to go far back, and obtain a correct understanding of the way in which, at the time in question, the Queen and her principal advisers viewed the situation of affairs and course of events, so far as the troubles in America were concerned. Nor in attempting this is it necessary to enter into any elaborate analysis of the character of Queen Victoria necessarily drawn from the most general sources of information. It is sufficient for present purposes to call attention to a very noticeable article, entitled "The Character of Queen Victoria," which appeared in the *Quarterly Review* shortly after her death.[1]

This article, the authorship of which, only surmised, has never been publicly avowed, was evidently prepared by a practised writer, probably in collaboration with some woman, presumably of rank, who enjoyed long and peculiar means of intimate observation of the royal family. From what is said in this paper, — which at the time occasioned a great deal of talk in England, — several points of much significance in the present connection may safely be educed. Neither naturally, nor under the shaping influence of the Prince Consort, did the Queen have any bias towards democracy. It was Francis Joseph of Austria who on some occasion remarked, "Royalty is my business"; and Queen

[1] Referred to by Mr. Morley in his *Life of Gladstone* (Vol. II, p. 425) as "the remarkable article in the *Quarterly Review*," No. 386, April, 1901, p. 320.

Victoria might well have so said. Throughout her entire life she bore herself in the spirit of the apothegm; and towards democracy in all its aspects and wherever existing, she felt an instinctive aversion. An ingrained Jacobite, one of her "strongest traits was her partiality for the Stuarts; she forgave them all their faults. She used to say, 'I am far more proud of my Stuart than of my Hanoverian ancestors'; and of the latter indeed she very seldom spoke." She would permit of no disparagement of even poor old James II; and Dean Stanley used to say that, in character, she much resembled Queen Elizabeth, — whom by the way, she particularly disliked. "When she faces you down with her 'It must be,'" the Dean declared, "I don't know whether it is Victoria or Elizabeth who is speaking." In the social life of the Palace, also, there was nothing of the *bourgeois* Queen about Victoria. She was insistent on Court etiquette; and the picture given in the article in the *Quarterly* of the German evenings at Windsor is extremely suggestive. "The Royalties stood together on the rug in front of the fire, a station which none durst hold but they; and amusing incidents occurred in connection with this sacred object." Thus the Queen was utterly devoid of what may be termed sympathy for those democratic institutions of which the American Union was the great exponent among the nations, or for any movement in that direction. On the other hand, she had an instinctive dread of war, and of all foreign complications likely to result in war. Moreover, she had in 1860 been gratified, and even touched, by the warm welcome everywhere extended to the Prince of Wales by the great English-speaking community across the Atlantic. The recollection of it was still fresh in memory when the issues of the Civil War presented themselves. A single thing more remains to be said. Queen Victoria was in one important respect the true grandchild of George III, our old revolutionary *bête noir*. To quote again, and for the last time, from the article in the *Quarterly:* "No one that knew her late Majesty well will be inclined to deny that her extraordinary pertinacity, her ingrained inability to drop an idea which she had fairly seized, might naturally have developed into obstinacy. By nature she certainly was what could only be called obstinate, but the extraordinary number of opposite objects upon which her will was incessantly exercised saved her from the consequences of this defect." This final saving clause was of course naturally limited to normal conditions. It would be wholly safe, on the other hand, to surmise that the latent peculiarity of character here alluded to would, in her case as in the case of her grandfather, become morbidly active in presence of sufficiently exciting causes, or under an excessive nervous strain.

Such was the Queen, a factor in the political conditions of her kingdom which no minister or combination of ministers was, during her long reign, ever able to ignore or even override. The royal sphere might be limited, and closely hedged about; but it was there, and within it her Majesty was supreme.

During the Civil War the so-called Palmerston-Russell ministry was in power. Formed in June, 1859, with an understanding between the two chiefs that either who might be sent for would accept office under the other, it was "looked upon as the strongest administration ever formed, so far as the individual talents of its members were concerned."[1] And this fact of the individuality and character of those composing the ministry became subsequently of great importance in deciding the policy to be pursued at several very critical diplomatic junctures; for the Palmer-

[1] Ashley, *Lord Palmerston* (ed. 1879), II, 364.

ston-Russell ministry remained in the firm control of the government from June, 1859, until the death of Lord Palmerston in October, 1865, following the collapse of the Confederacy. The three leading characters in it were Lord Palmerston, Premier, Lord John Russell, — created Earl Russell in July, 1861, — Secretary for Foreign Affairs, and Mr. Gladstone, Chancellor of the Exchequer.

In the first place, as respects Lord Palmerston. It has always been assumed that, from the very commencement of our troubles, his sympathies were with the Confederates, and that his instincts as a member and representative of the British privileged classes were hostile to the more democratic North. There can be no question that this was so. Nevertheless, during the earliest stages of the struggle, and before the *Trent* affair gave a decided adverse bent to the Premier's feelings, there was room for question. At first he seems to have regarded both parties to the quarrel with indifference, and, apparently, equal dislike. He cared not which whipped. Even as late as October 18, — only twenty-one days before the seizure of Mason and Slidell, — the Premier thus wrote to the Foreign Secretary: "As to North America, our best and true policy seems to be to go on as we have begun, and to keep quite clear of the conflict between North and South. . . . The love of quarrelling and fighting is inherent in man, and to prevent its indulgence is to impose restraints on natural liberty. . . . I quite agree with you that the want of cotton would not justify such a proceeding. . . . The only thing to do seems to be to lie on our oars and to give no pretext to the Washingtonians to quarrel with us, while, on the other hand, we maintain our rights and those of our fellow countrymen." [1]

Thus Palmerston was writing to Earl Russell, he then

[1] Ashley, *Palmerston*, II, 411.

being at Broadlands and the Foreign Secretary in attendance on the Queen, who was still at Balmoral. Meanwhile Mr. John Lothrop Motley was at that juncture in Great Britain. He had in August been appointed to the Austrian mission, and, on his way to Vienna, necessarily passed through England. Mr. Seward, newly installed in his office of Secretary of State, was then eager to inform himself through all possible channels [1] as to the state of affairs in Europe, and the views of our conflict held by public men, especially those of Great Britain and France. Mr. Motley's English acquaintance was exceptionally large; indeed, there were few persons he could not reach. Deeply interested in the Union cause, he now made frequent reports of a semi-official character to the Secretary of State. In them is the following account of interviews and conversations with Earl Russell and the Queen, and the writer's impressions as to the views and tendencies of Palmerston: —

"I had addressed a note to Lord Russell (who, as I understood, was at his country house called Abergeldie in the north of Scotland) saying that I had just returned to this country from America and that, before I departed for Vienna, I should be glad to accept an invitation often made by him, that I should visit him in Scotland. The answer came by return of post, that he would be delighted to see me at once, and that he hoped I would stay as long as I could.

"On the ninth of September I reached Abergeldie, where, however, my engagements did not permit me to stay longer than a day and a half. During this time, I had many full conversations with him of several hours' duration. I believe that we discussed the American question in all its bearings, and he was frank and apparently sincere in his expressions of amity towards the United States, and in deprecation of a rupture or of serious misunderstanding. . . .

"I spoke to him of the report alluded to by the editor of the

[1] *Supra*, 364–365.

Spectator, that England would recognize the Confederacy in November. He smiled, and said that it was a pure fiction; that no such purpose existed. He discussed this matter at considerable length and alluded to the practice of nations to recognize *de facto* governments, when they had become facts; observing that such things went more rapidly in modern times than they did of old; but saying distinctly, and repeating it many times, that the government were not thinking of recognizing the Southern Confederacy at present. . . .

". . . He did not wonder at our determination to put down the insurrection; but added that it was of so extensive a character, and was spread over so wide a surface, as to make our task seem a very formidable one. Five millions of people he thought hard to subdue, when fighting on their own soil; but he had no disposition to prejudge the case. He admitted the possibility of our efforts being successful, but thought that the effect of the Bull's Run affair would be to encourage the Confederates. He spoke very reasonably of that event, and did not attribute any great consequence to the panic, because it was well known that this was not uncommon among raw levies and volunteers, who might afterwards become the best of soldiers. He thought that much less effect had been produced in England by the defeat and the rout, than by the circumstance of so many regiments leaving on the eve of active operations, because their term of enlistment had expired. . . .

"Of course the subject of blockade was discussed. I said that in the Southern States there was the utmost confidence expressed that Great Britain would break our blockade, so soon as the cotton famine became imminent. It was notorious that the whole insurrection had been founded upon the theory that Great Britain could not exist without American cotton, and that therefore she could be relied upon to come to their rescue, after the United States should have effectually blockaded the cotton ports. The South believes itself possessed of the power of life and death over England by means of this single product, and therefore felt sure of forcing her into an alliance and into hostility to the United States. On the other hand, there was doubtless great uneasiness on the subject in the free states. To blockade the coast was one of the most indisputable of belligerent rights, and a forcible infringement by neutral governments of an effectual blockade was of course tantamount to a declaration of war. There was much anxiety therefore lest the stress of cotton should lead to war on the part of Great Britain. In this case, the consequences to humanity would be most disastrous. Without reference to the damage which each nation might inflict on the other, it was sufficient to intimate that the first effect of an infringement of the blockade and consequently of war made on the United States by Great Britain or by France, or by both united, would be a proclamation of universal emancipation of the slaves. . . .

". . . He was well aware, he said, of the power which the South thought itself possessed of over foreign nations by means of their cotton, and he sympathized with the general impatience of England under this supposed monopoly. The government was doing, would do, what it could to foster the production of cotton in India and other countries, and he felt hopeful of the result. He alluded to the resolution taken by the South to forbid the exportation of cotton, and showed me a familiar note to himself from Lord Palmerston on that subject, saying — 'We are up to that dodge.' . . .

"On the morning after my arrival, Lord Russell mentioned to me at breakfast, that the Queen, then residing at Balmoral, about a mile and a half from Abergeldie, was aware that I was making him a brief visit and that I was to leave early next morning. She had accordingly sent to say that the Prince Consort as well as herself would be pleased if I would come to Balmoral that afternoon. . . .

"In the afternoon he took me to Balmoral in the carriage, and we were received by the Prince Consort in the most informal and agreeable manner. The conversation was of some twenty minutes' duration, and was strictly limited to commonplace subjects, without reference to politics; but the Prince Consort took especial pains, I thought, to be polite and friendly, and certainly produced a most pleasing impression upon me. While we were conversing, the door opened, and her Majesty walked, quite unattended, into the room, dressed in plain, black morning costume. The Prince Consort presented me, and I was received with much affability; the Queen making a gracious observation in regard to myself, which I forbear to repeat, and then speaking at once, and with warmth, of the great pleasure which she had derived from the reception which the Prince of Wales had met with in America last year. The Prince Consort also expressed himself with eagerness on this subject, and alluded to the very great delight which the young Prince himself had experienced in his tour and in the friendly greeting which he had received from our nation.

"Nothing else, worthy to be repeated, was said, but I thought it my duty to mention the incident; for it seemed intended as a mark of respect and goodwill to the United States. . . .

"On our way back, I observed to Lord Russell that the Queen and Prince Consort seemed carefully to have abstained from an allusion to politics.

"He said — 'Yes — of course — for neither would choose to appear as interfering with the constitutional advisers of the crown.' He added, however, that the Prince had asked him, on his coming into the room, a few minutes before I was introduced, 'well, what about recognition,' or something to that effect; and that he had answered, 'no, we are not thinking of that at present; we are not prepared to recognize the Southern confederacy.' 'I suppose you mean,' said the Prince Consort, 'that you don't intend to pledge yourself for all time never to do it, whatever events might happen.' 'Yes,' answered Lord Russell, 'we can't look into all the future — but, for the present, we have no intention of recognizing them.'"

The next letter from Mr. Motley was dated "Vienna, Nov./61." In it he wrote: —

"In the present administration and its supporters, I know that we have many warm friends, warmer in their sentiments towards us than it would be safe for them in the present state of parties to avow. Lord Palmerston is not one of these friends. He knows little of our politics or condition, and cares less for them; and he is reckless of consequences should we give him good and popular cause of quarrel. But he is too adroit to place himself technically and flagrantly in the wrong; and therefore all fears that there would be a forcible infringement of our blockade have always seemed to me quite groundless."

It is important to note the date — September 9, 1861 — of the visit and conversations thus so graphically described. It was two months to a day before the occurrence of the *Trent* affair, and eighty days only before all England was set aflame by the arrival (November 27) of the news of that affair. The attitude towards things American of the British ministry at the earlier date was thus explicitly set forth. It certainly presented no grounds for complaint on our part. The glimpse given of the royal family is also suggestive.

Up to this time (September, 1861), the recently appointed American minister, Mr. Adams, had met Lord Palmerston merely in an official capacity and in the most formal way. He had been in London nearly five months; but he had arrived when the season was already well advanced towards its later stages, and had seen the Premier only on state occasions, or from the gallery of the House of Commons. Towards the end of September he had made a flying visit to Scotland at the invitation of Earl Russell, and had been the guest of the latter at Abergeldie Castle for a single day (September 25), occupied with official business. Mr. Motley had preceded him as a guest by about two weeks. While there he had seen nothing of the royal family. Subsequently, on the 9th of November, he had been one of the guests and speakers at the Lord Mayor's dinner, at which the Premier was a prominent figure. What the Premier says at the annual Guild-hall dinner is apt to be significant. On this occasion Mr. Adams listened with the keenest interest. The struggle in America was the issue then uppermost in all men's minds, the cotton market was excited, and it was not improbable that the policy of the government might be shadowed forth in anticipation of the meeting of Parliament. The impression left on Mr. Adams's mind was favorable. He referred to what Lord Palmerston said as being marked by his "customary shrewdness," adding, "He touched gently on our difficulties; and, at the same time, gave it clearly to be understood that there was to be no interference for the sake of cotton." This was on the 9th of November; and, the very day before, the steamer *Trent* had been stopped in the Old Bahama Channel, some four thousand miles away, and Messrs. Mason and Slidell taken from her. Eighteen days later, on the 27th, the occurrence became known in England. On the 12th, three days after the occurrence in the West Indian waters, and fifteen days before it was known in England, the first, as also the last, personal interview between Mr. Adams and Lord Palmerston took place. Of it, Mr. Adams immediately afterwards made the following diary record: —

"*Tuesday*, 12*th November*, 1861: — Received a familiar note from Lord Palmerston asking me to call at his house and see him between one and two o'clock. This took me by surprise, and I speculated on the cause for some time without any satisfaction. At one o'clock I drove from my house over to his, Cambridge House in Piccadilly. In a few minutes he saw me. His reception was very cordial and frank. He said he had been made anxious by a notice that a United States armed vessel had lately put into Southampton to get coal and supplies.[1] It had been intimated to him that the object was to intercept the two men, Messrs. Slidell

[1] The United States steamer *James Adger*, Commander John B. Marchand, had left New York October 16, under orders to intercept, if possible, the Confederate steamer *Nashville*, which ran the blockade at Charleston on the night of October 10, 1861, and was falsely reported to have Messrs. Mason and Slidell on board, presumably destined for some European port. The Confederate commissioners in fact left Charleston on the *Theodora*, also a Confederate vessel, two days later, on the night of October 12. The following day they arrived at Nassau, their immediate destination; and thence went to Cuba, still on the *Theodora*, landing at Cardenas. The orders under which Commander Marchand sailed were issued under an entire misapprehension of facts, and his instructions related exclusively to the *Nashville*. See *Official Records of the Union and Confederate Navies in the war of the Rebellion*, I, 128, 224–227.

and Mason, who were understood to be aboard the British West India steamer expected to arrive to-morrow or next day. He had been informed that the Captain, having got gloriously drunk on brandy on Sunday, had dropped down to the mouth of the river yesterday, as if on the watch. He did not pretend to judge absolutely of the question whether we had a right to stop a foreign vessel for such a purpose as was indicated. Even admitting that we might claim it, it was yet very doubtful whether the exercise of it in this way could lead to any good. The effect of it here would be unfavorable, as it would seem as if the vessel had come in here to be filled with coal and supplies, and the Captain had enjoyed the hospitality of the country in filling his stomach with brandy, only to rush out of the harbor and commit violence upon their flag. Neither did the object to be gained seem commensurate with the risk. For it was surely of no consequence whether one or two more men were added to the two or three who had already been too long here. They would scarcely make a difference in the action of the government after once having made up its mind. He was then going on to another question, when I asked leave to interrupt him so far as to reply on this point. I would first venture to ask him if he would enlighten me as to the sources of information upon which he imputed the intention of Captain Marchand to take such a step. His Lordship answered that he had no positive information, but that his belief rested on inferences of the motive for sending the vessel so far, and the coincidence in her time of departure. To this I remarked that Captain Marchand had been to see me, and had shown me the instructions under which he sailed. The object of the government had been, upon receiving information that the steamer *Nashville* from Charleston had succeeded in breaking the blockade and was proceeding with these men on a voyage to Europe, to despatch vessels in several directions with the design of intercepting and capturing her. I presumed that no objection could exist to such a proceeding on our part. His Lordship assented, though he did not seem to have heard of the *Nashville* or to understand its destination. I then said that the *James Adger* had been sent in this direction, but finding no news of the *Nashville*, and learning that the two emissaries had stopped at the West Indies, Captain Marchand had written to me his intention to return to the United States. I would, however, remark that I had urged him to follow up a steamer called the *Gladiator* which had been fitted up and despatched from London with contraband of war for the insurgents. Though sailing under British colors, I advised him to seize her on the first symptom of destination to a harbor in the United States. His Lordship did not deny my right, but he intimated that the proof ought to be well established. I said that my government had no desire to open questions with this country. On the contrary I think they would do all in their power to avoid them. But I could not deny that these proceedings in England were excessively annoying, and that there would spring up a strong desire to arrest them as decisively as possible. His Lordship then passed to the case of Mr. Bunch, the consul at Charleston. . . . We then passed into more general conversation, in the course of which I ventured to ask if it was to be presumed that the two governments of France and Great Britain were acting in concert in regard to the United States. He said, Yes. I then mentioned my having received in my latest despatch notice that M. Mercier had apprised my government that the French stood in need of cotton. Was I to understand that this was in concert too? His Lordship said that he was aware of the French government having directed a suggestion to be made, that it would be glad to have cotton, but it was nothing more, and Lord Lyons had not any direction to join in it. I replied that I so understood it, but that I could not but regret such steps as they formed the only foundation upon which the insurgents rested their hopes of success.[1] Mr. Yancey in his speech at the fishmongers' dinner had sufficiently expressed it, but in point of fact I had reason to know that he and his associates had been indefatigable in their representations of the certainty of interference in their behalf. It was this view of the subject which created the irritation in the United States. If we could be left entirely to ourselves, the issue would not be long doubtful. To this his Lordship made the common remark among his countrymen that we might perhaps coerce and subdue them, but that would not be restoring the Union. I answered that such was not our desire. What we expected to do was to give them

[1] *Supra*, 255.

an opportunity of making an unbiased decision. We believed that this was a conspiracy which had blown up a great rebellion. A short time would test the sense of the whole community. If the presence of a force adequate to protection did not develop a counter movement to return to the Union, I did not believe that pure coercion would be persevered in. I did not, however, add my conviction that slavery as a political element must be completely expunged before there can be any hope of permanent peace. I then took my leave and returned home." [1]

This record certainly shows Lord Palmerston in no attitude of hostility to America. On the contrary, he distinctly went out of his way to give a friendly intimation calculated to forestall and prevent the doing of something which was unfortunately already done, but which is now universally admitted to have been the super-zealous act of well-nigh incredible folly on the part of a highly indiscreet and ill-balanced naval officer. And Lord Palmerston did this, too, in a very kindly way. There was in his manner nothing either rough or brusque, or in any way offensive. On the contrary, it was marked by much characteristic *bonhomie*. Mr. Adams so accepted it, and even began to relax in his suspicions of the Premier.

Meanwhile, Mr. Adams did not know that only the day before the Premier had been in solemn conference with Lord Chancellor Westbury, Dr. Lushington and the three official Law Officers of the Crown, to consider the very contingency he now suggested. And, furthermore, much to his regret, as well as surprise, he had been then advised that, according to the principles of international law accepted in English courts, and practised and enforced by

[1] Mr. Adams's official account of this highly significant interview is in a despatch to the Secretary of State, dated November 15, 1861. Never printed in the Diplomatic Correspondence, it is to be found almost in full in *War Records*, Serial No. 115, pp. 1078, 1079.

Great Britain, a belligerent had a right to stop and search any neutral not being a ship of war suspected of carrying enemy's despatches. Consequently, either Commander Marchand or Captain Wilkes, on accepted English principles of law, might stop the *Trent*, search her, and if Messrs. Mason and Slidell, their despatches and credentials, were found on board, "either take them out, or seize the packet and carry her back to New York for trial."[1] The Premier, fully advised as to the law in the case, was thus doing his utmost to prevent the occurrence of that which, unknown to either himself or Mr. Adams, had already happened. The next glimpse we get of Palmerston, he appears in quite another character. It is from the recently published *Memoirs* of Sir Horace Rumbold. The *Trent* was stopped November 8; the interview between Mr. Adams and the Premier at Cambridge House was on the 12th; the news of what had taken place on the 8th reached London on the 27th. Sir Horace Rumbold says:[2] "As soon as the news reached England, a Cabinet Council was summoned, and I had it on the same day from Evelyn Ashley that Lord Palmerston, on entering the room where the Ministers met in Downing Street, threw his hat on the table, and at once commenced business by addressing his colleagues in the following words: 'I don't know whether you are going to stand this, but I'll be d——d if I do!' The ultimatum demanding the surrender of the prisoners was decided upon there and then, and sent out within two days (on the following Sunday)."

Into what subsequently occurred in the so-called *Trent* affair it is not, for present purposes, necessary to enter. It is matter of history. The royal family was then at Windsor,

[1] Dasent, *John Thadeus Delane*, II, 36.
[2] *Recollections of a Diplomatist*, II, 83.

having left Balmoral October 22. The Prince Consort began to sicken on the 1st of December; he died on December 14. As is well known, his very last public act was to soften down the asperities of the despatch to Lord Lyons as originally drawn up by the Foreign Secretary, and, according to usage, submitted to the Queen before transmission. Full details on this subject may be found in Sir Theodore Martin's *Life* of the Prince Consort. It is sufficient here to say — but to emphasize it is of importance in the matter under discussion — the last working hours of the Prince were anxiously devoted to an effort to preserve friendly relations between Great Britain and the United States. That might well have been considered his dying injunction to the Queen. The Prince was buried on the 23d of December; and when, on the 9th of the following month, Lord Palmerston officially communicated to her Majesty the intelligence that the *Trent* affair was happily solved, she promptly reminded him of the fact that "this peaceful issue of the American quarrel was greatly owing to her beloved Prince." [1]

In America active military operations had then ceased, and the two parties to the conflict were preparing for a supreme trial of strength when the coming season should open. Europe was looking on; a universal mourning for the Prince Consort overshadowed Great Britain; the stoppage of cotton shipments by the Federal blockade was beginning to make itself felt in the manufacturing districts of both England and France; the combined French, Spanish and English movement on Mexico was in preparation; the expediency and consequent probability of a joint movement of European powers looking to a recognition of the Confederacy and their subsequent intervention in our Civil War

[1] Lee, *Victoria*, p. 382.

was under discussion; no active movement to that end had, however, yet been initiated. The Queen herself, much broken by the death of her husband, and both mentally and physically in a condition causing profound solicitude, attended to her public duties and transacted business with her ministers as had been her habit, but naturally had to be treated by them with great consideration. Morbid excitement was feared, and anything which might in any way conduce thereto was carefully avoided.

This condition of affairs lasted all through both the winter and spring of 1862, — the months immediately following the death of the Prince Consort. During that time there is no reason whatever to suppose that, as a question of policy, any issue growing out of the American difficulties was brought to the Queen's notice. She had no occasion to express herself; and, weighed down by domestic affliction, her mind was intent on other things. During those months, however, the cotton famine reached its worst stages both in Great Britain and France; and, contemporaneously, the Union operations underwent severe reverses. As a natural result, the question of recognition, and consequent intervention, became urgent. The French Emperor publicly favored this course, repeatedly and persistently urging the British government to take the initiative, and signifying his readiness to coöperate.[1] The struggle in America was the uppermost subject of interest throughout Europe, and especially in Great Britain, where the tide of sympathy ran strongly with the Confederates in what was looked upon as their gallant struggle for independence against overwhelming odds of men and resources. The condition of the Queen, though not discussed openly, was well understood in court circles. She was unequal to any nervous strain.

[1] Rhodes, *United States*, IV, 94, n., 346.

QUEEN VICTORIA AND THE CIVIL WAR 401

This was recognized by the Confederate emissaries in London as a serious obstacle in the way of that recognition for which they were praying. They were also well informed on this point; probably far better informed than the American minister, for at least four out of five of the ministry and members of Parliament, and almost the entire court circle, were strong sympathizers with the Confederacy. Accordingly, on February 28, 1862, James M. Mason, the Confederate commissioner in London, wrote to Mr. Hunter, the Richmond Secretary of State: "In political circles it is thought the condition of the Queen has much to do with the manifest reluctance of the Ministry to run any risk of war by interference with the blockade. It is said that she is under great constitutional depression, and nervously sensitive to anything that looks like war. Indeed, much fear is entertained as to the condition of her health." And a few days later (March 11) to the same effect: "Many causes concur [in bringing about a general support of the ministry in its policy of non-intervention]. First, the prevailing disinclination in any way to disturb the mourning of the Queen. The loyalty of the English people to their present Sovereign is strongly mixed up with an affectionate devotion to her person. You find this feeling prevalent in all circles and classes." Finally, writing on the 31st of July following, Mason says: "The Queen remains in great seclusion, and it is more than whispered that apprehension is entertained lest she lapse into insania." [1]

That summer the Queen passed at Osborne, at Balmoral, and at Windsor; but early in the autumn (September) she went over to Germany, and was for a short time at Gotha, returning to England October 26. Earl Russell was in

[1] *The Public Life and Diplomatic Correspondence of James M. Mason*, 264, 265, 315.

attendance there upon her; and the crisis in American affairs, so far as European intervention was concerned, then occurred.

It came about in this wise: — Referring to the outcome of the so-called Pope, or second Bull Run, campaign before Washington in August, 1862, Lord Palmerston wrote to Earl Russell, then (September 14) in attendance at Gotha, suggesting whether the time had not come "for us to consider whether, in such a state of things, England and France might not address the contending parties and recommend an arrangement upon the basis of separation." This suggestion strongly commended itself to the Foreign Secretary, who replied on the 17th that he was decidedly of the same mind as the Premier: "I agree with you that the time is come for offering mediation to the United States government, with a view to the recognition of the independence of the Confederates. I agree further that, in case of failure, we ought ourselves to recognize the Southern States as an independent State. For the purpose of taking so important a step, I think we must have a meeting of the Cabinet. The 23d or 20th would suit me for the meeting." To this very emphatic acquiescence in his views, Lord Palmerston six days later, on the 23d, wrote back: "Your plan of proceedings . . . seems to be excellent. . . . As to the time of making the offer [of mediation] if France and Russia agree — and France, we know, is quite ready and only waiting for our concurrence — events may be taking place which might render it desirable that the offer should be made before the middle of October." Lord Russell now left Gotha and returned to London, Lord Granville relieving him in attendance on the Queen.

It has been surmised[1] that it was at this juncture, if ever,

[1] Mass. Hist. Soc. *Proceedings*, Second Series, XVIII, 145, 153.

that the incident occurred of which Prince Leopold retained the boyish recollection upon which President Eliot based his "credibly reported" statement. A mystery did indeed hang over the outcome of events at that most curiously critical period — a mystery the American minister was unable at the time to penetrate, in fact never did penetrate — but which admitted of an altogether natural explanation on the hypothesis that the incident narrated by Prince Leopold then occurred. It seemed not at all impossible in view of the solicitude felt over her mental as well as physical condition, that the whole course of events might have turned on the individual attitude of the widow of Prince Albert. The surmise was erroneous. The Queen had nothing to do with that particular sequence of events. There is no evidence that she in any way concerned herself in it. On the contrary, in so far as she was not absorbed by her widow's grief, her mind was intent on other things much nearer home. The solution of the mystery, sought elsewhere, is found in Lord Granville's correspondence, as set forth in his recently (1905) published *Life* by Lord Edmond Fitzmaurice.

The concurrence and course of events can be briefly stated. Throughout the months of July and August, 1862, the cause of the Union had sustained a series, almost unbroken, of reverses. The Confederacy had not only made good its right to be recognized as a belligerent, but it was a victorious belligerent. The Mexican expedition of the French Emperor having overrun that country, he was urging upon the British Cabinet an aggressive attitude towards the United States which would inevitably have proved the first step toward a direct armed intervention, and the consequent breaking of the blockade. The great Lancashire cotton famine, necessarily incident to the blockade and confidently relied on throughout the Confederacy to compel intervention in its behalf, was at its height. If gold in New York stood at a premium of 50, cotton stood at one of 200 in Liverpool. The looms were idle, and a long and sustained wail of famine and pitiable agony went up from the most crowded districts of Great Britain. Whether the fact was realized in America or not, the hour of crisis was at hand; and the issue was to be settled, not on the banks of the Potomac, as generally assumed, but in Downing Street, London.

The two weeks after Lord Russell's return to London from Gotha were utilized by him in the preparation of an elaborate, though confidential, Cabinet circular in direct furtherance of the mediation programme. In this circular the question was plainly put to those composing the Cabinet, whether in the light of what had taken place in America and the condition of distress prevailing throughout the manufacturing districts of England and France, it was not the duty of Europe "to ask both parties, in the most friendly and conciliatory terms, to agree to a suspension of arms for the purpose of weighing calmly the advantages of peace" — and so forth and so on, in the somewhat unctuous parlance usual with philanthropic, but interested, neutrals.

Mr. Gladstone was at this time Chancellor of the Exchequer, and next to the Premier, Lord Palmerston, and the Foreign Secretary, Earl Russell, the most influential member of the Cabinet. He was now consulted as to the proposed programme, and gave his hearty approval to it. It entirely met the views he at that time entertained and did not hesitate to express. The cry of agony coming up from the cotton spinning districts appealed to his strong humanitarian sympathies; he, like Lord Palmerston, was fully convinced that a reëstablishment of the Union was impossible as well as undesirable; finally, by that subtle process of reasoning always characteristic of him, he had persuaded himself that the victory of the slave-owner would result in the downfall of slavery. There was in Russell's attitude a certain coldness of political conviction, as in that of Palmerston there was apparent an element of cynical hesitation; but Gladstone seems at this juncture to have thrown himself into the proposed movement with that fervor of sympathetic conviction always characteristic of him. Nor was he chary of utterance, as he afterwards, in the day of his sackcloth and ashes, had good cause to remember and admit. For instance, he thus a few weeks later, in reply to a letter, wrote to Cyrus W. Field in terms unmistakably Gladstonese setting forth "the heavy responsibility you [Americans of the North] incur in persevering with this destructive and hopeless war at the cost of such dangers and evils to yourselves, to say nothing of your adversaries, or of an amount of misery inflicted upon Europe such as no other civil war in the history of man has ever brought upon those beyond its immediate range." The writer then went on thus to set forth the wickedness of any further continuance of our efforts towards a reëstablishment of the Union: "The impossibility of success in a war of conquest of itself suffices to make it unjust. When that impossibility is reasonably proved, all the horror, all the bloodshed, all the evil passions, all the dangers to liberty and order, with which such a war abounds, come to lie at the door of the party which refuses to hold its hand and let its neighbor be. You know that in the opinion of Europe that impossibility has (in the present case) been proved." [1]

The concurrence of Mr. Gladstone in the proposed programme rendered assurance doubly sure; for, as Lord Gran-

[1] Mass. Hist. Soc. *Proceedings*, Second Series, XX, 470, n.; *Harper's Monthly Magazine* (May, 1896), Vol. XCII, p. 847.

ville had a few months before, and in another connection, written to Lord Canning: "He [Gladstone], Johnny [Russell] and Pam [Palmerston] are a formidable phalanx when they are united in opposition to the whole Cabinet in foreign matters." And in the present case a large majority of the Cabinet were with "the formidable phalanx." It was now that the wholly unforeseeable, the strangely unexpected, occurred. The meeting of the Cabinet was fixed for the 23d of October. Mr. Adams got an inkling of what was on foot, and was greatly disturbed. "For a fortnight," he wrote, "my mind has been running so strongly on all this night and day that it seems almost to threaten my life." He had good reason for his anxiety, however extreme. The tension was becoming strained to the extent that something, it would seem, must break, and that soon. For, weeks previously, apprehending just such an emergency as was now impending, Mr. Adams had written home asking for specific instructions for his guidance if what he apprehended should occur. Those instructions he had in due time received from Secretary Seward; they were explicit. To make the narrative intelligible and fully set forth the extreme character of the crisis then impending, these instructions must be quoted at some length. Even at the interval of half a century they bear reading; for, carrying the standard entrusted to him high and with a firm hand, the Secretary bore himself in a way of which his country had cause to be proud. The paper read in part as follows: —

"If the British government shall in any way approach you directly or indirectly with propositions which assume or contemplate an appeal to the President on the subject of our internal affairs, whether it seems to imply a purpose to dictate, or to mediate, or to advise, or even to solicit or persuade, you will answer that you are forbidden to debate, to hear, or in any way receive, entertain, or transmit any communication of the kind. You will make the same answer whether the proposition comes from the British government in combination with any other power.

"If you were asked an opinion what reception the President would give to such a proposition, if made here, you will reply that you are not instructed, but you have no reason for supposing that it would be entertained.

"If contrary to our expectations the British government, either alone or in combination with any other government, should acknowledge the insurgents, while you are remaining without further instructions from this government concerning that event, you will immediately suspend the exercise of your functions, and give notice of that suspension to Earl Russell and to this department. I have now in behalf of the United States and by the authority of their chief executive magistrate performed an important duty. Its possible consequences have been weighed, and its solemnity is therefore felt and freely acknowledged. This duty has brought us to meet and confront the danger of a war with Great Britain and other states allied with the insurgents who are in arms for the overthrow of the American Union. You will perceive that we have approached the contemplation of that crisis with the caution which great reluctance has inspired. But I trust that you will also have perceived that the crisis has not appalled us."

It was with these ringing instructions before him that Mr. Adams, with such fortitude as he could command, now awaited the outcome he was powerless in any material way to affect. The special Cabinet meeting was called for the 23d of October; to all outward appearance and in all human probability that was the fateful day; the ordeal must then be faced. The programme for it was arranged.

The day came; and passed. Upon it nothing happened. The wholly unexpected had again occurred.

What had taken place? Why was the carefully prepared programme, so world-momentous and far reaching, suddenly, quietly abandoned? It is a curious story; in diplomatic annals scarce any more so. It was, it will be remembered — for dates in this connection are all-important — the 23d of October that had been assigned for the special Cabinet meeting, and sixteen days before, on the 7th of that month, Mr. Gladstone delivered that famous Newcastle speech in which he declared that Jefferson Davis had "made a nation," and that the independence of the Confederacy and dissolution of the American Union were as certain "as any event yet future and contingent could be." That speech, a marvel of indiscretion, — or, as Mr. Gladstone himself subsequently expressed it, "a mistake of incredible grossness," — though at the moment it caused in the mind of Mr. Adams deep despair, in reality saved the situation. It was for the Union a large cash prize drawn in fortune's lottery.

Speaking for himself, — "playing off his own bat," as Lord Palmerston would have expressed it, — Mr. Gladstone had foreshadowed a ministerial policy. The utterance was inspired; in venturing on it Mr. Gladstone unquestionably supposed, as he had good cause to know, he spoke the minds of both Lord Palmerston and Lord Russell. In another connection the principle of the so-called "collectivity" of the British Cabinet is discussed by Lord Edmond Fitzmaurice in his *Granville* (II, 322), and the point made that ministers are in nowise free to put forward each "his own views at large public meetings and elsewhere." This Mr. Gladstone had now done. Moreover, it was notorious in ministerial circles that the Prime Minister and the Chancellor of the Exchequer were not in general harmony. On the contrary, Lord Palmerston disliked and habitually thwarted Mr. Gladstone; and Mr. Gladstone instinctively distrusted Lord Palmerston. A year before, the two had been "in violent antagonism" on financial questions. "For two months," Granville wrote, "Gladstone has been on half-cock of resignation. . . . Palmerston has tried him hard once or twice by speeches and Cabinet minutes, and says that the only way to deal with him is to bully him a little; and Palmerston appears to be in the right."

A species of Cabinet *modus vivendi* was then arrived at, and had since been more or less observed; but the two men were by nature antagonistic. They instinctively disliked each other. Gladstone was plainly the coming man; but Palmerston, so to speak, held the fort, nor did he propose to vacate it in Gladstone's favor. It was a case of armed Cabinet observation. Under these circumstances the Chancellor of the Exchequer had in the autumn of 1862 gone on what proved to be a sort of triumphal progress through the northern counties. It amounted to a popular ovation; and, not unnaturally, his colleagues, especially his chief, took cognizance of it. Then came the Newcastle indiscretion. From his long subsequently published diary entries, it appears that what Mr. Gladstone then said was no hasty, impromptu utterance, but had been well and repeatedly considered. The inference is unavoidable. Distrusting the stability of the Premier's purpose, the Chancellor of the Exchequer intended to force his hand, thus clinching the thing. In so purposing, Mr. Gladstone had, as a member of the government, committed an offence against official propriety. Apparently it did not take the Premier long to make up his mind that the offender must be disciplined, and that severely; so he proceeded at once to intimate to Sir George Cornewall Lewis, also a member of the Cabinet and Gladstone's parliamentary rival as the coming man, that if he (Lewis) did not take this function on himself, it must devolve on the head of the government in person. On the 14th of October, therefore, Sir George Lewis, speaking at Hereford as the unrecognized mouthpiece of the Premier, very pointedly controverted the position taken by his colleague one week before at Newcastle. The hand of the Premier was on the Cabinet lever. The blind goddess had intervened for the preservation of the American Union!

The Cabinet meeting called for the 23d, the outcome of which had been settled in advance by the concurrence of the Premier, the Foreign Secretary and the Chancellor of the Exchequer — Palmerston, Russell and Gladstone — was for the nonce necessarily postponed, and never afterwards notified. Mr Gladstone had been "called down," — had received a distinct intimation that he was neither the ministry nor yet its accredited mouthpiece; and explanations were in order. None the less, as the secret working of the springs and wires which brought about the final result are now made apparent, the magnitude and imminence of the danger at that juncture threatening the cause of the Union are revealed. It was a case of touch and go!

Perhaps the most curious feature of the episode is, however, that Mr. Adams was at the moment altogether wrong in his understanding of the influences at work. He thought Palmerston the evil genius of the situation, and the source of hostile machinations; in his belief, Earl Russell was, on the whole, America's friend. In reality it was, as we now know, the other way. At the critical moment Russell, disregarding Gladstone's indiscreet disclosures, was disposed to go forward in the policy of recognition and intervention; it was Palmerston who hesitated and called a halt. The Premier was not disposed to forego the opportunity of disciplining an indiscreet colleague whom he thoroughly disliked, even though by so doing the recognition of the Confederacy was postponed. In the event, that postponement proved final. Then and there the dice had unknowingly been cast. Nearly three years later, when the Confederacy was in its death agony, General Robert E. Lee mournfully confessed that he had never believed it could in the long run make good its independence "unless foreign powers should directly or indirectly assist it in so doing."

Recurring, however, to what may not inappropriately be termed the Victorian legend in this connection, there is nothing whatever to indicate that the Queen ever felt any personal interest in the American struggle, or, after the Prince Consort's death (December, 1861) sought to influence in the slightest the policy of the ministry in regard to it. On this point the *Life of Lord Granville* affords conclusive evidence. Had she evinced such interest, or exerted any influence on the ministry, it would have been through Lord Granville; for in all such contingencies "Lord Granville was her mainstay in the Cabinet. On him the Queen relied, and she did not rely in vain."[1] The personal correspondence which took place between the Queen and Granville at about this time is as curious as it is conclusive on the point under discussion. On her part it is touching in its outbursts, — its appeals for sympathy and aid. For instance, on one occasion during the Schleswig-Holstein complications of 1864, writing from Balmoral, she refers to certain "dangerous steps which Lord Palmerston and Lord Russell would on several occasions have plunged us into," and authorizes Lord Granville to show her letter and enclosures "to any of his colleagues (excepting Lord Palmerston and Lord Russell) whom he thinks it useful to communicate them to"; and then in closing the Queen breaks out: "Oh, how fearful it is to be suspected — uncheered — unguided and unadvised — and how alone the poor Queen feels! Her friends must

[1] Fitzmaurice, I, 477.

defend her." And again: "Alone and unaided . . . she writes to Lord Granville as a faithful friend and not as a minister, to hear from him his opinion." Finally, in a letter from Osborne: "The Queen suffers much, and her nerves are more and more easily shattered, and her rest broken. . . . If Lord Granville only reflects, he will understand how terrible her position is! But though all this anxiety is wearing her out, it will not shake her in her firm purpose of resisting any attempt to involve this country in a mad and useless combat." Such were her relations with Lord Granville in 1864, when really interested in the successive issues raised by the gradual development of Bismarck's plans; but any indications or expressions of a similar character are wholly wanting as respects American affairs in September and October, 1862. Lord Granville was then in personal attendance upon her on the Continent; and there for the express purpose of communicating with her on questions of business. Lord Russell sent him notice of the Cabinet meeting called for October 23; and October 1 Granville wrote to his colleague, Lord Stanley of Alderley, — familiarly "Ben," — that Palmerston had already broached the idea of an offer of mediation and subsequent recognition; and he adds: "I have written to Johnny my reasons for thinking it decidedly premature. I, however, suspect you will settle to do so! Pam [Palmerston], Johnny [Russell] and Gladstone would be in favour of it; and probably Newcastle. I do not know about the others. It appears to me a great mistake." Here, in a familiar letter, is no reference whatever to the Queen, her condition, her wishes or her views, — no intimation that she feels any interest in the question at issue, or the policy to be adopted. In a prior official letter to Lord Russell, of September 27, 1862, Granville had discussed the question of intervention at length and in detail, but in it also there was no reference to the Queen. This silence is conclusive, so far as negative evidence can ever be accepted as conclusive. Apparently, another and very pleasing tradition must be dismissed from history as, at best, unauthenticated.

INDEX

Abeken, on Bazeilles, 287.
Ability, military, 1777, 115.
Aboukir, 57.
Acland, Sir Henry, 383.
Adair, John, 189.
Adams, Charles Francis, money needed for rams, 347; fears war, 357; meetings with Forbes, 358; on Evarts' mission, 363; and Queen Victoria, 377, 379, 381; criticised, 368, 370; on diplomatic agents, 366, 370; message from Dayton, 376; visits Lord Russell, 393; relations with Palmerston, 393; interview, 394; instructions on mediation and recognition, 406; mentioned, 256, 354.
Adams, Henry, 197 n., 353.
Adams, John, on cavalry, 75; describes a hussar, 82.
Adams, John Quincy, on separation, 225.
Africanism and the South, 230.
Agents, diplomatic, in Europe, 360, 364.
Alabama, 248, 357.
Albany, N.Y., 117, 134, 144.
Albert, Prince Consort, death of, 379; modifies Lord Russell's despatch, 383, 399; sees Motley, 391; on recognition, 392.
Alexander, Edward Porter, 312.
Alexandra, 357, 359, 363.
Allegiance, to State or nation, 208, 211, 212, 214, 215, 296, 298.
Alva, Duke of, 173.
Anson, George, 182.
Appomattox, surrender at, 326.
Arget, d', 1.
Army, continental, at New York, 25, 28; parade through Philadelphia, 75, 136; cavalry, 83 n.; at Morristown, 123; marching of, 160; British, evacuates Boston, 25; at New York, 28; on Long Island, 29. Strength of, 243. Of the Potomac, position of danger, 308; of Northern Virginia, 313; last days, 323, 326. See Confederacy.
Arnold, Benedict, 63, 71, 87.
Artillery on Long Island, 56.
Ashford, Conn., 2.
Ashley, Evelyn, 398.

Aspinwall, William H., mission to Europe, 354, 356.
Bacon, Francis, on posterity and foreign nations, 244.
Bagehot, Walter, on Washington, 166.
Balancing of blunders, 2, 23, 119, 123, 128, 151.
Bancroft, George, on Bunker Hill, 20; on Pulaski, 83; mentioned, 208 n.
Baring Brothers and Company, 352, 356; deposit of bonds, 359, 371.
Barnard, John Gross, 274.
Barren Hill, 94.
Baskingridge, 69.
Bates, Joshua, 352, 359.
Batteries at New York, 28.
Baylor, George, 75, 79.
Bayonet, dislike of, 92 n.
Bazeilles, 287.
Beauregard, Pierre Gustave Toutant, in Virginia campaign, 268, 271, 273.
Belknap, Jeremy, on Bunker Hill, 19.
Belle Isle, 57.
Bennington, Vt., 91, 135.
Berlin, 142.
Bigelow, John, 357, 365.
Bingham, Robert, 340.
Birkenhead, *see* Laird rams.
Birmingham, 78.
Bismarck, Otto, fürst von, 287.
Blackwood's Edinburgh Magazine, 244, 263.
Bladensburg, battle of, 175, 176; influence at New Orleans, 186, 188.
Blake, Robert, 57.
Bland, Theodorick, 75, 79.
Blockade, in Revolution, 121 n., 153; in Civil War, 246; Hammond on, 250; cotton and, 257; believed impossible, 315; effective, 316, 320; Lord Russell on, 390.
Bloomingdale, N.Y., 30.
Blücher, Gebhard Leberecht, von, 281.
Blunders, balancing of, 2, 119, 123, 128, 151.
Boats, concentration at New York, 42.
Boers, cavalry, 93, 98; area, population and fighting force, 239.

416 INDEX

Bonds, five-twenties, 355, 371.
Boston, council of war, 5; evacuation, 24.
Box, —, major, 34.
Braddock, Edward, 63.
Brandywine, battle of the, 72, 78, 87, 140, 146.
Bravay and Co., 363.
Breastworks, as defences, 15.
Breed's Hill, 3, 7.
Breslau, 143.
Brooklyn, interior lines, 29; defence of, 26, 32; cavalry of service, 65.
Buckle, Henry Thomas, 219 n.
Buford, Abraham, 104.
Bugeaud, Marshal, on English infantry, 190.
Bull Run, effect of, 390.
Bulloch, James Dunwoody, 363.
Bummers, Sherman's, 266, 289.
Bunch, Robert, consul, 255, 396.
Bunker Hill, British plan, 3, 5, 18; position of Americans, 3, 4; American plan, 5, 6, 13; consequences of defeat, 6; commander, 7; favorable to Americans, 11; Howe's conduct criticised, 18; strategy discussed, 19; results, 13; effect on Washington, 56.
Burgoyne, John, 144; army, 119; moves from Canada, 73, 124; situation of, 131; crushing of, 131, 133, 135; spoils of, 136.
Burnside, Ambrose Everett, 268, 308.
Burrard, Sir Harry, 100.
Busaco, 174.
Butler, Benjamin Franklin, in Virginia campaign, 267; instructions to, 269; takes command, 270; fails at Walthall Junction, 271; rejects advice, 272; driven from Drewry's Bluff, 273; opposes Gillmore, 274; recommendations upon, 274, 275, 278; quarrels with Smith, 275; cowes Grant, 276; relieved, 278; measure of service, 279.
Butt-head, 10.

Cabinet, British, collectivity, 408.
Cæsar, 14.
Calhoun, John Caldwell, 222, 293.
Cambridge, Mass., 6, 10.
Camp, Continental, sanitary condition, 135, 145.
Carlyle, Thomas, 1, 143 n.
Carolinas, campaign in, 103.
Carrington, Henry Beebee, 20, 41, 42, 43.
Cavalry, in Revolution, 59; favorable field, 62, 74; in colonies, 63; at Brooklyn, 65; results of a want of, 70; volunteer, 70 n.; in Continental army, 75, 83 n.; Continental Congress, 82; requirements to command, 86; Clinton's march, 97; cost, 92, 99; British advantage, 105; delay in using, 108.
Census of 1860, 235.
Chamberlain, Daniel Henry, 205, 207.
Chancellorsville, 78.
Character, influence of, 291; defined, 292.
Charlatan, Lee a, 58.
Charles, Prince, 142.
Charleston, S. C., 203; address in, 227; misfortunes, 228.
Charlestown, Mass., 2, 3, 5.
Charlestown Neck, 7, 18.
Chase, Salmon Portland, 208 n.; meets Chittenden, 347; mission of Forbes, 354, 355; mystifies Chittenden, 373.
Chatrian, Alexandre, 163.
Chesapeake Bay, 76.
Chittenden, Lucius E., career, 345; story of the bonds, 346, 371; time of incident, 356; disproved, 372.
Choate, Joseph Hodges, 382.
Citizenship, question of, 298.
City Point, Va., 269.
Clay, Cassius Marcellus, 366.
Clinton, Sir Henry, 102; advises Gage, 5, 9; Howe, 10; lands on Long Island, 29, 55; supersedes Howe, 94, 96; moves to New York, 95; up the Hudson, 124; on Howe's movements, 126 n.; at New York, 50, 131, 134, 144.
Clive, Robert, 101, 102.
Cochrane, Alexander Forester Inglis, at New Orleans, 196; on Ross, 200.
Coddington, William, 204.
Codrington, Edward, 195, 197.
Cold Harbor, 273.
Collectivity of British Cabinet, 408.
Collier, Sir George, on Howe, 52.
Common law, 299.
Concord, effect on Howes, 56.
"Conda" navy, 250.
Confederacy, Southern, cavalry, 93; arguments for, 204; causes of fall, 234, 244, 314; fighting force, 237, 241, 282; conscription, 284; supplies, 324; agents in Europe, 363; on Forbes mission, 370; recognition, 390, 392, 399, 400, 403.
Confederation, States under, 209.
Confidence of South, 259.
Confucius, 292 n.
Congress, Continental, 82, 138.

INDEX 417

Connecticut light horse, 64, 92.
Conscript de 1813, 163.
Conscription, in South, 284; Webster on, 339.
Constitution, divided sovereignty, 210.
"Contemporary Opinion of the Howes," 110.
Conway, Moncure Daniel, 369.
Copenhagen, 57.
Cornwallis, Charles, Earl, 105, 126 *n.*, 148 *n.*; flanks Washington, 78; at the Brandywine, 101; retreat, 150.
Corunna campaign, 114.
Cotton, as king, 252, 254, 255, 256, 314; blockade, 257; dependence of South, 314, 319; Lancashire famine, 317, 403; intervention and, 394; defeated, 258, 260; loan, 359; need in France, 396.
Councils of war, 6, 138, 164.
Cowpens, 92, 106.
Craufurd, Robert, march of, 110, 141.
Cromwell, Oliver, 14, 63, 72, 113, 115.

Dana, Charles Anderson, 277.
Daun, Leopold Joseph Maria, Count von, 143.
Davis, Jefferson, Gladstone on, 234; at Greensboro, 241, 323, 327.
Davout, Louis-Nicolas, 280.
Dayton, William Lewis, 256, 376.
Delaware, defences, 156, 157.
Democracy and history, 111.
Desertion in Confederacy, 286.
Devens, Richard, 20.
Digging by soldiers, 16.
Dilatoriness of Howe, 34, 36, 38, 45.
Diplomats, classified, 364.
Dorchester Heights, 56.
Dragoons in Europe, 82.
Drewry's Bluff, 273.
Dunbar, battle of, 163.
Dupont, Samuel Francis, 257 *n.*
Du Portail, Louis Le Begue, 147.

Edinburgh Magazine, Blackwood's, 244, 263.
Eliot, Charles William, 382, 383.
Elizabeth, Queen, 386.
Elkton, 76, 144.
Elson's *History*, 206 *n.*
Emerson, Ralph Waldo, 292, 337.
Erckmann, Emile, 163.
Europe, change of opinion, 263.
Eutaw Springs, 108.
Evarts, William Maxwell, mission of, 363, 370.
Everett, William, 2.
2 E

Fabius and Fabian tactics, 49, 71, 74.
Farragut, David Glasgow, 248, 249.
Ferguson, Patrick, at King's Mountain, 107 *n.*; invents breech-loading rifle, 107 *n.*
Field, Cyrus West, 405.
First Troop of Philadelphia, 75.
Firth, Charles Harding, 164 *n.*
Fisher, Sydney George, 62, 95; on American history, 110; on authorities, 118 *n.*; on Lee's plan, 121.
Fiske, John, 211 *n.*; on Bunker Hill, 20; retreat from Long Island, 41; on Washington, 61.
Fitchett, W. H., 129, 180.
Fitzmaurice, Lord Edmund, 403.
Flanking movements, 77, 79 *n.*
Flatbush, L. I., 29.
Fleet, British, 36, 44, 47, 57, 121.
Forage, abundant, 65.
Forbes, John Murray, 353; mission to Europe, 354; meets Chase and Welles, 355; interviews with C. F. Adams, 358; returns, 371.
Foreigners, condescension of, 262.
Formby, John, 90 *n.*
Forrest, Nathan Bedford, 70, 90 *n.*; on strategy, 115.
Forster, William Edward, 382.
Fort Du Quesne, 86; Edward, 132; Fisher, 322; Mifflin, 141, 157; Montgomery, 50; Moultrie, 22, 56, 57.
Fortescue, John William, 127 *n.*
"Fortifications," 198.
Fox, Gustavus Vasa, 361.
France, alliance with, 1778, 152; recognition of Confederacy, 400, 403.
Franklin, Benjamin, on Pulaski, 83 *n.*; on capture of Philadelphia, 149.
Frederick the Great, 14, 98, 139, 140; on cavalry, 68, 72; on Princeton, 72 *n.*; rapidity of movement, 142; after Saratoga, 154.
Frothingham, Richard, 20.

Gage, Thomas, 102; operations, 6; rejects Clinton's advice, 9; character, 10, 14; at Bunker Hill, 16.
Galloway, Joseph, on blockade, 121 *n.*; on Howe, 147.
Garibaldi, Giuseppe, commission for, 366.
Gates, Horatio, 53; in Saratoga campaign, 74, 133; cavalry, 102.
Generals, sacrifice of, 246.
Generalship, 177.
Genius, military, 14.
George III, 387.

INDEX

Georgiana, 359.
Germain, George Sackville, on Howe, 148.
Germantown, 72, 88.
Germany, Hessians, 358, 371.
Gettysburg, 141 *n.*; Lee at, 306, 312.
Ghent, treaty of, 196.
Gilbert-town, 106.
Gillmore, Quincy Adams, in Virginia campaign, 269; urges Butler to attack, 272; relieved of command, 274.
Gladiator, 376.
Gladstone, William Ewart, 388; on American constitution, 213; predicts success of South, 235; approves mediation, 404; letter to Field, 405; rivalry with Palmerston, 408.
Gleig, George Robert, 179.
Glover, John, 39, 48.
Görlitz, 143.
Goethe, Johann Wolfgang, 267.
Gordon, William, 20.
Gordy, John Pancoast, 211 *n.*, 214.
Government, centralized, fear of, 209.
Gowanus Cove, 32.
Grant, James, 94.
Grant, Ulysses Simpson, 126 *n.*, 308; Virginia campaign, 267, 273; Butler's relations, 275, 276, 277, 278; at Appomattox, 326.
Granville, Lord, 403; relations to Queen Victoria, 411; on mediation, 412.
Gravesend, L. I., 29, 31.
Graydon, Alexander, 61.
Great Britain, recognition of Confederacy, 390, 392.
Greene, George Washington, 167.
Greene, Nathanael, 76, 149; illness on Long Island, 31, 55; plan of defence, 32; advises evacuation of Manhattan, 49, 51; on militia, 52; cavalry, 93, 105, 108; horses, 96; Southern campaign, 102; on Howe, 159; on Philadelphia, 164; on Washington, 167; character of, 171.
Greensboro conference, 241, 323.
Grey, Charles, at Paoli, 81.
Grouchy, Emmanuel, 280.
Guilford Court House, 108, 150.
Gun, magazine, 16.
Gustavus, Adolphus, 14.

Hagood, Johnson, 271.
Halleck, Henry Wager, 274, 275, 276.
Hamilton, Alexander, on cavalry, 90 *n.*; on Revolution, 111; on Washington, 112; on blockade, 122 *n.*; and Constitution, 212.

Hammond, James Henry, on cotton is King, 252, 314; on blockade, 250.
Hampton Roads, 121, 153.
Hannibal, 14.
Harcourt, William, 69.
Harlem Heights, death of Knowlton, 2.
Hartford Convention, 212, 221 *n.*
Hatteras Inlet, 248.
Haverswerda, 72.
Hawkes, Edward, 57.
Hay, John, 353, 366.
Health of soldiers, 135.
Heath, William, on mounted patrols, 65.
Henry, of Prussia, 72, 143.
Henry, Prince, 382.
Hero worship, 113.
Hewitt, Abram Stevens, character of, 375; on Queen Victoria and the United States, 376.
Highlands on Hudson, 118.
History, accuracy of relations, 179; perspective, 233.
Holmes, Oliver Wendell, 303.
Hood, John Bell, 261.
Hooker, Joseph, 78, 308.
Horry, Peter, 71.
Horses in colonies, 62, 96.
Houghton, Richard Monckton Milnes, Lord, 380.
Houston, David Franklin, 223 *n.*
Howe, Richard, Lord, 25, 27, 44, 148 *n.*
Howe, Sir William, at Bunker Hill, 10, 18; on Staten Island, 25, 27, 56; dilatory movements, 10, 34, 45, 52, 147; strategy, 53 *n.*; southern move, 54, 73, 125, 148 *n.*; in New Jersey, 74; at the Brandywine, 77, 80, 101; in Philadelphia, 87, 94, 127, 140, 159; cavalry, 100; at New York, 117, 123; neglect of blockade, 122 *n.*; plan of campaign, 119, 120, 124, 131; Burgoyne and, 127; on Washington, 133; character of, 168.
Hudson River, 50, 64, 121.
Huger, Isaac, 184 *n.*
Hughes, Sarah Forbes, 354.
Hussar, German, 82.

Immigrants, army and factories, 245; naturalization, 221.
Index, Confederate organ, 318; on *Uncle Tom's Cabin*, 320; on continuance of war, 326.
India, cotton production, 391.
Infantry, British, at New Orleans, 190.
Intelligence, British, on Long Island, 28.
Intervention, foreign, in Civil War, 246, 315, 320. *See* Recognition.

INDEX   419

Intrenchments, Breed's Hill, 14; in war, 15; at New York, 26; on Long Island, 35.
Iredell, James, 214 n.
Irving, Washington, 61, 139, 165.

Jackson, Andrew, at New Orleans, 176, 185, 187, 192.
Jackson, Thomas Jonathan, 78, 308.
Jägers, 92 n.
Jamaica Road, Long Island, 33, 55, 65, 66.
James II, 386.
James Adger, 394 n., 395.
Jay, John, 293; advises desolation of New York, 49, 50; on Charles Lee, 58.
Johnson, Bradley Tyler, on Southern confidence, 251.
Johnston, Joseph Eggleston, on employing negroes, 239 n.; on end of war, 241, 243, 325.
Jones, J. William, 206 n.
Joseph [Bonaparte], King, 134.
Jourdan, Jean Baptiste, 134.
Junot, Andoche, 100.

Kearsarge, 248.
Kentucky resolves of 1798, 220, 297.
King's Mountain, 89, 92, 93, 106.
Kips Bay, N. Y., 30, 51, 67.
Knowlton, Thomas, 2, 8.
Kutuzoff, Michael Larivonovitch Golenitchef, 145.

Lafayette, Marquis de, 76; at Barren Hill, 94; at the Brandywine, 147; on Washington, 168.
Laird rams, 347; time of delivery, 356; Confederate funds, 359; denounced by Welles, 362.
Lambert, John, at New Orleans, 194.
Lancashire cotton famine, 258, 317, 319, 403.
Latour, Arsène Lacarrière, 200 n.
Latta, James W., 340.
Lawyers on Constitution, 209.
Lee, Charles, "plan" of campaign, 21, 151; on repulse of Parker, 22; sent to New York, 24; on abandoning New York, 50, 54; acclaimed, 58; captured, 68; on cavalry, 68 n.; at Monmouth, 98; on authority of Washington, 134; importance of Philadelphia, 149; on Howe's campaign, 152; on Howe, 170 n.
Lee, Henry, 61, 82, 105; on Camden, 102; at Cowpens, 107; on loyalty to State, 303.

Lee's legion, 89, 96, 99.
Lee, Robert Edward, 16, 308; order No. 73, 266, 306; a man of character, 292; charge of traitor, 295, 303; manumits slaves, 304; on secession, 301, 304; military ability, 306; at Gettysburg, 306, 310, 312; successful retreat, 313; quality of army, 316; its needs, 321, 322; recognizes the end, 325, 327, 329; at Appomattox, 326; decides for self, 328; college president, 332; under reconstruction, 336; in family, 337; on foreign intervention, 411.
Legion, Lee's, 89.
Le Marchant, —, 182.
Leopold, Prince, on Queen Victoria, 383, 403.
Leuthen, 142.
Lever, Charles, on Civil War, 263.
Lewis, George Cornewall, 409.
Lexington, Mass., 91.
Light horse, 66 n., 70.
Ligny, 12.
Lincoln, Abraham, order on Butler, 276; assassinated, 326, 327.
Lincoln, Benjamin, 135.
Lines of communication, interior, 122, 138, 144, 162.
Little Round Top, 141 n.
Livermore, Thomas Leonard, estimates of Confederate army, 238 n., 287.
Lodge, Henry Cabot, on Union, 205, 215.
London Chronicle, 18.
Long Island, battle of, 22; strategy, 29; sufferings of Continental army, 37; storm and rain, 37, 38, 45; retreat from, 41; merits of, 48.
Longstreet, James, 141 n.
Louis XIV, 267.
Low, Seth, 376.
Lowell, James Russell, 262.
Luck in war, 1.
Lunch hour, result, 52.
Lushington, Stephen, 397.
Lützen, Pinto's description, 163.

Maclean, W. Neil, 19.
McClellan, George B., 246, 308.
McCrady, Edward, 104, 105.
McLane, Allan 97, 99.
McMahon, Marie E.-P.-M., 16.
Madison, James, on Constitution, 212, 215 n.; on divided interests, 217.
Mahon, Stanhope Philip Henry, Lord, 101.
Marblehead, Mass., regiment, 39, 48.
Marchand, John B., 394 n., 395, 398.

March to sea, Sherman's, effect upon Europe, 262; vandalism, 265.
Marching, influence upon army, 135; Morgan's, 140; Continental army, 160.
Marion, Francis, 71, 105.
Marlborough, John Churchill, Duke of, 14, 98.
Marmont, Duke of Ragusa, at Salamanca, 178, 181.
Marshall, John, 293; on Brandywine affair, 146; on Delaware defences, 156; influence on Union, 219 n., 220.
Martin, Sir Theodore, 399.
Mason, James Murray, Conway and, 369; taken from *Trent*, 394, 398; on Queen Victoria, 401.
Massachusetts, differences in, 1639, 203.
"Massacre" at Paoli, 80, 92 n.
Massena, André, 178 n.
Maucune, —, 179, 181.
Mauduit, Israel, on Howe, 18.
Maxwell, Sir Herbert, on Salamanca, 180, 181.
Meade, George Gordon, 72, 268; against cavalry, 73; in Virginia campaign, 269; at Gettysburg, 307, 309, 313.
Mediation, Seward's instructions to Adams, 406. *See* France and Great Britain.
Meigs, Montgomery Cunningham, 274.
Men, influence of, 218.
Mercier, —, 396.
Mexico, European ambitions in, 399, 403.
Mifflin, Thomas, 38, 39, 65, 66 n.
Militia, unreliability of, 35, 37, 51, 132, 189.
Mississippi River, importance of, 185; west bank, 187.
Mobile, 249.
Mollwitz, 68.
Moltke, Helmuth, 16, 263.
Monmouth Court House, 98.
Montaigne, Michel, on force of laws, 203.
Montgomery, Richard, 63.
Moore, George Henry, Lee's plan, 121 n.
Moore, Sir John, 114.
Mordecai, Alfred, 276.
Morgan, Daniel, 71, 85, 87, 99; influence, 89; on cavalry, 100 n.; at Cowpens, 107; sent northward, 139, 140, 145.
Morgan, David, 188.
Morris, Gouverneur, 50.
Morristown, N. J., 117.
Moscow, abandoned by Russians, 145.
Motley, John Lothrop, visits Lord Russell, 389; sees the Queen, 391; on Palmerston, 392.
Moylan, Stephen, 75, 79.
Murray, Mrs., 52 n.

Napier, Charles, on Busaco, 174; on Pakenham, 175, 195.
Napier, Sir William Francis Patrick, 114; on Scott's error, 61; on Craufurd's march, 141 n.; on great captains, 142; Peninsular War, 143 n.; on Salamanca, 178, 181.
Napoleon, 14, 16, 139, 140, 154; at Ligny, 12; sayings, 107, 243, 307; in 1812-1813, 120; Russian campaign, 129; on rapidity of movement, 147; at Elba, 183; at Waterloo, 12, 280.
Napoleon III, and the South, 376, 400.
Nashville, 394 n., 395.
Nationality, growth of, 214, 216, 221, 227, 297, 299.
Navy, Rhodes on service of, 247.
Negroes and the South, 230; in Confederacy, 239; enlistment of, 323.
Nelson, Horatio, 57.
Newcastle speech of Gladstone, 408.
New Jersey, Howe in, 74.
New Orleans, battle of, 174; tactics, 185; influence of Bladensburg, 186, 188; effect in Europe, 196; capture of, 248.
New York, campaign in 1776, 22; strategic centre, 24, 116; commanded by sea, 24, 25; prevailing winds, 36; meteorological condition, 44; should not be held, 49; devastation of, 50; Clinton's force at, 131.
North, nationalization of, 221; clemency to South, 335.

Officers, British, character of, 177.
Olney, Stephen, 33.
Opinion, contemporary, 244.

Pacificator of Europe, Frederick the Great, 1.
Pakenham, Sir Edward, at Busaco, 175; record of, 176; at Salamanca, 178; chosen for American campaign, 184; Wellington on, 183; Smith on, 184; bravery, 184; plan of action, 187; error, 188, 193; influence against, 195.
Palmerston, Henry John Temple, Viscount, criticised by *Index*, 320; ministry, 387; death, 388; attitude towards the North, 388, 392, 396; on Marchand, 394; interview with Adams, 394; on *Trent* affair, 398; on

INDEX 421

intervention, 402, 410; dislike of Gladstone, 408.
Paoli "massacre," 80, 92 *n.*
Parker, Sir Peter, 22, 36, 57, 126.
Parthian tactics, 71, 92, 98.
Parton, James, on British officers, 177.
Patriotism, 113.
Patrol, mounted, 65, 66; need of, 79.
Patterson, David T., at New Orleans, 188.
Peasants in arms, 287.
Pemberton, John Clifford, 308.
Perkins, James Breck, 161 *n.*, 165 *n.*
Peterhoff, 357, 359.
Philadelphia, first troop of, 75; Howe's objective, 75, 126, 128; occupied, 87, 140; strategic position, 117, 129, 149, 162.
Pickens, Andrew, 71, 105.
Pickens, Francis Wilkinson, 254 *n.*
Pickering, Timothy, 47 *n.*, 90 *n.*; on Washington, 112, 167.
Pickett's charge, Gettysburg, 311.
Picton's division, 178.
Pierce, Edward Lillie, on recollections as history, 344, 378.
Plevna, 18.
Plowed Hill, 7.
Plutarch, on King Pyrrhus, 318.
Pontgibaud, Count de Moré, 122 *n.*
Pope, Alexander, 207.
Pope, John, 308.
Port Royal, 248.
Porter, David Dixon, 249; on Butler, 279.
Posterity and foreign nations, 244.
Prescott, William, 2, 7, 9, 11, 14.
Princeton, 67.
Progress, Stephen on, 229.
Prospect Hill, 7, 8.
Providence defined, 217.
Pulaski, Casimir, statue, 59; not known to Washington, 60; Washington and Franklin on, 83 *n.;* character, 85; at the Brandywine, 83; demands rank, 83 *n.;* on cavalry, 84 *n.,* 87; at Germantown, 88.
Putnam, Israel, at Bunker Hill, 8, 10; on the Yankee, 17; at New York, 25, 52; in Brooklyn, 55; in the Highlands, 118; incompetence, 141.
Pyrrhus, death of, 318.

Quatre Bras, 15.

Ragusa, Duc de, *see* Marmont.
Rainbow, 52.
Ranger, American, 91, 92 *n.,* 99.

Rapalye's negro, 48.
Rashness of ignorance, 6.
Rawdon, Francis, Lord, 105.
Rawle, William, 297, 340.
Read, J. C., on *Uncle Tom's Cabin,* 319.
Recognition, Seward's instructions to Adams, 407.
Recollections, as source of history, 344.
Reconnoitring extraordinary, 76.
Reconstruction, evil period of, 326, 335.
Red Hook, 36, 39.
Reed, Joseph, 39, 40.
Reid, Whitelaw, on Sherman's march, 289.
"Remarks upon General Howe's Account," 18.
Renegades to flag, some historical, 305.
Retreat from Long Island, 41.
Revere, Paul, 63.
Revolution, history of, 110, 111.
Rhett, Edmund, 256.
Rhode Island, 204, 224.
Rhodes, James Ford. *History,* 232; on success of North, 234; neglects sea power, 247; on Sherman's march, 265; on Grant's Virginia campaign, 268; on Butler, 279; on Lee, 294 *n.*
Rifle and riflemen, 89, 91, 92 *n.*
Ropes, John Codman, at Waterloo, 280.
Rosebery, Lord, 113.
Ross, Robert, 175, 183, 200.
Rossbach, 142.
Royalists in States, 103.
Rumbold, Sir Horace, 398.
Rupert, Prince, 63, 70, 92.
Russell, Lord John, Earl, alleged interview with Adams, 377; despatch modified by Prince Albert, 383, 399; conversation with Motley, 389; on recognition, 392; on mediation, 402, 410; circular on, 404.
Russell, William Howard, Southern opinion of Yankees, 251 *n.;* on Southerners, 253.
Rutledge, Edward, 50.

Sadowa, 78.
St. Clair, Arthur, 118
Salamanca, battle of, 178.
Salt, price at Philadelphia, 121 *n.*
Sandy Hook, 25.
Sanford, Henry Shelton, 366.
Santa Cruz de Teneriffe, 57.
Saratoga, 73.
Savannah, Ga., 104.
Schiller, Johann C. F., 267.
Schofield, John McAllister, 261.
Schuyler, Philip, 133, 135, 144.

422   INDEX

Scott, John Morin, 58.
Scott, Walter, *Napoleon*, 61.
Scott, Winfield, 73, 303.
Sea power, 247.
Secession, ethics of, 203; right of, 216, 295, 340; peaceable, 224, 301.
Sedan, 15.
Sedgwick's corps, 141 *n.*, 312.
Seward, William Henry, meets Chittenden, 347; organizes intelligence service, 364; defends Wilson, 368; Motley's reports, 389; instructions on mediation, 406.
Seydlitz, Friedrich Wilhelm von, 68.
Shaler, Nathaniel Southgate, 384 *n.*
Sheldon, Elisha, 75, 79.
Sheridan, Philip Henry, on cavalry, 73, 90 *n.;* on war, 287.
Sherman, William Tecumseh, 72, 308; march to sea, 261; effect in Europe, 262; Reid on, 289; on war, 289.
Shoe leather in war, 134.
Slavery, African, 300; influence on nationalization, 217.
Slidell, John, taken from *Trent*, 394, 398.
Sloane, William Milligan, 129.
Smith, Adam, on rebels and heretics, 335.
Smith, Goldwin, on American Union, 205, 215.
Smith, Sir Harry, on Pakenham, 184, 187; at New Orleans, 194.
Smith, Jacob Hurd, orders to devastate, 288.
Smith, William Farrar, in Virginia campaign, 268; Grant's opinion of, 270; urges Butler to attack, 272; recommendations upon, 274, 276; relieved, 276; on Butler, 279.
Smith, Zachary Frederick, 199 *n.*
Soldier, British, character, 70.
South, the nationalization, 217, 221; negro and, 230; strength of army, 236; self-conscious, 250, 257; idea of the North, 251, 254; confidence in cotton, 314.
South Africa, cavalry, 63; war, 93, 98, 104, 325.
Sovereignty, where found under Constitution, 208, 220, 224; divided, 210, 299; question of, 296, 302.
Spottsylvania, battle of, 272.
Squadron, 61.
Staff, general, 119, 171.
Stanley, Arthur Penrhyn, on Queen Victoria, 386.
Stanley, Edward John, Baron, 412.
Stark, John, 135.

State, right to withdraw from Union, 205, 226; under Confederation, 209; sovereignty, 209, 226, 297; allegiance, 213; citizenship, 298.
Staten Island, 25, 27.
Stedman, Charles, 61, 95; on Bunker Hill, 20; criticises Howe, 53, 124, 168; on Long Island, 66 *n.;* on King's Mountain, 106.
Stephen, Leslie, on progress, 229.
Stephens, Alexander Hamilton, on cotton, 260.
Steuben, Baron, on Washington, 112.
Stiles, —, 308.
Stirling, Lord, captured, 33, 46.
Stowe, Harriet Beecher, and book, 319.
Stragglers to Sherman's army, 265, 289.
Strategy, defined, 115; new system developed, 14, 64, 122; of British, 120; of Americans, 122; at New Orleans, 185, 192.
Stuart, Gilbert, 91.
Sullivan, John, on Long Island, 31, 55; captured, 33, 66; pays for patrols, 66, 79.
Sumner, Charles, 362; assault on, 255; denunciation of Lee, 293; criticised by Clay, 367; on Wilson, 368.
Sumter, Thomas, 71, 105.
Sylla, on vicissitudes of war, 114.
Symmetry, 20.
Sympathizers in Confederate army, 238.

Tactics, at New Orleans, 185, 192, 193.
Tappan Sea, 27.
Tarleton, Banastre, 61, 82; at capture of Lee, 69, 71; cavalry of, 103 *n.;* at Waxhaws, 104; in southern campaign, 108.
Taylor, Hannis, 343.
Tennyson, Alfred, Lord, 207.
Texas, as refuge for Confederacy, 242, 326.
Theodora, 394 *n.*
Thomas, George Henry, 71, 303.
Thomières, 181.
Thoreau, Henry David, 292 *n.*
Thornton, William, 201.
Ticonderoga, 118, 131.
Tilly, John Tzerklaes von, 267.
Tocqueville, Alexis de, 213, 298, 341.
Tolstoi, 145.
Torres Vedras, 17.
Tower, Charlemagne, 95.
"Traveller," Lee's horse, 331.
Treasury, loose methods, 372.
Trent affair, 380, 383, 394; Hewitt on, 376; right of, 397.

INDEX 423

Trenton, 67.
Trescot, William Henry, 256.
Trevelyan, George Otto, 62; on retreat from Long Island, 10; on weather at New York, 44; on the Brandywine, 78; on Paoli, 81, 92 *n.;* on campaign of 1777, 88; on cavalry, 89; on Clinton's withdrawal from Philadelphia, 96, 97, 98; on history of Revolution, 109; on Howe, 168.
Trumbull, Jonathan, sends mounted men, 64.
Trumbull Jonathan, Jr., 221 *n.*
Trumbull, Joseph, 153.
Tryon, William, 28, 81.
Tucker, Josiah, on American Union, 218.
Tyler, Lion Gardiner, 216; on Confederate forces, 282.

Ulm, 136.
Uncle Tom's Cabin, in England, 319.
Union, dissoluble, 205.
Urban, d', 182.

Valley Forge, 88, 146, 149.
Valori, Count de, 1.
Van Tyne, Claude Halstead, 339.
Victoria, Queen, intervention, 376; alleged assurance to Adams, 377; character, 385; unsympathetic for democracy, 385; obstinacy, 385; unable to transact public business, 379, 400, 403; sees Motley, 391; on the continent, 401; relations with Granville, 411; no proof of interest in America, 412.
"View of Evidence," 18.
Vimeiro, Wellington at, 100.
Virginia, intrenchments in, 15; horses, 96; sovereignty, 210; resolves, 1798, 220, 221 *n.;* states rights, 302.
Vittoria, 134.

Wales, Prince of (Edward VI), visit to America, 376, 386.
Walker, Leroy Pope, boast of, 251.
Walker, Robert John, 560.
Wallabout Bay, 32.
War, luck in, 1; use of intrenchments, 15; in colonies, 63; is hell, 265, 288, 327; defined, 287.
Ward, Artemas, 8, 14.
Warren, James, 82.
Washington, George, on Long Island, 14, 22, 31; takes command at New York, 25; problems of defence, 25; desperate situation on Long Island, 34, 38, 40; responsible for strategy, 41, 55; motives, 54; in command on Long Island, 55; on militia, 55, 132; prestige in danger, 57; idea of organization, 60; refuses to employ horsemen, 64, 92; military career, 71; want of alertness, 72; moves southward, 75; reconnoitres, 76; on cavalry and Pulaski, 83 *n.;* failure to value cavalry, 87; Congress and cavalry, 89 *n.;* interest in horses, 91; learns caution, 95; at Monmouth, 99; at Yorktown, 100; character of, 51, 112; at Morristown, 117, 123; failure to grasp Howe's strategy, 128, 129, 132, 137, 154; authority of, 133, 163, 164 *n.;* Northern department and, 138; errors in strategy, 145; after Saratoga, 154; on Delaware defences, 156; learns strategy, 161; councils of war, 164; cult, 166; Pickering's opinion of, 167; characterized, 170; on States, 209 *n.;* influence on Union, 219 *n.*, 220.
Washington, William, 102, 105.
"Washington and Cavalry," 110.
Washington College, Lee as president, 332.
Washington reminiscences, unhistorical, 344.
Waterloo, battle of, 12, 280; absence of intrenchments, 15.
Waxhaws, affair at, 104.
Wayne, Anthony, at Paoli, 80.
Weather conditions at New York, 44.
Webster, Daniel, on sovereignty, 221 *n.*, 297, 339.
Weed, Thurlow, 365, 369, 383.
Weems, Mason Locke, 166.
"Weems Dispensation," 110.
Wehla, 143.
Welles, Gideon, sends Forbes and Aspinwall to England, 354, 355, 372; on buying ships, 362.
Wellington, Arthur Wellesley, Duke of, 15, 140; at Torres Vedras, 17, 49; at Vimeiro, 100; allowance of shoes, 134; at Salamanca, 178; on war correspondents, 180; on Pakenham, 183; to be sent to America, 184; had he been at New Orleans, 201.
Westbury, Richard Bethell, Baron, 397.
West Point, 340.
White, Anthony Walton, 102.
White's Tavern, 69.
Wigfall, Louis Trezevant, on assault on Sumner, 255.
Wilderness, battle of, 272.
Wilkes, Charles, 398.

William of Orange, 112, 172.
William II, on war, 288.
Wilmington, Del., 121, 127, 153.
Wilmington, N. C., fall of, 249, 322.
Wilson, Charles L., 367.
Wilson, Henry, 274.
Wilson, James Harrison, 277.
Windsor, home life of Queen Victoria, 386.
Winter Hill, 7.
Winthrop, John, 203, 292.

Winthrop, Robert Charles, 226.
Wolfe, James, 72, 169.
Woodward, P. Henry, 8 *n*.

Yancey, William Lowndes, on cotton, 260, 396.
Young, Pierce Manning Butler, on war, 288.
Yorktown, Va., 113, 150, 161.

Ziethen, Johann Joachim von, 68.

WILKES COLLEGE LIBRARY